A Handbook of
American Military History

Second Edition

A Handbook of American Military History

Second Edition

From the Revolutionary War to the Present

EDITED BY

Jerry K. Sweeney

CONTRIBUTORS

Kevin B. Byrne
Jerry M. Cooper
James L. Crowder
John M. Lindley
Jerry K. Sweeney
David J. Ulbrich
William J. Woolley

UNIVERSITY OF NEBRASKA PRESS
LINCOLN AND LONDON

© 1996 by Jerry K. Sweeney
Chapter 7 © 2006 by the Board of Regents of the University of Nebraska

Library of Congress Cataloging-in-Publication Data
A handbook of American military history: from the Revolutionary War to the
present / edited by Jerry K. Sweeney; contributors, Kevin B. Byrne . . . [et
al.].—2nd ed.
p.   cm.
Includes bibliographical references and index.
ISBN-13: 978-0-8032-9337-3 (pbk.: alk. paper)
ISBN-10: 0-8032-9337-2 (pbk.: alk. paper)
1. United States—History, Military—Handbooks, manuals, etc.   I. Sweeney,
Jerry K.   II. Byrne, Kevin B.
E181.H23   2005
355.00973—dc22   2005032825

Contents

Preface

This work is concerned with the military history of the United States since the first stages of a revolt against the consequences of British colonial rule. It begins with otherwise unremarkable events which proved of seminal importance and reaches its climax with the end of the most defining historical process of recent decades—the Cold War. The Revolutionary War established enduring ideological parameters for the United States, but the closing years of twentieth century found the nation abandoning the verities of one age for the uncertainties of another, as it sought not to reorder its priorities but to determine their composition. This handbook is intended to serve a general public interested in American military history as well as students engaged in course work in that area. The various sections focus on the multiple facets of the regular American military establishment in peace and war and the various degrees between them. Although considerable efforts were undertaken in the interest of clarity, the work continues to presuppose some familiarity with the subject.

The handbook consists of seven chronological sections—each of which contains an introductory essay describing the dominant themes, a chronology of events, a summary of important military operations, selected biographic treatments, and a select annotated bibliography. The reader will also find a glossary of commonly used terms and acronyms. The seven sections exist somewhat independently of one another, in accord with the assumption the reader will ofttimes consult the work with a specific intention. This work is not designed to be read in the fashion of a monograph, although it may be used to supplement a general survey of the American military experience.

Chronology

The chronological section focuses on significant incidents, engagements and developments, and circumstances so unique as to otherwise warrant comment. Unless noted, a specific entry denotes the date when an institution or individual undertook a particular action, or an incident took place. Thus, an entry such as: "Congress creates a marine corps" indicates that the Second Continental Congress approved legislation establishing a corps of marines on a specific date; "USS *Ranger* defeats *Drake* (Br.)" reveals that an American naval vessel defeated an opponent on a particular day, and "Levi Woodbury (Secretary of the Navy)" denotes when that individual took his oath of office. Obviously, the decision as to what to include in this area is open to dispute in that the historical process is affected by a variety of factors and the importance assigned thereto is subject to conflicting interpretation. This section provides a rapid review of the military history of the United States, and serves to illustrate the chronological interaction which often exists between disparate circumstances. It also furnishes singular information of a temporal nature to assist persons consulting time-sensitive materials. Generally speaking, every effort was made to use local times and dates. In consequence, the attack on Pearl Harbor by the air and naval forces of Japan is presented as occurring on December 7, 1941, while the Japanese attack on American installations in the Philippine Islands is listed as December 8, 1941. Any reference to the something or someone being "first" refers, unless otherwise stipulated, only to the armed forces of the United States.

Military Operations

This section provides a concise treatment of some of the military operations which appear in the earlier section. The selection criteria were twofold, the inclusion of readily recognizable operations and those actions which specialists judge crucial to American military history. In most cases, the two criteria converged, but when spatial constraints intruded, greater weight was accorded the first criterion. Some may object to the exclusion of particular operations or with the decision to cover actions beyond the normal battlefield environment—as in the numerous references to the movement of troops to deal with race riots and labor disputes. Nevertheless, the scope of American military history is constantly expanding, and this work strives to reflect at least a portion of that evolving tableau.

Biographical Notes

The biographical notes do not present a complete appraisal of the whole of American military history. Rather, the intent is to assist the reader toward a greater appreciation of at least a portion of those influential personalities that time and circumstance served to render relatively obscure. The exploits of individuals of the first rank are presented in a more cursory fashion, inasmuch as their achievements are such as to need little amplification. Those who wish to delve further into the life and times of such persons will find a useful bibliographic citation at the end of the entry.

Although by far the majority of those examined in this section served in the armed forces of the United States, the biographic coverage also includes some individuals who were not members of the American military establishment.

Selected Reading List

The reading lists were compiled to be useful to each of several audiences, students, gifted amateurs and professionals. They are not intended to be comprehensive, and they include popular and scholarly works. Bibliographies and other reference sources appear regularly, but biographies are generally excluded insofar as they may be readily approached through any card catalogue. The principal historiographic trends in American military history are presented at intervals so as to place the listed works in context. Unfortunately, many otherwise outstanding monographs could not be discussed; therefore, the reader is enjoined to carefully peruse the bibliography of any work consulted. Recent books are given preference over older works, and the lists are organized topically for easy access.

Closing Remarks

No single work can provide all the information a potential user might seek. Our goal is to provide a wide range of essential information in a concise format and thereby facilitate additional investigation. We envisage this work as the first step in an otherwise lengthy journey, and only occasionally the end of the trip.

Kevin B. Byrne
Jerry M. Cooper
James L. Crowder
John M. Lindley
Jerry K. Sweeney
William J. Woolley

Acknowledgments

The authors wish to thank their colleagues and friends for their assistance and support in the preparation of this work. In particular:

South Dakota State University for release time and funding essential to the completion of this project.

Robert L. Cavanagh for service above and beyond the call of duty.

And, special thanks to our wives and children, especially the former and particularly the latter.

K.B.B.
J.M.C.
J.L.C.
J.M.L.
J.K.S.
W.J.W.

A Handbook of
American Military History

Second Edition

1

The Building Period: 1775–1815

The American Republic took shape in a time of conflict. From the onset of hostilities with Great Britain until the Senate approved the Treaty of Ghent Americans strove to reach a consensus governing military affairs. The colonial experience bequeathed to the new republic an ideology suspicious of professional soldiers and centralized political authority—a legacy of a century and a half of military practice largely controlled from the colonial capitals. While the colonies asserted a universal militia obligation, they largely relied on temporary volunteer forces recruited through bounties and the threat of conscription, to defend their borders and prosecute war. Attitudes and practices which evolved during the colonial years persisted through the War of 1812, profoundly influencing the development of military institutions.

When the colonies faced the realities of war with Britain in 1775 they confronted the need to create centralized administrative agencies as well as military forces to conduct war. Given the inherited suspicions of a strong government and standing armies, establishing a small regular force to give cohesion to the colonial war effort proved difficult. The vicissitudes of war forced Anglo-Americans to abandon temporarily their Whiggish fears of a standing army, but the Continental Army under George Washington suffered throughout the war from the lack of proper logistical, financial, and manpower support. Without an executive branch, the Continental government fumbled in its attempts to create effective administrative agencies. Supply, finance, and recruitment devolved back to the states in the last three years of the war. Ironically, the United States won its independence largely because its military and political power was so widely dispersed the British found it virtually impossible to destroy the rebellion militarily at an acceptable cost.

The new republic faced serious military problems in the three decades following independence. European powers, notably Great Britain, displayed scant respect for the new nation's sovereignty. The end of the war saw a burst of westward expansion which provoked conflict with Native Americans as far west as the Mississippi River. Internal upheaval posed a third challenge. The wartime confederation government proved unable to meet the financial, political, diplomatic, and military difficulties of independence. Adoption of the Constitution in 1787 established a federal government which held great potential power, not the least in military affairs.

Potential power became real only as the Washington administration responded to specific challenges. The Federalists assumed power with a military program articulated as early as 1783, but implemented it in piecemeal fashion. While the War Department appeared as one of the first executive agencies, a permanent standing army was not established until *ad hoc* volunteer and militia forces failed to quell conflicts with Native Americans in Ohio in the early 1790s. A permanent navy and Navy Department appeared at the end of the decade in response to French interference with American merchant shipping. Federalists also oversaw the establishment of government arsenals and the beginnings of a coastal fortification system. Their singular failure came in attempts to establish a centrally controlled militia. The Militia Act of 1792 left the citizen soldiery under state and local control, denying the federal government a reserve force for a full century and more.

Despite the acrimonious rhetorical battle between Federalists and Jeffersonian-Republicans over the power of the federal government, Republicans did not deviate in any substantive way from basic Federalist military policy. Indeed, Thomas Jefferson supplied the final element of the latter when he oversaw creation of the United States Military Academy. While Jeffersonians kept the Federalist structure, they drastically reduced military appropriations and adopted a passive defense policy with an emphasis on coastal defense and naval gunboats. This policy severely hampered the conduct of the War of 1812 which by its very nature called for offensive land operations into Canada and protection of American shipping on the high seas. Victory came largely for the same reasons as in 1783. American geography, the distance from Europe to North America, and the decentralized nature of the United States yet again confounded the British.

The United States emerged from the War of 1812 with its independence and sovereignty firmly established. It possessed as well a military-naval policy built upon the experiences of the previous forty years which would serve it to the end of the nineteenth century. Americans now accepted permanent military and naval forces under the control of federal executive agencies. The right of the central government to conduct war went unquestioned. If the federal government held greater military power by 1815 when compared to the powers of the Continental Congress, it was a power restrained, however. The army and navy remained small and inadequately financed, and the states continued to organize, recruit, and officer wartime army regiments through volunteering.

Chronology

1775

Apr	19	Battles of Lexington and Concord
Apr	19	Rebel army besieges Boston
May	10	Rebel forces seize Ft. Ticonderoga
May	12	Rebel forces seize Crown Point
Jun	12	First naval battle of the Revolutionary War (Rebel *Unity* defeats *Margaretta*)
Jun	14	Congress creates an army
Jun	15	George Washington (General of the Armies)
Jun	17	Battle of Bunker/Breed's Hill
Jul	3	Washington takes command of the Continental Army
Aug	24	First armed vessel "fitted out in the service of the U.S." (*Hannah*)
Aug	28	Rebel forces advance on Montreal (Montgomery's column)
Sep	6	First rebel "prize of war" (Rebel *Hannah* captures British *Unity*)
Sep	11	Rebel forces advance on Quebec (Arnold's column)
Oct	13	Congress creates a navy
Nov	9	Arnold's column reaches Quebec
Nov	10	Congress creates a marine corps
Nov	10	Samuel Nicholas (Commandant, Marine Corps)
Nov	13	Rebel forces occupy Montreal
Nov	19	Arnold's column withdraws to Point Aux Trembles
Nov	23	Congress authorizes letters of *marque and reprisal* against British vessels in government service
Nov	28	Congress adopts first "navy regulations"
Dec	2	Rebel forces besiege Quebec—ends May 6, 1776
Dec	3	*Alfred* commissioned (first ship Continental Navy)
Dec	13	Congress authorizes construction of thirteen frigates
Dec	14	Congress establishes Marine Committee
Dec	22	Esek Hopkins appointed Commander-in-Chief of the Fleet
Dec	31	Arnold and Montgomery unsuccessfully assault Quebec

1776

Mar	3	First amphibious operation—New Providence Island, Bahamas
Mar	4	Rebel forces occupy Dorchester Heights

Mar 17 British forces evacuate Boston
Mar 23 Congress authorizes letters of *marque and reprisal* against all
        British vessels
Apr 4 Continental Navy captures first enemy warship (*Columbus*
        defeats *Hawk*, Br.)
Apr 7 *Lexington* defeats *Edward* (Br.)
May 9 *Wasp* defeats *Betsy* (Br.)
Jun 8 Battle of Trois Riveres—ends Jun 9
Jun 9 Rebel forces withdraw from Montreal
Jun 13 Congress establishes Board of War and Ordnance
Jun 28 British Navy attacks Ft. Moultrie
Jul 2 Congress asserts that the "united colonies" are independent
Jul 2 British forces land on Staten Island
Jul 27 USS *Lexington* defeats *Lady Susan* (Br.)
Aug 22 British forces land on Long Island
Aug 27 USS *Providence* defeats *Britannia* (Br.)
Aug 27 Battle of Long Island
Aug 29 U.S. forces evacuate Long Island
Sep 7 *Turtle* (submersible) attempts underwater attack on British
        squadron
Sep 15 British forces land on Manhattan Island
Sep 16 Battle of Harlem Heights
Oct 11 Naval action—L. Champlain—ends Oct 13
Oct 18 Battle of Pelham
Oct 27 First Battle of Ft. Washington
Oct 28 Battle of White Plains
Nov 10 USS *Alfred* and USS *Providence* capture *Active* (Br.)
Nov 16 Second Battle of Ft. Washington
Nov 20 U.S. forces evacuate Ft. Lee
Nov 29 First vessel Continental Navy arrives European waters (USS
        Reprisal)
Dec 12 Congress authorizes one regiment of light dragoons
Dec 26 British forces occupy Newport
Dec 26 Battle of Trenton

1777

Jan 3 Battle of Princeton
Jan 5 First use of maritime mines—Delaware River
Jan 6 U.S. forces enter winter quarters—Morristown, NJ
Feb 7 British government authorizes letters of *marque and reprisal*
        against U.S. vessels
Jun 7 USS *Hancock* and USS *Boston* defeat *Fox* (Br.)
Jun 18 British forces depart St. Johns, Canada, to invade U.S.

Jul	4	First "stars and stripes" aboard U.S. warship (USS *Ranger*)
Jul	6	British forces reoccupy Ft. Ticonderoga
Jul	7	Battle of Hubbardton
Jul	8	*Rainbow, Flora* and *Victor* (Br.) defeat USS *Hancock*
Aug	3	British forces besiege Ft. Stanwix—ends Aug 23
Aug	4	Horatio Gates (Commander, Northern Army)
Aug	6	Battle of Oriskany
Aug	16	Battle of Bennington
Sep	11	Battle of Brandywine Creek
Sep	19	Battle of Saratoga/Freeman's Farm/Bemis Heights—ends Oct 17
Sep	19	*Alert* (Br.) defeats USS *Lexington*
Sep	26	British forces occupy Philadelphia
Oct	1	Naval action—Delaware River—ends Nov 22
Oct	4	Battle of Germantown
Oct	22	Battle of Ft. Mercer—ends Nov 21
Nov	10	Battle of Ft. Mifflin—ends Nov 15
Dec	19	U.S. forces enter winter quarters—Valley Forge, PA

1778

Jan	27	U.S. forces assault New Providence Island—Bahamas
Feb	23	Friedrich von Steuben arrives Valley Forge, PA
Feb	14	First unchallenged recognition U.S. flag by foreign government (USS *Ranger* by *Robuste*, Fr.)
Mar	7	USS *Randolph* explodes during battle with *Yarmouth* (Br.)
Mar	9	*Ariadne* (Br.) and *Ceres* (Br.) defeat USS *Alfred*
Mar	11	First recorded dismissal from a military service for homosexual activity (Gotthold F. Enslin, USA)
Mar	19	First uniform drill by the model training brigade of the Continental Army (Friedrich von Steuben)
Apr	24	USS *Ranger* defeats *Drake* (Br.)
Jun	18	British forces evacuate Philadelphia
Jun	28	Battle of Monmouth Courthouse
Aug	29	First significant combat by African American unit (Battle of Quaker Hill)
Dec	29	British forces occupy Savannah

1779

Feb	23	Battle of Vincennes—ends Feb 25
Mar	3	Battle of Briar Creek
Mar	29	Congress accepts *Regulations for the Order and Discipline of the Forces of the U.S.* (F. von Steuben)

May   7   USS *Providence* defeats *Diligent* (Br.)
May   9   British forces raid Hampton Roads, VA area—ends May 11
Jun 18   First organized campaign against Native Americans by USA—
          ends Oct 15
Jul 16   Battle of Stony Point
Jul 25   Combined operation—ends Aug 13—Penobscot Bay
Aug 29   Battle of Newtown
Sep 23   USS *Bonhomme Richard* defeats *Serapis* (Br.)
Oct   9   Franco-American forces unsuccessfully assault Savannah
Oct 28   Congress establishes Board of Admiralty
Dec   1   U.S. forces enter winter quarters—Morristown, NJ

1780

Apr   1   British forces besiege Charleston—U.S. forces surrender May
          12
May 29   Battle of Waxhaws
Jul 13   Horatio Gates (Commander, Southern Department)
Aug 16   Battle of Camden
Oct   7   Battle of King's Mountain
Oct 30   Nathanael Greene (Commander, Southern Department)

1781

Jan   1   Mutiny among Pennsylvania Line—ends Jan 10
Jan 17   Battle of Cowpens
Jan 20   Mutiny among New Jersey Line—ends Jan 27
Feb   7   Congress replaces Board of War and Ordnance with Depart-
          ment of War
Mar   1   Articles of Confederation ratified by sufficient states
Mar 15   Battle of Guilford Courthouse
Apr 14   *Roebuck* (Br.) and *Orpheus* (Br.) defeat USS *Confederacy*
Apr 25   Battle of Hobkirk Hill
May 29   USS *Alliance* defeats *Atalanta* and *Trepassey* (Br.)
Jul   6   Battle of Green Springs
Aug 29   *Iris* (Br.), formerly USS *Hancock*, and *General Monk* (Br), for-
          merly US privateer *General Washington*, defeat USS *Trumbull*
          (last of the original U.S. frigates)
Sep   7   Richard Morris (Agent of Marine)
Sep   8   Battle of Eutaw Springs
Sep 28   U.S. forces besiege Yorktown—ends Oct 19
Oct 21   USS *Indian* defeats *Venus* (Br.)
Oct 30   Benjamin Lincoln (Secretary at War)

1782

Apr	8	*Hyder-Ally* (Pennsylvania Navy) defeats *General Monk* (Br.)
Jul	11	British forces evacuate Savannah
Aug	7	Badge of Military Merit (Purple Heart) established
Sep	11	Battle of Ft. Henry—ends Sep 13
Dec	14	British forces evacuate Charleston

1783

Feb	4	U.K. ceases hostilities—U.S. agrees on Apr 11
Mar	10	USS *Alliance* vs. *Sybil* (Br.)
Mar	24	Congress recalls all U.S. armed vessels
Sep	3	Treaty ends war with the United Kingdom
Nov	25	British forces evacuate New York City
Dec	4	British forces evacuate Staten Island and Long Island
Dec	23	G. Washington resigns as Commander-in-Chief

1784

Jun	2	Congress disbands Continental Army
Jun	3	Congress creates a standing army (First American Regiment)
Nov	1	Robert Morris retires as Agent of Marine

1785

Mar	8	Henry Knox (Secretary of War)
Jun	3	USS *Alliance* sold (no U.S. Navy until USS *United States* launched in 1797)

1786

Oct	20	Congress authorizes another army (3-year enlistment)

1789

Aug	7	Congress establishes the Department of War and Navy
Aug	7	Congress establishes the Lighthouse Establishment (later Lighthouse Service)
Sep	12	Henry Knox (Secretary of War)
Sep	29	Congress creates a standing army based on existing force

1790

Aug	4	Congress establishes Revenue Cutter Service (USRCS)
Oct	19	Battle of Eel River/Heller's Corners (punitive campaign)
Oct	22	Battle of Kekionga (punitive campaign)

1791

Mar	21	First commissioned officer USRCS (Hopley Yeaton)
Jul	23	First revenue cutter launched (USRCS *Massachusetts*)
Nov	4	Battle of the Wabash (punitive campaign)

1792

May	2	Calling Forth Act—made permanent Feb 28, 1795; expanded Mar 2, 1799, and Mar 8, 1807
May	8	Militia Act

1794

May	27	Congress provides for construction of six frigates
Jun	30	Battle of Ft. Recovery (punitive campaign)
Aug	20	Battle of Fallen Timbers (punitive campaign)
Oct	20	U.S. forces dispatched to western Pennsylvania (civil unrest)

1795

Jan	2	Timothy Pickering (Secretary of War)

1796

Jan	27	James McHenry (Secretary of War)

1797

May	10	USS *United States* (first ship launched under the naval provisions of the U.S. Constitution)
Jul	1	Congress authorizes use of revenue cutters to defend U.S. & U.S. vessels

1798

Apr	30	Congress creates a Department of the Navy
May	28	Naval war with France begins
Jun	18	Benjamin Stoddert (Secretary of the Navy)
Jul	7	USS *Delaware* defeats *La Croyable*, Fr. (first ship taken by USN in naval war)
Jul	9	Congress authorizes letters of *marque and reprisal* against French vessels
Jul	12	William Burrows (Commandant, Marine Corps)
Aug	22	USS *United States* defeats *Sans Pareil* (Fr.)
Sep	4	USS *United States* defeats *Jalouse* (Fr.)
Nov	20	*Insurgent* and *Volontaire* (Fr.) defeat USS *Retaliation*

1799

Feb	9	USS *Constellation* defeats *L'Insurgente* (Fr.)
Mar	2	Congress authorizes the assignment of Revenue Service vessels to the Secretary of the Navy
Mar	2	Congress authorizes the payment of bounty money to USN personnel—abolished Mar 3, 1899
Mar	15	U.S. forces dispatched to Bucks County, PA (civil unrest)
Mar	26	USS *United States* defeats *La Tartueffe* (Fr.)
Jun	22	USRC *Eagle* vs. *Revenge* (Fr.)
Jun	28	USS *Merrimack* defeats *Magicienne* (Fr.)

1800

Jan	1	Naval action—Santo Domingo (USS *Experiment*)
Feb	1	USS *Constellation* vs. *Vengeance* (Fr.)
Feb	27	USRC *General Greene* bombards Jacmel, Haiti
Apr	23	Congress authorizes the payment of prize money to USN personnel—abolished Mar 3, 1899
May	11	USS *Constitution* defeats *Sandwich* (Fr.)
May	13	Samuel Dexter (Secretary of War)
Sep	30	Treaty ends naval war with France
Oct	12	USS *Boston* defeats *Le Berceau* (Fr.)

1801

Mar	5	Henry Dearborn (Secretary of War)
May	14	Tripoli declares war on U.S. (War with the Barbary Pirates)
Jul	27	Robert Smith (Secretary of the Navy)
Aug	1	USS *Enterprise* defeats *Tripoli* (Tripoli)

1802

Mar	16	Congress establishes United States Military Academy—opens Jul 4, 1802

1803

Jun	22	USS *John Adams* defeats *Meshouda* (Tripoli)
Aug	26	USS *Philadelphia* defeats *Mirboka* (Morocco)
Oct	31	USS *Philadelphia* captured by naval forces of Tripoli
Nov	12	Naval blockade—Tripoli

1804

Feb	16	USS *Philadelphia* destroyed by U.S. forces—Tripoli harbor

Mar 21 USS *Siren* captures *Transfer* (Tripoli)
Aug   3 Naval bombardment—Tripoli—ends Sep 4

1805

Mar   2 Congress authorizes the construction of twenty-five harbor
         defense gunboats with an additional authorization on Dec 18,
         1807
Mar   8 U.S. forces leave Alexandria, Egypt for Tripoli
Apr 27 U.S. forces seize Derna (combined operation)
Jun   4 Peace treaty ends war with Tripoli

1807

Jun 22 USS *Chesapeake* attacked by *Leopard* (Br.)

1809

Mar   7 William Eustis (Secretary of War)
May 15 Paul Hamilton (Secretary of the Navy)

1811

May 16 USS *President* vs. *Little Belt* (Br.)
Nov   7 Battle of Tippecanoe Creek (punitive campaign)

1812

May 16 USA abolishes flogging—revived Mar 2, 1833; abolished Aug
         5, 1861
Jun 18 United States declares war on the United Kingdom
Jun 26 Congress authorizes letters of *marque and reprisal* against
         British vessels.
Jun 29 USRC *Jefferson* defeats *Patriot* (Br.)
Jul   9 USS *Hornet* defeats *Dolphin* (Br.)
Jul 17 *Shannon* (Br.) defeats USS *Nautilus*
Aug   9 British navy bombards Stonington, CT
Aug 13 USS *Essex* defeats *Alert* (Br.)
Aug 16 Ft. Detroit surrenders to British forces
Aug 19 USS *Constitution* defeats *Guerriere* (Br.)
Sep 12 Battle of Twelve Mile Swamp (punitive campaign)
Oct 13 Battle of Queenstown
Oct 18 USS *Wasp* defeats *Frolic* (Br.)
Oct 18 *Proictiers* (Br.) defeats USS *Wasp*
Oct 25 USS *United States* defeats *Macedonian* (Br.)
Nov   9 Naval bombardment—Kingston, Ontario

Nov 22 *Southhampton* (Br.) defeats USS *Vixen*
Dec 2 USS *Argus* defeats *Recovery* (Br.)
Dec 29 USS *Constitution* defeats *Java* (Br.)

1813

Jan 13 John Armstrong (Secretary of War)
Jan 19 William Jones (Secretary of the Navy)
Jan 21 Battle of Raisin River
Feb 24 USS *Hornet* defeats *Peacock* (Br.)
Mar 3 Army adopts "bureau system" for administration
Apr 27 Combined operation—York/Toronto
May 27 Combined operation—Queenstown Heights
May 28 Combined operation—ends May 29—Sackett's Harbor
Jun 1 *Shannon* (Br.) defeats USS *Chesapeake*
Jun 22 Naval action—James River (Battle of Craney Island)
Jul 13 USS *Essex* captures British Pacific whaling fleet
Jul 14 USS *Greenwich* defeats *Seringapatam*, Br. (*Greenwich* commanded by John M. Gamble, USMC)
Jul 30 Combined operation—York/Toronto
Aug 7 Naval action—L. Ontario—ends Aug 11
Aug 14 *Pelican* (Br.) defeats USS *Argus*
Sep 5 USS *Enterprise* defeats *Boxer* (Br.)
Sep 10 Naval action—L. Erie
Sep 11 Naval action—L. Ontario
Sep 28 Naval action—L. Ontario
Oct 4 USRC *Vigilant* captures *Dart* (Br.) by boarding
Oct 5 Battle of Thames
Oct 5 Naval action—L. Ontario
Oct 25 Battle of Chateauguay
Nov 3 Battle of Tallushatchee (punitive campaign)
Nov 9 Battle of Talledega (punitive campaign)
Nov 11 Battle of Chrysler's Farm
Dec 10 U.S. forces burn Newark, Ontario
Dec 29 British forces burn Buffalo

1814

Mar 27 Battle of Horseshoe Bend (punitive campaign)
Mar 28 *Phoebe* and *Cherub* (Br.) defeat USS *Essex*
Apr 29 USS *Peacock* defeats *Epervier* (Br.)
Jun 8 Naval action—St. Leonard's Creek—ends Jun 10
Jun 22 USS *Independence* launched (first ship-of-the-line)
Jun 28 USS *Wasp* defeats *Reindeer* (Br.)

Jul   5   Battle of Chippewa
Jul   11   *Leander* (Br.) defeats USS *Rattlesnake*
Jul   25   Battle of Lundy's Lane
Aug 1   Naval action—Patuxent River
Aug 13   Battle of Ft. Erie—ends Sep 21
Aug 24   Battle of Bladensburg
Aug 24   British forces occupy Washington, D.C.—withdraw Aug 26
Sep   1   USS *Wasp* defeats *Avon* (Br.)
Sep   3   USS *Tigress* captured by British boarding party—L. Huron
Sep   5   USS *Tigress* (under British control) captures USS *Scorpion*—
           L. Huron
Sep   11   Naval action—L. Champlain
Sep   13   Battle of North Point
Sep   13   British bombard Ft. McHenry—ends Sep 14
Sep   16   U.S. forces land Barataria Island (punitive expedition)
Sep   21   USS *Wasp* defeats *Atlante* (Br.)
Sep   26   *Carnation, Plantagenet,* and *Rota* (Br.) defeat U.S. privateer
           General Armstrong—ends Sep 27
Sep   27   James Monroe (Secretary of War)
Oct   29   USS *Fulton* I (first steam-powered warship launched)
Dec   14   Naval action—L. Borgne
Dec   23   Combined operation—Bayou Bienvenu
Dec   24   Treaty ends war with the United Kingdom
Dec   28   Battle of New Orleans—ends Jan 8, 1815

1815

Jan   15   *Endymion, Majestic, Pomone,* and *Tenedos* (Br.) capture USS
           President
Jan   16   Benjamin Crowninshield (Secretary of the Navy)
Jan   19   Naval action—L. Borgne—ends Jan 21
Feb   7   Congress establishes the Board of Naval Commissioners
Feb   8   Battle of Ft. Bowyer—ends Feb 12
Feb   20   USS *Constitution* defeats *Cyane* (Br.) and *Levant* (Br.)
Mar   2   U.S. declares war on Algiers
Mar   23   USS *Hornet* defeats *Penguin* (Br.)
Jun   17   USS *Guerriere, Constellation, Ontario,* and *Epervier* defeat
           Mashouda (Algiers)
Jun   30   USS *Peacock* v. *Nautilus* (Br.)
Jul   3   Treaty ends war with Algiers
Aug 1   William Crawford (Secretary of War)
Dec   10   First training school for naval officers established—
           Charlestown, MA

Military Operations

BATTLES OF LEXINGTON AND CONCORD (Apr 19, 1775). These battles in Massachusetts were the first military engagements of the American Revolution. Ordered to destroy the rebel supply depot at Concord, Lt. Col. Francis Smith sent Maj. John Pitcairn's detachment ahead to Lexington, where Capt. John Parker's militia confronted them. Parker's forces scattered, leaving him and seven others dead. The British returned to Boston from Concord exhausted, however, as snipers inflicted heavy casualties.

BATTLE OF BUNKER/BREED'S HILL (Jun 17, 1775). Despite orders to fortify Bunker Hill overlooking Boston, the Americans instead chose Breed's Hill, closer to the city. Attacking frontally, British troops dislodged the rebels in fierce, bloody combat and then successfully assaulted the reserves on Bunker Hill. To the surprise of the victors, the rebels fought tenaciously; the British suffered over 1,100 casualties, about 50 percent of the force. Gen. William Howe, horrified by the carnage, grew cautious for the rest of the war.

BATTLE OF LONG ISLAND (Aug 27–28, 1776). Wanting desperately to control New York City, Gen. George Washington fortified it and Brooklyn Heights on Long Island. Gen. William Howe's superior force outflanked the American troops in Brooklyn on the 27th. Gen. William Alexander's soldiers then held long enough for Washington to evacuate his remaining troops the next day, while Howe deliberated. In mid-September, Washington fended off British attacks while retreating to Harlem Heights at the north end of Manhattan. Although Howe wanted a decisive battle, his army was unable to pursue.

ATTACKS ON TRENTON AND PRINCETON (Dec 26, 1776–Jan 3, 1777). Gen. George Washington crossed the Delaware on Christmas night to attack British army garrison at Trenton. The Americans achieved total surprise and captured 1,000 British troops with negligible losses. On January 2, Gen. Lord Charles Cornwallis arrived with 6,000 troops; apparently trapped, the Americans slipped away in the night and moved on to Princeton. There, on January 3, they prevailed against three regiments of reinforcements which offered stiff resistance. Washington achieved victory and successfully avoided confrontation with Howe's main force.

SARATOGA CAMPAIGN (Jun 18–Oct 17, 1777). Gen. John Burgoyne's army drove south, reoccupying Fort Ticonderoga on July 6, while a smaller force of British and Iroquois under Lieut. Col. Barry St. Leger and Chief Joseph Brant drove east from Lake Ontario. Burgoyne pursued the Americans, but at Bennington, Vermont, they rallied and withstood two assaults on August 16, killing 200 and capturing 700. St. Leger's force, meanwhile, was stopped at Oriskany (August 6) and Fort Stanwix (August 22) by hard fighting and trickery. Under Gen. Horatio Gates, who replaced Gen. Philip Schuyler, the Americans stopped Burgoyne's advance in two battles near Freeman's Farm on Bemis Heights, the decisive second battle fought on October 7. Burgoyne subsequently accepted Gates' terms, surrendering an army of 5,000 men on October 17. A turning point, Saratoga convinced France to enter the war and caused a revision of British command and strategy.

BATTLE OF GERMANTOWN (Oct 4, 1777). Keeping his best 3,000 troops in Philadelphia, Gen. William Howe sent 9,000 soldiers north to Germantown. Gen. George Washington attacked with superior numbers. His army almost achieved surprise; after intense fighting, the British regained control when Gen. Lord Charles Cornwallis arrived from Philadelphia. Disappointed, Washington retreated but discouraged Cornwallis from following up. While the Americans suffered about 1,000 casualties, the British lost 535. Howe's victory was empty; his troops returned to Philadelphia for the winter, and the Americans quartered at Valley Forge.

BATTLE OF MONMOUTH (Jun 28, 1778). Gen. Henry Clinton evacuated Philadelphia to assume a defensive position in New York. As his forces left, the Americans followed. At Monmouth Courthouse, Gen. George Washington ordered Gen. Charles Lee's troops to advance, but upon meeting the main force, Lee retreated. Washington personally assumed command and his force repulsed several counterattacks, but was unable to mount another offensive. Essentially a draw, the battle did not deter the British from reaching New York, and it led to Lee's court-martial.

BATTLE OF VINCENNES (Feb 23–25, 1779). Col. George Rogers Clark led a small force into the West, occupying Kaskaskia on July 4, 1778. Col. Henry Hamilton was sent to rebuild a fort, which he named Fort Sackville, near Vincennes. Clark's Americans and Frenchmen marched 180 miles and, concealing their numbers, attacked on February 23. Hamilton's Native American allies deserted in the face of Clark's fierceness, and the fort surrendered on the 25th. Although Clark never mounted an offensive against Detroit, he secured part of the West for the Americans.

BATTLE OF STONY POINT (Jul 15–16, 1779). After Gen. Henry Clinton easily captured the American fort in May, Gen. George Washington ordered a surprise attack led by Gen. Anthony Wayne. The Americans marched during the night of July 15–16 and achieved their mission, killing sixty-three and capturing the rest of the garrison. American casualties numbered twenty-three. Washington then wisely withdrew his forces rather than allow Clinton to engage him in a major battle.

USS *BONHOMME RICHARD* DEFEATS HMS *SERAPIS* (Sep 23, 1779). Commanding a squadron headed by the *Bonhomme Richard*, a refitted French ship, Capt. John Paul Jones attacked a British convoy of cargo ships and two warships in British home waters. The *Richard* chased the *Serapis*, commanded by Capt. George F. Pearson, and the two ships engaged in battle on the night of the 23rd. Jones' sailors suffered heavy casualties but won the engagement, then transferred to the *Serapis* as the *Richard* sank. The action won British respect for American naval fighting ability, while Jones' challenging "I've not yet begun to fight," inspired successive generations of American sailors.

BATTLE OF CAMDEN (Aug 16, 1780). As Gen. Horatio Gates advanced on Camden, South Carolina, Gen. Lord Charles Cornwallis moved out to meet him. Each force surprised the other. Both drove forward, the British line holding firm and the American eventually buckling, but not without a staunch effort by regulars under Baron de Kalb. American losses totaled 600, the British about half that. Gates' army was destroyed, however, and his reputation never recovered.

BATTLE OF KING'S MOUNTAIN (Oct 7, 1780). American mounted militia, under the joint command of Col. Isaac Shelby, Col. William Campbell, Col. Benjamin Cleveland, Col. Charles McDowell and Col. John Sevier, caught Maj. Patrick Ferguson's corps of 1,000 Loyalists at King's Mountain. Advancing on foot, the backwoodsmen closed in on three sides and soundly defeated the Loyalists. Episodes of American revenge, such as the hanging of nine Loyalists after the fight, marked the battle. The defeat caused Gen. Lord Charles Cornwallis to move back to South Carolina.

BATTLE OF COWPENS (Jan 17, 1781). Heading a new American army, Gen. Nathanael Greene forced the pursuing Gen. Lord Charles Cornwallis to divide his troops. Gen. Daniel Morgan's forces made a stand at the Cowpens, South Carolina, against Col. Banastre Tarleton's advancing soldiers. Morgan devised an ingenious plan: his militia formed the front line, fired twice, then moved to the rear as if retreating, leaving the American regulars to trap the charging British. Almost half of Tarleton's 1,200 troops were killed or captured, and the rest hastily retreated. Frustrated by the defeat, Cornwallis cut his ties to his base and took to the offensive.

BATTLE OF GUILFORD COURTHOUSE (Mar 15, 1781). Gen. Nathanael Greene advanced his 5,000 troops of mostly militia to do battle with Gen. Lord Charles Cornwallis' army of 2,000 professional soldiers. Although Greene attempted to duplicate Gen. Daniel Morgan's strategy at Cowpens, his army could not carry the day. The outcome was not conclusive, though, as the British suffered 500 casualties and were too weak to follow the retreating Americans. Cornwallis became convinced he should carry the war into Virginia.

YORKTOWN CAMPAIGN (Aug 1–Oct 19, 1781). Moving into Virginia, Gen. Lord Charles Cornwallis fortified Yorktown, between the James and York rivers. Gen. George Washington assembled an army of 16,000 American and French troops which hemmed in the British forces. The Comte de Grasse's fleet of twenty-eight ships, meanwhile, sailed into Chesapeake Bay on August 30, defeated a British squadron on September 5, and coordinated with Washington's forces to isolate Cornwallis. The bombardment opened on October 9, and when relief from Gen. Henry Clinton in New York did not appear, Cornwallis surrendered unconditionally on the 19th. The capitulation effectively ended the military phase of the Revolution.

BATTLE OF FALLEN TIMBERS (Aug 20, 1794). A few miles from British-held Fort Miami (present-day Toledo), a force of Native Americans led by Chief Blue Jacket planned to trap Gen. Anthony Wayne's well-trained army at a fortification made of fallen trees. Uncovering the trap, Wayne's mounted riflemen and infantry attacked, causing a general retreat. The British refused to protect the fleeing Native Americans in Fort Miami. The battle led to cession by twelve tribes of much of the Ohio territory in the Treaty of Greenville in 1795.

DESTRUCTION OF THE USS *PHILADELPHIA* (Feb 16, 1804). Tripoli had declared war on the United States in 1801. While chasing an enemy ship near the harbor of Tripoli, the American frigate *Philadelphia* ran aground on October 31, 1803. The Tripolitans imprisoned the crew and floated the ship, bringing her into port. Lt. Stephen Decatur convinced Com. Edward Preble to allow him to sail into Tripoli, destroy the ship, and fight his way out, which he did on February 16, 1804. The mission, which Adm. Horatio Nelson reportedly called "the most bold and daring act of the age," was a complete success.

BATTLE OF TIPPECANOE CREEK (Nov 7, 1811). The brother of Shawnee chief Tecumseh, Tenskwatawa opposed the Americans and gathered followers at Prophet's Town, on Tippecanoe Creek. Gen. William Henry Harrison, the territorial governor of Indiana, sought to strike first, but was himself surprised outside Prophet's Town. Harrison's army managed to recover and hold, and two days later razed the village. American propaganda trumpeted Harrison's victory, which ended organized Native American resistance in the Northwest, although sporadic warfare continued.

SURRENDER OF FORT DETROIT (Aug 16, 1812). Gen. William Hull's troops cut a path to Fort Detroit to begin one phase of a planned four-pronged assault on Canada. Gen. Isaac Brock advanced to counteract him. When Brock threatened Detroit with uncontrollable Native American allies, opened a bombardment, and marched militia dressed as regulars within sight of the fort, Hull surrendered his army of 2,500 without a shot. The defeat shocked Americans, who thought Canada was easily vulnerable.

USS *CONSTITUTION* DEFEATS HMS *GUERRIERE* (Aug 19, 1812). About 750 miles out of Boston, Capt. Isaac Hull's aggressive action surprised Capt. James Dacres. The guns of the *Constitution* severely damaged the British ship, while musket fire took a toll on each side. Dacres capitulated; his emptied ship was set afire. Hull's victory offset news of his uncle's debacle at Detroit and proved that the navy could fight out of port. Several other single-ship engagements occurred before the British blockade took effect in 1814.

BATTLE OF QUEENSTON HEIGHTS (Oct 13, 1812). A second prong of the attack on Canada was launched from Niagara. Gen. Alexander Smyth failed to lead his troops into Canada as ordered. (He was dismissed from the service.) Gen. Stephen Van Rensselaer's dangerous night crossing of the Niagra to take Queenston, meanwhile, failed when Gen. Isaac Brock's troops arrived from Fort George. The Americans fought well, but militia reinforcements refused to come to their aid. Brock was killed in action.

ATTACK ON YORK/TORONTO (Apr 27, 1813). The American victory at York, the capital of Upper Canada, was more symbolic than strategic. Gen. Roger Sheaffe's small force withdrew under naval bombardment and an assault led by Gen. Zebulon Pike. The Americans suffered 300 casualties (Pike was killed), but they looted houses and burned two parliament buildings. Although some Canadians may have engaged in the destruction, the incident enraged many Canadians.

HMS *SHANNON* DEFEATS USS *CHESAPEAKE* (Jun 1, 1813). Capt James Lawrence, with an inexperienced crew, on the *Chesapeake* engaged Capt. Philip Broke's highly-trained sailors on HMS *Shannon*. Without much attempt at maneuver, the two vessels shot it out at close range. In fifteen minutes the British won. Lawrence, however, uttered the phrase "Don't give up the ship," before he died, and his words joined those of John Paul Jones as mottoes of the American navy.

BATTLE OF LAKE ERIE (Sep 10, 1813). The American forces gained control of the lake with this victory. The British, under Capt. Robert Barclay were outnumbered, nine vessels to six, but used their superiority in long-range guns to advantage at first. When Capt. Oliver Perry's ship, the USS *Lawrence*, was disabled, he courageously transferred his flag to the USS *Niagara*, which then broke through the British line and raked all six ships. By the end of the fighting, the British fleet surrendered.

BATTLE OF THE THAMES (Oct 5, 1813). Gen. William Henry Harrison's army met Gen. Henry Procter's retreating troops near Chatham on the Thames River. The Americans opened with a charge by mounted riflemen, which routed the startled British. The Shawnee chief Tecumseh was killed in battle, ending the threat of his Native American confederacy. Harrison hoped to drive more deeply into Canada, but returned to Detroit for the winter.

BATTLE OF HORSESHOE BEND/TOHOPEKA (Mar 27, 1814). Only one-eighth Creek, William Weatherford (Chief Red Eagle) nevertheless led a faction of that tribe against encroaching white settlers. The resulting war culminated at Horseshoe Bend. The Native Americans fortified the peninsula with a palisade. Gen. John Coffee and a group of Cherokees attacked from the rear, while Gen. Andrew Jackson's main force bombarded, then stormed, the fortification. Insofar as 800 Creeks died in this engagement, it was the most costly defeat in the history of the Native American resistance. The battle broke the back of the Creek war effort. Jackson, commanding Tennessee militia, later accepted a commission in the regular army.

BATTLE OF CHIPPEWA (Jul 5, 1814). American regulars, trained by Gen. Winfield Scott, demonstrated admirable military qualities not shown before in the war. Gen. Jacob Brown sought the battle, despite inferior numbers. Meeting the enemy in fairly open terrain, the Americans held their ground in the face of heavy fire, and their bayonet charge forced the British to retreat. British losses amounted to 500, the Americans 300. The value of the victory was more psychological than strategic, but no less real for that.

BATTLE OF LUNDY'S LANE (Jul 25, 1814). As at Chippewa, the armies met in open terrain. The fighting was heavy and continued into the night, with the Americans repulsing three British charges. As the Americans withdrew to replenish supplies, they lost the small hill for which they were fighting. Both sides suffered 900 casualties. The victory went to Gen. Gordon Drummond, but the ability of the American regulars to fight in open fields was a notable development.

BATTLE OF FORT ERIE (Aug 15, 1814). The British opened a siege of the reinforced fort on August 13, and launched a night assault two days later. Hand-to-hand combat produced a bloody battle, but the attackers withdrew, losing about one-third of their force. Gen. Gordon Drummond ended the siege on September 21, the battle having blunted his offensive toward the American Northwest.

BATTLE OF BLADENSBURG AND BURNING OF WASHINGTON (Aug 24–26, 1814). The British won the battle in three separate actions. In the heaviest fighting, Com. Joshua Barney, who destroyed his cornered fleet on the 22nd, led his sailors well, inflicting 500 casualties to 100, but capitulated on the 24th. Gen. William Winder withdrew his entire force behind Washington, and that evening Gen. Robert Ross' army marched into the city and burned several government buildings. Having insulted American pride, Ross left the smoldering city on the 26th.

BATTLE OF LAKE CHAMPLAIN (Sep 11, 1814). This British land and sea operation against Plattsburg on Lake Champlain produced a major naval engagement. Capt. Thomas Macdonough used every advantage magnificently, but the fighting on the lake was nonetheless intense. Eventually all the British ships were scuttled, as was the USS *Saratoga*. Gen. Sir George Prevost, convinced of the importance of controlling the lake, retreated after a few failed thrusts at the American fortifications. The defeat ended British plans for an invasion.

ATTACK ON BALTIMORE (Sep 12–14, 1814). Gen. Robert Ross began a land assault on the 12th, but was slowed by Gen. John Stricker's brigade. The next day, Adm. Sir Alexander Cochrane's fleet opened a bombardment of Fort McHenry, which withstood a tremendous shelling. Gen. Samuel Smith's defenses held, and on the 14th the British withdrew. Francis Scott Key, watching the action in the harbor, was moved to write his poem, "The Star Spangled Banner."

BATTLE OF NEW ORLEANS (Jan 8, 1815). Both sides were unaware that their nations had already agreed to peace, but Americans gained immense satisfaction from Jackson's stunning victory. Britain's powerful invasion force confronted Jackson's motley army, which fortified lines across the principal, narrow approach to the city. Although hostilities began on December 23, the British main advance came in the early morning of January 8. By 8:30 A.M., the battle was over. The British had lost about 2,000 men, one-third of the force, the Americans seven dead and six wounded. American newspapers trumpeted the "glorious victory," lionizing Gen. Andrew Jackson and leaving the impression that the United States won the war.

Biographical Notes

ALLEN, ETHAN (1738–1789). As the leader of Vermont's Green Mountain Boys, Allen with the help of Benedict Arnold and local militia captured Fort Ticonderoga on Lake Champlain on May 10, 1775. Allen was subsequently captured by the British during the ill-fated Montreal campaign. He gained his freedom in a prisoner exchange and returned home.

BAINBRIDGE, WILLIAM (1774–1833). A sailor from the age of fifteen, Bainbridge fought the British in the American Revolution and the Barbary pirates from 1798 to 1805. He commanded the frigate USS *Philadelphia* at Tripoli in 1803 where the ship ran aground and he was captured. Released in 1805, he helped make peace with the pirates. Bainbridge subsequently commanded the USS *Constitution* in its victory over the British frigate *Java* (1812).

BARNEY, JOSHUA (1759–1818). A Revolutionary War naval officer, Barney fought the British many times. He is best known for his skill in capturing the bigger *General Monk* in 1782. In the War of 1812 he resourcefully hindered the British advance on Washington, D.C. and then fought in the Battle of Bladensburg (1814) where he was wounded and taken prisoner.

BIDDLE, JAMES (1783–1848). Biddle served with Capt. William Bainbridge in the war with Tripoli and along with his commander was captured and imprisoned (1803). He commanded the sloop USS *Wasp* and captured the British *Frolic* (1812) and subsequently outfought the British with the sloop *Hornet* (1815). In 1845 he negotiated the first treaty between the United States and China.

BUSHNELL, DAVID (1742?–1824). Bushnell built a small one-man submarine that was called *Bushnell's Turtle* (later the *American Turtle*). He armed it with detachable gun powder mine that could be screwed into the hull of an enemy ship. His submarine went into action in New York (1776) and New London (1777) harbors, but it failed to do any significant damage.

CLARK, GEORGE ROGERS (1752–1818). Clark explored parts of Kentucky prior to the Revolutionary War. Commissioned in the militia, Clark captured, lost, and recaptured Vincennes fort in Illinois in 1778–1779. He is largely credited with holding much of the Old Northwest for the United States for the remainder of the war. He subsequently participated in several failed military and colonization schemes in the West.

CORBIN, MARGARET (1751–1800). When her husband, John Corbin, was killed by Hessian soldiers while firing a field gun near Fort Washington on November 16, 1776, Margaret Corbin took his place until brought down by her own wounds, which left her permanently disabled. The American forces subsequently surrendered their position, but Corbin was not taken prisoner. In 1779 the Continental Congress granted her a soldier's half-pay pension for life and in 1783 she was formally mustered out of the Continental Army. Corbin is sometimes confused with Mary McCauley ("Molly Pitcher").

DECATUR, STEPHEN (1779–1820). Born in Maryland, Decatur led a daring raid on the harbor of Tripoli in the Barbary Wars to burn the captured frigate USS *Philadelphia* (February 16, 1804). He subsequently helped negotiate peace in 1805. During the War of 1812 Decatur commanded the USS *United States* which captured the British frigate *Macedonian* (1812), a great victory. In 1815 his squadron put an end to all piracy by the Barbary States.

ESTAING, CHARLES, COMTE DE (1729–1794). A French naval commander, the Comte d'Estaing first tried to block the British fleet under Admiral Richard Howe in New York (1778). He later fought the British at Savannah (1779) in aid of Gen. Benjamin Lincoln and was wounded. He was guillotined in 1794 in Paris during the French Revolution.

GATES, HORATIO (c. 1728–1806). Born in England, Gates saw service in the British Army during the French and Indian War where he met George Washington. Washington encouraged Gates to take up land in Virginia (1772). Gates sided with the colonies at the outbreak of the Revolutionary War and was commissioned a brigadier general. He was subsequently promoted to major general (1776), succeeded Gen. Philip Shuyler in northern New York, and with the help of Benedict Arnold defeated Gen. John Burgoyne's British forces at the Battle of Saratoga (1777). Gates was subsequently linked to the scheme known as the Conway Cabal, named after Gen. Thomas Conway, which sought to replace Washington as commander with Gates. Gates' degree of involvement in this intrigue is unclear and although the plot failed, he continued to serve in the Continental Army. He subsequently lost the disastrous battle of Camden (1780) to Gen. Lord Charles Cornwallis and was relieved of command. In 1782 Congress, without inquiry, ordered Gates back into service under Washington, whom he served loyally for the remainder of the war.

GRASSE, FRANCOIS-JOSEPH-PAUL, COMTE DE (1722–1788). A French admiral, de Grasse fought the British in the American Revolution in the West Indies (1779–1780). He successfully prevented the British from providing naval support to the besieged Gen. Lord Charles Cornwallis at Yorktown (1781) by operating off the mouth of the Chesapeake Bay. This helped Washington to force Cornwallis to surrender.

GREENE, NATHANAEL (1742–1786). Raised a Quaker, the Society of Friends expelled Greene for his interest in military affairs. He was commissioned a brigadier general in the Continental Army (1775) and then promoted to major general (1776) at the time he was defending New York City. Greene served with distinction in the Battles of Trenton (1776), Brandywine (1777), Germantown (1777), and Monmouth (1778). When Benedict Arnold's plot to betray West Point came to light in 1780, Greene served as president of the court-martial that condemned Col. John Andre, a British spy, to death by hanging. Late in 1780 Greene relieved Gen. Horatio Gates as commander of the army in the South. He subsequently fought British Gen. Charles Cornwallis in a strategic retreat that culminated in victory at Cowpens (1781). His army then fought at Guilford Courthouse, Hobkirk Hill, Eutaw Springs, and the siege of Charleston (1781–1782) when the British finally withdrew at the end of the war.

HARRISON, WILLIAM HENRY (1773–1841). His victory over the tribal coalition organized by Tecumseh at the Battle of Tippecanoe Creek was a severe blow to the Native American effort to resist the settlement of the frontier. Harrison was subsequently elected President of the United States (1840), but died after one month in office. James A. Greene, *William Henry Harrison: His Life and Times* (1941).

HOPKINS, ESEK (1718–1802). A merchant sea captain and successful privateer during the French and Indian War, Hopkins was named commodore of the fledgling Continental Navy in 1775. Ordered to sail to the Chesapeake Bay, Hopkins chose instead to operate in the Bahamas where he captured valuable war material at New Providence (1776). Hopkins and his fleet then returned to New England fighting British naval forces inconclusively. The Continental Congress subsequently grew dissatisfied with Hopkins' lack of results, censured him (October 1776), suspended him from command (March 1777), and dismissed him from naval service (January 1778).

HUMPHREYS, JOSHUA (1751–1838). When the American Revolution broke out in 1775, the Continental Congress called on Joshua Humphreys, an accomplished shipbuilder, to refit eight small merchant vessels for the command of Esek Hopkins. Humphreys was later appointed the first U.S. naval constructor (1794–1801). He prepared plans and supervised the re-building of the U.S. Navy as authorized by Congress in 1794. The new frigates (USS *Constitution, President, United States, Chesapeake, Constellation,* and *Congress*) were the nucleus of the naval forces that fought the War of 1812. The success of Humphrey's ships proved the value of his innovative ship design ideas which were widely copied.

JACKSON, ANDREW (1767–1845). Although he was already famous for punitive expeditions against Native American tribes, his defense of New Orleans (1815) against a British assault made him a living legend. He later served as President of the United States (1829–1837). Robert Remini, *Andrew Jackson and the Course of American Empire, 1767–1821* (1977).

JONES, JOHN PAUL (1747–1792). While aboard the USS *Bonhomme Richard,* a squadron under his command attacked a British convoy (1779). A desperate battle ensued between Jones' ship and the British frigate *Serapis* which led the British commander to surrender. Samuel E. Morison, *John Paul Jones: A Sailor's Biography* (1959).

KNOX, HENRY (1750–1806). Friend and adviser to George Washington, Knox began his military career in 1772 in Boston. Commissioned a colonel and given command of the Continental Army's artillery in 1775, he successfully transported fifty-five artillery pieces 300 miles from Fort Ticonderoga to Boston. Knox was promoted to brigadier general and major general (1781), was present at nearly all major battles in the north, and served at Yorktown at the war's end. In May 1783 Knox organized the Society of the Cincinnati and succeeded Washington as commander of the army (1783–1784). He was elected Secretary of War by the Congress under the Articles of Confederation (1785) and was reappointed as Secretary of War in 1789 with the ratification of the U.S. Constitution. He served until his resignation and return to private life in 1794.

KOSCIUSKO, TADEUSZ/THADDEUS KOSCIUSKO (1746–1817). Born in Belorussia, Kosciusko began his military career in Warsaw and later studied engineering in Paris. When the American Revolution broke out, he applied to Benjamin Franklin for help in getting a commission from the Continental Congress. He joined the Continental Army in 1776, serving with distinction at Ticonderoga, Saratoga (1777), and in the Carolinas with Gen. Nathaniel Greene (1780–1782) as chief engineer. In 1783 he received the thanks of Congress, permanent citizenship, and appointment as a brigadier general. In 1784 he returned to Poland and subsequently led Polish forces in rebellion against the Russians (1794). Kosciusko was captured and imprisoned (1794–1796). Prior to his death, he worked continuously to gain freedom for Poland and set a personal model by using his own money to buy freedom for slaves in the United States.

LAWRENCE, JAMES (1781–1813). Lawrence entered the U.S. Navy as a midshipman in 1798. He subsequently served as second in command to Stephen Decatur in the raid to destroy the captured USS *Philadelphia* in Tripoli harbor (1804) during the Barbary Wars. In the War of 1812 Lawrence commanded the USS *Hornet* (1812–1813) raiding British commerce and defeating the brig *Peacock* with superior tactics. Promoted to captain, Lawrence took command of the USS *Chesapeake*. When the USS *Chesapeake* engaged the British *Shannon* outside Boston harbor (1813), Lawrence was mortally wounded. He told his men: "Don't give up the ship," as he was carried below. This famous appeal gave Lawrence heroic stature among naval commanders.

LEWIS, MERIWETHER (1774–1809). Lewis began his military career in 1794 when, as a member of the Virginia militia, he took part in the suppression of the Whiskey Rebellion. He subsequently came to know Lt. William Clark, who was to be his future partner in westward exploration. In 1801 President Thomas Jefferson made Capt. Lewis his private secretary and began preparations to seek a land route across the continental United States, particularly the territory recently purchased from France. In 1803 Congress authorized the money for the expedition. Lewis requested that Clark be given joint command of the exploring party. The Lewis and Clark expedition subsequently went up the Missouri River (1804), crossed the Great Divide, and then descended the Clearwater, Snake, and Columbia Rivers to the Pacific (1805). They returned to St. Louis in the fall of 1806. The expedition is credited with providing great knowledge of the flora, fauna, terrain, Native American tribes, and mineral resources of the Louisiana Purchase. It also greatly strengthened U.S. claims to the Oregon Territory. The journals of this expedition were subsequently published in 1814.

LINCOLN, BENJAMIN (1733–1810). When the Revolutionary War began, Lincoln was a brigadier general in the Massachusetts militia. He commanded troops engaged in the siege of Boston (1776) and was later commissioned major general in the Continental Army (1777). He fought under Gates at Saratoga (1777) and was wounded. Following his recovery, he was given command in the South where in 1779 he laid siege to Savannah with the help of the French fleet under the Comte d'Estaing. Lincoln and his army were subsequently captured in Charleston (1779) by Sir Henry Clinton, but he later gained freedom in a prisoner exchange and fought with Washington in the victory at Yorktown (1781). When Shays' Rebellion broke out in Massachusetts in 1787, Lincoln commanded the force that suppressed the rebels. In 1788–1789 he actively worked to persuade Massachusetts to ratify the proposed U.S. Constitution.

McCAULEY, MARY LUDWIG HAYS (1754–1832). Known as "Molly Pitcher" Molly Ludwig married John Hays in Carlisle, Pennsylvania in 1769. Hays was a member of the 7th Pennsylvania Regiment at the Battle of Monmouth Courthouse (1778), when he collapsed at his artillery post from the heat. Molly, who along with the wives of other soldiers, was assisting the artillerymen with pitchers of drinking water, took Hays' place at his cannon and served for the remainder of the battle. Having earned the nickname "Molly Pitcher," she later married John (or George) McCauley after Hays died in 1789. In 1822 the Pennsylvania legislature voted her a pension of $40 per year for her heroism at Monmouth.

MACDONOUGH, THOMAS (1783–1825). Macdonough joined the U.S. Navy in 1800 as a midshipman. He subsequently served under Capt. William Bainbridge and Lt. Stephen Decatur in the Tripolitan War. When the War of 1812 broke out, Macdonough was given command of a small fleet on Lake Champlain (1812–1814) and successfully defeated the British squadron at Plattsburg (September 11, 1814) to help save Vermont and New York from occupation by British troops.

McGILLIVRAY, ALEXANDER (1759?–1793). McGillivray, the son of a Scottish merchant and a French-Creek princess, was born and grew up in the South. Because his father was pro-British during the American Revolution, McGillivray returned to his mother's tribe, where her lineage assured him a position of leadership. The British gave him the rank of colonel and he promoted Native American attacks on frontier settlements. After the war McGillivray worked repeatedly to form a confederation of southern tribes to push back white settlers. Beginning in 1783 he also sought Spanish help against the advance of the Americans, including inciting attacks on settlements in 1785–1787. McGillivray negotiated a peace treaty with the United States (1790), which he subsequently repudiated (1792) when Spain offered him better terms.

MARION, FRANCIS (1732?–1795). Marion saw his initial military service against the Cherokee in 1759 and 1761. Commissioned as a captain in 1775, Marion was promoted to lieutenant colonel when his South Carolina militia unit was mustered into the Continental Army in 1776. From 1777 to the end of the war, he served in command of militia troops harassing the British. Marion fought with Gen. Benjamin Lincoln at Savannah (1779) and Charleston (1780) and with Gen. Horatio Gates at Camden (1780). Marion developed a technique to attack larger bodies of British troops with sudden raids and then to escape into the nearby swamps and forests. This earned him the nickname "Swamp Fox." In 1781 he rescued the American forces surrounded by the British at Parker's Ferry and then took part in the Battle of Eutaw Springs in September of that year.

MONTGOMERY, RICHARD (1738–1775). Born in Dublin, Montgomery joined the British Army in 1756. He served with Gen. Jeffrey Amherst's forces in the capture of Louisbourg (1758) and in Gen. James Wolfe's capture of Montreal (1760). In 1772 he left the army and emigrated to New York (1773). A strong supporter of American independence, Montgomery was commissioned a brigadier general in the Continental Army (1775). He served in Gen. Philip Schuyler's campaign to capture Montreal. When Schuyler fell ill, Montgomery took command. His troops captured Montreal in November 1775. The following month, Montgomery joined Col. Benedict Arnold's force in attacking Quebec in a snowstorm on December 31. Montgomery was killed in that assault, which failed.

MORGAN, DANIEL (1736–1802). Morgan first fought Native Americans for the British (1763–1764), before fighting the British as a leader in the Continental Army. He served under Benedict Arnold in the failed assault on Quebec (1775) and was captured. Following his return in a prisoner exchange (1776), he fought with Gen. Horatio Gates at Saratoga (1777) and Gen. George Washington at Philadelphia. In 1780 Morgan was assigned to Gates. When Gates was replaced by Gen. Nathanael Greene, Morgan, now a brigadier general, had command in North Carolina. He brilliantly defeated the British at Cowpens (1781). After the war, Morgan commanded the Virginia militia that helped suppress the Whiskey Rebellion (1794) in western Pennsylvania.

PERRY, OLIVER HAZARD (1785–1819). Older brother of Matthew C. Perry, another famous U.S. naval officer, Oliver H. Perry began his naval career in 1799. He served in the naval war with Tripoli and then helped enforce the Embargo Act of 1807. In early 1813 Perry received orders to Erie, Pennsylvania, to build and equip a naval fleet for Lake Erie. In September Perry's force engaged the British in the Battle of Lake Erie.

Despite the destruction of his flagship, the USS *Lawrence*, Perry transferred his command to the USS *Niagara* and continued the fight, eventually forcing the British to surrender. After the battle Perry sent Gen. William Henry Harrison his famous message: "We have met the enemy and they are ours."

PREBLE, EDWARD (1761–1807). Preble fought as a youthful sailor against the British in the American Revolution. In 1798 he took a commission in the U.S. Navy and fought in the naval war with France (1800). Preble then took command of the USS *Constitution* (1803) and sailed to Tripoli where he blockaded the harbor and sent Lt. Stephen Decatur to burn the captured USS *Philadelphia* (1804). In subsequent attacks in August and September of that year, Preble forced the Tripolitans to seek peace. He is also credited with creating the first working tactical naval squadron in his operations against Tripoli.

ST. CLAIR, ARTHUR (1736–1818). Born in Scotland and trained in the British Army, St. Clair then settled in western Pennsylvania (1762). As a brigadier general, he fought with the New Jersey militia at Trenton (1776) and Princeton (1777). Promoted to major general, he subsequently fought British Gen. John Burgoyne at Fort Ticonderoga. He secretly abandoned Ticonderoga and came back later to defeat Burgoyne. He was much criticized, saw little action in the remainder of the war, but was completely acquitted in a court-martial in 1778. After the war he served in state politics in Pennsylvania and in the U.S. Congress. When the Northwest Ordinance of 1787 created the Northwest Territory, he served as its governor (1787–1802). As governor, St. Clair negotiated the Treaty of Fort Harmar (1789) which was very unfavorable to the Native Americans. War broke out with the advance of white settlers, and St. Clair, who was in command of poorly trained militia, was badly defeated near Fort Wayne (1791). St. Clair was exonerated, but President Thomas Jefferson removed him from office in 1802 for criticizing the legislation that created the state of Ohio.

SHAYS, DANIEL (1747?–1825). As a soldier in the American Revolution, Shays served with distinction at Bunker Hill, Ticonderoga, Saratoga, and Stony Point. Although he was commissioned a captain in the Massachusetts militia in 1777, Shays resigned and settled in Pelham, Massachusetts in 1780. Severe economic depression after the war and the failure of the Massachusetts legislature to take action for redress of grievances among the farmers of western Massachusetts led Shays to join in armed rebellion in 1786. Shays was but one of several leaders, but the insurrection was named for him, mainly because of an armed confrontation at Springfield on September 26. Although a troubled peace followed, actual fighting occurred with the militia at Springfield on January 25, 1787. Gen. Benjamin Lincoln then routed the rebels at Petersham (February 21) and Shays fled to Vermont. Shays was condemned to death *in absentia*, but he petitioned for and received a pardon in 1788. Shays' Rebellion did hasten economic reforms and helped persuade many leaders that the United States needed a stronger central government that could deal with such uprisings.

STEUBEN, FRIEDRICH VON (1730–1794). Born in Prussia, von Steuben began military service at an early age. When his military career in Europe stalled, von Steuben got Silas Deane and Benjamin Franklin, American agents in France, to provide him with letters of introduction to General Washington. He reported to Washington at Valley Forge (1778) and quickly proved to be an effective drillmaster, bringing discipline and order to the Continental Army. Congress appointed him Inspector General with the rank of major general later in 1778. Gen. von Steuben fought at the battles of Monmouth and Yorktown (1781), where he commanded a division under Marquis de Lafayette. After the war he became an American citizen (1783) and received a lifetime annual pension from the U.S. Congress (1790).

STODDERT, BENJAMIN F. (1751–1813). Stoddert served in the Pennsylvania militia from 1777–1779 when he was appointed secretary of the Board of War (1779–1781) of the Continental Congress. After the war he settled in Georgetown, Maryland, buying a partnership in a merchant firm. Because of his success as a real estate investor, George Washington and others asked Stoddert to act confidentially as the agent for the new government in buying large tracts of land on which the federal capital city of Washington was to be built. His care in handling this task prevented a frenzy of land speculation. Stoddert later was appointed the first secretary of the U.S. Navy (1798–1801) and drafted the legislation that provided for the re-establishment of the Marine Corps (1798).

TECUMSEH, or TECUMTHA, or TIKAMTHI (1768–1813). A chief among the Shawnees, he was born in the area that is now Ohio. Tecumseh's father was killed in a battle with white colonists in 1774. Tecumseh was a prominent warrior in the turmoil involving the expansion of white settlement along the frontier during and after the Revolution. But he also took an effective stand against the practice of torture and killing of captives. Tecumseh refused to participate in negotiations leading to the Treaty of Greenville because he believed lands belonged to all Native Americans and could not be sold or ceded by their chiefs. This stand gained Tecumseh a wide reputation as an orator. Beginning in 1808, Tecumseh attempted to form a confederation to oppose white settlement. He and his brother, Tenskwatawa, known as the "The Prophet," preached a return to the traditional ways—free of white practices. William Henry Harrison, governor of Indiana Territory, put pressure on the fragile confederacy in an effort to gain more land by treaty. While Tecumseh was away, Harrison negotiated with other Native Americans at Tippecanoe Creek (1811), but the Prophet led an attack on Harrison's forces that brought defeat. Tecumseh then sought help unsuccessfully from the British (1812). He was subsequently killed at the Battle of the Thames (1813).

TRUXTON, THOMAS (1755–1822). Truxton sailed in command of several privateers during the American Revolution, capturing a number of British prizes. Following the war, he went back to merchant service (1783–1794) until he was commissioned as a captain in the U.S. Navy during the undeclared naval war with France (1798–1800). In command of the USS *Constellation*, Truxton defeated the French frigates *Insurgente* (1799) and *La Vengeance* (1800). He is credited with helping to set standards of discipline and in maintaining high morale in the new U.S. Navy.

WASHINGTON, GEORGE (1732–1799). His appointment as General of the Armies (1775) was another milestone in a distinguished career of public service that climaxed in his selection as the first President of the United States. Don Higginbotham, *George Washington and the American Military Tradition* (1985).

WAYNE, ANTHONY (1745–1796). Anthony Wayne had a long and distinguished military career that included service in the American Revolution in the expedition to Canada (1776) and battles of Ticonderoga (1776), Brandywine (1777), Germantown (1777), and Monmouth (1778). He led the attack that captured the British garrison at Stony Point (1779) and helped protect West Point following Benedict Arnold's treasonous plot. Wayne also fought at Yorktown (1781). He retired in 1783, served in the U.S. House from Georgia (1791–1792), and was later appointed by President Washington as a major general to deal with the turmoil involving whites and Native Americans on the Ohio frontier. After much training, his troops decisively engaged the Native Americans in the brief Battle of Fallen Timbers (1794). Without British aid, the Native American leaders soon lost their will to resist and agreed in the Treaty of Greenville (1795) to open much of their land to white settlement. Wayne earned his nickname of "Mad Anthony" because some soldiers saw his tactical boldness and personal courage in battle as reckless.

Selected Reading List

Reference and General Works

Bloomfield, Howard V. L. *The Compact History of the United States Coast Guard* (1966). Bloomfield's history is written for a popular audience and emphasizes coast guard operations, especially those linked with American military activities.

Capron, Walter C. *The U. S. Coast Guard* (1965). This is a largely institutional history that emphasizes the development of the wide range of coast guard activities.

Coffman, Edward M. *The Old Army: A Portrait of the American Army in Peacetime, 1784–1898* (1986). Coffman's social history of the Army includes women associated with the army as well as soldiers and officers. A second volume is promised.

Coletta, Paolo E. *An Annotated Bibliography of U. S. Marine Corps History* (1986). Coletta includes all works in which there is significant reference to Marine Corps activities in this subject guide to over 3,900 books, articles, and dissertations.

Coletta, Paolo E. *A Bibliography of American Naval History* (1981). Coletta provides a chronologically organized list of nearly 4,900 books, articles and dissertations dealing with the history of the navy.

Cresswell, Mary A. and Carl Berger. *The United States Air Force: An Annotated Bibliography* (1971). This is an annotated subject guide to nearly 1,000 books, articles, and sources dealing with air force history.

Davis, Lenwood G. and George Hill. *Blacks in the American Armed Forces, 1776–1983: A Bibliography* (1985). Davis and Hill compiled an extensive list of nearly 2,400 books, articles, and dissertations in which one can find significant reference to the black military experience in America.

Glines, Carroll V., Jr. *The Compact History of the United States Air Force* (1980). Glines presents an institutional history of the development of the air force with an emphasis on operations, particularly those during World War II.

Hagan, Kenneth J. and William R. Roberts, eds. *Against All Enemies: Interpretations of American Military History from Colonial Times to the Present* (1986). While the books by Matloff and Weigley listed below provide the best introductions to the operational and institutional history of the army, this collection of essays by major authorities provides a view of the latest interpretations of each of the major periods in the history of the army.

Higham, Robin, ed. *A Guide to the Sources of United States Military History* (1975, with supplements published in 1981, 1986, and 1993). This is the most comprehensive and detailed overall guide to American military history available. It includes a subject guide to books, articles, and dissertations covering all armed services. All sections are introduced by a lengthy historiographical essay.

Hill, Jim D. *The Minute Man in Peace and War: A History of the National Guard* (1964). While Hill is clearly sympathetic to the Guard, this is still the most comprehensive history of the institutional development of the National Guard available.

Johnson, Charles. *African-American Soldiers in the National Guard: Recruitment and Deployment During Peacetime and War* (1992). Johnson provides an examination of African American Guard units from 1877 to 1949, focussing in particular on their military achievements and the efforts to integrate the Guard.

Lane, Jack C. *America's Military Past: A Guide to Information Sources* (1980). This is a brief, but handy, annotated selected guide to nearly 1,800 books and articles limited largely to the history of the army.

Love, Robert W. *History of the U.S. Navy* (1992). This two-volume survey is currently the most comprehensive institutional history of the U.S. Navy available. The focus is on the politics of policy and strategy formation with emphasis on the roles and activities of major statesmen and officers. However, operations and the development of technology are also covered.

Matloff, Maurice. *American Military History* (1973, reprinted and partially revised). Matloff provides a traditional military history focussed almost entirely on army operations and written primarily for cadets.

Millett, Allan R. and Peter Maslowski. *For the Common Defense: A Military History of the United States of America* (1984, rev. expanded 1994). The authors include in this text the experiences of all combat services of the armed forces with a nod to the emphasis now being given to the relationship of armed forces and society.

Millett, Allan R. *Semper Fidelis: The History of the United States Marine Corps* (1980). Millett has written a survey of Marine Corps history from the American Revolution to the present including institutional and political developments as well as operations.

Moskin, T. Robert. *The U.S. Marine Corps Story* (1977). Moskin's popular narrative history is focused almost entirely on operations and contains a wealth of anecdotal material.

Nalty, Bernard C. *Strength for the Fight: A History of Black Americans in the Military* (1986). This is a survey of the black experience in the American armed forces from colonial times to the present with a special focus on the process of integration.

Natkiel, Richard. *Atlas of American Military History* (1986). Natkiel covers the period from the French and Indian War to the Panama Intervention with a collection of maps at both the tactical and strategic level together with pictures and brief accompanying text.

Spiller, Roger J., et al., eds. *Dictionary of American Military Biography* (1984). This is a three-volume collection of short biographies of military figures from all services and major service-related civilians from the colonial period forward.

Weigley, Russell F. *The American Way of War: A History of United States Military Strategy and Policy* (1973). Weigley offers an interpretive study of the development of American military thought and practice in regard to strategy.

Weigley, Russell F. *History of the United States Army* (1967). This is the best institutional history of the army with special focus on its relationship with the American tradition of the citizen-soldier.

Colonial America

For a long time the work on the military history of colonial America tended to be limited to either the involvement of the colonies in the seventeenth and eighteenth century European wars for empire or conflicts with the Native Americans. While interest in these two areas continues, the focus in each is tending to shift. Works on imperial wars are now more concerned with setting the colonial conflicts into larger international contexts, while works on the conflicts with Native Americans now show an increased interest in, and sympathy for, their side of the struggle.

Moreover, in the past two decades, historians have also begun to take a major interest in the colonial militias. While such works continue to survey the military operations of the militias, there is also interest in their institutional development within the framework of individual colonial societies. In addition, some historians now argue that in the eighteenth century some militias were beginning to evolve into semi-professional military forces. As a result, the Americans entered the Revolution in 1775 with far more experience with military organizations and operations than has previously been thought.

Reference and General Works

Ferling, John. *Struggle for a Continent: The Wars of Early America* (1993). This is a fairly traditional survey of the wars fought against Native Americans and among Europeans in Colonial America with emphasis on actual military operations. The approach is modernized with more emphasis on the nature and brutality of the experience.

Leach, Douglas E. *Arms for Empire: A Military History of the British Colonies in North America, 1607–1763* (1973). Leach surveys both the imperial wars and important conflicts with Native Americans as well as analyzing the development of colonial militias.

Lydon, James G. *Struggle for Empire: A Bibliography of the French and Indian Wars, 1739–1763* (1983). Lydon's annotated guide covers the entire colonial period far more amply than its title implies.

Shrader, Charles R. *Reference Guide to United States Military History, 1607–1815, Volume One* (1991). Shrader's guide provides an introduction to early American military organizations, short biographies of leaders, descriptions of major events and a bibliography.

The Struggle for Empire

Dunnigan, Brian L. *Siege 1759—the Campaign Against Niagara* (1986). In this campaign history related to the wars for empire, Dunnigan argues that the siege was carried on in a largely European fashion.

Jennings, Francis. *Empire of Fortune: Crowns, Colonies, and Tribes in the Seven Years War in America* (1988). Jennings sets the war into a larger political context and argues that military success in the conflict rested more with the ability to gain Native American allies than with winning engagements.

Peckham, Howard H. *The Colonial Wars, 1689–1762* (1964). Peckham's is one of the most detailed of the earlier military accounts of the colonial counterparts of the major eighteenth century European wars.

Frontier Struggle with the Native Americans

Bourne, Russell. *The Red King's Rebellion: Racial Politics in New England, 1675–1678* (1990). While Bourne does consider the social and racial aspects of King Philip's War, his emphasis is on military operations.

Malone, Patrick M. *The Skulking Way of War: Technology and Tactics Among the New England Indians* (1991). With its focus on the Pequot War (1636–1637) and King Philip's War (1675–1676) Malone studies the impact of the introduction of white military technology, especially gunpowder weapons, on Native American military culture in southern New England. He finds that Native Americans adapted easily and early to the use of these weapons, adapting them to their own needs and habits.

Peckham, Howard H. *Pontiac and the Indian Uprising* (1947). This is still the classic account of the best known of the eighteenth century Native American uprisings. The focus is on Pontiac for whom Peckham has great respect.

Naval Histories

Lydon, James G. *Pirates, Privateers, and Profits* (1970). Lydon emphasizes the entrepreneurial side of privateering focusing on New York as the major privateering center in America.

Swanson, Carl E. *Predators and Prizes: American Privateering and Imperial Warfare, 1739–1748* (1991). While Swanson limits his study to King George's War, this is still the best current study of American privateering in the colonial period.

Militia and Society

Ahearn, Marie L. *The Rhetoric of War: Training Day, the Militia, and the Military Sermon* (1989). Following the lead of historians who argue that training day was used as a means of socializing the militia, Ahearn analyzes the role played by the sermons read on those days as part of the process.

Anderson, Fred. *A People's Army: Massachusetts Soldiers and Society in the Seven Years' War* (1984). Anderson argues that the perceived quality of the Massachusetts militia was largely a product of the soldiers' attitudes concerning war and militia service.

Dederer, John M. *War in America to 1775: Before Yankee Doodle* (1990). This is chiefly an intellectual history of how colonial Americans thought about war. Dederer argues that the American view of war was based on prevailing European ideas as modified by both the American frontier experience and growing liberal ideology.

Ferling, John E. *A Wilderness of Miseries: War and Warriors in Early America* (1980). Ferling claims that colonial America faced frequent violence of considerable magnitude and explores the impact this had on society.

Higginbotham, Don. *George Washington and the American Military Tradition* (1985). Higginbotham provides a useful bridge between the American colonial military tradition and the Revolution by arguing that Washington's ambitions as a young officer to serve in a strictly regular army were mellowed by later experiences to produce a commander capable of working with both professional and citizen soldiers.

Melvoin, Richard I. *New England Outpost: War and Society in Colonial Deerfield* (1989). For most of the seventeenth century Deerfield faced frequent violent contact with Native Americans. This book is a study of how the town organized for this conflict and the impact it had on society.

Selesky, Harold E. *War and Society in Colonial Connecticut* (1990). Selesky argues that during the two centuries prior to the Revolution the Connecticut militia evolved from an amateur self-defense force to a semi-professional participant in the European wars for empire.

Shea, William L. *The Virginia Militia in the Seventeenth Century* (1983). In this book Shea studies the institutional and operational history of the Virginia militia with emphasis on the social politics of recruitment and organization of such forces.

Titus, James. *The Old Dominion at War: Society, Politics, and Warfare in Late Colonial Virginia* (1991). Titus continues Shea's approach by analyzing Virginia's participation in the French and Indian War with primary focus on the social politics of militia mobilization.

The American Revolution

For several decades after World War II, the American Revolution was treated from a nationalist perspective with emphasis on great men and great battles, especially in the northern theater and in the early years of the war. Starting in the 1970s, under the impact of both the bicentennial celebration of the Revolution and the experiences of the Vietnam War, the nationalist tone began to diminish while the orientation given to work in this area began to broaden in several directions. Interest in the operational side of the war shifted to the southern theater and to the later years of the war. More attention was paid to the internal revolutionary character of the political struggle and greater emphasis was given to the institutional development of the army and navy, to the experience of ordinary combatants, and to the involvement of women and minority groups in the war.

Reference and General Works

Black, Jeremy. *War for America: The Fight for Independence, 1775–1783* (1991). While Middlekauf's work noted below is the current major historical treatment of the Revolution, Black provides a useful brief military and political history of the war. Along with traditional topics, the problems of the British, the naval war, the militia, and tories are all covered.

Blanco, Richard L. *The American Revolution 1775–1783: An Encyclopedia* (1993). This two-volume reference is made up of over 800 entries of persons, events and concepts relating to the Revolution as well as over fifty maps and a chronology. Articles are arranged alphabetically, range from a paragraph to several pages in length, and are concluded with short bibliographies.

Gephart, Ronald M. *Revolutionary America, 1763–1789: A Bibliography* (1984). This annotated two-volume subject guide to over 20,000 books, articles, dissertations, and sources is by far the most exhaustive bibliography currently available on the Revolution.

Middlekauff, Robert. *The Glorious Cause: The American Revolution, 1763–1789* (1982). Middlekauff's book is highly detailed while his interpretation adheres to the nationalist tradition. His coverage of the major campaigns and battles is excellent.

Smith, Myron J., Jr. *Navies in the American Revolution: A Bibliography* (1973). Smith lists nearly 1,600 books, articles, and dissertations with occasional annotation and a subject index.

Symonds, Craig L. *A Battlefield Atlas of the American Revolution* (1986). Symonds provides a full-page map accompanied by a page of text for each of nearly 40 engagements.

American Armed Forces and Campaigns

Bill, Alfred H., *The Campaign for Princeton, 1776–1777* (1948). Bill's popular narrative history of the Trenton-Princeton campaign is told with reverence for Washington.

Bliven, Bruce. *Battle for Manhattan* (1956). Bliven provides a highly detailed narrative account of the campaign for a general audience.

Carp, E. Wayne. *To Starve the Army at Pleasure: Continental Army Administration and American Political Culture, 1775–1783* (1984). Carp argues that the weakness in the administration of the Continental Army lay in the political culture of the times and in the radical whig ideology of the Revolution.

Chidsey, Donald B. *Victory at Yorktown* (1962). Despite its title, this book is a history of the entire final phase of the war beginning with Arnold's treason at West Point.

Davis, Burke. *The Cowpens-Guilford Courthouse Campaign* (1962). Davis provides a general audience with a traditional operational history of Greene's major campaign in the south with focus on the commanders.

Furneaux, Rupert. *The Battle of Saratoga* (1971). Furneaux's book deals with both sides of the entire campaign from its inception to the surrender of Burgoyne with an emphasis on personalities and leadership.

Hatch, Robert M. *Thrust for Canada: The American Attempt on Quebec in 1775–1776* (1979). Hatch's book is written for a general audience and includes all northern military operations from the capture of Fort Ticonderoga to the Battle of Valcour Island.

Lumpkin, Henry. *From Savannah to Yorktown: The American Revolution in the South* (1981). Lumpkin's book represents the shift of more recent scholarship on military operations from its earlier focus on the campaigns in the north to those in the south.

Martin, David G. *The Philadelphia Campaign, September 1777–June 1778* (1993). This is a popular history of the military actions surrounding the British capture and later withdrawal from Philadelphia. The focus is on operations which are studied from a command perspective.

Martin, James K. and Mark E. Lender. *A Respectable Army: The Military Origins of the Republic, 1763–1789* (1982). Martin and Lender analyze the efforts to sustain the Continental Army in the war arguing that these precipitated the development of later nationalist and federalist political orientations.

Neumann, George C. *A History of Weapons of the American Revolution* (1967). Neumann provides an encyclopedic survey of weapons used in the Revolution with over 1,000 illustrations and descriptions.

Palmer, Dave R. *The Way of the Fox: American Strategy in the War for America, 1775–1783* (1975). Palmer argues that Washington's strategy in the Revolution was more complex than mere defensive fabianism and shifted to meet the character of the war.

Pancake, John S. *This Destructive War: The British Campaign in the Carolinas, 1780–1782* (1985). Pancake argues that the war in the south was as much a civil war as a regular one and was fueled more by traditional local feuds than by ideologies.

Risch, Erna. *Supplying Washington's Army* (1981). In this topical study of the efforts to supply the Continental Army, Risch argues that the problems were more the fault of an inept Congress than the product of corruption in army administration.

Rossie, Jonathan, G. *The Politics of Command in the American Revolution* (1975). Rossie uses the political conflict between Gates and Schuyler in the northern theater as the basis for a broader study of command relations in the Continental Army.

Royster, Charles. W. *A Revolutionary People at War: The Continental Army and American Character, 1775–1783* (1979). Royster's highly original and detailed study of the relationship of the Continental Army with the values of the society and of the Revolution provided some of the inspiration for later works on the impact of revolutionary ideology on the war effort.

Selby, John E. *The Revolution in Virginia, 1775–1783* (1988). Selby looks at the Revolution from the point of view of an individual state, focusing on military operations as well as on the efforts of the political leadership in Virginia to create a new administrative structure while also mobilizing the resources needed to fight the war.

Sosin, Jack M. *The Revolutionary Frontier, 1763–1783* (1967). Sosin argues that military operations in the west should be viewed as part of the efforts of the local elites to build a stabilized community.

Stryker, William S. *The Battle of Monmouth* (1927, reissued in 1970). Stryker's book is a popular and detailed narrative account of the campaign and battle with emphasis on the role of Washington.

Wood, W. J. *Battles of the Revolutionary War, 1775–1781* (1990). Wood uses the analysis of a group of selected battles to study American tactics, leadership, and organization in the war.

Wright, Robert K. *The Continental Army* (1983). Wright provides an objective description of the development of both the organization and the early tactical doctrine of the Continental Army.

Naval War

Coggins, Jack. *Ships and Seamen of the American Revolution* (1969). Coggins provides an encyclopedic survey of the ships, gear, men, tactics, and actions of both navies.

Fowler, William M., Jr. *Rebels Under Sail: The American Navy During the Revolution* (1976). Fowler's book is a topical analysis of the operations and administration of the Continental Navy written for a general audience.

Miller, Nathan. *Sea of Glory: A Naval History of the American Revolution* (1974). Miller attempts to cover all aspects of the naval war in the Revolution including activities of the Continental Navy, state navies, and privateers. Although the focus is on operations Miller does include material on the lives of officers and sailors.

Smith, Charles R. *Marines in the Revolution: A Pictorial History* (1975). Smith reviews a wide range of episodes in the war where marines played a significant role.

Stivers, Reuben E. *Privateers and Volunteers: The Men and Women of Our Reserve Naval Forces, 1776 to 1866* (1973). Stivers uses a detailed and wide-ranging account of maritime and riverine combat to argue that the Naval Reserve can trace its heritage back to privateering.

Impact of the War on Social Groups

Blumenthal, Walter H. *Women Camp Followers of the American Revolution* (1952, 1974). So far, no major book on women's participation in the military side of the war has appeared except for this short and discursive account of the activities of wives, sweethearts and prostitutes in the armies of both sides.

Frey, Sylvia R. *Water from the Rock: Black Resistance in a Revolutionary Age* (1991). Frey argues that the American Revolution precipitated widespread resistance to slavery in the form of actual African American military participation in the war on both sides especially in the southern campaigns in the later years. The failure of this movement redirected African American resistance towards cultural struggle.

Graymont, Barbara. *The Iroquois in the American Revolution* (1972). Graymont traces the Iroquois' early attempts to remain neutral in the war and their later entry as a British ally, arguing that the Iroquois Confederation was fatally weakened by a conflict into which it was only reluctantly drawn.

Kaplan, Sidney and Emma N. *The Black Presence in the Era of the American Revolution* (1989). This is a series of short biographies of individual African Americans in the Revolution and subsequent decades. Following the same approach as Frey, the focus of the study shifts from military participants in the war to religious and intellectual leaders afterwards.

Rosswurm, Steven. *Arms, Country, and Class: The Philadelphia Militia and "Lower Sort" During the American Revolution, 1775–1783* (1988). Rosswurm claims that the lower classes in Philadelphia played a significant role in both the military and political dimensions of the war.

The Early Republic, 1783–1812

Unlike the case of the American Revolution, where there has been a considerable change in the direction of historical interest and interpretation during the past two decades, historical writing about the American military experience in the early years of the republic is relatively unchanged. Work in this area continues to be dominated by narratives of efforts to suppress domestic unrest, military involvement in conflicts abroad, and conflict with the Native Americans on the frontier. The only significant changes in recent historical work have been a growing interest in the institutional development of the army and navy, the social evolution of the officer class in the navy, and a concern for the interaction between popular mentalities and military policy similar to that seen in the work of Royster, Martin, Lender, and Carp on the American Revolution.

Reference and General Works

Fredriksen, John C. *Shield of Republic/Sword of Empire: A Bibliography of United States Military Affairs, 1783–1846* (1990). Fredriksen's guide contains reference to nearly 6,800 books, articles, and dissertations dealing with the early history of all services as well as the major military events of the period.

Foreign Wars and Domestic Unrest

Nash, Howard P., Jr. *The Forgotten Wars: The Role of the U. S. Navy in the Quasi War with France and the Barbary Wars, 1798–1805* (1968). Nash argues that both wars demonstrate the importance Americans placed on the freedom of maritime trade.

Palmer, Michael A. *Stoddert's War: Naval Operations During the Quasi-War with France, 1798–1801* (1987). Palmer's work is marked by the attention given to the international context of the quasi-war as well as his argument that Stoddert exercised control and direction over all operations.

Slaughter, Thomas P. *The Whiskey Rebellion: Frontier Epilogue to the American Revolution* (1986). Slaughter's work includes both the political and military dimensions of the conflict and is now considered the best work on the topic.

Tucker, Glenn. *Dawn Like Thunder: The Barbary Wars and Birth of the U. S. Navy* (1963). Tucker provides one of the better studies of the Barbary Wars with some attention given to the North Africans as well as the Americans.

Native American Conflicts on the Frontier

Horsman, Reginald. *The Frontier in the Formative Years: 1783–1815* (1970). This survey of political, diplomatic, and social aspects of frontier society was written to provide a broad context for understanding military operations there.

Prucha, Francis P. *The Sword of the Republic: The Unites States Army on the Frontier, 1783–1846* (1969). Prucha argues that the army was developed at this time chiefly as an instrument of westward expansion.

Sword, Wiley. *President Washington's Indian War: The Struggle for the Old Northwest, 1790–1795* (1985). This is a traditional survey of the early struggles with the Native Americans in the Old Northwest with attention given to the larger diplomatic context of the conflict.

Tebbel, John W. *The Battle of Fallen Timbers, August 20, 1794* (1972). Tebbel provides a traditional narrative account of Wayne's victory against the Native Americans of the Northwest written for a general audience.

Institutional Development of the Armed Forces

Crackel, Theodore J. *Mr. Jefferson's Army: Political and Social Reform of the Military Establishment, 1801–1809* (1987). Crackel argues that Jefferson undertook a major reform of the army in order to transform it from a Federalist into a Republican institution.

Cress, Lawrence D. *Citizens in Arms: The Army and the Militia in American Society to the War of 1812* (1982). As is the case with Stuart, below, Cress is interested in the impact of ideology on the formation of military policy. Cress stresses the impact of radical whig ideology on the development of ideas regarding a citizen soldiery during the early decades of the republic.

Fowler, William M. *Jack Tars and Commodores: The American Navy, 1783–1815* (1984). In this popular history of the early navy, Fowler places his emphasis on the lives of the sailors.

King, Irving H. *The Coast Guard Under Sail: The U.S. Revenue Cutter Service, 1789–1865* (1989). King provides a history of the service from its founding until the introduction of steam, stressing its dual role in providing support for traditional naval functions as well as protection of revenue and maritime support functions.

Kohn, Richard H. *Eagle and Sword: The Federalists and the Creation of the Military Establishment in America, 1783–1802* (1975). Kohn discusses the efforts of the Federalists to build a strong and centrally controlled army in the 1790's as a function of their ideology.

McKee, Christopher. *A Gentlemanly and Honorable Profession: The Creation of the U.S. Naval Officer Corps, 1794–1815* (1991). Following the ideas suggested in Peter Karsten's book noted in the next chapter on the development of a sense of professionally defined class consciousness among naval officers, McKee examines the training and socialization of the post-Revolutionary War generation of naval officers.

Stuart, Reginald C. *War and American Thought from the Revolution to the Monroe Doctrine* (1982). Like Cress, Stuart extends into the history of the early republic the tendency seen in Royster's work to stress the role of ideology in the formation of American military policy.

Symonds, Craig L. *Navalists and Antinavalists: The Naval Policy Debate in the United States, 1785–1827* (1980). Symonds provides a study of the debate between the "blue water" and harbor defense schools of thought in congress concerning the development of American naval organization, force and strategy.

Tucker, Spencer C. *The Jeffersonian Gunboat Navy* (1993). Tucker provides a highly descriptive analysis of the gunboats built for the U.S. Navy between 1800 and 1812 and their operational service in the Mediterranean and in the War of 1812.

Ward, Harry M. *The Department of War, 1781–1795* (1962). Ward provides an objective history of the building of the administration of the War Department and its role in the Whiskey and Shays' rebellions and in the Native American wars.

War of 1812

Historical work on the War of 1812 is still largely confined to operational histories of the entire war. Substantial campaign and battle studies appear only occasionally, while related political and social questions or the institutional development of the services still attract little attention.

General Works

Berton, Pierre. *Flames Across the Border: The Canadian-American Tragedy, 1813–1814* (1981). Berton provides a Canadian view of the experience of the war and of the social and emotional environment in which it was fought.

Caffrey, Kate. *The Twilight's Last Gleaming: Britain vs. America, 1812–1815* (1977). This is a popular account of the war written for British readers covering both the origins and the military operations of the war.

Elting, John R. *Amateurs to Arms! A Military History of the War of 1812* (1991). This is an operational history of both the land and maritime aspects of the war written from the point of view that the war began as a bungled affair fought by amateurs. However, in 1814 a new generation of professionals began to take over and thereby considerably improved the conduct of the war.

Hickey, Donald R. *The War of 1812: A Forgotten Conflict* (1989). Hickey's book represents a recent trend to view the war in its domestic and political as well as military and diplomatic aspects.

Horsman, Reginald. *The War of 1812* (1969). Horsman's book represents the earlier traditional and mostly military presentation of the war with special attention given to British strategy.

Mahon, John K. *The War of 1812* (1972). Mahon provides a basic and detailed narrative of military operations of the war on land and sea.

Stagg, John C. A. *Mr. Madison's War: Politics, Diplomacy, and Warfare in the Early American Republic, 1783–1830* (1983). Stagg argues that the war was, in both its origins and conduct, a product of domestic politics and outlooks but sees it more as a product of Madison's policies than of ideology.

Campaigns

Everest, Allan S. *The War of 1812 in the Champlain Valley* (1981). Everest's book is an episodic history of the war as seen from the local level.

Gilpin, Alec R. *The War of 1812 in the Old Northwest* (1958). Gilpin's book is still considered one of the best regional studies of the war.

Graves, Donald E. *The Battle of Lundy's Lane: On the Niagara in 1814* (1993). This is a command-centered narrative of the battle set in the context of both the 1814 Niagara campaign and the war itself. The book is scholarly but written in a style accessible to lay readers.

Owsley, Frank L., Jr. *Struggle for the Gulf Borderlands: The Creek War and the Battle of New Orleans, 1812–1815* (1981). Owsley links Jackson's campaign against the Creeks to the larger war concerns of the Americans, the Spanish, and the British.

Reilly, Robin. *The British at the Gates: The New Orleans Campaign in the War of 1812* (1974). Reilly's largely military account of the New Orleans campaign is written in the context of the final year of the war with attention given to both sides.

Stanley, George F. G. *The War of 1812: Land Operations* (1983). Stanley surveys the military operations on the Canadian border from a Canadian point of view.

Sugden, John. *Tecumseh's Last Stand* (1985). Sugden provides a survey of the war in Western Ontario in 1812–1813 with emphasis on the Battle of the Thames.

Naval War

Forester, C. S. *The Age of Fighting Sail: The Story of the Naval War of 1812* (1956). This is a history of the naval war written for a general audience by a British novelist. It focuses on actions of the regular navy with emphasis on American commanders.

Garitee, Jerome R. *The Republic's Private Navy: The American Privateering Business as Practiced by Baltimore During the War of 1812* (1977). Following the example set by Lydon's study of colonial privateering, Garitee focuses on Baltimore and emphasizes the business end of privateering.

2

The Institutional Period: 1816–1865

In many respects American military policy in these years remained markedly similar to the pattern established by 1815. When confronted with conflict the nation mobilized volunteers to expand the standing army and navy. After 1816, however, the armed services developed as mature institutions, establishing methods and practices which endured for decades.

The army's early history was marked by unpredictable changes in strength, poor administration, political preference in officer appointments, and a lack of knowledgeable commanders. When John C. Calhoun became secretary of war in 1817 he centralized administration by placing logistical bureaus, created during the War of 1812, directly under the control of his office. He also established the office of commanding general in 1821, given to the senior general in the army, to provide the Secretary of War with military advice and oversee field operations. In addition, reforms at the United States Military Academy during Calhoun's tenure provided the foundations of a basic professional education for new officers.

The effect of Calhoun's reforms and the obvious fact that the nation intended to maintain a regular army created an institution which attracted and retained able men in the officer corps. Winfield Scott, commanding general from 1841 through 1861, for all his flaws, set the pattern of an evolving professionalism within the officer corps. Scott encouraged promising officers to pursue military studies and established standard operating procedures, governing rules and regulations. Admittedly, much of daily army life was dull and undemanding, and living conditions at frontier posts were uninviting if not outright uncomfortable. Many promising men left the service, but others remained to establish a tradition of military professionalism.

While the peacetime army remained small, the force was sufficient to meet the nation's peacetime military needs. Serving mainly on the frontier, the army fostered national expansion through exploration, road building and river clearance, and fought Native Americans resisting the movement westward. The Corps of Engineers and the Topographical Engineers provided expertise in exploration, surveying and construction.

Smaller than the army, more isolated from public attention than the soldiers, the navy evolved more slowly institutionally than did the army. It adopted a bureau system in 1824 in order to centralize administration but failed to name a "commanding admiral." The United States Naval Academy was not founded until 1845. Prior to that date officers were commissioned directly from civil life or earned their commissions through the midshipman system. Meeting the challenges of rapidly changing naval technology, in gunnery, steam propulsion, and iron hull construction forced the sea service to move beyond the old system of learning to sail and fight through the direct experience of sailing and fighting.

The nature of the naval service hindered institutional development. In peacetime the navy served largely overseas to represent American commercial interests, protect citizens and their property, and explore and chart unknown waters. The navy's wartime service was two-fold: to protect American coasts and attack enemy commercial shipping. Given these peacetime and wartime roles, the navy served in small squadrons across a wide geographic area with only a slow and tenuous communications link with the Navy Department. Such service gave a great deal of independence to squadron and ship commanders, and made it difficult to impose central control over the entire force.

Although the armed forces matured institutionally and fostered a form of professionalism in these years, neither service responded easily to the outbreak of war. Regular duty in peace for both services was highly routinized and carried on in widely scattered posts or ports. War required centralized activity and quick decisions. Scattered regiments or squadrons must be concentrated for combat. For the army, state volunteer regiments filled with raw recruits and ill-prepared officers had to be organized and taught the rudiments of field duty. Neither service had agencies to prepare for mobilization, wartime expansion, or operational planning. The lack of institutional means to move the regular forces from a peacetime footing to war status reflected national policy and the decentralized nature of the federal government as much as it did failings within the armed forces.

Under these circumstances, the response to war followed a familiar pattern. At the onset of hostilities regular forces were too small to meet the demands of war. Therefore, Congress would authorize the president to call upon the states for volunteers and appropriate funds to enlarge the navy. Active land operations awaited the organization and equipment of the volunteers. Initial combat produced either defeat or stalemate, although such was not the case during the Mexican War, where strategic indecision hampered American efforts. After a series of campaigns, as the volunteers learned to fight and the army either adjusted to war demands or removed the incompetent and found younger, more able officers to command, the system began to work. Ultimately, a sound strategy was devised and the war fought with greater effectiveness. For the navy, the Mexican War posed few problems, but the Civil War challenged the navy as much as it befuddled the army.

Despite the evident flaws in the American military system, the United States won the Mexican War and prevailed again in 1865. Winfield Scott's strategic leadership in the Mexico City campaign and the contribution of many junior officers who were West Point graduates gave the nation victory in 1847. West Pointers and other former regular army officers dominated the high commands in the Federal and Confederate armies from the very onset of combat in 1861. The organizational efforts to place two field armies in Mexico, and the ability of both northern and southern military departments to organize, field, and support vast armies over four years stands in sharp contrast to American failings during the War of 1812. The Union navy's capacity to expand its force five-fold, to adapt to coastal and riverine warfare, and adjust to steam propulsion on a broad scale reveal a similar institutional maturity. As with the army, naval high command in the North fell almost exclusively to regulars from the peacetime service. Success in the Mexican and Civil Wars indicated clearly the effects of fifty years of institutional development.

Chronology

1816

Jul   27   U.S. forces seize Ft. Apalachicola, FL (punitive campaign)

1817

Jul   28   Sylvanus Thayer (Superintendent, USMA)
Oct   8   John Calhoun (Secretary of War)
Nov 30   Apalachicola Massacre (punitive campaign)

1818

Apr   7   U.S. forces seize St. Marks, Spanish Florida
May 28   U.S. forces seize Pensacola, Spanish Florida

1819

Jan   1   Smith Thompson (Secretary of the Navy)
Mar   3   Anthony Gale (Commandant, Marine Corps)

Nov   3   First warship arrives China (USS *Congress*)

1820

Oct 17   Archibald Henderson (Commandant, Marine Corps)
Dec 12   John Calhoun proposes "expansible army" concept to
          Congress

1821

Jun   1   Jacob Brown (Commanding General of the Army)
Nov   5   USS *Alligator* defeats *Marianna Flora/Mariano Faliero* (Port.)

1823

Feb 14   USS *Sea Gull* (first steam warship to see combat enters active
          service)
Sep 16   Samuel Southard (Secretary of the Navy)

1824

May 24   First USA postgraduate school established (Artillery School of
          Practice)
Aug 16   First use of the phrase "national guard" to designate a militia
          unit (7th NY Regiment)

1825

Mar   7   James Barbour (Secretary of War)

1826

Sep   3   First warship to circumnavigate globe—returns Jun 8, 1830
          (USS *Vincennes*)

1828

May 26   Peter Porter (Secretary of War)
May 29   Alexander Macomb (Commanding General of the Army)

1829

Mar   9   John Eaton (Secretary of War)
Mar   9   John Branch (Secretary of the Navy)

1830

Sep   1   Dennis Hart Mahan joins the faculty of the USMA
Dec   8   Whiskey eliminated from the enlisted ration (USA)

1831

May	23	Levi Woodbury (Secretary of the Navy)
Aug	1	Lewis Cass (Secretary of War)
Aug	24	U.S. forces dispatched to Suffolk, VA (civil unrest)

1832

Feb   6   U.S. forces (USS *Potomac*) land Kuala Batu, Sumatra (punitive action)
Apr 26   Black Hawk War—ends Sep 30
Jul   21   Battle of Wisconsin Heights (punitive campaign)
Aug   2   Battle of Bad Axe River (punitive campaign)

1833

Mar   2   1st dragoon regiment established

1834

Jan 29   First use of troops during a period of labor unrest (Chesapeake-Ohio Canal Strike)
Jul   1   Mahlon Dickerson (Secretary of the Navy)

1835

Jun 30   Battle of Anahuac (Texas Independence)
Oct   2   Battle of Gonzales (Texas Independence)
Oct 28   Battle of Mission Concepcion (Texas Independence)
Nov 24   Texas creates a navy
Dec 18   Battle of Black Point (punitive campaign)
Dec 28   Dade "massacre" (punitive campaign)
Dec 31   Battle of Withlacoochee River (punitive campaign)

1836

Jan 14   *Independence* commissioned (first ship Texas Navy)
Jan 17   Battle of Dunlawton (punitive campaign)
Feb 23   Battle of the Alamo—ends Mar 6 (Texas Independence)
Feb 28   Battle of Camp Izard—ends Mar 6 (punitive campaign)
Apr 21   Battle of San Jacinto—ends Apr 22 (Texas Independence)
Apr 27   Battle of Thlonotosassa (punitive campaign)
Jun   9   Battle of Cuscawalla Hammock (punitive campaign)
Jul 12   First naval officer commissioned as an engineer (Charles H. Haswell)
Jul 19   Battle of Welika Pond (punitive campaign)
Sep 18   Battle of San Felasco Hammock (punitive campaign)

Oct   5   Benjamin Butler (Secretary of War)
Nov 21   Battle of Wahoo Swamp (punitive campaign)

1837

Jan   23   First Battle of L. Ahapopka (punitive campaign)
Jan   27   Battle of the Hatchee-Lustee (punitive campaign)
Mar   7   Joel Poinsett (Secretary of War)
Apr   17   Naval action—Brasos de Santiago (USS *Natchez*)
Apr   17   *Vencedor del Alamo* and *Libertador* (Mexico) defeat *Independence* (Texas)
Apr   27   Last remaining ships Texas Navy wrecked—Galveston, TX
Jun   2   Battle of Tampa Bay (punitive campaign)
Jul   18   Largest sailing warship launched (USS *Pennsylvania*)
Sep   10   Battle of Mosquito Inlet (punitive campaign)
Oct   22   Osceola seized under flag of truce
Dec   13   USS *Fulton* II commissioned (first purpose designed steam warship to see active service)
Dec   25   Battle of Lake Okeechobee (punitive campaign)

1838

Jan   15   Battle of Jupiter River (punitive campaign)
Jan   24   Battle of Lockahatchee (punitive campaign)
Jun   17   Battle of Newnansville (punitive campaign)
Jul   1   James Paulding (Secretary of the Navy)
Aug 18   U.S. South Sea Surveying and Exploring Expedition departs—returns Jun 10, 1842
Dec   25   USS *John Adams* bombards Kuala Batu, Sumatra (punitive action)

1839

Jan   1   USS *John Adams* bombards Muki, Sumatra (punitive action)
Mar 23   *Zavala* commissioned (first ship commissioned in the second Texas Navy)
Jul   23   Battle of Caloosahatchee River (punitive campaign)

1840

Mar 28   Battle of Ft. King (punitive campaign)
Jun   2   Battle of Chocachatti (punitive campaign)
Jul   12   U.S. forces (USS *Peacock*) land Fiji Islands (punitive expedition)

1841

Feb   25   U.S. forces (USS *Peacock*) land Samoan Islands (punitive expedition)

Mar 5 John Bell (Secretary of War)
Mar 6 George Badger (Secretary of the Navy)
Apr 9 U.S. forces (USS *Peacock*) land Drummond Island (punitive expedition)
Jul 5 Winfield Scott (Commanding General of the Army)
Oct 11 Abel P. Upshur (Secretary of the Navy)
Oct 12 John Spencer (Secretary of War)

1842

Jan 25 Battle of Dunn's Lake (punitive campaign)
Apr 19 Second Battle of L. Ahapopka (punitive campaign)
Jul 4 First test of an electrically-operated underwater mine (Samuel Colt)
Aug 31 Board of Naval Commissioners abolished (Navy adopts "bureau system" for administration)
Oct 21 U.S. forces land Monterey, CA—ends Oct 23
Dec 1 Only ship-board executions for mutiny (USS *Sommers)*

1843

Mar 8 James Porter (Secretary of War)
Apr 30 Naval action—Campeche (first use of exploding shells)
May 16 Naval Action—Campeche (Texas & Mexico)
Jul 24 David Henshaw (Secretary of the Navy)
Aug 9 First steam powered Atlantic passage by warship—ends Aug 25 (USS *Missouri)*
Sep 9 USS *Princeton* commissioned (first screw-driven warship)
Dec 16 U.S. forces land Liberia (punitive expedition)

1844

Feb 15 William Wilkins (Secretary of War)
Feb 19 Thomas Gilmer (Secretary of the Navy)
Feb 28 Cast iron gun explodes aboard USS *Princeton*
Mar 26 John Mason (Secretary of the Navy)
Sep 29 USS *Michigan* commissioned (first iron-hulled ship)

1845

Mar 6 William Marcy (Secretary of War)
Mar 11 George Bancroft (Secretary of the Navy)
Oct 10 U.S. Naval School established (U.S. Naval Academy—Jul 1, 1850)

1846

Apr 25 Battle of Rancho de Carricitos

May   8   Battle of Palo Alto
May   9   Battle of Resaca de la Palma
May 13   U.S. declares war on Mexico
May 24   Naval bombardment—Tampico (USN undertakes numerous
          such actions during the war)
Jul   7   U.S. forces occupy Monterey, CA
Aug 18   U.S. forces occupy Santa Fe
Sep 10   John Mason (Secretary of the Navy)
Sep 21   Battle of Saltillo
Sep 21   Battle of Monterrey—ends Sep 24
Nov 15   U.S. forces occupy Tampico
Dec   6   Battle of San Pascual
Dec 25   Battle of El Brazito

1847

Jan   8   Battle of San Gabriel
Jan   9   Battle of La Mesa
Jan 10   U.S. forces occupy Los Angeles
Feb   3   Battle of Pueblo de Taos—ends Feb 5 (punitive campaign)
Feb 22   Battle of Buena Vista—ends Feb 23
Feb 28   Battle of Sacramento
Mar   9   Combined operation—Vera Cruz
Mar 10   U.S. forces besiege Vera Cruz—ends Mar 27
Apr 18   Battle of Cerro Gordo
Aug 20   Battle of Contreras
Aug 20   Battle of Churubusco
Sep   8   Battle of El Molino del Rey
Sep 13   Battle of Chapultepec—ends Sep 13
Sep 14   U.S. forces occupy Mexico City—ends Jun 12, 1848

1848

Feb   2   Treaty ends war with Mexico

1849

Mar   8   George Crawford (Secretary of War)
Mar   8   William Preston (Secretary of the Navy)

1850

Aug   2   William Graham (Secretary of the Navy)
Aug 15   Charles Conrad (Secretary of War)
Sep 28   Flogging abolished in USN

1852

Jul	15	B. F. Isherwood (Chief, USN Bureau of Steam Engineering)
Jul	26	John Kennedy (Secretary of the Navy)
Sep	30	First hydrographic voyage of Atlantic—ends Nov 12, 1853 (USS *Dolphin*)

1853

Mar	7	Jefferson Davis (Secretary of War)
Mar	8	James Dobbin (Secretary of the Navy)

1854

Mar	30	Battle of Cieneguilla (punitive campaign)
May	27	U.S. forces dispatched to Boston, MA (civil unrest)
May	27	Attorney General Caleb Cushing supports the use of federal troops as *posse comitatus*
Jul	13	Naval bombardment—San Juan del Norte (GreyTown), Nicaragua (USS *Cyane*)

1855

Mar	3	Congress authorizes the purchase of camels to carry USA freight western frontier
Apr	4	U.S. forces (USS *Plymouth*) land Shanghai, China (punitive expedition)
Jun	11	North Pacific Surveying and Exploring Expedition—ends Oct 19
Dec	3	Co. C, 4th Inf. engages hostile Native Americans while under command James E. Harrison, USRCS—near Seattle, WA

1856

Jan	26	Battle of Seattle (punitive campaign)
Apr	22	U.S. forces dispatched to Lawrence, KS (territorial conflict)
Jun	28	U.S. forces dispatched to Topeka, KS (territorial conflict)
Jul	19	Use of federal troops *posse comitatus* to control domestic violence within a state restricted (Caleb Cushing)
Aug	19	U.S. forces dispatched to Lecompton, KS (territorial conflict)
Sep	13	U.S. forces dispatched to Lecompton, KS (territorial conflict)
Sep	14	U.S. forces dispatched to Lawrence, Osawakee, & Hickory Point, KS (territorial conflict)
Sep	16	U.S. forces dispatched to Topeka, KS (territorial conflict)
Nov	20	Naval action—Barrier Forts, Canton, China—ends Nov 24

1857

Mar   5   Battle of Big Cypress Swamp (punitive campaign)
Mar   6   John Floyd (Secretary of War)
Mar   7   Isaac Toucey (Secretary of the Navy)
May 28   U.S. forces dispatched to Salt Lake City, UT (civil disorder)
Jun   1   U.S. troops dispatched to Washington, D.C. (civil disorder)
Jul   14   U.S. forces dispatched to Lawrence, KS (territorial conflict)
Jul   20   Battle of Devil's River (punitive campaign)
Jul   29   Battle of Solomon's Fork (punitive campaign)
Sep 26   U.S. forces dispatched to Lawrence, KS (territorial conflict)
Oct   19   U.S. forces dispatched to Lecompton, KS (territorial conflict)

1858

Apr 21   Battle of Painted Creek (territorial conflict)
Sep   1   Battle of Four Lakes (punitive campaign)
Oct   6   U.S. forces (USS *Vandalia*) land Fiji Islands (punitive
            expedition)

1859

Jan   7   John Harris (Commandant, Marine Corps)
Jun 25   Naval involvement—Pei Ho River, China
Oct   17   U.S. forces dispatched to Harpers Ferry, VA (civil disorder)

1860

Mar   6   U.S. forces (USS *Saratoga*) land Anton Lizardo, Mexico
            (punitive action)

1861

Feb 21   Stephen K. Mallory (Secretary of the Navy, C.S.A.)
Feb 21   Leroy Walker (Secretary of War, C.S.A.)
Mar   5   Simon Cameron (Secretary of War, U.S.A.)
Mar   5   Gideon Welles (Secretary of the Navy, U.S.A.)
Apr 12   Bombardment of Ft. Sumter—ends Apr 13
Apr 12   Naval action—Charleston (USRC *Harriet Lane* fires on
            Nashville)
Apr 15   President A. Lincoln issues a call for the militia to suppress an
            insurrection
Apr 19   President A. Lincoln proclaims a blockade of some
            Confederate ports—extends blockade Apr 27
May   6   Confederate Congress authorizes letters of *marque and reprisal*
            against U.S.A. vessels

May	28	I. McDowell (Commander troops south of Potomac River, USA)
Jun	2	P.G.T. Beauregard (Army of the Potomac, CSA)
Jun	3	Battle of Philippi
Jun	3	CSS *Sumter* commissioned (first commerce raider, CSN)
Jul	8	First use of naval mines by Confederate forces—Potomac River
Jun	9	U.S. War Department authorizes the use of women nurses in military hospitals
Jun	10	Battle of Big Bethel Church
Jun	22	First balloon reconnaissance—Falls Church, VA
Jul	20	J. E. Johnston (Army of the Potomac, CSA)
Jul	21	First Battle of Bull Run/Manassas Junction
Jul	22	U.S. Congress requires volunteer officers to face an efficiency examination by a board of officers
Aug	10	Battle of Wilson's Creek
Aug	15	G. B. McClellan (Army of the Potomac, USA)
Aug	28	Combined operation—ends Aug 29—Fts. Clark and Hatteras
Aug	31	Whiskey eliminated from the enlisted ration (USN)
Sep	17	Judah Benjamin (Secretary of War, C.S.A.)
Oct	12	Naval action—Head of Passes—Mississippi River
Nov	1	G. B. McClellan (Commanding General of the Army, USA)
Nov	5	Naval action—Hilton Head, SC—ends Nov 7
Nov	15	D. C. Buell (Army of the Ohio, USA)
Dec	21	U.S. Congress authorizes a Medal of Honor for naval and marine enlisted

1862

Jan	19	Battle of Mill Springs/Logan Cross Roads
Jan	20	Edwin Stanton (Secretary of War, U.S.A.)
Feb	6	Combined operation—Ft. Henry
Feb	7	Combined operation—ends Feb 8—Roanoke Island
Feb	12	Combined operation—ends Feb 16—Ft. Donelson
Feb	21	Battle of Valverde
Feb	25	USS *Monitor* commissioned (first U.S. iron-clad to see combat)
Mar	3	Combined operation—ends Apr 8—New Madrid/Island No. 10
Mar	5	CSS *Virginia* commissioned
Mar	7	Battle of Pea Ridge/Elkhorn Tavern—ends Apr 8
Mar	8	CSS *Virginia* v. USS *Congress* and USS *Cumberland*
Mar	9	USS *Monitor* v. CSS *Virginia*
Mar	11	G. B. McClellan relieved as Commanding General of the Army, USA
Mar	13	Combined operation—ends Mar 14—New Bern, NC

Mar 22   George Randolph (Secretary of War, C.S.A.)
Mar 23   Battle of Kernstown
Mar 26   Battle of Apache Canyon
Mar 28   Battle of Glorieta Pass
Apr 5   Battle of Yorktown—ends May 4
Apr 6   Battle of Shiloh/Pittsburg Landing—ends Apr 7
Apr 11   Combined operation—ends Apr 26—Beaufort, NC
Apr 16   Confederate Congress passes conscription law
Apr 18   Naval action—Fts. Jackson & St.Philip—ends Apr 24
Apr 21   Confederate States Naval Academy established
Apr 25   New Orleans, LA surrenders to U.S. forces
May 4   Battle of Williamsburg—ends May 5
May 8   Battle of McDowell
May 10   Naval action—Plum Point Bend—Mississippi River
May 23   Battle of Front Royal
May 25   Battle of Winchester
May 31   Battle of Seven Pines/Fair Oaks—ends Jun 1
May 31   Williams Rapid-Fire Gun deployed in Battle of Seven Pines/
         Fair Oaks (first successful combat use of true machine gun)
Jun 1   R. E. Lee (Army of Northern Virginia, CSA, formerly Army of
         the Potomac, CSA)
Jun 6   Naval action—Memphis—Mississippi River
Jun 8   Battle of Cross Keys
Jun 9   Battle of Port Republic
Jun 13   USS *Alligator* (first submarine accepted by USN)
Jun 25   Battle of Oak Grove/Henrico/King's School House/The
         Orchards
Jun 26   Battle of Mechanicsville/Ellison's Mill
Jun 27   Battle of Gaines' Mill/Chickahominy/Cold Harbor
Jun 29   Battle of Savage's Station/Allen's Farm
Jun 30   Battle of Frayser's Farm/White Oak Swamp
Jul 1   Battle of Malvern Hill
Jul 2   U.S. Congress requires military tactics in the curriculum of
         land-grant schools (Morrill Act)
Jul 3   Battle of Locust Grove
Jul 12   U.S. Congress authorizes a Medal of Honor for army enlisted
Jul 13   Battle of Murfreesboro
Jul 15   Battle of Apache Pass—ends Jul 16 (punitive campaign)
Jul 23   H. W. Halleck (Commanding General of the Army, USA)
Aug 9   Battle of Cedar Mountain/Slaughter Mountain
Aug 17   CSS *Florida* commissioned (first foreign-built CSN vessel)
Aug 18   Battle of Ft. Ridgely—ends Aug 24 (punitive campaign)
Aug 24   CSS *Alabama* commissioned

Aug 24 New Ulm massacre (punitive campaign)
Aug 28 Battle of Groveton
Aug 29 Second Battle of Bull Run/Manassas—ends Aug 30
Sep 1 Battle of Chantilly/Ox Hill
Sep 4 Army of Northern Virginia invades Maryland
Sep 14 Battle of Crampton's Gap
Sep 14 Battle of South Mountain
Sep 15 Battle of Harpers Ferry
Sep 17 Battle of Antietam/Sharpsburg
Sep 23 Battle of Wood Lake (punitive campaign)
Sep 27 1st Louisiana Native Guards (first USA African American regiment)
Oct 3 Battle of Corinth—ends Oct 4
Oct 8 Battle of Perryville/Chaplin Hills
Oct 16 U.S. Grant (Army of the Tennessee, USA)
Oct 28 Battle of Island Mounds (First combat by an African American unit-1st Kansas Colored Volunteers; later 79th U.S. Colored Infantry as of Dec 13, 1864)
Oct 30 W. S. Rosecrans (Army of the Cumberland, USA)
Nov 9 A. E. Burnside (Army of the Potomac, USA)
Nov 20 B. Bragg (Army of Tennessee, CSA)
Nov 21 James Seddon (Secretary of War, CSA)
Dec 12 USS *Cairo* sinks (first warship sunk by mine)
Dec 13 Battle of Fredericksburg
Dec 20 Battle of Holly Springs
Dec 26 USS *Red Rover* commissioned (first hospital ship, USN)
Dec 27 Battle of Chickasaw Bluffs/Walnut Hills—ends Dec 29
Dec 31 Battle of Stones River/Murfreesboro—ends Jan 3

1863

Jan 10 Combined operation—ends Jan 12—Ft. Hindman
Jan 17 Mangas Coloradas killed "trying to escape"
Jan 26 J. Hooker (Army of the Potomac, USA)
Jan 27 Battle of Bear River (punitive campaign)
Mar 3 U.S. Congress passes conscription law
Mar 3 U.S. Congress extends Medal of Honor to include Army officers (Navy & Marine officers added 1915)
Mar 3 U.S. Congress authorizes letters of *marque and reprisal* against C.S.A. vessels
Mar 7 E. K. Smith assumes command of Confederate forces west of the Mississippi River
Apr 7 Naval action—Charleston
Apr 9 1st Red River campaign—ends May 23

Apr 16   Naval action—Vicksburg—Mississippi River
Apr 17   B. H. Grierson's Raid—ends May 2
May   1   Battle of Chancellorsville—ends May 4
May   3   Battle of Salem Church—ends May 4
May 14   Battle of Jackson
May 16   Battle of Champion's Hill/Baker's Creek
May 17   Battle of the Big Black River
May 19   Siege of Vicksburg—ends Jul 4
May 22   Bureau of Colored Troops created by U.S. War Department
May 27   Battle of Port Hudson—ends Jul 9
Jun   9   First "true" cavalry engagement—Brandy Station/Fleetwood
          Hill/Beverly Ford
Jun 13   Battle of Winchester—ends Jun 15
Jun 28   G. G. Meade (Army of the Potomac, USA)
Jul   1   Battle of Gettysburg—ends Jul 3
Jul 10   Combined operation—ends Feb 18, 1865—Charleston, SC
Jul 13   U.S. troops dispatched to New York, NY (civil unrest)
Jul 16   Naval bombardment—Shimonoseki, Japan (USS *Wyoming*)
Jul 17   Battle of Honey Springs
Jul 24   Battle of Big Mound (punitive campaign)
Jul 26   Battle of Dead Buffalo Lake (punitive campaign)
Jul 28   Battle of Stony Lake (punitive campaign)
Sep   3   Battle of Whitestone Lake (punitive campaign)
Sep 19   Battle of Chickamauga—ends Sep 20
Oct 14   Battle of Bristoe Station
Oct 19   G. Thomas (Army of the Cumberland, USA)
Oct 24   W. T. Sherman (Army of the Tennessee, USA)
Nov 17   Siege of Knoxville—ends Dec 5
Nov 23   Battle of Orchard Knob
Nov 23   Battle of Indian Hill
Nov 24   Battle of Lookout Mountain
Nov 25   Battle of Missionary Ridge
Dec 27   J. E. Johnston (Army of Tennessee, CSA)

1864

Jan 12   Canyon de Chelly Expedition (punitive campaign)
Feb 17   CSS *H. L. Hunley* attacks USS *Housatonic* (presumably first
          submarine to sink a warship in combat)
Feb 24   U.S. Congress provides alternative service for conscientious
          objectors
Mar 10   2nd Red River Campaign—ends May 22
Mar 12   U.S. Grant (General in Chief of the Armies of the U.S.)
Mar 26   J. B. McPherson (Army of the Tennessee, USA)

Apr 12   Ft. Pillow Massacre/Battle of Ft. Pillow
May 4   Battle of Drewry's Bluff—ends May 16
May 5   Battle of the Wilderness—ends May 7
May 5   Naval action—Albemarle Sound
May 5   Battle of Rocky Face Ridge—ends May 11
May 6   First commissioned Native American general officer
         (Stand Watie, CSA)
May 7   Battle of Spotsylvania Court House—ends May 20
May 11   Battle of Yellow Tavern
May 13   Battle of Resaca/Sugar Valley/Oostenaula—ends May 16
May 15   Battle of New Market
May 23   Battle of North Anna/Hanover Junction—ends May 27
May 31   Battle of Cold Harbor—ends June 12
Jun 9   Battle of Petersburg—ends June 18
Jun 10   Battle of Brice's Cross Roads/Tishomingo Creek/Guntown
Jun 10   Jacob Zeilin (Commandant, Marine Corps)
Jun 15   Cherokee Mounted Rifles capture SS *J. R. Williams* with a
         cavalry charge
Jun 18   Siege of Petersburg—ends April 2, 1865
Jun 19   USS *Kearsarge* defeats CSS *Alabama*
Jun 27   Battle of Kenesaw Mountain
Jul 17   J. B. Hood (Army of Tennessee, CSA)
Jul 20   Battle of Peach Tree Creek
Jul 22   Battle of Atlanta
Jul 28   Battle of Killdear Mountain/Tahkahokuty (punitive campaign)
Jul 30   Battle of the Crater/Petersburg Mine Assault
Aug 5   Naval action—Mobile Bay
Aug 31   Battle of Jonesboro—ends Sep 1
Sep 5   Multi-national naval bombardment—Shimonoseki, Japan—
         ends Sep 8
Sep 19   Battle of Opequon/Third Battle of Winchester
Sep 22   Battle of Fisher's Hill
Oct 5   Battle of Allatoona
Oct 7   CSS *Florida* "removed" from Bahia, Brazil by USS *Wachusett*
Oct 19   CSS *Shenandoah* commissioned
Oct 19   Battle of Cedar Creek/Belle Grove
Oct 23   Battle of Westport (largest engagement west of Missouri)
Oct 25   Battle of Marais De Cygnes
Nov 29   Sand Creek Massacre (punitive campaign)
Nov 15   March to the Sea—ends Dec 21
Nov 25   First Battle of Adobe Walls (punitive campaign)
Nov 30   Battle of Franklin
Dec 15   Battle of Nashville—ends Dec 16

1865

Jan	7	Battle of Julesburg (punitive campaign)
Jan	13	Battle of Ft. Fisher—ends Jan 15 (only successful full-scale amphibious assault against a fortified position)
Feb	4	John Breckinridge (Secretary of War, C.S.A.)
Feb	6	R.E. Lee (General in Chief of the Armies of the C.S.A.)
Feb	6	2nd & 3rd U.S. Volunteers—inactivated Nov 13, 1866 (galvanized yankees)
Feb	25	J. E. Johnston (Army of Tennessee, CSA)
Mar	7	Battle of Kinston—ends Mar 10
Mar	7	First African American commissioned officer in the USRCS (Michael Healy)
Mar	13	Confederate Congress authorizes enlistment of African Americans in CSA
Mar	19	Battle of Bentonville—ends Mar 21
Mar	22	J. H. Wilson's Raid—ends Apr 20
Mar	25	Battle of Ft. Steadman
Mar	30	Battle of Five Forks—ends April 1
Apr	2	Battle of Petersburg
Apr	2	Battle of Selma
Apr	6	Battle of Sayler's Creek/Harper's Farm
Apr	9	Battle of Appomattox Courthouse/Clover Hill
Apr	9	Army of Northern Virginia, CSA surrenders
Apr	26	Army of Tennessee, CSA surrenders
May	4	Remaining Confederate forces east of the Mississippi River surrender
May	12	Battle of Palmito Ranch—ends May 13
May	26	Confederate Department of the Trans-Mississippi surrenders
Jun	22	CSS *Shenandoah* destroys U.S. whaling fleet in Bering sea—ends Jun 28
Jun	23	Last Confederate general surrenders (Stand Watie)

Military Operations

BATTLE OF THE ALAMO (Feb 23–Mar 6, 1836). American migrants in Mexico's Texas territory declared the area independent in 1836. Gen. Antonio Lopez de Santa Anna's large army besieged a force of about 200 rebels occupying the Alamo mission in San Antonio, which held for thirteen days. It fell on March 6 with no survivors, except a dozen women and children. The Mexicans stacked the corpses and burned them. The incident provided a rallying cry for the Texans and also for many Americans.

BATTLE OF SAN JACINTO (Apr 21, 1836). A contingent of Gen. Antonio Lopez de Santa Anna's army pursued Gen. Sam Houston's force toward the Sabine River. As the Mexicans encamped, awaiting reinforcements, the outnumbered Texans launched a surprise attack. Texan casualties numbered thirty; the Mexicans, 838, most of whom were killed in the battle. Santa Anna was captured while trying to flee. He withdrew all Mexican troops from Texas and granted it independence.

BATTLE OF PALO ALTO (May 8, 1846). Palo Alto saw the first significant battle of the Mexican War. Gen. Zachary Taylor, heavily outnumbered, encountered Gen. Mariano Arista's 6,000 troops on the afternoon of the 8th. Arista's cannons were ineffective, while Taylor's artillery stopped the Mexican advance and eventually drove Arista's army from the field. By nightfall, the Mexicans lost almost four times as many troops as the Americans, and Arista withdrew to a stronger defensive position.

BATTLE OF RESACA DE LA PALMA (May 9, 1846). The day after the victory of Palo Alto, Gen. Zachary Taylor attacked Gen. Mariano Arista's army despite the Mexicans' superior numbers. Taylor's speed and decisiveness worked to his advantage. The Americans launched a frontal assault following a successful cavalry charge. The fighting was confused, intense, and bloody; the Mexicans were routed across the Rio Grande. Arista's casualties numbered 1,200 to Taylor's 150.

BATTLE OF MONTERREY (Sep 21–24, 1846). Nature and Mexican efforts made Monterrey in Northern Mexico a fortress. Gen. Zachary Taylor divided his army, despite facing a superior force. On September 20, Gen. William J. Worth began a flanking movement around the city; the following day, his attack in the rain succeeded, cutting off any means of retreat. On the 23rd, Taylor advanced with the main force and invaded the city. After bitter street fighting, Gen. Pedro Ampudia surrendered under lenient terms the next day.

BATTLE OF SAN GABRIEL (Jan 8–9, 1847). Col. Stephen Kearny's troops made an overland march to join Com. Robert Stockton's combined force. Stockton then advanced with his small army and met the Mexicans drawn up along the San Gabriel River on the 8th. Using the battle cry of "New Orleans" (fought on that day in 1815), the Americans prevailed, as they also did the following day in another battle. Stockton thus regained control of southern California for the Americans, occupying Los Angeles on the 10th.

BATTLE OF BUENA VISTA (Feb 22–23, 1847). With 20,000 men, Gen. Antonio Lopez de Santa Anna advanced on Gen. Zachary Taylor's position. Mistakenly thinking the Americans were fleeing, the Mexicans instead found them waiting near Buena Vista in a defensive position chosen by Gen. John Wool. On the 22nd, the fighting was inconclusive. The next day, the Mexicans made three heavy assaults and the Americans one. Both sides were exhausted, but Taylor staved off defeat with timely reinforcements. Santa Anna's withdrawal ended the fighting in Northern Mexico.

SIEGE OF VERA CRUZ (Mar 9–27, 1847). Gen. Winfield Scott and Com. P.S.P. Conner, models of interservice cooperation, landed a force unopposed on March 9, but eschewed a frontal assault on the heavily fortified city. Instead, Scott's troops isolated the city, and American naval and siege guns pounded the city around the clock, from March 22 to 25. The garrison formally surrendered on the 27th. American casualties were fewer than 100.

BATTLE OF CERRO GORDO (Apr 17–18, 1847). Gen. Antonio Lopez de Santa Anna's army of 12,000 held this strong defensive position in front of Gen. Winfield Scott's advancing troops. Gen. David Twiggs fought a small engagement on the 17th. On April 18, Scott ordered Twiggs to attack the flank, while another contingent crossed steep mountains, gained the Mexican rear undetected, and attacked; the battle became a rout. Three thousand Mexican troops were captured, the rest fleeing into the mountains.

BATTLE OF CHAPULTEPEC (Sep 12–13, 1847). The fortified castle on the hill of Chapultepec was a major obstacle before Mexico City. On the 12th, Gen. Winfield Scott opened a bombardment, but realized that assault was required. Divisions under Generals William J. Worth, Gideon J. Pillow, and John Quitman attacked from three directions on the 13th. Despite several serious mistakes, the Americans managed to storm the castle. American troops continued on to the gates of Mexico City. By nightfall, Worth's division had entered the city, and a demoralized Gen. Antonio Lopez de Santa Anna withdrew. American troops occupied the city on September 14, ending the last major battle of the war.

ATTACK ON FORT SUMTER (Apr 12, 1861). Located on an island in Charleston harbor, the fort had more symbolic than military value. On April 11, Gen. Pierre G.T. Beauregard was ordered to demand the surrender of Sumter, which was about to be reprovisioned. Maj. Robert Anderson refused, and at 4:30 A.M. on the 12th, Confederate batteries opened fire. Thirty-three hours later, Anderson capitulated. Neither side sustained a death, but the American Civil War had begun.

FIRST BATTLE OF BULL RUN/MANASSAS (Jul 21, 1861). Northern opinion and expiring three-month enlistments pressed Gen. Irvin McDowell to engage the Confederates. Using railroad lines, Gen. Joseph E. Johnston added 12,000 soldiers to Gen. Pierre G.T. Beauregard's army in time for the battle, and then assumed nominal command. McDowell devised a solid plan and almost succeeded, but the inexperience of his troops proved too great. His attack on the 21st stalled; after heavy fighting, a

Confederate counterattack precipitated a Union rout. The green Confederate troops, however, were unable to follow up.

BATTLE OF WILSON'S CREEK (Aug 10, 1861). Gen. Nathaniel Lyon aggressively split his force and attacked the Confederate encampment. His troops carried the battle until the smaller of his forces mistook Confederate soldiers for comrades, withheld their fire, and were in turn routed. The Confederates proceeded to pound the main force, which held for a time, then retreated, leaving Missouri open to invasion.

ATTACK ON FORT HENRY (Feb 6, 1862). Gen. Ulysses S. Grant and Flag Officer Andrew Foote planned a combined attack, but heavy rains slowed the ground forces. The shelling from Foote's fleet of seven ships, however, was sufficient to batter the fort. Gen. Lloyd Tilghman, who had sent most of the garrison to nearby Fort Donelson prior to the engagement, surrendered his remaining force. The victory allowed the Federal forces to begin a deep penetration of the Confederacy along the Tennessee River.

ATTACK ON FORT DONELSON (Feb 12–16, 1862). The Union commanders hoped to duplicate their victory at Fort Henry, but Confederate guns disabled several of Flag Officer Andrew Foote's ships, which attacked on the 14th. The Confederates almost broke out on the 15th, but hesitated and the Union lines held. The next day, Gen. Ulysses S. Grant demanded an unconditional and immediate surrender; thus, his nickname "Unconditional Surrender" Grant. The Confederates complied. The fall of Fort Donelson forced the Confederacy to abandon Kentucky and led to the loss of a considerable portion of Tennessee. Northerners received news of the victory with great celebration, and Grant was promoted to Major General.

USS *MONITOR* V. CSS *VIRGINIA* (Mar 8–9, 1862). For the first time in naval warfare, both ships were iron-clad. The *Monitor* was of a completely new design, while the CSS *Virginia* was built from the hull of the captured USS *Merrimack*. On its first mission (March 8) the *Virginia* destroyed two blockade ships and ran three aground at Hampton Roads. The next day the *Monitor* arrived. A three-hour battle exhausted both crews. Neither ship was severely damaged, but the Confederates failed to break the Union blockade.

BATTLE OF SHILOH/PITTSBURG LANDING (Apr 6–7, 1862). Gen. Albert Sidney Johnston's advance caught Federal troops off guard on April 6. His force bent the Union line but did not break it, as Gen. Ulysses S. Grant, reinforced by Gen. Don Carlos Buell and later Gen. Lew Wallace, rallied the troops. Johnston was killed and Gen. Pierre G.T. Beauregard assumed command of the Confederate forces. The following morning, Grant's counterattack regained lost ground, but his troops were unable

to follow the retreating Confederates. Each side lost 1,700 men killed
and 8,000 wounded in fearsome fighting.

JACKSON'S SHENANDOAH VALLEY CAMPAIGN (May 8–June 9, 1862).
Gen. Thomas J. Jackson used speed and terrain in textbook fashion to
confound Union plans. Feinting towards Richmond, his army back-
tracked and defeated a smaller Union force at McDowell (May 8) and
surprised an outpost at Front Royal (May 23). As Gen. Nathaniel Banks
retreated, the Confederates struck at Winchester on the 25th, breaking
the Federal lines. With Federal armies closing in behind him, Jackson
quickly retreated, turning to fight at Cross Keys on June 8 and Port Republic on June 8–9. Despite the overwhelming forces arrayed against
him, Jackson withdrew safely to join Lee on the Peninsula.

BATTLE OF SEVEN PINES/FAIR OAKS (May 31–Jun 1, 1862). As the Federal forces prepared to besiege Richmond, Gen. Joseph E. Johnston's army
attacked on the 31st, driving the Union troops back at Seven Pines until
halted at Fair Oaks. The following day's fighting was indecisive, as the
Confederates were forced back, suffering greater casualties. Johnston
was wounded in the fighting and replaced as the commander of the
Confederate Army of the Potomac by Gen. Robert E. Lee. This decision
was, ironically in view of later developments, widely unpopular within
the Confederacy.

BATTLES OF THE SEVEN DAYS (Jun 26–Jul 1, 1862). Gen. Robert E. Lee
aggressively assaulted at Mechanicsville (June 26), but took heavy losses.
While Gen. Thomas J. Jackson was uncharacteristically timid, Gen.
George McClellan was characteristically so. The following day, Lee's
army broke through Union lines at Gaines' Mill. As McClellan retreated,
Confederate attacks at Savage's Station (June 29) and Glendale (June 30)
failed to destroy the Federals. At Malvern Hill (July 1), Union artillery
produced a bloodbath, stopping the Confederate advance, but McClellan
refused to counterattack. Confederate casualties numbered 20,000 to the
Union's 16,500. Lee's forces won outright only a single engagement in
the Seven Days, but McClellan's retreat resulted in a strategic victory
for Lee.

SECOND BATTLE OF BULL RUN/MANASSAS (Aug 29–30, 1862). Gen.
Robert E. Lee divided his force, sending Gen. Thomas J. Jackson on a
daring maneuver against the Federal supply depot at Manassas (August 27). Encountering Jackson two days later, Gen. John Pope ordered
six heavy assaults, which failed. Pope attacked again on the 30th, but
Gen. James Longstreet's troops arrived in time to assault the Union flank.
Pope, receiving no help from Generals George McClellan or Fitz-John
Porter, retreated back toward Washington. The humiliating defeat cost
the North 16,000 casualties to the South's 9,200. The battle led to Lee's
invasion of Maryland.

BATTLE OF ANTIETAM/SHARPSBURG (Sep 17, 1862). The bloodiest day of the war, casualties numbered about 22,000 men. Gen. Robert E. Lee invaded Maryland and promptly divided his forces. Gen. George McClellan, with a larger army and a copy of Lee's plans, failed to exploit opportunities as the battle raged. Gen. A.P. Hill's reinforcements arrived from Harpers Ferry and halted a Union advance, which allowed Lee to retreat the following night, unmolested but unsuccessful. The outcome stopped Britain from recognizing the Confederacy, allowed Lincoln to announce the Emancipation Proclamation, and resulted in the Union president's removal of McClellan from command for the second and final time.

BATTLE OF FREDERICKSBURG (Dec 13, 1862). Gen. Robert E. Lee's smaller force occupied a strong defensive position on Marye's Heights. After having moved swiftly, Gen. Ambrose Burnside's army of 120,000 was delayed in crossing the Rappahannock, but finally made several frontal assaults, to no avail. Union losses numbered 12,500 to 5,000 Confederate, as the Confederate generals provided superior leadership. The demoralized Burnside was transferred.

BATTLE OF STONES RIVER/MURFREESBORO (Dec 31, 1862–Jan 2, 1863). Outnumbered Confederate forces assaulted the Union troops on December 31 in desperate fighting, but were repulsed. After a day's respite, Gen. Braxton Bragg launched an attack which went well until Union artillery stopped him. On the 3rd, he retreated. Each side lost about one-third of its army, but Gen. William Rosecrans turned near-defeat into victory.

BATTLE OF CHANCELLORSVILLE (May 1–4, 1863). Both Gen. Robert E. Lee and Gen. Joseph Hooker divided their armies; Lee did so twice. With Union forces to his front and rear, Lee sent Gen. Thomas J. Jackson's "foot cavalry" around Hooker's flank on May 2. That afternoon, Jackson's attack surprised the Federals but he was wounded and later died. Although Hooker's force outnumbered Lee's two to one, Hooker's nerve completely broke under Confederate attack on the 3rd, and he retreated. Lee then defeated the other part of Hooker's army (May 3–4). Hooker completed the retreat on the 6th. While the victory was "the Virginian's greatest triumph," the death of Jackson was costly.

SIEGE OF VICKSBURG (May 19–Jul 4, 1863). Gen. Ulysses S. Grant manifested daring and persistence in moving his army and supplies south of Vicksburg. Living off the land, he defeated Confederate troops at Raymond (May 12) and Jackson (May 14), and turned west. Victorious again at Champion's Hill (May 16), Union troops surrounded Vicksburg. Two assaults (May 19 and 22) failed. With the aid of Adm David Porter's gunboats, Grant besieged the "Gibraltar of the West." It fell on July 4. The victory, which split the Confederacy in two, was a turning point in the war for the Union effort.

BATTLE OF GETTYSBURG (Jul 1–3, 1863). Gen. Robert E. Lee's army encountered Union troops near this Pennsylvania town on July 1, the Confederates initially pushing the Federals back. The following day Confederate armies attacked the Union flanks, but were denied. Lee then
attacked the center on the 3rd; after the war's heaviest artillery duel, the
Confederates launched a violent, unsuccessful charge against Cemetery
Ridge. Although labeled "Pickett's charge," Gen. George Pickett neither
led the charge nor was his the only division involved. Gen. George Gordon Meade was victorious, but cautious, failing to launch a full counterattack. The Union suffered 23,000 casualties, the Confederates 28,000
(one-third of Lee's army), but the outcome raised morale in the Union
as Meade finally had stopped Lee.

BATTLE OF CHICKAMAUGA CREEK (Sep 19–20, 1863). Having evacuated Chattanooga (September 9), Gen. Braxton Bragg tried to ensnare
Gen. William Rosecrans. Gen. James Longstreet's divisions, arriving by
train, made a difference for the South. Fighting on the 19th was inconclusive, but the Confederates breached the Union line on the 20th. Only
the leadership of Gen. George H. Thomas (the "Rock of Chickamauga")
prevented a thorough rout. This final victory for a Confederate offensive, however, was without strategic value, as the South suffered 18,000
casualties.

BATTLES OF CHATTANOOGA (Nov 24–25, 1863). Gen. Ulysses S. Grant
took the initiative against the Confederates' near-impregnable position
to end the stalemate which developed after the Battle of Chickamauga
Creek. On November 24, Gen. Joseph Hooker's division swept the Confederates off Lookout Mountain, while Gen. William T. Sherman's corps
attacked the other flank. The following day, as Sherman tried to advance,
Gen. George H. Thomas' veterans of Chickamauga made an unordered
assault against the Confederate center on Missionary Ridge and carried
the day. Only Gen. Patrick Cleburne's rear guard action saved Gen.
Braxton Bragg's army from total destruction. The battle was a stunning
success for Grant, and opened the door for an invasion of Georgia.

BATTLE OF THE WILDERNESS (May 5–6, 1864). Gen. Ulysses S. Grant
was General in Chief of the Armies of the U.S., but he chose to accompany the Army of the Potomac as it advanced against Gen. Robert E.
Lee. Lee attacked the Federals in thick woods on May 5, the fighting
setting fire to the undergrowth. Gen. Winfield Scott Hancock's all-out
assault on the 6th went well until Gen. James Longstreet's troops arrived, driving the Union troops back. The Union lost 17,000 men, the
Confederates 11,000, but Grant did not retreat. Instead, to the delight of
his veterans, he ordered his army to advance.

BATTLE OF SPOTSYLVANIA (May 7–20, 1864). Having skirmished on the
7th, the entrenched Confederates stopped a Union advance at

Spotsylvania on the 8th. On May 10, a second assault on Gen. Robert E. Lee's center almost succeeded. Two days later, Federal troops broke through, but were again driven back, while hand-to-hand fighting at the Bloody Angle cost both sides dearly. The week's fighting produced 18,000 Union and 12,000 Confederate casualties, but Lee's defenses held, as they did against another assault the following week. Union hopes, raised by Gen. Ulysses S. Grant's advance at the Wilderness, plummeted as the casualty lists were made public and as Lee's army did not break.

BATTLE OF COLD HARBOR (May 31–Jun 3, 1864). Gen. Ulysses S. Grant later regretted assaulting these well-entrenched Confederate lines. Having repeatedly failed to outflank Gen. Robert E. Lee, Grant finally went into battle when Gen. Philip Sheridan's cavalry captured the Cold Harbor crossroads on May 31 and pushed the Confederates back the next day. Having deployed on the 2nd, the Federals attacked on the 3rd, meeting withering fire. Most of the 7,000 Union casualties occurred within the first hour; the Confederates lost about 1,500. Lee's army fought with determination, while the Federals' morale was deeply shaken.

BATTLE OF THE CRATER (Jul 30, 1864). Colonel Henry Pleasants' ingenious plan to dig a mine shaft under Confederate trenches outside Petersburg and detonate 4 tons of explosives created a spectacular crater 30 feet deep. Gen. Ambrose E. Burnside's assault failed, however, as Union troops went into the crater and Confederate artillery slaughtered them. Gen. William Mahone's counterattack led to a confused, costly retreat for the Union, and Grant ended the attack.

BATTLES FOR ATLANTA (Jul 20–Sep 1, 1864). Atlanta's Confederate defenders attacked Gen. George H. Thomas' corps at Peachtree Creek on July 20, and two days later attempted to roll up Sherman's lines. Both efforts were costly failures. Although Gen. John B. Hood stopped the Federals at Ezra Church on the 28th, he misinterpreted Gen. William T. Sherman's next flanking effort as retreat. At Jonesboro on the 31st, Sherman's outnumbered troops turned back a Confederate attack and the next day successfully counterattacked. Fearing encirclement, Hood withdrew from Atlanta that night. The symbolic importance of the fall of Atlanta was profound for each side.

BATTLE OF MOBILE BAY (Aug 5–23, 1864). Demonstrating personal bravery, Adm. David Farragut led a Union force of fourteen wooden ships and four iron-clad monitors past three forts at the entrance to Mobile Bay on August 5. Farragut's stirring phrase, "Damn the torpedoes! Full speed ahead," entered naval lore. His fleet destroyed the Confederate vessels in the bay, and in combined operations captured the forts over the next three weeks. The city of Mobile held, but was nullified as a blockade-running port.

SAND CREEK MASSACRE (Nov 29, 1864). Chief Black Kettle's Cheyennes encamped at Sand Creek as prisoners of war, seeking amnesty from the

American government. Col. John Chivington nevertheless assaulted the peaceful village from all sides, slaughtering its 200 or so inhabitants and mutilating several at a cost of nine dead and thirty-eight wounded. Although the atrocity was a reprisal and in line with general American policy, subsequent investigations concluded the massacre was wanton.

BATTLES OF FRANKLIN AND NASHVILLE (Nov 30–Dec 16, 1864). Gen. John B. Hood, failing to capture Gen. John Schofield's retreating force at Spring Hill on November 29, ordered a disastrous frontal assault the following day on Federal entrenchments at Franklin. Yet as Schofield's troops joined Gen. George H. Thomas' army in Nashville, Hood advanced. On December 15, Thomas attacked, and by the next day he routed the Army of Tennessee in "one of the most crushing Union victories of the war."

ATTACK ON FORT FISHER (Jan 13–15, 1865). Gen. Ulysses S. Grant sent Gen. Alfred Terry's ground forces and a fleet of fifty-eight ships against the fort, which defended Wilmington, North Carolina, the Confederacy's last blockade-running port. A naval bombardment on the 13th and 14th opened the fight, and Terry attacked from front and rear on the 15th. The fort fell, sealing the Confederacy.

BATTLES OF SELMA AND COLUMBUS (Apr 2–16, 1865). Gen. James H. Wilson led "the best executed Union cavalry operation of the war." His troopers used innovative tactics and Spencer carbines to capture Selma, Alabama, an important manufacturing center, on April 2; 1,500 Union soldiers defeated Gen. Nathan Bedford Forrest's 7,000 defenders. On April 12, Wilson seized Montgomery, and four days later successfully assaulted Columbus, Georgia, with very light casualties. As Confederate President Jefferson Davis sought to flee the country, Wilson's troops captured him on May 10.

BATTLE OF APPOMATTOX (Apr 9, 1865). Union troops inflicted heavy losses on the Confederates at Sayler's Creek (April 6) and Gen. Philip Sheridan blocked Lee's advance at Appomattox Station two days later. When Gen. Robert E. Lee met the force on the 9th, he realized the futility of his position and surrendered the Army of Northern Virginia to Gen. Ulysses S. Grant, signalling the defeat of the Confederacy.

Biographical Notes

ANDERSON, ROBERT (1805–1871). A graduate of West Point (1825), Anderson first served in the Black Hawk War in Wisconsin (1832) and the Seminole War (1836–1838) in Florida. He saw subsequent action in the Mexican War (1847) under Gen. Winfield Scott. Selected to command Ft. Sumter in the mouth of Charleston, SC harbor in November 1860 in part because of his southern birth and proslavery attitude, Anderson informed the War Department the garrison there was insufficient in strength. He received no reinforcements nor instructions from Washington, but maintained a conciliatory stance toward the Confederate authorities. Following Anderson's refusal to surrender Sumter on April 11, 1861, the Confederates opened fire on the fort the next day. Anderson held out until April 14 when he could no longer defend the heavily damaged fort. Although he retired from the service in 1863 due to ill health, Anderson returned on April 14, 1865 to once more raise the Union flag over the recaptured Ft. Sumter.

ATKINSON, HENRY (1782–1842). Atkinson entered the U.S. Army in 1808 and by 1814 he had advanced to the rank of colonel in the infantry. Assigned by Secretary of War John C. Calhoun to lead an exploratory expedition to the West in 1819, Atkinson got as far as what is now Council Bluffs, Iowa. In 1825 Atkinson led a second expedition westward this time reaching the mouth of the Yellowstone and also meeting trader William H. Ashley and his "mountain men," as his fur trappers were called. Seven years later, Atkinson commanded Army regulars and volunteers in the Black Hawk War (1832). As field commander, he defeated Black Hawk and his allies at Bad Axe, in present-day Wisconsin. Atkinson later was in charge of the removal of the Winnebagos from Wisconsin to Iowa (1840).

BARTON, CLARISSA HARLOWE (1821–1912). She was a Civil War nurse for the Union Army who helped to organize the American Association of the Red Cross (1881). William E. Barton, *The Life of Clara Barton* (2 vols., 1922).

BEAUREGARD, PIERRE GUSTAVE TOUTANT (1818–1893). He was the architect of the Confederate victory at First Bull Run, and succeeded to command of the Army of Mississippi with the death of Gen. Albert S. Johnston on the first day of the Battle of Shiloh (April 6, 1862). T. Harry Williams, *P.G.T. Beauregard: Napoleon in Grey* (1954).

BICKERDYKE, MARY ANN BALL (1817–1901). Following the death of her husband in 1859, Mrs. Bickerdyke supported herself by the practice of "botanic" medicine. When the Civil War broke out in 1861, Bickerdyke volunteered as a collector of medical supplies for the relief of wounded soldiers at a makeshift army hospital in Cairo, Illinois. Because conditions in the hospital were extremely primitive, she took on the task of cooking, cleaning, and caring for the wounded. Her success in Cairo won her the support of Generals Grant and Sherman in 1862 along with an alliance with the U.S. Sanitary Commission. Grant gave Bickerdyke a rail pass for free transportation anywhere in his command as she sought to care for the wounded on the western front. Through her efforts to organize medical care, secure supplies, and provide for the wounded, she earned the name "Mother" Bickerdyke. When incompetent officers or physicians failed to support their wounded men or her efforts, she succeeded in having several dismissed. After the war's end, Bickerdyke worked to help those in need in Chicago (1866–1867), Kansas (1867–1869), and New York City (1870). In 1886 Congress voted her a pension.

BLACK HAWK (1776–1838). *Native American name* MAKATAIMESH-EKIAKIAK. Born near present-day Rock Island, Illinois, Black Sparrow Hawk succeeded his father as chief of the Sauks about 1788. Black Hawk resented the American settlers, especially after William Henry Harrison, then governor of the Indiana Territory, negotiated a treaty in 1804 that ceded all Sac and Fox land east of the Mississippi River to the United States. During the War of 1812 Black Hawk supported the British by serving with the Shawnee chief, Tecumseh. After settling in what is now Iowa, Black Hawk and about 1,000 followers attempted to return to their homeland in Illinois in 1832. The white settlers grew alarmed and fighting broke out with the troops of Gen. Henry Atkinson, thus beginning the so-called Black Hawk War. The Native Americans retreated into Wisconsin and were badly defeated at Bad Axe River (1832). Black Hawk was captured and imprisoned. In 1833 he dictated his autobiography that fully stated the Native American resentment of white settlers on tribal lands. Black Hawk was subsequently placed (1833) in the custody of Keokuk, a pro-United States Sac chief, in Iowa.

BRAGG, BRAXTON (1817–1876). As commander of the Confederate Army of Tennessee he is credited with victory at the Battle of Chickamauga, but defeat at the Battle of Missionary Ridge which lifted the siege of Chattanooga, TN (1863). Grady McWhiney, *Braxton Bragg and Confederate Defeat: Field Command* (1969).

BROWN, JACOB JENNINGS (1775–1828). When the War of 1812 started, Brown, who had been active in the militia in western New York, successfully repelled British attacks at Ogdensburg (1812) and Sackett's Harbor (1813). He was given a commission as a brigadier general in the U.S. Army, took part in the failed attempt to capture Montreal, and with Gen. Winfield Scott invaded Canada again in 1814. This time the U.S. forces were successful in the Battles of Chippewa and Lundy's Lane, where Brown was badly wounded. His forces retired to Ft. Erie and withstood British siege. Brown was subsequently appointed the first Commanding General of the U.S. Army (1821–1828).

BURNSIDE, AMBROSE EVERETT (1824–1881). He rapidly rose to command of the Union's Army of the Potomac after the Battle of Antietam (1862), but was disgraced and dismissed after the Battle of Fredericksburg (1862). William Marvel, *Burnside* (1991).

BUTLER, BENJAMIN FRANKLIN (1818–1893). A lawyer by training, Butler was a delegate from Massachusetts to the 1860 Democratic national convention. He bolted the party to help nominate John C. Breckinridge for president instead of Stephen Douglas. Butler entered Union service at the outbreak of war in 1861. He was subsequently promoted to major general and given command of Ft. Monroe, Virginia. There he declared escaped slaves to be "contraband" of war. He then commanded the land forces in the assault on New Orleans (1862) where he became military governor. Butler's arbitrary actions in that port city caused an outcry of protest and charges of corruption. The Confederate government declared Butler an outlaw and he was later recalled from his post. Reassigned to command of the Army of the James, he lost the battle of Drewry's Bluff (1864) and was unable to assist Grant in the Richmond-Petersburg campaign (1864). Gen. Grant subsequently removed him from command in January 1865. Butler then won election to the U.S. House of Representatives as a Radical Republican (1867–1875) and as a Greenbacker (1877–1879). He was involved in the impeachment trial of President Andrew Johnson and was a strong supporter of President U.S. Grant.

CLARK, WILLIAM (1770–1838). The younger brother of George Rogers Clark, William Clark fought against the Native Americans during several military campaigns including the Battle of Fallen Timbers (1794). Invited by Capt. Meriwether Lewis to share command of an expedition to explore the Louisiana Territory and to seek a land route to the Pacific, Clark was fully Lewis's equal throughout the long trip. Lewis and Clark left St. Louis in 1804, reached the mouth of the Columbia river in 1805, and returned to St. Louis in 1806. During this time, Clark specialized in mapmaking and in studying the natural history of the areas they explored. He played a major role in collecting the official and personal records of the expedition. Clark later served as a brigadier general of militia and superintendent of Indian affairs for the Louisiana Territory (1807–1821) and as governor of the Missouri Territory (1813–1821). Throughout the 1820s, Clark participated in efforts to settle permanently all territorial disputes with the Native Americans. This involved him in the suppression of the Winnebagos (1827) and the Sauk (1832).

COLT, SAMUEL (1814–1862). Beginning in 1830 Colt began work to develop a repeating pistol that would automatically involve a revolving set of chambers, each of which would successfully align with a single barrel. Colt received English and French patents for his idea in 1835 and a U.S. patent in 1836. He then founded the Patent Arms Manufacturing Company (1836) to make his invention by mass production of completely interchangeable parts, assembly-line procedure, and end-of-the-line inspection. Unfortunately, despite the proven success of the Colt revolver in the Seminole campaign (1837), Colt's company failed to interest the army in his product and the business failed in 1842. The Mexican War subsequently produced a demand for his "six-shooters" and Colt subcontracted with Eli Whitney to make the revolvers. These orders and others from around the world later made a fortune for Colt. His revolver was a key technological development in small-arms weaponry and played a major role in the settlement of the West.

DAHLGREN, JOHN ADOLPHUS BERNARD (1809–1870). After more than sixteen years of duty at sea, Dahlgren, then a lieutenant, was assigned to the Washington Navy Yard as ordnance officer (1847). At the Navy Yard he began a program of experimentation and ordnance testing that led to the development of the Dahlgren gun, nicknamed the "soda-water bottle." This 11-inch gun was thicker at the breech and curved to a thinner size at the muzzle. The smooth curve from breech to muzzle also improved the strength of the gun by regularizing the cooling process. Cast solid and bored smooth, Dahlgren guns were first installed in shore batteries (1851) and then on ships (1857). Promoted to captain in 1862, Dahlgren served as Chief of the Bureau of Ordnance (1862–1863, 1868–1869). Dahlgren went to sea in 1863 as a rear admiral in command of the South Atlantic Blockading Squadron. His forces assisted in the capture of Savannah in 1864.

DIX, DOROTHEA LYNDE (1802–1887). A philanthropist and reformer, Dorothea Dix headed a school for girls in Boston (1821–1836) and led an extensive and exhausting campaign to reform state institutions for the insane (1841–1843) in Massachusetts and elsewhere. In the 1850s Dix worked hard, but unsuccessfully, to persuade the U.S. Congress to set aside a parcel of public land whose income could be used for the care of the insane. Appointed superintendent of nurses in the Union Army in 1861, Dix had a frustrating and controversial experience dealing with the problems of the army's medical service. She set up and staffed hospitals, helped stockpile supplies, and did much good, but Dix also became involved in bitter disputes resulting from her sometimes arbitrary way of dealing with problems. Because of this friction, the Secretary of War intervened and from October 1863 to 1866 Dix functioned with considerably lessened authority.

EADS, JAMES BUCHANAN (1820–1887). James Eads, a highly productive inventor and engineer, made a fortune from the diving bell he invented to use in salvaging steamboats sunk in the Mississippi and other rivers (1848–1857). When the Civil War broke out, Eads proposed building a fleet of armor-plated gunboats for controlling the Mississippi River (1861). When the War Department contracted with Eads to build eight gunboats, his firm did so on time in sixty-five days. These gunboats helped secure the Mississippi for the Union. After the war Eads built the first bridge across the Mississippi at St. Louis (1867–1874) and developed a jetty system in 1879 that helped to keep the river channel at a proper depth for navigation.

ERICSSON, JOHN (1803–1889). Born in Sweden, Ericsson received training as an engineer in the Swedish army. In 1826 he built and experimented with steam engines in London and built a steam locomotive (1829) and other inventions. In the 1830s Ericsson focused his efforts on ship design and propulsion. He built and tested a ship in 1837 that was the first successful propeller-driven commercial vessel. When Capt. Robert F. Stockton of the U.S. Navy contracted with Ericsson to build another such ship, the Swedish engineer migrated to New York (1839). Ericsson's ideas resulted in the *Princeton* (1844), the first warship with a screw propeller. Ericsson became an U.S. citizen in 1844. He subsequently designed and built the ironclad *Monitor* (1862) that fought the Confederate ironclad *Virginia* (formerly the *Merrimack*) at Hampton Roads. The *Monitor* was powered solely by steam and screw propeller-driven. Constructed entirely of iron, heavily armored, and armed with heavy guns fitted to a revolving turret, Ericsson's ironclad inaugurated a new era in naval warfare. In 1878 Ericsson built the *Destroyer*, a ship that could launch underwater torpedoes from a gun on its bow.

FARRAGUT, DAVID GLASGOW (1801–1870). The first Hispanic American to reach flag rank in the U.S. Navy, Farragut began naval service shortly after his adoption by Capt. David Porter. He served in the War of 1812 and the Mexican War as well as a variety of posts at sea. At the outbreak of the Civil War, Farragut was ordered to capture New Orleans. This he accomplished despite many obstacles in April 1862. Promoted to rear admiral, Farragut spent two years blockading the Gulf Coast and helping the Union armies to secure the Mississippi River. In 1864 Farragut led the assault on Mobile Bay, which was heavily mined and protected by Ft. Morgan. When one of the Union warships struck a mine (or torpedo as it was then called) which destroyed the vessel, Farragut shouted "Damn the torpedoes! Full speed ahead, Drayton" and headed his ship into the minefield. No more mines exploded and Farragut's squadron quickly forced the Confederate defenders to surrender. Promotion to vice admiral and admiral (1866) followed Farragut's success at Mobile Bay.

FOOTE, ANDREW HULL (1806–1863). Foote spent twenty undistinguished years of naval service in the Caribbean, Pacific, and Mediterranean before coming to prominence for his efforts beginning in 1843 to abolish the traditional grog (or rum) ration on ships of the U.S. Navy. At the same time he also campaigned against the slave trade on the African Coast. Foote's *Africa and the American Flag* (1854) summarized his opposition to this practice. Following service in China, Foote was put in command of naval operations on the vital upper Mississippi River (1861). There his gunboats and mortarboats greatly assisted Gen. U.S. Grant in taking Ft. Henry and Ft. Donelson (1862). Despite being wounded in the fighting around Ft. Donelson, Foote later participated in Gen. John Pope's campaign to take Memphis and to open the way for the Union to move down the Mississippi.

FORREST, NATHAN BEDFORD (1821–1877). Largely self-educated, Forrest was a brilliant Confederate general. He enlisted as a private at the outbreak of the war and rapidly rose through the ranks fighting Gen. U.S. Grant's forces along the Mississippi at Ft. Donelson (1862) and Shiloh (1862), where he was severely wounded. Promoted to brigadier general, Forrest spent much of 1862–1863 carrying out raids on Union forces in Tennessee and Kentucky. In the spring of 1863 he captured an entire Union cavalry brigade near Rome, Ga. Forrest then fought in the battle of Chickamauga (1863) before turning once again to carrying out highly effective raids on Union forces in Tennessee, Alabama, Mississippi, and Georgia. In 1864 Forrest participated in Gen. John B. Hood's disastrous Nashville campaign. As the Confederate armies began to withdraw further southward in the face of overwhelming Union strength, Forrest and his men fought effective rearguard actions up to the time of Gen. Lee's surrender to Grant (1865).

FOX, GUSTAVUS VASA (1821–1883). Fox entered naval service in 1838 and served until 1856 when he resigned to work for a Massachusetts textile mill. When the Confederacy demanded the surrender of Ft. Sumter in Charleston, S.C. harbor, Fox was asked to develop a plan to relieve the Union garrison. President James Buchanan vetoed the plan, and although President Abraham Lincoln approved it later, time had run out for the Ft. Sumter garrison. Not long afterward, Fox was appointed chief clerk of the Navy Department and, on August 1, 1861, Assistant Secretary of the Navy. From then until he resigned in 1866, Fox provided wise counsel and advice to Navy Secretary Gideon Welles on a wide range of naval issues. Fox encouraged development and use of ironclad monitors, and the assignment of Capt. David G. Farragut to the campaign against New Orleans (1862). Following the war, Fox headed a diplomatic mission to Russia before returning to private business.

FREMONT, JOHN CHARLES (1813–1890). Although known primarily as an explorer, he played a major role in the conquest of California during the Mexican War. He was the first Republican nominee for President and held various commands in the U.S. army during the Civil War. Allan Nevins, *Fremont: Pathmaker of the West* (1939).

GORGAS, JOSIAH (1818–1883). A graduate of West Point (1841), Gorgas took part in the Mexican War and served in various army posts involving the ordnance service. When the Civil War began, Gorgas resigned his commission and entered the service of the Confederacy as the chief of its ordnance service. Because the Confederacy had limited stockpiles of arms and ammunition and could not depend on captured Union matériel, Gorgas quickly worked to set up a rudimentary and highly decentralized system of manufacturing and distribution involving mines, mills, and factories to provide a flow of arms and munitions to the Confederate armies. Although some war supplies reached Confederate forces via blockade runners, Gorgas's work to provide bullets, powder, small arms, and cannon for the entire course of the war was remarkable given the political, financial, and other handicaps he faced.

GRANT, ULYSSES S. (1822–1885). After victories in the West, he was appointed General in Chief of the Armies of the United States (1864) and orchestrated the final defeat of the Confederate Army of Northern Virginia at Appomattox Court House (1865). He served as President of the U.S. (1868–1876). William S. McFeely, *Grant: A Biography* (1981).

GRIERSON, BENJAMIN HENRY (1826–1911). Grierson enlisted as a private in the Illinois cavalry at the outbreak of the Civil War. During 1862–1863, Grierson, by then a colonel, led his cavalry on numerous raids into Tennessee, Louisiana, and Mississippi that contributed greatly to Gen. U.S. Grant's campaign to capture Vicksburg, Mississippi (1863). Following the surrender of Vicksburg, Grierson's cavalry raids concentrated in Tennessee and Mississippi as the Union forces chased Confederate Gen. Nathan Forrest's men across the lower South. At the time of Forrest's defeat in July 1864, Grierson was a Union division commander. After the war Grierson reverted to the rank of colonel and served in a variety of posts on the Western frontier—most particularly with the 10th Cavalry.

HALLECK, HENRY WAGER (1815–1872). After service in the West he was appointed Commanding General of the U. S. Army in 1862. He was an excellent administrator but a poor field commander. He also composed highly successful books on the military art and on international law. Stephen E. Ambrose, *Halleck: Lincoln's Chief of Staff* (1962).

HOOKER, JOSEPH (1814–1879). He succeeded Gen. Burnside as commander of the Union's Army of the Potomac after the defeat at Fredericksburg (1863), only to be defeated himself at the Battle of Chancellorsville (1863). Walter H. Hebert, *Fighting Joe Hooker* (1944).

ISHERWOOD, BENJAMIN FRANKLIN (1822–1915). An engineer and naval officer, Isherwood began his adult life working for a railroad and studying engineering from his stepfather. He was appointed to the newly established Engineer Corps of the U.S. Navy in 1844. During the Mexican War, Isherwood served on the navy's first screw-propeller driven vessel, the *Princeton*, which had been built by John Ericsson. He took part in several battles during the conflict with Mexico, but his greatest contributions came in the Civil War as the U.S. Navy's Engineer-in-Chief. In 1859 he published *Engineering Precedents*, a study of steam power plants. This was followed in 1863 and 1865 by two volumes of *Experimental Researches in Steam Engineering* in which Isherwood broke new ground in the design and construction of steam engines. In his role as the navy's foremost engineer, Isherwood built a fleet of steam-powered vessels that grew to over 600 by the war's end. He was also responsible for building the fast *Wampanoag*-class sloops that proved to be excellent in blockade and commerce-raiding work.

JACKSON, THOMAS JONATHAN (1824–1863). Although he earned the sobriquet "Stonewall" at First Bull Run (1861), he became famous for his lightning campaigns. He proved exceedingly valuable to R. E. Lee and the Army of Northern Virginia until his death in battle (1863). Lenoir Chambers, *Stonewall Jackson* (1959)

JOHNSTON, ALBERT SIDNEY (1803–1862). As commander of the Confederate Department of the West, he took responsibility for successive losses in that area in 1862. He oversaw the Confederate success on the first day of the Battle of Shiloh but died before the reversal on the next. Charles P. Roland, *Albert Sidney Johnston: Soldier of Three Republics* (1964).

JOHNSTON, JOSEPH EGGLESTON (1807–1891). As commander of the Confederate Army of the Potomac, he was far more successful on the defense than the offense. He performed creditably in the Peninsula against Gen. G. B. McClellan and later in Georgia against Gen. W. T. Sherman. Gilbert E. Govan and James W. Livingood, *A Different Valor: The Story of General Joseph E. Johnston, C.S.A.* (1956).

KEARNY, STEPHEN WATTS (1794–1848). Kearny began his military career in the War of 1812. He then served in various parts of the western frontier, reaching the rank of colonel in 1836. In 1842 he took command of the Third Military Department which then comprised most of the Great Plains area. When the Mexican War broke out, Gen. Kearny went first to the New Mexico territory (1846) and then on to California to join forces with Commodore Robert F. Stockton in southern California. When the Californians surrendered in January 1847 to Lt. Col. John C. Fremont, Stockton and Kearny quarreled over who was the final authority in this newly conquered territory. Authorities in Washington supported Kearny, who then removed Fremont, whom Stockton had appointed governor, and court-martialed him for insubordination and other offenses. Fremont resigned from the army and Kearny became military governor. From pacified California, Kearny went to Mexico and served briefly (1848) as governor general of Vera Cruz and then of Mexico City before he caught the tropical disease that led to his death.

LEE, ROBERT EDWARD (1807–1870). As commanding general of the Confederate Army of Northern Virginia (1862–1865) he was the most important field commander in the Confederacy. His surrender to Gen. U. S. Grant at Appomattox Court House marked the end of significant military operations by the Confederate States of America. Douglas S. Freeman, *R.E. Lee* (4 vols., 1934–1937).

LETTERMAN, JONATHAN (1824–1872). Trained as a physician, Letterman entered the medical department of the U.S. Army in 1849. He went to Florida and saw service in the campaign against the Seminole. He then served on the western frontier before being ordered to duty with the Army of the Potomac (1861). By mid-1862 Letterman was medical director of that army. Reorganizing the medical service of the Army of the Potomac, Letterman greatly improved the treatment of wounded, the management of first-aid stations and field and base hospitals. He secured control of the ambulance corps under the medical service rather than the quartermaster corps and set up a vastly improved system for medical supply. The value of Letterman's work was demonstrated at the Battle of Fredericksburg (1862) when the Union forces sustained 12,000 casualties. By 1864 the U.S. Congress officially established the Letterman system as the model for all Union armies. After the war Letterman published his *Medical Recollections of the Army of the Potomac* (1866).

LONGSTREET, JAMES (1821–1904). He was Gen. R. E. Lee's most trusted subordinate from the beginning to the end of the war. His actions, positive and negative, at the Battle of Gettysburg continue to spark heated controversy. William S. Piston, *Lee's Tarnished Lieutenant: James Longstreet and His Place in Southern History* (1987).

MAHAN, DENNIS HART (1802–1871). Mahan entered West Point in 1820, where he was a brilliant student. In fact, Superintendent Sylvanus Thayer appointed Mahan an acting instructor in mathematics before his graduation. Commissioned in the engineering corps in 1824 and assigned to the faculty at West Point, Mahan studied in France from 1826 to 1830. He then returned to West Point where he served until his death as a professor of civil and military engineering. While at West Point, he wrote numerous textbooks which soon became standard works for students. Mahan's adherence to high educational and engineering standards helped to build a program of high quality at West Point and set new standards of excellence in engineering in the United States. Mahan's principles and teaching influenced many classes of West Point cadets, particularly those who became Union or Confederate generals in the Civil War. Rather than retire from teaching in 1871, Mahan committed suicide.

MALLORY, STEPHEN RUSSELL (1813?–1873). Although Mallory was born in Trinidad, his family moved to the United States about 1814 and settled in Key West, Florida in 1820. Mallory grew up with a knowledge and love of the sea which he combined with the practice of law. Appointed customs inspector by President Andrew Jackson in 1833, he became Collector of Customs in 1845. Then in 1851 the Florida legislature elected Mallory to the U.S. Senate where he participated vigorously in naval reform legislation. Mallory was reelected in 1857 and became chair of the committee on naval affairs, but he resigned his seat when Florida seceded from the Union, went home to Pensacola, and worked hard to resolve the sectional dispute peacefully. However, in early 1861 Mallory accepted appointment from President Jefferson Davis as the Secretary of the Navy for the Confederacy. In this post Mallory actively pushed for the construction of ironclad warships, such as the *Merrimack* (Confederate *Virginia*), which fought the Union *Monitor* in 1862. He also supported the development of improved torpedoes and submarines. Although Mallory had great vision for the Confederate navy, many of his ideas and plans went unrealized due to lack of resources or to Union military successes. At the end of the war, Union forces took Mallory prisoner and he was held for nearly a year before he was paroled (1866) and returned to Pensacola.

MCCLELLAN, GEORGE BRINTON (1826–1885). As commanding general of the U.S. Army of the Potomac and Commanding General of the U.S. Army, he was the most important individual in the Union war effort until his removal from command (1862). McClellan was an effective administrator, but his field operations were singularly flawed. Stephen W. Sears, *George B. Mcclellan: The Young Napoleon* (1988).

MEADE, GEORGE GORDON (1815–1872). He inherited command of the Union Army of the Potomac immediately prior to the Battle of Gettysburg and retained that position, unlike his predecessors, until the end of the war. Freeman Cleaves, *Meade of Gettysburg* (1960).

MEIGS, MONTGOMERY CUNNINGHAM (1816–1892). Although commissioned in the artillery after graduation from West Point (1836), Meigs subsequently transferred to the engineers and spent sixteen years in a variety of posts doing engineering work. In 1852 Meigs was given charge of building the Washington Aqueduct, a tremendous job. He supervised various public works projects in Washington, including the building of the wings and the dome of the U.S. Capital. With the coming of the Civil War, Meigs was promoted to brigadier general and made Quartermaster General of the U.S. Army. In this post Meigs was responsible for the procurement of food, clothing, and equipment other than ordnance used by the army. He also had charge over all transportation (by road, rail, river, sea or pack animal) and the construction and maintenance of a variety of army installations. Meigs' Quartermaster Department maintained key supplies and support to various Union commanders, such as Generals Grant and Sherman, throughout the war.

OSCEOLA (c. 1804–1838). Probably born of Creek parents in Georgia, Osceola later moved to Florida where he may have fought Gen. Andrew

Jackson in the First Seminole war (1817–1818). Osceola opposed the removal of the Seminoles westward in the face of white expansion in the 1830s. In the Second Seminole War he established himself as a leader of the Native American resistance. For two years Osceola used guerilla tactics to hide his people in the swamps of the Everglades and to mount quick raids on army troops sent to find him. In October 1837 Osceola agreed to meet with Gen. Thomas S. Jesup under a flag of truce, but when Osceola and others met with Jesup, he arrested and imprisoned them despite a public outcry over Jesup's trick. Osceola died in prison in early 1838 and although the Seminoles continued sporadic resistance to the whites, they were no longer a significant threat.

PERRY, MATTHEW CALBRAITH (1794–1858). The brother of Oliver Hazard Perry, his most notable achievement was his successive voyages to Japan to secure American access to that previously closed society (1852). In the course of his second voyage, Perry negotiated the unprecedented Treaty of Kanagawa (1854). Samuel E. Morison, *"Old Bruin:" Commodore Matthew C. Perry, 1794–1858* (1967).

POPE, JOHN (1822–1892). Although successful in the West, he accepted defeat at the Second Battle of Bull Run (1862) while in command of the U.S. Army of Virginia. Wallace J. Schultz and Walter N. Trenerry, *Abandoned by Lincoln: A Military Biography of General John Pope* (1990).

PORTER, DAVID DIXON (1813–1891). The son of Capt. David Porter and foster brother of David Glasgow Farragut, David Dixon Porter went to sea at an early age with his father. He joined the U.S. Navy in 1829 as a midshipman serving on various ships and in the Mexican War. Early in 1861 Porter was about to resign when he was given command of the *Powhattan* and ordered along with Army Capt. Montgomery Meigs to mount a relief mission to Ft. Pickens, Florida. Porter went on to blockade duty on the Gulf Coast and a major role in the campaign to capture New Orleans (1862). Porter's ships helped open the mouth of the Mississippi and to take New Orleans. Porter then operated northward on the Mississippi in support of Gen. U.S. Grant's siege of Vicksburg (1863). Promoted to rear admiral, Porter took part in other campaigns on the western rivers and in late 1864 took command of the North Atlantic Blockading Squadron. His ships participated in both naval operations against Ft. Fisher in North Carolina. Although Porter continued his naval service in various posts after the war ended, he became increasingly frustrated in the 1870s with the navy's limited role and influence in peacetime.

SCOTT, WINFIELD (1786–1866). He is considered by many the most significant field commander between Revolutionary and Civil Wars. His exploits during the War of 1812 are legendary, and his campaign to capture Mexico City serves as a model of limited warfare. Charles W. Elliot, *Winfield Scott: The Soldier and the Man* (1937).

SEMMES, RAPHAEL (1809–1877). Semmes began his naval career in 1826, studied law on the side, and had routine assignments until the Mexican War. He took part in the landing at Vera Cruz (1847) and marched to Mexico City with Gen. Winfield Scott's army. Following his service in Mexico, Semmes practiced law in his home near Mobile, Alabama, until the start of the Civil War when he joined the Confederate navy (1861) as a commander. He operated in the Gulf, Caribbean, and along the East Coast raiding merchant ships and taking numerous prizes. Blockaded in Gibraltar, Semmes was ordered to go to England where he took command of the British-built cruiser *Alabama*. He then operated in the Atlantic harassing Union shipping and taking many prizes. By June 19, 1864 when the *Alabama* encountered the Union sloop *Kearsarge*, Semmes had captured or destroyed 64 ships. The *Kearsarge* sank the *Alabama*, but Semmes was rescued by a British yacht. Returning to the South, Semmes was ordered to assist in the defense of Richmond, VA in command of the naval forces on the James River. The fall of Richmond ended Semmes' naval career. The damage that the *Alabama* and other Confederate vessels constructed in neutral Britain did to Union commerce led to a diplomatic imbroglio known as the *"Alabama* claims." The dispute was settled by arbitration in 1872.

SHERIDAN, PHILIP HENRY (1831–1888). His campaign to severely curtail the Confederate presence in the Shenandoah Valley of Virginia was a crucial element in the U.S. victory in the East. Paul Hutton, *Phil Sheridan and his Army* (1985).

SHERMAN, WILLIAM TECUMSEH (1821–1891). He was Gen. U.S. Grant's able subordinate at the Battle of Shiloh and the Siege of Vicksburg. His "march to the sea" after the capture of Atlanta, GA (1864) helped convince supporters of the Confederacy that their efforts to achieve independence were doomed. Charles E. Vetter, *Sherman: Merchant of Terror, Advocate of Peace* (1992).

SMALLS, ROBERT (1839–1915). Smalls was born into slavery in Beaufort, South Carolina. He received rudimentary schooling prior to being pressed into the Confederate navy at the opening of the Civil War. Serving as wheelman on the armed frigate *Planter*, Smalls commandeered the ship on May 13, 1862 and escaped Charleston to deliver the ship to the Union. This heroism won Smalls, his family, and a dozen other slaves their freedom. President Abraham Lincoln appointed Smalls pilot in the Union navy. He participated in the attack on Charleston, South Carolina and was promoted to captain (1863) for his bravery. From 1863 to 1866 he was the highest ranking African American officer in the U.S. Navy. Following the war Smalls pursued a successful career in South Carolina politics, eventually winning election as a Republican to the U.S. House of Representatives (1875). He served in that position until 1887 except for 1879–1881. Always an advocate of civil rights for African Americans, Smalls fought the gradual imposition of segregation in the South until his death in 1915.

SMITH, EDMUND KIRBY (1824–1893). An 1845 graduate of West Point, Smith fought in many of the major battles of the Mexican War (1846–1847). Duty at West Point (1849–1852) was followed by assignments on the frontier where he took part in several campaigns. Smith resigned from the U.S. Army in March 1861 to take a commission as a colonel of cavalry in the Confederate army. Serving first in the Army of the Shenandoah, Smith was badly wounded at Manassas (1861) and then in 1862 took command of the Department of East Tennessee. He briefly cleared the Cumberland Gap area of Union forces and fought frequently in the Tennessee-Kentucky area. Early in 1863 Smith took command of the Trans-Mississippi Department, which was most of Arkansas, Louisiana, Texas, and the Indian Territory. The fall of Vicksburg in July 1863 to Gen. U.S. Grant left Gen. Smith in virtual civil and military command in Texas. Smith's efforts to maintain trade with Europe via the port of Galveston was essential to the continued Confederate struggle. Despite a deteriorating situation in Texas, Smith was the last department head to surrender (May 1865).

STUART, JAMES EWELL BROWN (1883–1864). He was a Confederate cavalry commander best known for his daring raids on Union forces in the East. Stuart served Gen. R. E. Lee with distinction, but his absence in the weeks prior to the Battle of Gettysburg led to questions concerning his leadership. Emory M. Thomas, *Bold Dragoon: The Life of J.E.B. Stuart* (1986).

TAYLOR, ZACHARY (1784–1850). Although he saw service in the War of 1812, Taylor is best remembered for battles early in the Mexican War—especially the Battle of Buena Vista (1847). He was elected President in 1848, and died in office. K. Jack Bauer, *Zachary Taylor: Soldier, Planter, Statesman of the Old Southwest* (1985).

THOMAS, GEORGE HENRY (1816–1870). He won fame as the "Rock of Chickamauga" in consequence of his actions after the penetration of the Union line (1863) by Confederate forces. Troops under his command achieved impressive victories at Missionary Ridge (1863) and the Battle of Nashville (1864). Francis F. McKinney, *Education in Violence: The Life of George H. Thomas and the History of the Army of the Cumberland* (1961).

TOMPKINS, SALLY LOUISA (1833–1916). Sally Tompkins grew up in Richmond, Virginia in a wealthy family. At the outbreak of the Civil War she established a private hospital, known as Robertson Hospital, at her own expense and operated it for the duration of the war. When the Confederate government sought to close all private hospitals in the fall of 1861, President Jefferson Davis commissioned Tompkins a captain in the cavalry. This move not only circumvented the governmental order, it also made Tompkins the only woman to hold a commission in the Confederate military. Known thereafter as "Captain Sally," Tompkins had the cooperation of the army and was able to operate a very effective and efficient hospital. Out of the more than 1,000 patients treated at Robertson Hospital between 1861 and the end of the war, only 73 died, a remarkable record.

WALKER, MARY EDWARDS (1832–1919). Mary Walker overcame many hurdles to graduate from Syracuse Medical College in 1855. She later married Albert Miller and practiced medicine with him until war broke out. Then she volunteered as a nurse in a Washington hospital while she sought an appointment to the army medical service. In September 1863 Gen. George H. Thomas appointed her assistant surgeon in the Army of the Cumberland, probably the only woman holding such a position in the Civil War. Walker had been a follower of Amelia Bloomer from an early age and an ardent advocate of dress reform. Consequently she wore the standard uniform of an officer while serving in Tennessee. In 1864 she also fell prisoner for several months to the Confederates. Awarded a Medal of Honor in 1865, Walker continued her reformist efforts for the rest of her life. Because she insisted on wearing male attire, she was often arrested for doing so. Walker became increasingly eccentric with time, but even after her Medal of Honor was revoked (for the lack of documentation) by an army board in 1917, she continued to wear it.

WARREN, GOUVENEUR KEMBLE (1830–1882). A graduate of West Point (1850), topographical engineer, and Civil War general, Warren served throughout the eastern theater of war. He participated in the Peninsula campaign of 1862, the Battle of Antietam (1862), and served as chief engineer for the Army of the Potomac (1863). His alert action on the second day of the Battle of Gettysburg (July 2, 1863) helped repel a heavy assault by Confederate Gen. James Longstreet's soldiers. Warren continued fighting in various engagements in and around Washington in 1864, particularly Gen. U.S. Grant's Wilderness campaign. As commander of Grant's V Corps, Warren fought at Cold Harbor and Petersburg, but in April 1865 he was summarily relieved of command by Gen. Philip H. Sheridan. After the war he went back to service as a topographical engineer while seeking a court of inquiry in an effort to clear his name. Eventually his request was granted and the court found fully in Warren's favor, but the publication of this finding came after Warren's death in 1882.

WATIE, STAND (1806–1871). Originally Degataga Oowatie or Uwetie, a member of the Cherokee tribe, Watie's name Degataga was roughly translated as "stand." His father's name Oowatie or Uweti became Watie in English. Watie's older brother was Elias Boudinot, the editor of the *Chero-*

kee Phoenix from 1824 to 1835. Watie was educated at a mission school and was a signer of the Treaty of New Echota (1835) in which the Cherokees gave up all lands east of the Mississippi. Although Watie supported removal to the west, most Cherokees did not. When Gen. Winfield Scott supervised the removal of the Cherokees in 1838–1839, Watie narrowly escaped assassination. His brother Boudinot and the other signers were not so lucky. When the Civil War began, Watie was living in the Indian Territory (Oklahoma). He supported the Confederate cause and soon was given the rank of colonel in command of a regiment of Cherokees. Even though the majority of Cherokees rejected any alliance with the Confederacy in 1863, Watie and his troops fought frequently in Indian Territory, Arkansas, and Missouri. The most audacious act attributed to the Cherokee Rifles was the capture of the steamship *J. R. Williams* while it was underway (1864). Watie was promoted to brigadier general in 1864. He was the last Confederate general to surrender to the Union forces.

WILKES, CHARLES (1798–1877). Following service in the merchant marines, Wilkes entered naval service in 1818. He held routine assignments at sea and ashore until 1838 when he was appointed to command a naval scientific expedition to the South Pacific. Wilkes' command included six ships and a number of scientists. The expedition travelled along both coasts of South America and headed across the Pacific to Australia (1839) and on to Antarctica. Wilkes claimed to have sighted land in Antarctica, but many years passed before this discovery was substantiated and the area known as Wilkes Land. Sailing northward in 1840, Wilkes' squadron landed at the Fiji and Hawaiian Islands before exploring the west coast of North America, which helped bolster U.S. claims to the Oregon Territory. From North America the Wilkes expedition headed west to the Philippines, South Africa, Brazil and then to New York, arriving in June 1842. From 1844 to 1861, Wilkes edited or wrote more than 20 volumes detailing his explorations and the findings of his team. The Civil War sent Wilkes back to sea where in 1861 he forcibly removed two Confederate diplomats, James M. Mason and John Slidell, from the British mail ship *Trent*. Wilkes was a hero, but the Union disavowed his actions and released Mason and Slidell to avoid offending the neutral British governent.

WILSON, JAMES HARRISON (1837–1925). An 1860 graduate of West Point, Wilson was one of the Civil War's "boy wonders" because he rose to the rank of major general five years after his graduation. Wilson fought at Port Royal, S.C. (1861), Ft. Pulaski, Ga. (1862), Vicksburg (1863), and Missionary Ridge in the Chattanooga campaign (1863). In the spring of 1864, Wilson led cavalry troops in the Wilderness campaign and then in and around Petersburg, Va. He also fought with Gen. Philip Sheridan in

the Shenandoah Valley. In October 1864 Wilson was named chief of cavalry for Gen. William T. Sherman, then fighting in Mississippi. There
Wilson pursued Confederate general Nathan B. Forrest, whom he defeated at Ebenezer Church, Alabama (1865). Troops under Wilson's command also captured Confederate president Jefferson Davis (May 1865)
near Irwinville, Ga. After the war, Wilson engaged in railroad construction and management. He later volunteered for duty in the Spanish-
American War, serving in Puerto Rico and Cuba (1898), and in the China
Relief Expedition (1900).

WOOL, JOHN ELLIS (1784–1869). Wool joined the U.S. Army early in the
War of 1812. He fought at Queenston Heights, Quebec (1812), and
Plattsburg, N.Y. (1813). In 1816 he was promoted to colonel and appointed
inspector general of the army, a post he held for twenty-five years. Wool
participated in the removal of the Cherokee in the mid-1830s and served
with distinction in the Mexican War by supervising the training of 12,000
volunteers and serving as a general in Zachary Taylor's army. He was
Taylor's second-in-command at the Battle of Buena Vista (1847). After
the war Wool held various assignments including responsibility for leading Army troops in the Yakima War in the mid-1850s. In the Civil War he
served for two years as commander of the Department of Virginia, the
Middle Department, and the Department of the East before retiring in
1863.

Selected Reading List

Antebellum Period: 1815–1861

Most of the trends noted in American military history in the early years
of the republic in the previous chapter also appear in the antebellum period. The area of greatest interest remains operations. This is particularly
true for army history which is dominated by the issues of westward expansion, the associated conflicts with Native Americans, and the Mexican
War. Only in the occasional histories of West Point do army historians share
the fascination of their naval colleagues with the growing profes-
sionalization of the service in this period.

In the areas of dominant interest, the traditional concerns regarding the
role of the army in westward expansion have been expanded recently by
interest in the economic impact on a region of garrison occupation. More
important, under the influence of Prucha and Utley, histories of conflicts
with the Native Americans have become more scholarly and show more
interest in, and sympathy for, the vanquished tribes.

Institutional and Social

Coakley, Robert W. *The Role of Federal Military Forces in Domestic Disorders, 1789–1878* (1988). Coakley's book consists of a set of topical studies of instances of federal military involvement in domestic unrest beginning with the Whiskey Rebellion.

Cunliffe, Marcus. *Soldiers and Civilians: The Martial Spirit in America, 1775–1865* (1968). Cunliffe examines the social development of the army within the context of broader social and cultural trends in the nation.

Cutrer, Thomas W. *Ben McCulloch and the Frontier Military Tradition* (1993). Cutrer uses his biography of McCulloch as a vehicle to portray the growing competition between the older volunteer military tradition still extant in the west during the antebellum period and the rising professionalism in the east focussed on West Point.

Gillett, Mary C. *The Army Medical Department, 1818–1865* (1987). Gillett's institutional study of the development of the Medical Department also pays particular attention to its relation to the changing state of medical knowledge at the time.

Guttridge, Leonard F. *The Commodores: The United States Navy in the Age of Sail* (1969). Guttridge presents an institutional history of the navy from its beginning to the Civil War with a focus on its leadership, its politics, and its ships.

Karsten, Peter. *The Naval Aristocracy: The Golden Age of Annapolis and the Emergence of Modern American Navalism* (1972). Karsten's book is a controversial social history that argues that antebellum American naval officers saw themselves as an elite group and were primarily motivated by a search for power and prestige.

Langley, Harold D. *Social Reform in the United States Navy, 1798–1862* (1967). Langley's work represents an earlier and less critical social history of the Navy than that of Karsten and also includes study of sailors.

Morrison, James L. *"The Best School in the World:" West Point in the Pre-Civil War Years, 1833–1866* (1986). Morrison's study of West Point covers the years in which most Civil War officers attended and tries to assess the impact the Academy had on them.

Skelton, William B. *An American Profession of Arms: The Army Officer Corps, 1784–1861* (1992). In this social history of the officer corps of the U.S. Army, Skelton argues that military professionalism began to appear and become deeply rooted in the decades between the War of 1812 and the Civil War.

Smith, Merritt, R. *Harpers Ferry Armory and the New Technology: The Callenge of Change* (1977). Smith argues that institutional structures and attitudes led the armory to resist mechanization and changes in technology.

Todorich, Charles. *The Spirited Years: A History of the Antebellum Naval Academy* (1984). Todorich argues that in this period the academy was struggling to establish itself as the focal point of naval professionalism.

The Army and Navy in Westward and Oceanic Expansion

Frazer, Robert W. *Forts and Supplies: The Role of the Army in the Economy of the Southwest, 1846–1861* (1983). Frazer claims that the army supply system, especially its purchases of cereals and forage, had a significant impact on the economy in New Mexico.

Goetzmann, William H. *Army Exploration in the American West, 1803–1863* (1959). Goetzmann surveys the role of the army, and especially the topographical engineers, in the exploration of the trans-Mississippi west.

Prucha, Francis P. *Broadax and Bayonet: The Role of the United States Army in the Development of the Northwest, 1815–1860* (1953). Prucha's work was a pioneering effort to describe both the social and institutional development of the army on the frontier in this period as well as its use as an instrument of westward expansion.

Schubert, Frank N. *Vanguard of Expansion: Army Engineers in the Trans-Mississippi West, 1819–1879* (1980). Schubert describes the institutional development of the Corps of Engineers as well as its activities in opening up the West.

Stanton, William R. *The Great United States Exploring Expedition of 1838–1842* (1975). Stanton provides a history of the Charles Wilkes' expedition to map Pacific Islands and parts of Antarctica as an example of the navy's participation in scientific research in the nineteenth century.

Native American Wars

Buker, George E. *Swamp Sailors: Riverine Warfare in the Everglades, 1835–1842* (1975). Buker provides not only an account of the navy's role in the Second Seminole War but fits that action into the larger context of the evolution of the navy's approach to war.

Chalfant, William Y. *Cheyennes and Horse Soldiers: The 1857 Expedition and the Battle of Solomon's Fork* (1989). Chalfant provides a highly detailed account of the army's first encounter with the Cheyenne, seeing the entire conflict as a product of a clash of cultures.

Eby, Cecil D. *"That Disgraceful Affair:" The Black Hawk War* (1973). Eby provides a scholarly introduction to the Black Hawk War that is sympathetic to the Sacs.

Mahon, John K. *History of the Second Seminole War, 1835–1842* (1967, rev. ed. 1991). Mahon still provides the best account of the Second Seminole War giving significant attention to the nature of Seminole society and to the organizational development of the army during the war.

Peters, Virginia B. *The Florida Wars* (1979). Peters brings together a survey of the three wars fought in Florida between 1810 and 1858 arguing that all were similar in their being linked to Seminole removal.

Utley, Robert M. *Frontiersmen in Blue: The United States Army and the Indian, 1848–1865* (1967). Utley describes the entire range of relations between the army and the Native Americans in this period portraying the army sympathetically as an often frustrated peace keeper.

The Texan and Mexican Wars

The study of the Mexican War is still dominated by Justin Smith's massively researched two-volume work published in 1919 so that most subsequent work on the military aspects of the war remains focused on operations. These works vary from one another largely in emphasis and contexts. On the other hand, there has been little interest shown so far in either social or institutional aspects of the war.

Bauer, K. Jack. *The Mexican War, 1846–1848* (1974). While Bauer provides some coverage of the political aspects of the war, his is largely a military account including guerrilla operations found on the fringes of the formal campaigns.

Connor, Seymour V. and Odie B. Faulk. *North America Divided: The Mexican War, 1846–1848* (1971). Connor and Faulk are more concerned with the political struggles in Washington but do deal with the military history of the war.

Eisenhower, John S. D. *So Far from God: The U.S. War with Mexico, 1846–1848* (1989). Eisenhower uses a lively writing style to make his history accessible to a general audience. He provides a largely military account of the war set within a broader political context.

Johannsen, Robert W. *To the Halls of the Montezumas: The Mexican War in the American Imagination* (1985). While Johannsen goes into some aspects of the fighting in Mexico, his main concern is how the Mexican War was seen by the American public.

Lavender, David S. *Climax at Buena Vista: The American Campaigns in Northeastern Mexico, 1846–1847* (1966). Lavender has written an account of the northern campaign in Mexico for a general audience. The book is focussed on the Battle of Buena Vista and is highly positive toward Taylor.

Long, Jeff. *Duel of the Eagles: The Mexican and U.S. Fight for the Alamo* (1990). This is the most recent history of the siege. It is an objective narrative that is mildly critical of both sides.

McCaffrey, James M. *Army of Manifest Destiny: The American Soldier in the Mexican War, 1846–1848* (1992). This is a social history of the volunteers who fought in the Mexican War. McCaffrey surveys soldier's treatment and experiences from recruitment through discharge with special emphasis on their attitudes towards the Mexican enemy.

Smith, Justin H. *The War with Mexico* (2 vols., 1919). While Smith's work is
   highly partisan, its level of research makes it still the dominant history
   of the war.
Tutorow, Norman E. *The Mexican-American War: An Annotated Bibliography*
   (1981). Tutorow provides an annotated and topically organized compilation of over 4,500 entries that includes archives, books, articles, dissertations, and sources in English, Spanish, German, and French.

Civil War: 1861–1865

The accumulated literature on the Civil War is massive, exceeding 50,000
volumes by one estimate, with hundreds being added each year. Most works
continue to be concerned with traditional interpretations of operations and
focus on leadership, although a few of the more recent studies have tried
to follow John Keegan's approach to combat study and examine conflicts
from the perspective of the soldiers.

Outside of this area, following Thomas Connelly's two-volume history
of the Army of Tennessee, there has appeared a growing interest in the
institutional history of the armies and navies of both sides as well as analyses of several particular smaller units. In the area of social history, three
decades after the publication of Bell Wiley's seminal social histories of the
common soldiers, historians are finally taking an interest in the everyday
lives of those soldiers. Some, in fact, are going beyond Wiley's more descriptive approach to examine the impact of the combat experience on soldiers. Finally, there remains significant interest in the relationship of minority groups to the war. The earlier work of Cornish and Quarles on the
role of African Americans in the war has been supplemented by newer
works focussed on the African American experience in the war. Ella Lonn's
pioneering work on ethnic minorities in the war published over forty years
ago is now being supplemented by new work in that area.

Reference

Esposito, Vincent J. *The West Point Atlas of the Civil War* (1962). This is still
   the classic battlefield atlas of the war, with narrative text accompanying
   the maps.
Murdock, Eugene C. *The Civil War in the North: A Selective Annotated Bibliography* (1987). Murdock provides a compilation of over 5,600 entries,
   topically organized, including books, articles, dissertations, sources, and
   fiction.
Nevins, Allan, et al. *Civil War Books: A Critical Bibliography* (2 vols., 1967,
   1969). Nevins' guide, while now dated, is still useful. It is limited to
   books, but covers over 5,700 of them organized topically and annotated
   critically.

Smith, Myron J., Jr. *American Civil War Navies: A Bibliography* (1972). Smith provides an alphabetical list by author of over 2,800 entries including books, articles, and dissertations.

Symonds, Craig L. *A Battlefield Atlas of the Civil War* (1983). The Symonds atlas is a handy guide for the layman. It includes maps of every significant engagement together with narrative text and photographs.

General and Interpretive Histories

Beringer, Richard E., et al. *Why the South Lost the Civil War* (1986). This is an interpretive study of the war by four noted authors who argue that a lack of will rather than resources accounted for the failure of the Confederacy.

Hattaway, Herman, and Archer Jones. *How the North Won: A Military History of the Civil War* (1983). Hattaway and Jones present an interpretive approach to the war with the focus more on strategy and campaigns than on battles and tactics.

McPherson, James M. *Battle Cry of Freedom: The Civil War Era* (1988). This is currently considered the best single-volume history of the war. It is characterized by its broad approach looking at the domestic as well as military aspects of the war.

Nevins, Allan. *The War for the Union* (4 vols., 1959–1971). Nevins' work is now considered the best multi-volume history of the period. It is balanced and goes well beyond operations to cover the political, social and economic aspects of the war.

The Armies: Institutions and Organizations

Connelly, Thomas L. *The Army of Tennessee* (2 vols., 1967, 1971). Connelly's organizational history of the army stresses personalities and internal political wrangling as well as operations.

Daniel, Larry J. *Cannoneers in Gray: The Field Artillery of the Army of Tennessee, 1861–1865* (1984). Daniel argues that the problems of the Army of Tennessee, inadequate supplies and poor leadership, were reflected in its artillery.

Daniel, Larry J. *Soldiering in the Army of Tennesee: A Portrait of Life in a Confederate Army* (1991). Looking at the Army of Tennessee from the perspective of the common soldier, Daniel argues that the social origins of the men as well as the frequent changes of leadership account for the relatively poor performance of the army.

Glatthaar, Joseph T. *The March to the Sea and Beyond: Sherman's Troops in the Savannah and Carolinas Campaigns* (1986). Glatthaar argues that the devastating character of Sherman's campaign in Georgia and the Carolinas was principally the product of the veteran character of his troops. In the book he describes the formation of this character and its impact on soldiers' behavior and attitudes.

McMurry, Richard M. *Two Great Rebel Armies: An Essay in Confederate Military History* (1989). McMurry compares the success of the Army of Northern Virginia with the failure of the Army of Tennessee, arguing that the main difference lay in the leadership of each army.

Mitchell, Reid. *The Vacant Chair: The Northern Soldier Leaves Home* (1993). Arguing that the Union soldier never "left home" insofar as he made a major effort to recreate his community within his unit, Mitchell examines how the 19th-century vision of community in America colored the soldiers' outlooks on all aspects of military life and activity.

Nolan, Alan T. *The Iron Brigade: A Military History* (1983). Nolan studies the social composition and leadership as well as the operations of the midwestern unit so famous for its courage and fighting ability.

Radley, Kenneth. *Rebel Watchdog: The Confederate States Army Provost Guard* (1989). Radley examines the duties of the provost guard in mediating between the Confederate armies and civilians.

Reese, Timothy J. *Sykes' Regular Infantry Division, 1861–1864: A History of Regular United States Infantry Operations in the Civil War's Eastern Theater* (1990). Most units in the Civil War were made up of state volunteers, so that 2nd Division, Fifth Corps was unusual since it was made up of regulars. This is a social and military history of the unit.

Starr, Stephen Z. *The Union Cavalry in the Civil War* (3 vols., 1980–1985). This is the definitive work on the development and activities of the Union cavalry. The first two volumes cover the war in the East while the third covers the war in the West.

Welcher, Frank J. *The Union Army, 1861–1865: Organizations and Operations. Vol.I: The Eastern Theater* (1989); *Vol. II: The Western Theater* (1993). Welcher offers an encyclopedic account of all military units in the Union army down to the brigade level.

The Armies: Command, Strategy, and Tactics

Connelly, Thomas L. and Archer Jones. *The Politics of Command: Factions and Ideas in Confederate Strategy* (1973). This is a study of the Confederate decision making process at the highest level focusing on the competing factions around Davis trying to influence the development of strategy.

Griffith, Paddy. *Battle Tactics of the Civil War* (1989). Griffith's study of tactics concludes that artillery and cavalry played a greater role in battles than previously thought and discounts the impact of the introduction of the rifle.

Hensel, Howard M. *The Sword of the Union: Federal Objectives and Strategies During the American Civil War* (1989). This is largely a political analysis of the interaction between politics and grand strategy focused on Lincoln as the principal mediator between the two.

McWhiney, Grady and Perry D. Jamieson. *Attack and Die: Civil War Military Tactics and the Southern Heritage* (1982). The authors argue that Civil War commanders, especially Confederate, failed to adapt their tactics to the enormous advantage that new technology gave to the defense. They blame the Confederate failure on Celtic traditions in the southern culture.

Woodworth, Steven E. *Jefferson Davis and His Generals: The Failure of Confederate Command in the West* (1990). Arguing that the western theater was decisive in the war, Woodworth explains the Confederate failure there in terms of both the command relations between Davis and his western generals and the battlefield performance of the latter.

The Armies: Weapons

Coggins, Jack. *Arms and Equipment of the Civil War* (1962). Coggins provides a basic and well-illustrated introduction to army and navy weapons.

Davis, Carl L. *Arming the Union: Small Arms in the Civil War* (1973). Davis surveys Union arms technology and procurement pointing out the impact of changing arms technology on the war.

Hagerman, Edward. *The American Civil War and the Origins of Modern Warfare Ideas, Organization, and Field Command* (1988). Hagerman sees the "modernness" of the Civil War principally in the new arms technology that developed there and provides an encyclopedic survey of the impact of those technologic advances on the character of the war.

Campaigns and Battles

Castel, Albert. *Decisions in the West: The Atlanta Campaign of 1864* (1992). This is a command-centered history of the campaign written in the present tense to convey to the reader the "fog of war" experienced by leaders. Castel is disappointed with most of the major commanders involved, but especially with Sherman.

Coddington, Edwin B. *The Gettysburg Campaign: A Study in Command* (1968). This is a massively researched narrative of the campaign with emphasis on command, giving Meade high marks.

Cooling, Benjamin F. *Forts Henry and Donelson: The Key to the Confederate Heartland* (1988). In this detailed campaign narrative, Cooling credits the Union victory to Grant's brilliance and Confederate bungling.

Cozzens, Peter. *No Better Place to Die: The Battle of Stones River* (1990). Following more recent trends, Cozzens places the battle within the context of the larger campaign and describes it from both commanders' and soldiers' perspectives.

Cozzens, Peter. *This Terrible Sound: The Battle of Chickamauga* (1992). Cozzens considers Chickamauga a useless battle for the Union and an empty victory for the Confederacy. His narrative of the campaign and battle is command centered and continues his efforts to rehabilitate Braxton Bragg's reputation.

Davis, William C. *Battle at Bull Run: A History of the First Major Campaign of the Civil War* (1977). Davis' narrative account emphasizes the background, abilities, and character of officers on both sides, crediting them with considerable competence.

Fellman, Michael. *Inside War: The Guerrilla Conflict in Missouri During the American Civil War* (1989). Fellman offers a topical analysis of guerrilla fighting in Missouri taken, in part, from a sociopsychological point of view.

Furgurson, Ernest B. *Chancellorsville: The Souls of the Brave* (1992). Seeing the battle as more a series of clashes than a single engagement, Furgurson extends his narrative to the entire campaign. His focus is on both leadership and soldiers. The approach is scholarly but quite accessible to the lay reader.

Gragg, Rod. *Confederate Goliath: The Battle of Fort Fisher* (1991). Gragg's narrative of the siege and capture of the fort is set in the context of both the later years of the war and the history of the fort itself.

Hearn, Chester G. *Mobile Bay and the Mobile Campaign: The Last Great Battles of the Civil War* (1993). Hearn's basically operational narrative includes both the successful naval attack on Mobile Bay in the summer of 1864 and the siege of the city in 1865. Although written for the professional, it may be perused with profit by the lay reader.

Hennessy, John J. *Return to Bull Run: The Campaign and Battle of Second Manassas* (1993). This is a colorful command-centered narrative of the campaign and battle which follows the traditional interpretation in which Lee's leadership team is portrayed as a "well-oiled machine" while Pope was a bungler.

Hughes, Nathaniel C. *The Battle of Belmont: Grant Strikes South* (1991). Hughes argues that this battle fought in November 1861, had a significant impact on the development of Grant's military abilities.

Josephy, Alvin M. *The Civil War in the American West* (1992). Arguing that the Civil War was an experience that involved the entire west, Josephy provides narratives of military operations and Native American uprisings scattered all over the trans-Mississippi west.

Kerby, Robert L. *Kirby Smith's Confederacy: The Trans-Mississippi South, 1863–1865* (1972). Kerby argues that the collapse of the Confederate west was more a matter of a lack of will than a lack of resources.

Krick, Robert K. *Stonewall Jackson at Cedar Mountain* (1990). This is a highly detailed examination of the campaign that is adulatory regarding Jackson while critical of Pope.

Mahr, Theodore C. *The Battle of Cedar Creek: Showdown in the Shenandoah* (1992). Mahr argues that even though Sheridan outnumbered Early 3:1, it was still Early's overconfidence and Sheridan's intelligence that accounted for the decisive Union victory.

Matter, William D. *If it Takes All Summer: The Battle of Spotsylvania* (1988). This is a detailed narrative of the battle from a command point of view with special emphasis on the role of cavalry before and during the battle.

McDonough, James L. *Chattanooga: A Deathgrip on the Confederacy* (1984). This is a detailed narrative of the siege and its conclusion set in the context of the war in the western theater.

McDonough, James L. *Shiloh—In Hell Before Night* (1977). Currently the best narrative of the battle. This is a balanced account which emphasizes command decisions and sees the battle as the turning point in Grant's career.

McDonough, James L. and James P. Jones. *"War So Terrible:" Sherman and Atlanta* (1988). The authors provide a balanced military history with emphasis on strategy and tactics as well as on the personalities of the commanders.

McDonough, James L. and Thomas Connelly. *Five Tragic Hours: The Battle of Franklin* (1983). While the Battle of Franklin is discussed in some detail, the book is really a history of Hood's final campaign including the battle of Nashville.

Priest, John M. *Antietam: The Soldiers' Battle* (1989). This is one of the few Civil War battle studies presented from the perspective of the soldiers.

Rodick, Burleigh C. *Appomattox: The Last Campaign* (1965). Rodick offers a colorful narrative of the final military operations of the war in Virginia written for a general audience.

Scott, Robert G. *Into the Wilderness with the Army of the Potomac* (1985). Scott provides a highly detailed description of the Battle of the Wilderness from the perspective of both leaders and soldiers.

Sears, Stephen W. *Landscape Turned Red: The Battle of Antietam* (1983). This is a narrative of the campaign from a command point of view. It is best read in conjunction with John M. Priest listed above.

Sears, Stephen W. *To the Gates of Richmond: The Peninsula Campaign* (1992). This approach is command-centered and Sears is rather harsh in his judgement of McClellan. The book is scholarly but quite accessible for lay readers.

Shea, William and Earl J. Hess. *Pea Ridge: Civil War Campaign in the West* (1992). This is the first study of this trans-Mississippi campaign. Although the focus is on the commanders the vision of the campaign is extended to include soldiers' experiences, logistics, medical problems and similar matters.

Sommers, Richard J. *Richmond Redeemed: The Siege at Petersburg* (1981). Sommers provides a highly detailed history of the siege with emphasis on its last days.

Stackpole, Edward J. *Chancellorsville: Lee's Greatest Battle* (1958). Stackpole provides a detailed and vivid account of the action crediting Lee and Jackson while condemning Hooker.

Sword, Wiley. *Embrace an Angry Wind, The Confederacy's Last Hurrah: Spring Hill, Franklin and Nashville* (1992). In this popular history of the 1864 Tennessee campaign, Sword gives nearly as much attention to the soldiers as to the leaders, although his interpretation still places most of blame for the Confederate failure on Hood.

Tanner, Robert G. *Stonewall in the Valley: Thomas J. "Stonewall" Jackson's Shenandoah Valley Campaign, Spring 1862* (1976). Tanner provides a detailed popular account of the campaign from Jackson's perspective with the focus on personality.

Whan, Vorin E. *Fiasco at Fredericksburg* (1961). Whan follows the traditional interpretation of the battle, seeing its results as the product of blunders by Burnside and other Union generals.

Wheeler, Richard. *Sword over Richmond: An Eyewitness History of McClellan's Peninsula Campaign* (1986). Wheeler's book is a history of the March–July, 1862 campaign comprised of excerpts from original sources and highly critical of McClellan.

Naval Histories

Anderson, Bern. *By Sea and By River: The Naval History of the Civil War* (1962). This is a single-volume naval history of the war with heavy emphasis on strategy based on the idea that the blockade was the major naval contribution to the war.

Browning, Robert M., Jr. *From Cape Charles to Cape Fear: The North Atlantic Blockading Squadron During the Civil War* (1993). Browning presents a scholarly history of the squadron from its origins through its career as a blockading force to its participation in combined operations along the Confederacy's Atlantic coast.

Fowler, William M. *Under Two Flags: The American Navy in the Civil War* (1990). Fowler sees the naval war as decisive, and examines blockades, river operations, combined operations and raiders from a largely Union perspective.

Hoehling, A. A. *Thunder at Hampton Roads* (1976). Hoehling provides a detailed study of the engagement between the *Monitor* and the *Virginia*.

Jones, Virgil C. *The Civil War at Sea* (3 vols., 1960–1962). Jones' multi-volume history of the naval war covers all aspects and is written for a general audience.

Kern, Florence. *The United States Revenue Cutters in the Civil War* (1980). This is one of the few works dealing with the role of the Revenue Service, later the Coast Guard, in wartime. Kern describes the role of the revenue cutters in the naval war, noting participation in blockades, harbor defense, and tracking down privateers.

Milligan, John D. *Gunboats down the Mississippi* (1965). Milligan discusses the changing role of the Mississippi operations in Union strategy as well as providing a detailed survey of those operations with emphasis on Vicksburg.

Perry, Milton F. *Infernal Machines: Story of Confederate Submarines and Mine Warfare* (1965). Perry offers a somewhat episodic history of the Confederate development of submarines, torpedoes and mines.

Reed, Rowena. *Combined Operations in the Civil War* (1978). Reed argues that McClellan's amphibious operations in Virginia offered the Union its most effective war-winning strategy.

Robinson, William M., Jr. *The Confederate Privateers* (1928). This is a vivid history of the activities of distinct privateering vessels from the southern perspective and written for a general audience.

Spencer, Warren F. *The Confederate Navy in Europe* (1983). Spencer provides a broad political, diplomatic, and naval history of the efforts of the confederacy to obtain warships in Europe.

Still, William N., Jr. *Iron Afloat: The Story of Confederate Armorclads* (1971). Still argues that the failures of the Confederate navy and its shipbuilding programs were reflective of weaknesses of the confederacy itself.

Wells, Tom H. *The Confederate Navy: A Study in Organization* (1971). Wells describes the organizational structure of the Confederate navy including its origin, its institutional components and their function, and the men who ran it.

Wise, Stephen R. *Lifeline of the Confederacy: Blockade Running During the Civil War* (1988). This is the most authoritative book on the subject, discussing the ships, the crews and the public policies related to blockade running.

Soldiers in the War

Barton, Michael. *Goodmen: The Character of Civil War Soldiers* (1981). Barton makes a comparative study of the character and values of officers and men in both armies, noting both similarities and contrasts arising from cultural differences.

Frank, Joseph A. *"Seeing the Elephant:" Raw Recruits at the Battle of Shiloh* (1989). Influenced by Linderman's book, noted below, and by the claim that Shiloh was largely a "soldiers battle," Frank looks at the attitudes of the privates who fought at Shiloh and their impact on the action.

Glatthaar, Joseph T. *The March to the Sea and Beyond: Sherman's Troops in the Savannah and Carolinas Campaigns* (1985). In this social history of Sherman's army, Glatthaar argues that the background of the men and their experience in the war created a set of special characteristics and outlooks among the troops that had a significant impact on the character of the campaign.

Jones, Terry L. *Lee's Tigers: The Louisiana Infantry in the Army of Northern Virginia* (1987). Jones notes the ambiguous character of the Louisiana troops in Lee's army. They were both the source of turbulence and, at the same time, the most heroic fighters in the army.

Linderman, Gerald F. *Embattled Courage: The Experience of Combat in the American Civil War* (1987). Linderman examines the attitudes of soldiers on both sides to the concept of courage and how both changed during the war.

Mitchell, Reid. *Civil War Soldiers* (1988). A study of the impact of combat and other experiences on the outlooks and expectations of soldiers on both sides with a slight emphasis on the Confederates.

Robertson, James I. *Soldiers Blue and Gray* (1988). Robertson provides a descriptive social history of the experiences of soldiers in both armies from enlistment to discharge.

Wiley, Bell I. *The Life of Billy Yank* (1952) and *The Life of Johnny Reb: The Common Soldier of the Confederacy* (1943). Together these are still the classic social histories of the Civil War soldiers. They are encyclopedic in their coverage of all aspects of the soldier's social life.

Impact of the War on Special Social Groups

Burton, William L. *Melting Pot Soldiers: The Union's Ethnic Regiments* (1988). Burton discusses the experiences of soldiers, mostly German and Irish, in ethnic units in the Union army in the context of the overall experience of ethnicity in nineteenth century America.

Clinton, Catherine and Nina Silber. *Divided Houses: Gender and the Civil War* (1992). This anthology of essays provides the first serious examination of the impact of the war on gender roles in American society. Equal treatment is afforded both sides, while a concluding section covers the immediate postwar years.

Cornish, Dudley T. *Sable Arm: Negro Troops in the Union Army* (1956). Cornish analyzes the development of Union policy toward the use of African Americans in the armed forces in the war.

Gaines, W. Craig. *The Confederate Cherokees: John Drew's Regiment of Mounted Rifles* (1989). This is one of the few books dealing with Cherokee participation in the war. Drew's Cherokees were fiercely antislavery and most deserted to the Union.

Glatthaar, Joseph T. *Forged in Battle: The Civil War Alliance of Black Soldiers and White Officers* (1990). Glatthaar analyzes the evolution of the increasingly effective though always uneasy relationship between African American soldiers and their white officers.

Hall, Richard. *Patriots in Disguise: Women Warriors of the Civil War* (1993). Hall recounts stories of individual women who fought in the armies of both sides. Overall, he finds that most women took part in the combat not so much for adventure but to follow their soldier husbands into camp.

Hauptman, Laurence M. *The Iroquois in the Civil War: From Battlefield to Reservation* (1993). This is a social history of both Iroquois males who enlisted in the war and the women and others left behind. As was the case with other soldiers, the Iroquois tried to recreate a sense of community within the regiments in which they enlisted. At the same time, their absence weakened the home front.

Lonn, Ella. *Foreigners in the Confederacy* (1940) and *Foreigners in the Union Army and Navy* (1951). Both works are social analyses of immigrants who served in the armed forces and governments of both sides, including those who immigrated just to fight.

McPherson, James M. *The Negro's Civil War: How American Negroes Felt and Acted During the War for the Union* (1965). This is a broad collection of eyewitness accounts of all phases of African American contact with, or involvement in, the war aimed at providing a sense of the African American experience of the war.

Quarles, Benjamin. *The Negro in the Civil War* (1953). Quarles provides a number of narratives of the activities of African Americans in and behind the lines in both armies.

3

The Reform Period: 1866–1914

At the end of the Civil War, the United States possessed the largest, most experienced, active armed force in the world. Within two years that massive force was gone, its citizen volunteers back on the farm and in the factories. The army and navy returned to traditional duties with their organizations virtually unchanged, although Congress added two infantry and two cavalry regiments of African Americans to the army.

For the remainder of the nineteenth century the army served the nation much as it had before 1860. It served largely in the trans-Mississippi west policing or subduing Native Americans. In a series of campaigns beginning in 1866 and culminating in the late 1870s, soldiers broke the power of the Plains Indians and confined them to reservations. They repeated the process in the southwest in the early 1880s. As part of the effort to quell Native Americans the army assisted in the construction of the great transcontinental railroads.

The army also continued to act as the nation's police force. It faced frustration in enforcing Reconstruction policy in the south and most soldiers welcomed relief from that failed experiment. As Reconstruction ended, however, the army suppressed rioting railroad workers in 1877, performed similar service during the 1894 Pullman strike, and intervened in lesser labor upheavals through the early 1900s. On all other counts, postwar army life resembled an earlier era of mundane garrison duty in small posts scattered across the nation.

Naval service for twenty years after 1865 also reflected previous practice. The navy largely abandoned the iron hulled, steam powered ships acquired during the war and once again patrolled foreign stations in sail-driven wooden ships. Given the nature of overseas duty it made some sense to rely on the more easily maintained wooden vessels in a time of great technological change. Because the United States pursued a reactive foreign policy based on continental defense and noninvolvement in foreign wars the return to ante-bellum military and naval practice seemed reasonable in an era when the nation was blessed with the freest security in its history.

Change was inevitable in the long run, however. The navy responded first, moved in large part by the technological backwardness of its fleet. From the early 1880s through the turn of the century, naval officers worked to reform and modernize their service. Naval reform began as an educational effort with the founding of the Naval War College in 1884. Capt. Alfred Thayer Mahan turned his War College lectures into a best selling book, *The Influence of Sea Power on History*. This work argued that a major industrial power could achieve greatness only through command of the sea, and that goal could only be gained through a war fighting fleet composed of battleships. Mahan's argument found a receptive audience and by the turn of the century the nation was committed to building a major battleship navy commanded by educated officers schooled in strategic thinking.

Army officers also called for modernization and professional education, but faced greater difficulty in convincing the nation to reform the ground forces. Commanding General William T. Sherman and his protege Col. Emory Upton believed the tactical stalemate during the Civil War resulted from poorly trained volunteers led by officers who knew little about the strategic demands of modern war. Sherman sought to elevate the educational and intellectual perspectives of officers, and established the School of Application for Infantry and Cavalry in 1881 to begin that process. Upton's important study, *The Military Policy of the United States*, argued that modern war required leadership by trained officers and a general staff system to plan and direct war.

Reform in the army did not come until after 1900. War with Spain in 1898 revealed that while the navy was prepared to fight and win, the army lacked the means to mobilize a trained and equipped force ready for combat. With only some 27,000 officers and men, the regular force was too small to conduct even a limited war. President William McKinley called the National Guard to volunteer. While Guardsmen came forth by the thousands they were woefully unprepared. The Guard had evolved since 1865 largely to serve the states as industrial policemen, and their enthusiasm for imperial adventure could not make up for their lack of training. Furthermore, the army's decentralized bureau system fumbled mobilization and logistics, and its command arrangements hindered devising a successful strategy to take the war to Cuba.

The glaring failures in fighting the war, and the need to occupy the new imperial possessions in the Pacific and the Caribbean, led to military reform. President McKinley appointed Wall Street lawyer Elihu Root as Secretary of War to guide the army in its new duties. Root argued the army's purpose in peace was to plan and train for war. In order to do this effectively it needed a professionally educated officer corps, a planning agency, and a trained, reliable reserve. Relying in part on Upton's writings, he oversaw reform measures bringing the National Guard under partial federal control (the Militia Act of 1903), modernizing the army command (the General Staff Act of 1903), and furthering professional education through the establishment of the General Service and Staff College and the Army War College.

The so-called "Root Reforms" brought the managerial revolution to the army, but problems remained. Conservatives within the army fought the authority of the newly created chief of staff and the National Guard resisted strong federal control. Moreover, although Congress supported a land force after 1900, the army remained too small to protect overseas possessions and also carry out an effective peacetime training program. The navy fared better in the years 1900 to 1914, with an active shipbuilding program which gave the United States the third largest navy in the world.

Expansion in 1898 led the United States to redefine its foreign and military policies, to establish fortified bases in Cuba, the Philippines, and the Panama Canal Zone, and to extend its conception of security beyond the North American continent. For all these changes, however, and despite military and naval reform, in 1914 the United States remained more a regional than a world power. The army particularly would remain a force reflecting both policies of the past and present until challenged to fight a war in Europe.

Chronology

1866

Jul	25	First Hispanic American Admiral (David Farragut)
Jul	28	Congress authorizes formation of the 9th & 10th Cavalry, 38th, 39th, 40th & 4lst Infantry (African American units)
Dec	21	Battle of Lodge Trail Ridge (punitive campaign)

1867

Aug	1	Hayfield Fight—Ft Smith (punitive campaign)
Aug	2	Wagon Box Fight (punitive campaign)
Aug	17	Battle of Plum Creek (punitive campaign)

1868

Jun	1	John Schofield (Secretary of War)
Sep	17	Battle of Beecher's Island—ends Sep 25 (punitive campaign)
Oct	17	Battle of Beaver Creek (punitive campaign)
Nov	27	Battle of Washita River (punitive campaign)

1869

Mar   3   38th/39th Infantry become 24th Infantry & 40th/41st Infantry become 25th Infantry (African American units)
Mar   8   William Sherman (Commanding General of the Army)
Mar   9   Adolph Borie (Secretary of the Navy)
Mar 13   John Rawlins (Secretary of War)
Jun 26   George Robeson (Secretary of the Navy)
Jul   11   Battle of Summit Springs (punitive campaign)
Oct 25   William Belknap (Secretary of War)

1870

Jan 23   Battle of Marias River (punitive campaign)
Feb   9   Weather Service established as part of the Army Signal Service
Mar 28   U.S. forces dispatched to Brooklyn, NY (civil unrest)
May   4   Congress authorizes the issue of ordnance to land-grant schools for military instruction
Nov   2   U.S. forces dispatched to Brooklyn, NY (civil unrest)

1871

Jan 13   U.S. forces dispatched to New York, NY (civil unrest)
Apr 20   Congress establishes Life-Saving Service
Apr 30   Camp Grant massacre (punitive campaign)
Jun 10   U.S. forces land Kangwha Island, Korea—ends Jun 11 (punitive expedition)
Oct 12   Cochise agrees to live on a reservation

1872

Dec 28   Battle of Skull Cave (punitive campaign)

1873

Jan 16   Battle of the Stronghold (punitive campaign)
Apr 11   Edward R. S. Canby dies (only general of regulars killed in wars with Native Americans)
Mar 27   Battle of Turret Peak (punitive campaign)
May 18   Battle of Remolino (punitive campaign)

1874

Jun 27   Second Battle of Adobe Walls (punitive campaign)

1876

Sep 28   Battle of Palo Duro (punitive campaign)

Mar   8   Alphonso Taft (Secretary of War)
May 22   James Cameron (Secretary of War)
Jun 17   Battle of the Rosebud (punitive campaign)
Jun 25   Battle of the Little Big Horn (punitive campaign)
Jul   17   Battle of War Bonnet Creek (punitive campaign)
Jul   30   Battle of Zaragosa (punitive campaign)
Jul   31   Revenue Cutter Service School of Instruction established (Coast Guard Academy/Jan 28, 1915)
Sep   9   Battle of Slim Buttes (punitive campaign)
Nov   1   Charles McCawley (Commandant, Marine Corps)
Nov 25   Battle of the Tongue River (punitive campaign)

1877

Jan   8   Battle of Wolf Mountain (punitive campaign)
Mar 12   George McCrary (Secretary of War)
Mar 13   Richard Thompson (Secretary of the Navy)
Apr   3   Incident at Piedas Negras, Mexico
May   7   Battle of Muddy Creek (punitive campaign)
Jun 15   First African American graduate from the USMA (Henry Ossian Flipper)
Jun 17   Battle of White Bird Canyon (punitive campaign)
Jul   11   Battle of Clearwater River—ends Jul 12 (punitive campaign)
Jul   18   U.S. forces dispatched to Martinsburg, Grafton, & Keyser, WV (labor unrest)
Jul   21   U.S. forces dispatched to Baltimore, MD (labor unrest)
Jul   22   U.S. forces dispatched to Chicago, IL, Cumberland MD, & Washington, DC (labor unrest)
Jul   23   U.S. forces dispatched to St. Louis, MO & Philadelphia, PA (labor unrest)
Jul   25   U.S. forces dispatched to Chicago, IL (labor unrest)
Jul   26   U.S. forces dispatched to Indianapolis, Terre Haute & Vincennes, IN (labor unrest)
Jul   27   U.S. forces dispatched to East St. Louis, IL (labor unrest)
Jul   28   U.S. forces dispatched to Pittsburgh, PA (labor unrest)
Aug   1   U.S. forces dispatched to Scranton, Easton, Wilkes Barre, Reading, & Mauch Chunk, PA (labor unrest)
Aug   9   Battle of Big Hole River—ends Aug 10 (punitive campaign)
Sep   7   Crazy Horse killed
Sep 13   Battle of Canyon Creek (punitive campaign)
Sep 30   Battle of Snake Creek—ends Oct 5 (punitive campaign)
Oct   5   Chief Joseph surrenders

1878

Jun 12 Mackenzie Expedition enters Mexico—returns Jun 22
Jun 18 Congress passes the Posse Comitatus Act
Dec   7 First steam-powered warship to circumnavigate the globe—
          returns Aug 23, 1881 (USS *Ticonderoga*)

1879

Apr 11 U.S. forces dispatched to Hastings, NE (civil unrest)
Sep   6 Battle of Ojo Caliente (punitive campaign)
Sep 29 Battle of Milk Creek (punitive campaign)
Oct   1 National Guard Association created
Oct 27 Battle of Corralitos River (punitive campaign)
Dec 10 Alexander Ramsey (Secretary of War)

1880

Jan 24 First African American lighthouse keeper (Richard Etheridge)
Apr   7 Battle of Hembrillo Canyon—ends Apr 8 (punitive campaign)
May 23 Battle of Palomas River (punitive campaign)
Jul 30 Battle of Tinja de las Palmas (punitive campaign)

1881

Jan   7 Nathan Goff, Jr. (Secretary of the Navy)
Feb 27 Whiskey sales abolished on all USA installations
Mar   5 Robert Lincoln (Secretary of War)
Mar   7 William Hunt (Secretary of the Navy)
Jul 19 Sitting Bull agrees to live on a reservation
Aug 30 Battle of Cibicu Creek (punitive campaign)

1882

Mar   9 U.S. forces dispatched to Omaha, NE (labor unrest)
Apr 17 William Chandler (Secretary of the Navy)
Apr 23 Battle of Horseshoe Canyon (punitive campaign)
May   1 U.S. forces dispatched to Cochise County, AZ (civil unrest)
Jul 17 Battle of Big Dry Wash (punitive campaign)

1883

Nov   1 Philip Sheridan (Commanding General of the Army)

1885

Jan 24 Alfred Thayer Mahan assigned to the Naval War College

Mar 5 William Endicott (Secretary of War)
Mar 7 William Whitney (Secretary of the Navy)
Sep 4 U.S. forces dispatched to Rock Springs, WY (racial unrest)
Nov 6 U.S. forces dispatched to Seattle, WA (racial unrest)
Dec 2 U.S. forces dispatched to Salt Lake City, UT (civil unrest)

1886

Feb 10 U.S. forces dispatched to Seattle & Tacoma, WA (racial unrest)
Feb 16 U.S. forces dispatched to Promontory, UT (civil unrest)
Mar 9 U.S. forces dispatched to Des Moines, IA (civil unrest)
Jul 19 USS *Atlanta* commissioned (first steam and sail protected cruiser)
Sep 4 Geronimo agrees to live on a reservation

1888

May 17 First naval militia battalion established (Masschusetts Militia)
Aug 14 John Schofield (Commanding General of the Army)

1889

Mar 5 Redfield Proctor (Secretary of War)
Mar 6 Benjamin Tracy (Secretary of the Navy)
Mar 15 Hurricane strikes Apia, Samoa (USS *Trenton* & USS *Vandalia* wrecked; USS *Nipsic* damaged)
Jul 30 U.S. forces land Honolulu, HI (civil unrest)
Dec 14 Leonard Shepard (Captain-Commandant, USRCS)

1890

Apr 22 USS *Cushing* commissioned (first torpedo boat)
Dec 15 Sitting Bull killed
Dec 29 Incident at Wounded Knee (punitive campaign)
Dec 30 Battle of Drexel Mission (punitive campaign)

1891

Jan 30 Charles Heywood (Commandant, Marine Corps)
Mar 2 First congressional appropriation to purchase equipment for naval militia
Jun 15 U.S. forces dispatched to Bridgeport, CT (civil unrest)
Dec 17 Stephen Elkins (Secretary of War)

1892

Apr 12 U.S. forces dispatched to Johnson City, WY (civil unrest)

Jul   12   U.S. forces dispatched to Coeur d'Alene, Gem, Wardner,
           Wallace, Osburn, Murke, & Mullan, ID (labor unrest)

1893

Jan   16   U.S. forces (USS *Boston*) land Honolulu, HI (civil unrest)
Mar   5   Daniel Lamont (Secretary of War)
Mar   7   Hilary Herbert (Secretary of the Navy)
Aug   1   USS *New York* commissioned (first armored cruiser)
Sep   1   U.S. forces dispatched to Redlands, CA (civil unrest)

1894

Apr   13   U.S. forces dispatched to Council Bluffs, IA (labor unrest)
Apr   24   U.S. forces dispatched to Bozeman, MT (labor unrest)
Apr   26   U.S. forces dispatched to Forsyth, MT (labor unrest)
Apr   28   U.S. forces dispatched to Portland, OR (labor unrest)
Apr   29   U.S. forces dispatched to Spokane, WA (labor unrest)
May   19   U.S. forces dispatched to Oklahoma, Indian Terr. (labor unrest)
May   25   U.S. forces dispatched to Centralia & La Salle, IL (labor unrest)
May   26   U.S. forces dispatched to Pana, IL (labor unrest)
May   27   U.S. forces dispatched to Minonk, IL (labor unrest)
May   30   U.S. forces dispatched to Evans, IA (labor unrest)
Jun   5   U.S. forces dispatched to Carterville, IL (labor unrest)
Jun   7   U.S. forces dispatched to Pekin & Peoria, IL (labor unrest)
Jun   8   U.S. forces dispatched to Edinburg, IL (labor unrest)
Jun   9   U.S. forces dispatched to Pana, IL (labor unrest)
Jun   18   U.S. forces dispatched to Mt. Olive, IL (labor unrest)
Jun   30   U.S. forces dispatched to Trinidad, CO (labor unrest)
Jul   1   U.S. forces dispatched to Los Angeles, CA (labor unrest)
Jul   2   U.S. forces dispatched to Decatur & Danville, IL (labor unrest)
Jul   3   U.S. forces dispatched to Chicago & Mounds, IL (labor unrest)
Jul   4   U.S. forces dispatched to Raton, NM, Sioux City, IA, San Jose,
           Chico, Oakland, & Sacramento, CA (labor unrest)
Jul   5   U.S. forces dispatched to Springfield, IL (labor unrest)
Jul   6   U.S. forces dispatched to Chicago, IL (labor unrest)
Jul   7   U.S. forces dispatched to Spring Valley, IL, St. Paul, MN, Puget
           Sound, WA, & Hammond, IN (civil unrest)
Jul   9   U.S. forces dispatched to Wardner, ID (labor unrest)
Jul   10   U.S. forces dispatched to Coeur d'Alene, ID, Sacramento, &
           San Francisco, CA (labor unrest)
Jul   13   U.S. forces dispatched to Enid, Oklahoma Territory, & Truckee,
           CA (labor unrest)
Jul   16   U.S. forces dispatched to Dunsmuir, CA (labor unrest)

Jul 17 U.S. forces dispatched to Porta Costa, CA (labor unrest)
Jul 18 U.S. forces dispatched to Truckee, CA (labor unrest)
Jul 19 U.S. forces dispatched to Alameda, CA (labor unrest)
Jul 22 U.S. forces dispatched to Woodland, CA (labor unrest)
Jul 23 U.S. forces dispatched to Red Bluff, CA (labor unrest)

1895

Mar 19 Charles Shoemaker (Captain-Commandant, USRCS)
Aug 15 USS *Texas* commissioned (first battleship)
Oct 5 Nelson Miles (Commanding General of the Army)
Nov 20 USS *Indiana* commissioned (first ship designated as battleship)

1896

Aug 19 Naval War Board created

1897

Mar 5 Russell Alger (Secretary of War)
Mar 6 John Long (Secretary of the Navy)
Dec 15 First submarine powered by internal combustion engine
        demonstrated (*Argonaut*)

1898

Feb 15 USS *Maine* sinks (Havana, Cuba)
Apr 13 USS *Yosemite* commissioned (only ship crewed by naval militia
        to see combat in the Hispano-American War)
Apr 20 U.S. declares war on Spain
Apr 25 U.S. renounces the use of letters of *marque and reprisal* against
        Spain
Apr 27 Naval vessels bombard Mantanzas (the first of numerous
        operations against Spain's Caribbean installations)
May 1 Naval action—Manila Bay
May 2 U.S. forces land Cavite, Philippine Islands
May 3 U.S. forces land Corregidor Island, Philippine Islands
May 11 Naval action—Cienfuegos, Cuba
May 11 Naval action—Cardenas, Cuba
May 19 Spanish squadron arrives Santiago, Cuba
May 28 Naval blockade—Santiago, Cuba
Jun 3 Naval operation—Santiago, Cuba
Jun 10 U.S. forces land Guantanamo, Cuba
Jun 14 Battle of Cuzco
Jun 21 U.S. forces occupy Guam (USS *Charleston*)

Jun 22 U.S. forces land Daiquiri, Cuba
Jun 23 U.S. forces occupy Siboney
Jun 24 Battle of Las Guasimas
Jul   1 Battle of El Caney
Jul   1 Battle of Kettle Hill
Jul   1 Battle of San Juan Hill—ends Jul 2
Jul   3 Naval action—Santiago, Cuba
Jul 17 Santiago, Cuba surrenders to U.S. forces
Jul 17 Battle of Cavite, Philippine Islands
Jul 25 U.S. forces land Puerto Rico
Jul 31 Siege of Manila—ends Aug 13—Philippine Islands
Aug 12 USS *Arethusa* commissioned (first tanker)
Dec 10 Treaty ends war with Spain

1899

Feb   4 Philippine-American War begins
Feb   4 Manila campaign—ends Mar 17
Feb   8 Iloilo campaign—ends Feb 12
Mar   2 George Dewey (Admiral of the Navy)
Mar 24 Malolos campaign—ends Aug 16
Apr   8 Laguna de Bay campaign—ends Apr 17
Apr 10 Battle of Santa Cruz
Apr 21 First San Isidro campaign—ends May 30
May   2 U.S. forces dispatched to Wardner, ID (labor unrest)
May 15 Battle of San Isido
Jun 13 Zapote River campaign
Aug   1 Elihu Root (Secretary of War)
Oct   7 First Cavite campaign—ends Oct 13
Oct 15 Second San Isidro campaign—ends Nov 19
Nov   5 Tarlac campaign—ends Nov 20
Nov   6 San Fabian campaign—ends Nov 19
Dec   2 Battle of the Clouds (Tilad Pass)

1900

Jan   4 Second Cavite campaign—ends Feb 9
Feb 20 USS *Kearsarge* commissioned (only battleship not named for a state)
Mar 13 General Board of the Navy created
May 22 U.S. forces (USS *Newark*) join International Relief Expedition (Boxer Rebellion)
Jun 20 Siege of Allied Legations in (Peking) Beijing—ends Aug 14 (Boxer Rebellion)

Jul   7   U.S. forces land (Tangku) Tanggu (Boxer Rebellion)
Jul   9   Battle of (Tientsin) Tianjin—ends Jul 14 (Boxer Rebellion)
Aug   5   Battle of Pei-tsang (Boxer Rebellion)
Aug   6   Battle of (Yang-tsun) Yangtsun (Boxer Rebellion)
Aug 14   U.S. forces enter (Peking) Beijing (Boxer Rebellion)
Oct   12   USS *Holland* commissioned (first true submarine)

1901

Feb   2   Congress establishes Army Nurse Corps
Mar 23   Emilio Aguinaldo captured by U.S. forces
Sep 28   Battle of Balangiga
Nov 15   Battle of Sohoton River (Moro Rebellion)
Nov 16   W. S. Sims writes to President T. Roosevelt regarding battle-
          ship design and the state of naval gunnery
Nov 17   Battle of Caducan River

1902

Apr 16   U.S. forces (USS *Machias)* land Panama (first of several land-
          ings during Panama's revolt from Columbia)
May   1   William Moody (Secretary of the Navy)
May   2   Battle of Pandapatan (Moro Rebellion)
Oct   1   Battle of Macin—ends Oct 2 (Moro Rebellion)
Dec 22   USS *Maine* commissioned (first battleship designed to reach
          Philippine Islands)

1903

Jan 21   Congress revises 1792 Militia Act (Dick Act)
Feb 12   USS *Bainbridge* commissioned (first destroyer)
Feb 14   Congress establishes a general staff (USA)
Apr   6   Battle of Bacolod—ends Apr 8 (Moro Rebellion)
May   2   Lake Lano Expedition—ends May 10 (Moro Rebellion)
May   4   Battle of Taraca—ends May 5 (Moro Rebellion)
Jun 10   U.S. forces dispatched to Morenci, AZ (labor unrest)
Aug 15   Samuel Young (Chief of Staff, USA)
Sep 19   USS *Plunger* commissioned (first submarine purpose built for
          USN)
Oct   3   George Elliot (Commandant, Marine Corps)

1904

Jan   9   Adna Chaffee (Chief of Staff, USA)
Feb   1   William Taft (Secretary of War)

Jul   1   Paul Morton (Secretary of the Navy)

1905

Apr   1   Worth Ross (Captain-Commandant, USRCS)
Jul   1   Charles Bonaparte (Secretary of the Navy)
Oct   22   Battle of Malalag River (Moro Rebellion)

1906

Jan   15   John Bates (Chief of Staff, USA)
Mar   5   Battle of Bud Dajo—ends Mar 8 (Moro Rebellion)
Apr   14   J. Franklin Bell (Chief of Staff, USA)
Aug   13   Brownsville, Texas Incident (racial unrest)
Sep   13   U.S. forces land Cuba—ends Apr 1, 1909
Dec   17   Victor Metcalf (Secretary of the Navy)

1907

Aug   1   Signal Corps establishes an Aeronautical Division
Dec   7   U.S. forces dispatched to Goldfield, NV (labor unrest)
Dec   16   "Great White Fleet" departs Hampton Roads—returns Feb 22,
           1909

1908

Jan   10   USA contracts with Wright Bros. to build an aircraft
Feb   12   War Department creates Division of Militia Affairs (Militia
           Bureau, 1908; National Guard Bureau, 1933)
May   13   Congress establishes Navy Nurse Corps
Jul   1   Luke Wright (Secretary of War)
Aug   12   USA receives first airship (Dirigible No. 1)
Dec   1   Truman Newberry (Secretary of the Navy)

1909

Mar   6   George Meyer (Secretary of the Navy)
Mar   12   Jacob Dickinson (Secretary of War)
May   26   First flight Dirigible No. 1 with USA pilots
Aug   2   USA accepts first aircraft
Oct   26   First pilot (Frederic Humphreys, USA)
Dec   3   Richard Wainwright (Aide for Operations, USN)

1910

Jan   4   USS *Michigan* commissioned (first dreadnought)
Apr   4   USS *Delaware* commissioned (first warship without a tonnage
           stipulation imposed by Congress)

Apr 22   Leonard Wood (Chief of Staff, USA)
Aug 27   First test aircraft to ground radio-telegraphy
Nov 14   First aircraft to takeoff from a ship—lands Willoughby Spit, VA
          (Eugene Ely)

1911

Jan 18   First aircraft to land and takeoff from a ship (Eugene Ely)
Jan 26   First successful hydro-aeroplane flight (Glenn Curtiss)
Feb   3   William Biddle (Commandant, Marine Corps)
Apr 11   First Army pilot training school (College Park, MD)
Apr 12   First naval aviator (Theodore Ellyson)
May   8   USN completes purchase contract for first airplane
          (Curtiss A-1)
May 22   Henry Stimson (Secretary of War)
Jun 19   Ellsworth Bertholf (Captain-Commandant, USRCS\USCG)
Dec 17   Charles Vreeland (Aide for Operations, USN)
Dec 22   Siege of Bud Dajo—ends Dec 26 (Moro Rebellion)

1912

Jan 14   Jolo Expedition (Moro Rebellion)
Feb 17   Attorney General asserts that "in general" National Guard
          units may not serve outside the U.S.
Jul 16   Patent for an airborne torpedo release mechanism issued to
          Bradley Fiske, USN
Jul 26   First aircraft to ship radio-telegraphy
Aug   4   U.S. forces land Nicaragua—ends Jan 17, 1913
Aug 10   First use aircraft army maneuvers—Bridgeport, CT
Aug 24   Congress creates Army Reserve Corps
Aug 24   "Manchu Law" returns many staff officers to line units
Nov 12   First successful launch of an aircraft by a compressed air
          catapult (Theodore Ellyson, USN)

1913

Feb 11   Bradley Fiske (Aide for Operations, USN)
Mar   4   Compensation authorized for military flying
Mar   5   Lindley Garrison (Secretary of War)
Mar   5   1st Aero Squadron activated (USA)
Mar   5   Josephus Daniels (Secretary of the Navy)
Mar   5   First Marine aviator (Alfred A. Cunningham)
Apr 13   USS *Jupiter* commissioned (first electrically propelled warship)
Apr 13   First test of oil refueling procedures while underway (USS
          Arethusa & USS *Warrington*)

Jun 11   Battle of Bud Bagsak—ends Jun 15 (Moro Rebellion)
Jul   1   First military instruction camp for college students opens—
          Monterey, CA

1914

Feb 25   George Barnett (Commandant, Marine Corps)
Mar   1   Battle of Bud Tanu (Moro Rebellion)
Apr   9   Tampico Incident (USS *Dolphin*)
Apr 21   William Wotherspoon (Chief of Staff, USA)
Apr 21   U.S. forces land Vera Cruz—ends Nov 23
Apr 25   First use of naval aircraft in combat—Vera Cruz
Apr 28   First use of aerial photography in combat—Vera Cruz
Apr 28   U.S. forces dispatched to Trinidad, CO (labor unrest)
May   6   First aircraft damaged in a hostile action—Vera Cruz (Curtiss
          AH-3)
Jul   1   Office of Naval Aeronautics created (USN Division of Opera-
          tions)
Jul   1   Prohibition proclaimed for all ships and stations (USN)
Jul 18   Aviation Section created (Signal Corps, USA)
Nov   6   U.S. forces dispatched to Prairie Creek, AK (labor unrest)
Nov 16   Hugh Scott (Chief of Staff, USA)

Military Operations

BATTLE OF LODGE TRAIL RIDGE (Dec 21, 1866). Chief Red Cloud's
    Lakota harassed Colonel Henry Carrington's force at Fort Phil Kearny
    along the Bozeman Trail. Led by Chief Crazy Horse, the Lakotas en-
    snared a relief party under the over-confident Captain William Fetterman
    at Lodge Trail Ridge. Assaulted by more than 1,500 opponents, Fetterman
    and his command of eighty were engulfed and destroyed within an hour.
    The disaster stung the American public and evoked cries for revenge.
    The Fort Laramie treaty of 1868 temporarily ended the war on Red
    Cloud's terms.
BATTLE OF BEECHER'S ISLAND (Sep 17–25, 1868). Chief Tall Bull led
    between 600 to 700 Dog Soldiers, a Cheyenne warrior society, into battle
    in 1868. His forces met Maj. George A. Forsyth's company at the Arikara
    Fork of the Republican River in Colorado on September 17. After three
    unsuccessful assaults, the third resulting in the death of Chief Roman
    Nose, the Cheyennes besieged the Americans. Half of Forsyth's troops
    died in the engagement, but the other half were saved by a relief col-
    umn which arrived on the 25th. Although the battle had no overarching
    significance, it entered into the lore of both sides as a classic confronta-
    tion.

BATTLE OF WASHITA RIVER (Nov 27, 1868). One of three converging columns sent by Gen. Philip Sheridan against the Cheyennes in a winter campaign, Col. George A. Custer's Seventh Cavalry surrounded an encampment in the Washita valley. Before dawn, his troops attacked, destroyed the village, then held out against counterattacks from nearby villages. Chief Black Kettle was killed during the assault. Critics likened the attack to the Sand Creek massacre (1864), but Sheridan believed the outcome vindicated his strategy of the winter campaign.

BATTLE OF THE STRONGHOLD (Jan 16, 1873). Kintpuash's [Captain Jack] Modocs refused reservation life and sought refuge in the Stronghold, in the Lava Beds abutting Tule Lake. There, about fifty Modoc warriors held off eventually 1,000 troops. Lieutenant Colonel Frank Wheaton's force attacked this defensive position on January 16, losing thirty-seven soldiers while never sighting the enemy. In an attempt to seek a negotiated settlement, a meeting was arranged on April 11. But in the course of talks, Kintpuash killed Gen. Edward R.S. Canby, the only general of regulars killed in the wars with the Native Americans. Kintpuash was captured (June 1) and hanged (October 3).

BATTLE OF PALO DURO CANYON (Sep 28, 1874). This action was part of the Red River War, which erupted on the southern plains in 1874. Gen. Philip Sheridan sent three columns to subdue a coalition of Cheyennes, Kiowas, and Comanches involving Chief Mamanti, Chief Satanta, and Chief Medicine Arrows. Chief Mamanti convinced the assembly to seek shelter in Palo Duro Canyon in the Texas Panhandle. As Col. Ranald Mackenzie's cavalry approached the Native American village on the morning of the 28th, the inhabitants fled. Although the Americans killed only three people, they destroyed the village and almost 1500 horses. Relentlessly pursued by the American columns, individual parties surrendered between October and the following April; their leaders were imprisoned. The war ended hostilities on the southern plains.

BATTLE OF THE ROSEBUD (Jun 17, 1876). Gen. Philip Sheridan ordered Gen. George Crook to lead one of three converging columns against the Lakotas and Cheyennes. At Rosebud Creek, the Native American coalition attacked Crook. The Native Americans withdrew after a desperate six-hour battle. Although Crook claimed victory, his mauled force retreated to its supply base. This action allowed the Native Americans to concentrate against Lt. Col. George Custer, thereby condemning him to certain defeat if he engaged the enemy.

BATTLE OF THE LITTLE BIG HORN (Jun 25, 1876). Part of Gen. Philip Sheridan's three-pronged assault, Lt. Col. George A. Custer's Seventh Cavalry happened upon the unexpectedly large encampment of Lakotas and Cheyennes at the Little Big Horn River. Custer divided his force three ways. Custer's group was caught in a pincers movement and the entire force of 210 was dead within an hour, a second unit, under Maj. Marcus Reno, was severely handled as well, while those troops under Capt. Frederick Benteen were initially not engaged. The total defeat enraged the American public, which hailed Custer's embellished memory, and led to increased demands against the Native Americans.

BATTLE OF WHITE BIRD CANYON (Jun 17, 1877). This battle marked the beginning of the Nez Perce War. Chief Joseph and other Nez Perce chiefs reluctantly chose to resist reservation life. When some of Chief White Bird's warriors killed several settlers, Gen. Oliver O. Howard sent Capt. David Perry's cavalry to punish them. On September 17, Perry refused a truce. Although outnumbered, the Nez Perces nonetheless handed the Americans a stinging defeat; Perry lost over a third of his force. Howard cautiously pursued, giving rise to more engagements over several months.

BATTLE OF CLEARWATER RIVER (Jul 11–12, 1877). Gen. Oliver O. Howard's troops pursued the Nez Perces following the Battle of White Bird Canyon. The American soldiers surprised the outnumbered Nez Perces encamped on the Clearwater River on July 11, but Chief Toohoolhoolzote held his forces together under artillery attack until four other bands surrounded and besieged the attackers. The battle continued into the next day, when the Nez Perces broke off the engagement. Howard's victory was indecisive, and he continued to pursue his opponents.

BATTLE OF THE BIG HOLE RIVER (Aug 9–11, 1877). As the Nez Perces sought to escape the pursuing force led by Gen. Oliver O. Howard, Chief Looking Glass persuaded the other chiefs to encamp on the Big Hole River, where Col. John Gibbon's infantry surprised them on the morning of August 9. Their attack was initially successful, killing about ninety, including noncombatants. The Nez Perces successfully counterattacked, however, retaking the village and holding off the Americans for two days as the tribe escaped. Gibbon lost over seventy troops, and the Nez Perces continued their flight, with Howard's force still in pursuit.

BATTLE OF CANYON CREEK (Sep 13, 1877). Having trailed the Nez Perces for about 75 miles, Col. Samuel D. Sturgis' cavalry met the Nez Perces drawn up for battle near Canyon Creek. Using the terrain to their advantage, the Nez Perces stopped Sturgis' advance, as the tribe continued to escape up river. The cavalry suffered four dead and several wounded, and Sturgis called off his advance. The Nez Perces, whose flight later captured the imagination of the American people, pressed on, hoping to escape into Canada.

BATTLE OF SNAKE CREEK (Sep 30–Oct 5, 1877) Col. Nelson A. Miles' cavalry caught the Nez Perces encamped near Snake Creek, about thirty miles short of safety in Canada. Chief White Bird's warriors stopped the advance, but Miles besieged the Native Americans with superior numbers and captured their horses. As a snowstorm slowed the fighting for two days, Gen. Oliver O. Howard's force, which had pursued the Nez Perces for months, joined Miles. Several chiefs having been killed in the battle, and his people suffering from the weather, Chief Joseph surrendered to Miles on October 5. Ironically, although the white population was moved by the plight of the Nez Perces, the survivors were sent to the Indian Territory in violation of their truce.

INCIDENT AT WOUNDED KNEE (Dec 29, 1890). This incident was not truly a "battle" at all. The Seventh Cavalry intercepted Chief Big Foot's band, encamped near Wounded Knee Creek and peacefully heading for the Pine Ridge reservation. On the 29th, troopers surrounded the camp and proceeded to disarm the inhabitants, when an errant shot precipitated fierce fighting in close quarters. Artillery and rifle fire killed about 150 Native American men, women, and children, and wounded fifty more, at a cost of twenty-five dead and thirty-nine wounded. The episode marked the end of the wars with the Native American tribes.

PULLMAN STRIKE INTERVENTION (Jul 4–19, 1894). When a strike against the Pullman Sleeping Car Company widened into a strike against the railroads around Chicago, Attorney General Richard Olney urged President Grover Cleveland to send troops to protect interstate commerce and mail routes. Cleveland complied; on July 4, Gen. Nelson A. Miles took command of the arriving troops, which soon numbered almost 2,000. The railroad companies, in turn, attached mail cars to trains with Pullman cars. Serious rioting ensued. Although Miles was sympathetic to management, his troops carefully avoided violence, limiting their activity to protecting trains and keeping the mails moving. Federal intervention, however, was decisive and the strike crushed. The troops withdrew on the 19th.

BATTLE OF MANILA BAY (May 1, 1898). This naval engagement was the first battle of the Hispano-American War. The dispirited Adm. Patricio Montojo anchored his fleet in shallow water near Cavite to save the lives of his sailors and to spare Manila, but therefore out of range of Manila's covering fire. The American squadron slipped into the bay after midnight on May 1 and began its attack at dawn. Despite poor marksmanship, the stronger American fleet destroyed all five Spanish gunboats and several other ships. Montojo suffered 371 casualties; Dewey, nine wounded. The victory resulted in Com. George Dewey's promotion to admiral and whetted the American public's appetite for a quick, glorious victory over the Spanish.

BATTLE OF EL CANEY (Jul 1, 1898). Gen. William Shafter planned a quick victory over the small garrison at El Caney, after which his troops would reinforce the assault on San Juan Heights. El Caney proved to be naturally strong, its defenders determined. The frontal assault, under Gen. Henry Lawton, met stubborn resistance for eight hours. American artillery and a final charge eventually carried the day, but too late to assist at San Juan Heights. Because the garrison could easily have been isolated, it was "a bloody and unnecessary affair."

BATTLE OF SAN JUAN HEIGHTS (Jul 1, 1898). The Heights (Kettle and San Juan Hills) protected the important city of Santiago de Cuba. Gen. William Shafter's assault plan disintegrated, as Spanish gunners and terrain slowed the offensive and the Battle of El Caney dragged on. Infantry and dismounted cavalry (including the Rough Riders and courageous African American units) made an uncoordinated, costly approach. Gatling guns and persistence finally won out. Shafter's force suffered a surprisingly high 1,385 casualties and was too exhausted to assault the city. While the American press lauded and embellished the exploits of the Rough Riders, which fired the public's imagination, the staunchest fighting units were those comprised of African American troops.

BATTLE OF SANTIAGO DE CUBA (Jul 3, 1898). Adm. Pasqual Cervera attempted to break through the American blockade in daylight, but his fleet had to leave the harbor in line-ahead (column) and confront Adm. William Sampson's much more powerful force. Although some ships broke through, the Spaniards were outgunned and unable to utilize their superior speed. Five ships were run ashore and a sixth sunk. The victory gave the Americans command of the seas in the Caribbean.

SIEGE OF MANILA (Aug 13, 1898). With the American navy controlling Manila Bay and the followers of Filipino revolutionary leader Emilio Aguinaldo besieging the city, Gen. Wesley Merritt assembled an assault force. Com. George Dewey and Don Fermin Jaudenes (the Spanish Governor General) reached an unofficial agreement for Spanish surrender after an American show of force, as Jaudenes feared capitulating to Aguinaldo. On the 13th, Dewey's guns shelled Fort San Antonio Abad and ground forces encountered limited resistance. The garrison surrendered. Friction between the Americans and their Filipino allies, however, foreshadowed the Philippine-American war.

INCIDENT IN MANILA (Feb 4–5, 1899). The Americans refused to acknowledge President Emilio Aguinaldo's Filipino republic, as armies for both sides faced each other in Manila. The uneasy situation exploded on February 4, when an American sentry killed two Filipinos. Undisciplined fighting dominated that night and the following day; the Americans killed over three thousand indigenous people. Within a year, American forces in the Philippines numbered 70,000. The incident signaled the start of the Philippine-American War.

BATTLE OF BALANGIGA (Sep 28, 1901). This assault by guerilla forces, part of the Philippine-American War, took place on the island of Samar.

The Filipinos attacked on a Sunday morning, achieving total surprise. Only twenty of seventy-four American soldiers survived the bloody hand-to-hand fighting. American reporters likened the incident to the Alamo and Little Bighorn, thus enraging their readers. In response, Gen. Jacob Smith ordered an expedition under Major Littleton Waller to burn villages and kill anyone over ten years of age. The American public, ironically, reacted with horror when it learned of Waller's actions in carrying out Smith's order.

BATTLE OF CADUCAN RIVER (Nov 17, 1901). Following Gen. Jacob Smith's order to destroy Gen. Vincente Lukban's force, Maj. Littleton Waller discovered Lukban's headquarters in the Sohoton cliffs near the Caducan and divided his troops. His own unit was stopped by the terrain, but a second unit with a machine gun attacked from across the river and scaled the cliffs. The fighting was some of the fiercest of the Philippine-American War. Lukban's troops were killed or fled into the jungle.

MARCH TO BASEY (Dec 28, 1901–Feb 26, 1902). On December 28, Maj. Littleton Waller and fifty Marines set out to cross Samar from Lanang to Basey, searching for Emilio Aguinaldo's followers. By January 2, the Americans were lost. Waller ordered the infirm to return to Lanang and reached Basey on January 6. The infirm soldiers reached Lanang five days later, leaving behind Marines too sick to continue. The Filipino bearers for one group of ailing Marines rebelled, but a relief expedition from Lanang rescued twenty-three survivors on the 18th. The Marines rounded up several bearers and sent them in chains to Basey. Waller had ten of them executed on the 20th, and was later acquitted of murder charges, pointing to orders given him by Gen. Jacob Smith. Smith was court-martialled in May.

OCCUPATION OF VERA CRUZ (Apr 21–Nov 23, 1914). US-Mexican relations were already uneasy when on April 9, 1914, Mexican authorities mistakenly arrested eight American sailors from the USS *Dolphin* in Tampico. President Woodrow Wilson, having already decided to intervene in the Mexican civil war, demanded a public apology from Mexican president Victoriano Huerta. Subsequently learning of a shipment of arms about to be unloaded in Vera Cruz, Wilson ordered Adm. Frank F. Fletcher to send sailors and Marines to occupy the customs house in the city. He did so on April 21. When Gen. Gustavo Maass's forces counterattacked, Fletcher's guns opened fire. Five battleships and more land forces joined the occupation the next day. U.S. Army troops commanded by Gen. Frederick Funston landed on April 28 and the sailors ashore withdrew. Additional Marine forces landed on April 30 to replace those ashore, and the former were transferred to Army operational command on May 1. The occupation was popular with no one, and Wilson withdrew the troops after negotiation, on November 23.

Biographical Notes

AGUINALDO, EMILIO (1869–1964). One of the great Filipino revolutionaries, Aguinaldo, in 1895, joined a revolutionary group that took part in the effort to overthrow the Spanish government. Spain sent reinforcements to the Philippines and Aguinaldo and his forces retreated to the mountains north of Manila. Spanish representatives then persuaded the rebel leaders to go into exile in Hong Kong in return for the establishment of governmental reforms and a large sum of money. When war broke out between the United States and Spain in 1898, Commodore George Dewey assisted Aguinaldo and his exiles to return to their homeland. Aguinaldo quickly organized a revolutionary army and set up a rebel government near Manila. Although the U.S. subsequently required Spain to cede control of the islands to the U.S., Aguinaldo controlled much of the archipelago outside Manila and, as its first president, proclaimed the independence of the Philippines. Relations between the U.S. military occupation forces and the Aguinaldo government deteriorated when Aguinaldo refused to recognize U.S. sovereignty over the islands. The American military leaders soon began a systematic program to pacify the Philippines. The war of occupation that followed was very costly to both sides, but especially to the Filipinos. By 1901, President Aguinaldo found safety in northern Luzon, but the revolution was beginning to weaken. In March, Gen. Frederick Funston and four U.S. officers posed as captives of the Filipino army and infiltrated behind enemy lines to Aguinaldo's camp. When the party reached the camp on March 27, they took President Aguinaldo prisoner and returned to Manila. Aguinaldo now cooperated with the Americans and signed a proclamation urging other Filipinos to surrender and accept the sovereignty of the U.S. Aguinaldo subsequently retired from public life.

AINSWORTH, FREDERICK CRAYTON (1852–1934). Ainsworth's army career began in 1874 when he enlisted in the medical corps as an assistant surgeon. In 1886 Ainsworth was put in charge of the Record and Pension Division of the surgeon-general's office. He reorganized and streamlined the work of the division with such success that it gained public and congressional attention due to the widespread interest in veterans and pension issues. Ainsworth's career flourished and in 1892 he resigned his medical commission to take a line commission as a colonel in charge of the War Department's Record and Pension Office. This post increased Ainsworth's responsibilities and influence. By 1904 he achieved the rank of major general and in 1907 he became the Adjutant General, a position in which he wielded considerable power. When in 1912 Ainsworth clashed with the Chief of Staff, Gen. Leonard Wood, Secretary of War Henry L. Stimson moved to have Ainsworth court-martialled for insubordination. Ainsworth chose to retire rather than continue his efforts to oppose Wood's assertion of the power of the chief of staff.

BILLINGS, JOHN SHAW (1838–1913). Educated at Miami University of Ohio and the Medical College of Ohio, Billings obtained his M.D. in 1860. The following year he was commissioned in the U.S. Army and put in charge of a hospital in Philadelphia where he quickly learned the problems in army medicine. In April 1864 Billings was ordered to duty with the Army of the Potomac where he served unofficially as the medical statistician collecting and consolidating all sorts of reports, but then he was invalided back to Washington and assigned to the surgeon-general's office where he worked for thirty years. Billings had charge of the army medical library in Washington. There he built the collection from about 600 items in 1865 to more than 50,000 in 1873, using money turned in from army hospitals after the war. In 1880 Congress appropriated money to print what became the *Index Catalogue of Medical Literature* which Billings prepared with the assistance of Dr. Robert Fletcher. Together they published sixteen volumes—as well as a companion monthly guide to current medical literature called the *Index Medicus*. Billings helped plan the construction of the Johns Hopkins Hospital in Baltimore, establish the American Public Health Association in 1872, direct the analysis of the vital statistics of the federal census of 1880 and 1890, and served as the first director of the New York Public Library (1896–1913) following his retirement from the army (1895).

BLACK KETTLE (c. 1803–1868). *Native American name* MOKETAVATO. Born in the Black Hills in what is now South Dakota, Black Kettle, a chief of the Southern Cheyennes, tried to keep peace with the white settlers after the discovery of gold in the area of Colorado. In 1864 Black Kettle went to Denver seeking peace from Governor John Evans, who turned him down. Black Kettle was subsequently able to reach an agreement with Maj. Edward M. Wynkoop, commander of Ft. Lyon, Colorado, and the Cheyennes established a camp at Sand Creek, about forty miles from Ft. Lyon. Evans, in the meantime, authorized Col. John M. Chivington to raise a regiment of volunteers to deal with the Native Americans in the area. Chivington apparently got Wynkoop replaced at Ft. Lyon and then attacked the Cheyenne camp on November 29, 1864 with about 1,000 men. There the undisciplined Colorado volunteers slaughtered about 161 men, women, and children, burned the camp, and scalped and mutilated many of the dead. Black Kettle, who had raised a large American flag and a white flag at the outset of the attack, survived and again sought peace in 1867 when he signed the Treaty of Medicine Lodge. The following year Black Kettle moved his people to the Washita Valley in Kansas against the advice of Wynkoop, now an Indian agent. Because many of the Plains tribes, including the Cheyennes, resented the building of the transcontinental railroad across their territory, the army continued to use force to subjugate them. Black Kettle was unable to avoid this warfare and died on November 27, 1868, when Gen. George A. Custer's Seventh Cavalry killed most of Black Kettle's people in an attack on their camp.

CARTER, WILLIAM HARDING (1851–1925). Carter graduated from West Point in 1873 and for the next 24 years served with the army in the western United States, mostly in expeditions against Native Americans. He received the Medal of Honor in 1881 "for distinguished bravery in action" against the Apache. He then served twice in the Philippines. Carter was promoted to major general in 1909 and in 1913 mobilized his division in Texas in preparation for suppression of Mexican hostility. Carter retired in 1915, but he was called back to active service in 1917 for World War I. He retired again in the spring of 1918. Carter is best known as the author of *The American Army* (1915) and his work with Secretary of War Elihu Root in 1903 in the drafting of legislation that led to the reorganization of the army and the establishment of the army general staff.

CHAFFEE, ADNA ROMANZA (1842–1914). Enlisting in an Ohio volunteer regiment in 1861, Chaffee served throughout the Civil War fighting in many of the major battles in the eastern theater including Antietam and Gettysburg, where he was wounded and barely escaped capture. From 1867 to 1888 Chaffee served in the southwest taking part in numerous campaigns against the Apaches. He then saw service in Cuba during the Hispano-American War in command of a brigade. In July 1900 Chaffee took command of the troops sent as part of the International Relief Expedition to Beijing, China during the Boxer Rebellion. Chaffee's troops captured the gates of Beijing (Aug. 14, 1900) and were the first to relieve the besieged diplomatic legations. Promoted to major general in 1901, Chaffee became military governor and commander of U.S. forces in the Philippines, a post he held until the fall of 1902. In 1904–1906, Chaffee served as Chief of Staff of the army.

COCHISE (1812?–1874). Chief of the Chiricahua Apaches, Cochise and his people were in constant conflict with the Spanish and Mexican authorities when the southwestern U.S. was part of their territory. When the U.S. took possession of this land in 1850, relative peace lasted until 1861 when Cochise, falsely accused of having kidnapped a white child, was imprisoned. He escaped and took white hostages. When an exchange of hostages failed, both sides executed their hostages. Cochise then joined his father-in-law Mangas Coloradas, chief of the Mimbreño Apaches, in raids on the army and white settlers in Arizona. Along with about 500 warriors, Cochise and Mangas held Apache Pass (July 1862) against Gen. James Carleton and 3,000 California volunteers until they were temporarily routed by the army's artillery. When Mangas died in prison, Cochise led the Apache opposition fighting from the depths of the Dragoon Mountains. He continued his resistance to the white forces until September 1871 when Gen. George Crook used Apache scouts to track down Cochise and force him to surrender. Cochise refused to leave his tribe's ancestral lands when the Chiricahua were ordered to a reservation in New Mexico. When the army negotiated a new treaty in 1872, Cochise returned to the Chiricahua reservation in Arizona.

CRAZY HORSE (1842?–1877). *Native American name* TA-SUNKO-WITKO. He was a chief of the Oglala Lakotas who defeated Gen. G. Crook at the Battle of Rosebud Creek (1876) and Gen. G. A. Custer at the Battle of Little Big Horn (1876). Mari Sandoz, *Crazy Horse, the Strange Man of the Oglalas* (1942).

CROOK, GEORGE (1829–1890). After service in the Civil War, he returned to the West and fought Cochise (1871–1873), Crazy Horse, Sitting Bull and Geronimo (1882). Martin Schmitt, ed. *General George Crook: His Autobiography* (1960).

CURTISS, GLEN HAMMOND (1878–1930). In 1895 Curtiss opened a bicycle shop in Hammondsport, New York. Successful as a bicycle racer and then as a motorcycle racer, Curtiss developed an interest in aeronautics. He built engines for dirigibles and in 1907 became director of experimental work for the Aerial Experiment Association founded by Alexander Graham Bell. Curtiss built his first airplane, the *June Bug*, in 1908 and in that year also won the trophy for the first public airplane flight of a kilometer in the U.S. He then went on to win the New York *World's* $10,000 prize for a flight from Albany to New York City (1910) and one of his biplanes made the first successful takeoff from a ship. In January 1911 he fitted the *June Bug* (now called the *Loon*) with pontoon floats and successfully demonstrated the first practical seaplane. Later in 1911 Curtiss and his associates engaged in litigation with the Wright brothers over a patent for an aileron. The Curtiss group was awarded the patent, its most important contribution to aviation. During World War I the Curtiss Aeroplane and Motor Company produced more than 5,000 JN-4 ("Jenny") biplanes that were used at army and navy flight schools. In 1919 a Navy-Curtiss flying boat (NC-4), commanded by Lt. Cdr. Albert C. Read, made the first successful transatlantic flight. In 1929 the Curtiss firm merged with its former rival to become the Curtiss-Wright Company.

CUSTER, GEORGE ARMSTRONG (1839–1876). Custer's death alongside a substantial portion of the 7th Cavalry at the Battle of Little Big Horn (1876) overshadows all other aspects of his career—particularly his distinguished service in the Civil War. Robert M. Utley, *Cavalier in Buckskin: George Armstrong Custer and the Western Military Frontier* (1988).

DANIELS, JOSEPHUS (1862–1948). Josephus Daniels' father was a Whig and a Unionist in North Carolina in the Civil War. Killed in an ambush at the end of the war, the elder Daniels left his wife and three children near destitution. Educated in a one-room school, the young Daniels began a career in journalism in 1880. He was an outspoken champion of reform and the Democratic party. Daniels studied law and passed the bar exam in 1885, but he never practiced law. Instead he took over the *Raleigh State Chronicle*, a weekly newspaper, and continued to campaign for reform and Democratic politics. When the paper failed in 1892, he used his political connections to get a post in the Cleveland administration in Washington (1893–1895) and then returned to North Carolina to purchase the Raleigh *News and Observer*. Daniels' paper was progressive on most issues, but it also supported disenfranchisement of African Americans. Daniels' stature in Democratic politics continued to grow as he worked hard for the election of William Jennings Bryan for president. Bryan failed to win that office, but Woodrow Wilson did in 1912. In consequence of his support for Wilson, Daniels was appointed Secretary of the Navy. During his term as secretary (1913–1921), Daniels instituted a number of major personnel reforms and established the post of Chief of Naval Operations as an alternative to a naval general staff. He also guarded the navy's oil reserves at Teapot Dome from exploitation by private interests. In 1932, Daniels supported Franklin D. Roosevelt for president and subsequently served as ambassador to Mexico (1933–1941).

DEWEY, GEORGE (1837–1917). His victory over the Spanish fleet at the Battle of Manila Bay (1898) contributed significantly to the defeat of Spain during the Hispano-American War. Ronald Spector, *Admiral of the New Navy: The Life and Career of George Dewey* (1974).

EVANS, ROBLEY DUNGLISON (1846–1912). Evans entered the Naval Academy by a legal subterfuge at age of thirteen during the Civil War. On January 15, 1865, he was wounded four times while leading an assault by a company of marines on Ft. Fisher, but refused to go down from his wounds. Subsequently Evans fought for reinstatement after he was invalided out of the navy. Congress granted his request and Evans went on to a distinguished career that included invention of the signal lamp and effective advocacy for a steel navy. He also combined seamanship with practical diplomacy following the Valparaiso Incident (1891) in Chile when a mob killed several Americans. His defense of the sailors earned him the nickname "Fighting Bob." As commander of the battleship *Iowa*, his ship began the attack on the Spanish fleet at Santiago (1898). Promoted to rear admiral in 1901, Evans commanded the Battle Fleet that made a round-the-world cruise in 1907 to demonstrate American naval strength.

FISKE, BRADLEY ALLEN (1854–1942). Fiske graduated from the Naval Academy in 1874. He served in a succession of sea and shore assignments during which he demonstrated a genuine flair for invention. Fiske developed a system of electric communication for the interiors of warships, an electric range finder, an electric ammunition hoist, a naval telescopic sight, a system of wireless control of moving vessels, and an aircraft torpedo release mechanism. Although Fiske invented his telescopic sight in 1891, some officers saw no value to it. Nevertheless it became standard equipment by the outbreak of the Hispano-American War. Fiske was promoted to the rank of rear admiral in 1911, but his energy for invention, more than his various afloat commands, was his major contribution to the development of the U.S. Navy. Fiske had more than 60 inventions earn patents.

FLIPPER, HENRY OSSIAN (1856–1940). Born a slave in Georgia, Henry O. Flipper was the first African American graduate of West Point. Flipper entered the Military Academy in 1873 and endured four years of ostracism before graduating fifty in a class of seventy-six. Commissioned a second lieutenant, Flipper was ordered to the all-African American 10th Cavalry Regiment in the Indian Territory (Oklahoma). While serving at Ft. Davis in Texas, Flipper was accused of embezzling commissary funds (1881). Although he was found not guilty of embezzlement, the court did find him guilty of conduct unbecoming an officer and a gentleman. He was discharged from the army in 1882, but Flipper remained in the west working in engineering, mining, and surveying for various companies. Flipper tried to return to the army at the outbreak of the Hispano-American War in 1898, but he had no success. Flipper always maintained he was innocent of any crime and should not have been dismissed from the army. He attributed his conviction to white prejudice and tried repeatedly to clear his name. In 1976 the army posthumously exonerated Flipper and honored his years of service to his country.

FUNSTON, FREDERICK (1865–1917). Funston grew up in Kansas, and following a restless youth, volunteered in 1895 to aid Cuban revolutionaries against the Spanish government. Although he had no military training or qualifications, he served effectively for eighteen months in the Cuban guerilla forces rising to the rank of lieutenant colonel. Funston left Cuba in 1898 and returned to the United States. When war broke out with Spain, he was given command of the 20th Kansas Volunteer Regiment, which was sent to the Philippines. The regiment arrived too late to fight the Spanish, but Funston was soon fighting the Filipino forces led by President E. Aguinaldo. In 1899, Funston won the Medal of Honor at the Battle of Calumpit. In March 1901, Funston led a daring raid on President Aguinaldo's secret headquarters in northern Luzon province and captured the Filipino leader. Shortly thereafter Funston was promoted to brigadier general and given command of the Department of California. While serving in that post, he was in charge of the early phases of emergency military relief and rescue operations following the San Francisco earthquake (1906). In April 1914, he commanded the army forces involved in the occupation of Vera Cruz and subsequently commanded troops on the Mexican border (1915–1917) while Gen. John J. Pershing was pursuing Pancho Villa.

GATLING, RICHARD JORDAN (1818–1903). Trained in the mechanical arts by his father, Gatling became wealthy by the 1850s from his many agricultural inventions. When the Civil War broke out, he turned his mechanical genius to weapons of war. In late 1862, he patented the rapid-fire Gatling gun, which was the first practical machine gun. Later models could fire up to 350 rounds per minute via ten barrels clustered around a central revolving shaft. Crank-driven with an automatic feed and ejection system, the Gatling gun utilized newly developed brass cartridge shells. The War Department approved the gun for use too late for general service in the Civil War, but some guns were used by Gen. Benjamin F. Butler's Army of the James. In 1870 Gatling moved to Hartford, Connecticut to work with the Colt Patent Fire Arms Manufacturing Company in the improvement and manufacture of his gun. A motor-driven Gatling gun was built that could fire 3,000 rounds per minute. Eventually Gatling sold his patent rights to Colt. The Gatling gun did not see much use in combat because Hiram S. Maxim's fully automatic machine gun made it obsolete.

GERONIMO (1829–1909). *Native American name* GOYATHLAY. Born in Arizona, Geronimo grew up during the period when the Apaches were constantly at war. When the Chiricahua Apaches moved to a new reservation in 1876, Geronimo and his followers escaped to Mexico. For ten years Geronimo and his band raided settlements along the border. The army assigned Gen. George Crook to pursue Geronimo in the Sierra Madre Mountains. Crook was successful, but in 1885 Geronimo and others fled their reservation and this time it took Gen. Nelson A. Miles five months and 5,000 soldiers to recapture them (1886). President Grover Cleveland ordered Geronimo and his followers sent to Florida, then to Alabama, and finally to Ft. Sill, Oklahoma. Geronimo took up farming, became a Christian, and traveled to various expositions in 1904–1905. Although Geronimo tried to obtain permission to return to his ancestral lands before his death in 1909, the government refused his request.

GOETHALS, GEORGE WASHINGTON (1858–1928). A member of the West Point class of 1880, Goethals was commissioned in the engineers. He received further education in engineering before being assigned to several civil works projects on the Ohio, Cumberland, and Tennessee Rivers. He taught at West Point, served as chief engineer in Puerto Rico in the Hispano-American War, and spent four years (1903–1907) on the army's general staff. In 1907 President Theodore Roosevelt appointed Goethals chief engineer and chairman of the Isthmian Canal Commission with full authority to build the Panama Canal. At the height of construction, Goethals was in charge of a work force of over 30,000 civilians as well as numerous army officers and men. A tremendous feat of engineering, the canal opened to traffic on August 15, 1914, nearly six months ahead of schedule. President Woodrow Wilson appointed Goethals the first governor of the Canal Zone and a special act of Congress in 1915 promoted him to major general.

GORGAS, WILLIAM CRAWFORD (1854–1920). Educated at the University of the South (1875) and Bellevue Medical College in New York City, Gorgas joined the army medical corps in 1880. After he survived an attack of yellow fever in Texas, Gorgas was often stationed at army posts where the disease was prevalent. In 1898, he was ordered to Havana, Cuba, then occupied by U.S. forces. When Maj. Walter Reed, who was also in Cuba, demonstrated that yellow fever was transmitted by a species of mosquito, Gorgas rapidly eliminated the mosquito's breeding grounds and rid the city of the disease. In 1904, Col. Gorgas became chief sanitary officer of the Panama Canal Zone, which was plagued by yellow fever and malaria. By 1905, he had eliminated yellow fever and vastly improved overall sanitary conditions. From 1907 to 1914 Gorgas served on the Isthmian Canal Commission. In 1914, he was promoted to brigadier general and became surgeon general of the army. During World War I Gorgas headed the army medical services. He retired in 1918 and continued his work to eradicate yellow fever in South and Central America.

GREELY, ADOLPHUS WASHINGTON (1844–1935). With the outbreak of the Civil War, Greely enlisted in the 19th Massachusetts Volunteers. He fought in several major battles and three times sustained serious wounds. By 1864 he attained the rank of brevet major. Greely continued his army career after the war, and in 1881 he volunteered for a scientific expedition to Ellesmere Island in the Arctic. Greely's exploration team made extensive meteorological, oceanographic, and geographical observations and discovered Lake Hazen and Greely Fjord. Supply and relief ships were unable to reach the Greely party in 1882 and 1883 and when in 1884 relief vessels finally connected with the explorers, only Greely and six others (one of whom died shortly thereafter) had survived the ordeal. In 1886 President Grover Cleveland promoted Greely to brigadier general and made him Chief Signal Officer (1887). For 20 years Greely oversaw the construction of thousands of miles of telegraph lines and submarine cables. He also served as head of the U.S. Weather Service until 1891. In 1906, Greely supervised Army relief operations following the San Francisco earthquake. Just prior to his death in 1935, Greely was awarded the Medal of Honor in recognition of his many contributions to science.

HOLLAND, JOHN PHILIP (1840–1914). Born in Ireland, Holland emigrated to the United States in 1873 and settled in Paterson, New Jersey. There he resumed his work as a teacher and an inventor interested in submarines. The U.S. Navy rejected his plans for a submarine in 1875, but the Fenian Society, which was made up of Irish nationalists, financed further experiments. Holland built and tested his first submarine, the *Fenian Ram*, in 1881. Holland earned the technical, if not financial, support of naval officers in the 1880s and early 1890s. Finally, in 1895, the navy awarded Holland's company a contract to build a submarine. The resulting vessel was unsatisfactory. In 1898, Holland tried again, building the *Holland*, which had internal-combustion engines for surface power and electric motors powered by storage batteries for submerged propulsion. In addition Holland's vessel had rudder planes that enabled the boat to dive rather than sink passively. After rigorous tests, the navy accepted the *Holland* in 1900 as its first submarine. Holland went on to build several more submarines for the United States, Great Britain, Russia, and Japan.

JOSEPH (c. 1804–1904). *Native American name* INMUTTOOYAH-LATLAT. A Nez Perce chief, Joseph was born in Oregon in an area where gold was discovered in 1863. Although other tribes eventually agreed to cede their land to the white government, the Nez Perces refused. The government held that the treaty the other tribes had signed also applied to the Nez Perces. Upon the death of his father, Chief Joseph continued to resist the loss of ancestral lands to foreign settlement. In 1877 Gen. Oliver O. Howard issued an ultimatum ordering the Nez Perces to leave their land or face forcible removal. When some Nez Perce braves killed several persons, open warfare followed. Initially the Native Americans were successful against the white soldiers, but their strength waned. Joseph led his people on a masterful retreat over more than 1,500 miles moving toward Canada. Despite outfighting their pursuers, however, they failed to reach the border before Gen. Nelson A. Miles surrounded them on October 5, 1877 only 30 miles from their goal. Joseph surrendered with dignity and vowed to fight no more. The Nez Perces were sent to the Indian Territory (Oklahoma) and in 1885 were allowed to return to a reservation in the state of Washington.

LAWTON, HENRY WARE (1843–1899). Lawton enlisted in an Indiana regiment in 1861. He fought at Shiloh (1862), Stones River (1862–1863), Chickamauga (1863), and Atlanta (1864) where he won a Medal of Honor. Mustered out of the Union Army as a brevet colonel in 1865, Lawton briefly studied law before rejoining the regular army in 1867. He served in campaigns against the Native Americans in Texas and the Indian Territory (Oklahoma), and in 1886 while serving under Gen. Nelson A. Miles he captured Geronimo in the Sierra Madre Mountains of Arizona. At the start of the Hispano-American War, Lawton went to Cuba as a division commander under Gen. William R. Shafter. He fought effectively against the Spanish at Daiquiri, Siboney, Santiago, and El Caney. In early 1899 Lawton was ordered to the Philippines as a corps commander. Gen. Lawton's soldiers operated north of Manila pushing the Filipino forces back. He was killed in action in the Philippines on December 19, 1899.

LEA, HOMER (1876–1912). After two years at Stanford University (1897–1899), Lea left the U.S. for China. There he participated in the joint international expedition that relieved Beijing during the Boxer Rebellion. Lea won the support of the Chinese with his courage and knowledge of military history. Soon Lea was a general in charge of Chinese volunteers, but when the Chinese authorities learned of his work with the reform movement he fled to Hong Kong. In 1900, he met Sun Yat-sen and briefly served as his chief of staff. Lea returned to the U.S. in 1901, only to leave for China in 1904 and service as an adviser to Sun Yat-sen (1911–1912). Although he was offered the post of chief of staff in the Chinese army, Lea declined due to ill health. In *The Valor of Ignorance* (1909) Lea astutely predicted a future war between the United States and Japan that would begin with a Japanese attack on Hawaii.

LUCE, STEPHEN BLEECKER (1827–1917). Luce entered the navy as a midshipman in 1841, served in the Mexican War and the Civil War, and wrote a textbook called *Seamanship* (1863). Luce was a strong advocate of improving the training of sailors and naval officers. It was through his efforts that the navy was persuaded to establish the Naval War College in 1884 with Luce as its first president. Promoted to rear admiral in 1885, Luce took command of the North Atlantic Squadron in mid-1886 before retiring in 1889. Luce not only laid a sturdy foundation for the postgraduate education of naval officers at the War College, he also sought the appointment of superior faculty members, such as Capt. Alfred T. Mahan, who would provide a necessary intellectual stimulus to the officers' training course.

MACARTHUR, ARTHUR (1845–1912). In 1862 MacArthur joined the 24th Wisconsin Infantry and fought with distinction in Tennessee where he won the Medal of Honor (1863) and was severely wounded (1864). Before he was age 20 he was a brevet colonel. He re-entered the army in 1866 and served for more than twenty years in a variety of frontier posts. In May 1898 as a brigadier general of volunteers he took a brigade to the Philippines where they took part on the capture of Manila. He was then given charge of the operations against the forces of the Philippine Republic (1899). In 1900 MacArthur succeeded Gen. Elwell S. Otis as commander of the Division of the Philippines and military governor. He later instituted many democratic reforms in the territorial government. MacArthur returned to the United States in 1901, was promoted to major general, and subsequently served as an observer during the Russo-Japanese War (1904–1905). He retired in 1909 as the ranking general in the army. One of his sons was Douglas MacArthur.

MACKENZIE, RANALD SLIDELL (1840–1889). Although the son of a naval officer, Ranald Mackenzie graduated from West Point in 1862 first in his class. He distinguished himself at the second battle of Bull Run (1862), Fredericksburg (1862), Chancellorsville (1863), Gettysburg (1863) and Petersburg (1864). By age twenty-four he was a brigadier general of volunteers. He remained in the army after the war as colonel of the 4th cavalry. Mackenzie proved to be a master tactician and a formidable opponent. In the 1870s he participated in operations against the Cheyennes, Comanches, Kickapoos, Kiowas, and the Lakotas. In 1873, acting under orders, Mackenzie led a large formation into Mexico to end a threat from Kickapoo raiders. While serving under Gen. Philip H. Sheridan, Mackenzie defeated Red Cloud and Red Leaf in Nebraska and Dull Knife in the Bighorn Mountains (1876). These victories were instrumental in the final defeat of Crazy Horse and the Lakotas. With the rank of brigadier general, Mackenzie retired in 1884 due to ill health.

MAURY, MATTHEW FONTAINE (1806–1873). Maury joined the navy in 1825 and spent nearly nine years at sea including a circumnavigation of the world (1829–1830). In 1836 he published *A New Theoretical and Practical Treatise on Navigation*, but an accident in 1839 rendered him permanently lame and unfit for sea duty. Maury was appointed Superintendent of the Depot of Charts and Instruments in 1842 and in 1844 Superintendent of the Naval Observatory. An intensive study of winds and currents led Maury to publish numerous works reflecting his oceanographic studies. Maury's *The Physical Geography of the Sea and Its Meteorology* (1855) is considered the first textbook of modern oceanography. Maury's charts of the Atlantic seabed demonstrated the practicability of a trans-Atlantic telegraph cable. In April 1861 Maury resigned from the U.S. Navy and entered the service of the Confederate navy as a commander. In 1862 Maury went to England as a special agent of the Confederacy. During his three years in England, Maury secured a number of warships for the Confederacy. After the war Maury served in Mexico under appointment by the Emperor Maximilian. In 1868 he returned to the United States as professor of meteorology at the Virginia Military Institute (1868–1873).

MAXIM, HIRAM STEVENS (1840–1916). Born in Maine, Maxim showed an aptitude for mechanical invention at an early age. He earned his first patent in 1866 for a hair-curling iron. In 1878 he became the chief engineer of the United States Electric Lighting Co. in New York City. In the early 1880s he began work in London on a fully automatic machine gun, which he successfully built in 1884. The Maxim gun used the principle of a short recoil to produce a complete cycle, including reloading, in a single barrel. Maxim's weapon benefited greatly from the contributions of his brother, Hudson Maxim, who developed a smokeless powder. The gun could fire 660 rounds per minute with the ammunition supplied on a belt. The Maxim Gun Company and its successor organizations (particularly Vickers, Ltd.) sold their gun to every major nation. World War I demonstrated convincingly the effectiveness of the Maxim gun. Maxim became a British subject in 1900 and was knighted by Queen Victoria in 1901. Although Maxim is best known for his invention of the machine gun, he obtained more than 250 patents in Britain and the United States prior to his retirement (1911).

MILES, NELSON APPLETON (1839–1925). After the Civil War he spent many years on the frontier. He drove Sitting Bull into Canada after the Battle of Little Big Horn and captured Chief Joseph. During the Hispano-American War he supervised the invasion of Puerto Rico. Virginia W. Johnson, *The Unregimented General: A Biography of Nelson A. Miles* (1961).

PEARY, ROBERT EDWIN (1856–1920). Although he never saw combat, his attempts to reach the North Pole enlarged the human community's geographic knowledge of the Far North. John E. Weems, *Peary, the Explorer and the Man* (1988).

RED CLOUD (1822–1909). *Native American name* MAHPIUA LUTA. Born in north central Nebraska, Red Cloud was the chief of the Bad Face band of the Oglala Lakotas. In 1865 Red Cloud and the Oglalas resisted the building of the Powder River Road in Wyoming that was intended to open the mining region of western Montana. The Cheyennes, who had just suffered a massacre at Sand Creek, joined the Lakotas in fighting the construction party because the road cut through the rich hunting lands in the Bighorn Mountains. In 1866, the U.S. Army sought to negotiate with Red Cloud, but he broke off negotiations when he learned construction crews had entered the disputed territory. Two years of warfare followed with the proposed road under siege by the Native Americans. On December 21, 1866 Red Cloud's warriors killed 80 soldiers under the command of Capt. William J. Fetterman near Ft. Phil Kearney. Eventually in April 1868 a new treaty was negotiated that abandoned the Powder River Road and the territory north of the North Platte River was recognized as closed to white settlement or passage. When the army burned three forts as part of the treaty, Red Cloud settled in Nebraska having forced the army to concede. Thereafter he was an advocate of peace with the whites, but his influence waned and he moved to the Pine Ridge Agency in South Dakota.

SAMPSON, WILLIAM THOMAS (1840–1902). First in his class at the Naval Academy (1861), Sampson served as an instructor at Annapolis, survived an explosion when the ship on which he was serving struck a mine in Charleston harbor (1865), and had several tours of duty with the Atlantic and Asiatic Squadrons. From 1893 to 1897 Sampson was chief of the Bureau of Ordnance where much work was done to introduce smokeless powder to the navy and to improve gunnery training. In early 1898 Sampson served on the board that investigated the sinking of the *Maine* in Havana harbor. Promoted to rear admiral in March 1898, Sampson took command of the North Atlantic Squadron. Shortly thereafter war broke out with Spain and Sampson's ships blockaded Cuba. When Spanish Adm. Topete y Cervera and his squadron slipped by part of the blockading force commanded by Adm. Winfield S. Schley and entered the harbor of Santiago de Cuba, Sampson concentrated his force there. Just prior to a coordinated land-sea assault by U.S. forces, Cervera's squadron sortied from the harbor (July 3, 1898) and Schley's ships severely damaged the Spanish force in less than four hours. A controversy ensued in the press over whether Schley or Sampson should be credited for the naval victory.

SCHLEY, WINFIELD SCOTT (1839–1909). A 1860 graduate of the Naval Academy, Schley served throughout the Civil War, especially in the operations against Mobile, Ala. In 1884 Schley had command of the expedition sent to rescue the Arctic exploring party led by Lt. Adolphus W. Greely, who had been in Greenland since 1881. Schley found the survivors of the Greely party on June 22 after a perilous voyage. When the Hispano-American War broke out in 1898, Schley was given command of the "Flying Squadron" based in Hampton Roads, Virginia, which was to be ready to intercept any Spanish naval forces in the Atlantic or Caribbean. When Spanish Adm. Cervera was discovered heading for Cuba, Schley's squadron set out in pursuit. Although Schley was technically senior to Adm. William T. Sampson, Sampson was the naval commander in the area and he ordered Schley to blockade the southern Cuban parts. Cervera and his fleet avoided Schley and made Santiago before the blockade was fully in place. On July 3, 1898 while Sampson was ashore planning for a joint army-navy assault, Cervera's squadron sortied from the harbor. The U.S. ships made quick work of the Spanish fleet and the press and public gave Schley credit for the victory. When controversy followed, a naval court of inquiry found in Sampson's favor and against Schley (1902).

SIMS, WILLIAM SOWDEN (1858–1936). Born in Canada of American parents, Sims graduated from the Naval Academy in 1880. He spent the next seventeen years almost continuously at sea on the North Atlantic, Pacific, and China stations. In 1900, while again at sea on the China station, Sims met Capt. Percy Scott of the Royal Navy, the developer of a new gunnery technique called continuous-aim firing. Sims used Scott's ideas to press the navy for adoption of this technique. Between 1902 and 1907, Sims was inspector of target practice and in that job he was able to reduce gunnery firing times and to greatly increase accuracy. Sims' career prospered despite his advocacy of reforms. When the U.S. joined World War I in 1917, Sims, now a rear admiral, was President of the Naval War College. He was then put in command of the U.S. naval forces operating in European waters. In that post he worked vigorously to persuade the allies to adopt the convoy system of protection against German submarines. U.S. naval forces later took part in convoy-escort duties and mine-laying work.

SITTING BULL (1831?–1890). *Native American name* TATANKA IYOTAKE. A member of the Hunkpapa Lakota, he was first a warrior and later a medicine man. He was a leader, along with Crazy Horse and Gall, in the war that led to the Battle of Little Big Horn (1876). Robert M. Utley, *The Lance and the Shield: The Life and Times of Sitting Bull* (1993).

STERNBERG, GEORGE MILLER (1838–1915). Educated at Hartwick Seminary and Columbia University Medical School where he earned his M.D., Sternberg entered the army medical corps in May 1861. He participated in several early battles in the Peninsular campaign but then contracted typhoid fever which forced him to spend the rest of his war service in various military hospitals. While serving in Florida (1872–1875), Sternberg came in contact with yellow fever and found that he could improve the health of the local forces by moving them out of the infected area. He then published two articles reflecting his research on yellow fever, which he had himself caught in 1875. In 1879 the army sent Sternberg to Havana as a member of the Havana Yellow Fever Commission. There he worked with other distinguished physicians in the new science of bacteriology. By 1881 Sternberg was also studying the cause of pneumonia and in that year he and Louis Pasteur simultaneously reported the discovery of the pneumococcus, pneumonia's pathogenic agent. In 1885 Sternberg first demonstrated the plasmodium of malaria and in 1886 the bacilli of tuberculosis and typhoid fever. Sternberg had also been experimenting with disinfectants and following the publication of an essay on this subject in 1886, he was recognized as an authority. In 1893 Sternberg became Surgeon-General of the U.S. Army. In that post he established the Yellow Fever Commission (1900) headed by Maj. Walter Reed, who identified the mosquito *Aëdes aegypti* as the agent of transmission for yellow fever. Sternberg also established the Army Medical School, Dental Corps, Nurse Corps, and the Army Tuberculosis Hospital.

TAYLOR, DAVID WATSON (1864–1940). A graduate of Randolph-Macon College (1881), the Naval Academy (1885), and the Royal Naval College in England (1888), Taylor began designing ships of the new steel navy in 1888. Because naval engineers had few reliable scientific guidelines for ship design, Taylor concentrated on developing an experimental research program that would provide reliable data on ship design. In 1899, he built a testing basin for ship models in the Washington Navy Yard. From then until 1914 he headed the experimental work done there. Out of this research came his book *The Speed and Power of Ships* (1910) in which he set out what became known as the Taylor Standard Series, the first practical method to determine the relationship of engine power to a given hull design and the water-resistance characteristics of that hull design. Taylor became head of the Bureau of Construction and Repair in 1914, and was promoted to rear admiral in 1916. He was responsible for much of the U.S. naval construction involved in World War I. At the same time he became interested in aircraft design and along with Glen H. Curtiss developed the design for the Navy-Curtiss aircraft, one of which (NC-4), was the first aircraft to make a trans-Atlantic crossing (1919).

TERRY, ALFRED HOWE (1827–1890). A veteran of the Civil War, he held overall command of the expedition against the dissident tribal elements assembled alongside the Little Big Horn River in 1876. John W. Bailey, *Pacifying the Plains: General Alfred Terry and the Decline of the Sioux, 1868–1890* (1979).

YOUNG, CHARLES (1864–1922). Born in Kentucky of parents who were ex-slaves, Young grew up in Ohio. He entered West Point in 1884, the ninth African American to be appointed to the Academy and only the third to graduate prior to 1936. Encouraged by Lt. George Goethals, an engineering instructor, Young persevered, despite discrimination and academic difficulties, to earn a commission in 1889. Young then went to the west, serving in Nebraska and Utah. In 1894 Young received orders to Wilberforce University in Cleveland where he was a professor of tactics and military science for four years. During the Hispano-American War, Young served with the 9th Ohio Volunteer Infantry and the 9th Cavalry in Utah. The army promoted Young to captain in 1901 and sent him to the Philippines where he served for eighteen months, largely in jungle locations. Young went to Haiti as a military attache (1904–1907), the first African American to serve as an attache. A tour on the War Department General Staff (1907–1908) was followed by another tour in the Philippines (1908–1909) and service in Wyoming (1909–1911). Young served two years as military attache in Liberia (1912–1914) where he helped reorganize the Liberian Frontier Force and Constabulary, was injured by a bullet wound, and caught black water fever that left him greatly weakened. Young also served with Gen. John J. Pershing in the Punitive Expedition to Mexico (1916–1917). Yet in June 1917 when Young took his promotion examination for colonel, he was found physically unfit and sent to Letterman Hospital for more tests. Although the surviving medical evidence indicates Young suffered from high blood pressure and chronic nephritis (Bright's disease), he could not be convinced he was physically unfit for duty. Young retired on June 22, 1917 whereupon he was promoted to full colonel (because the medical standards did not apply). Young subsequently rode by horseback from Ohio to Washington, but he was unable to persuade the army to recall him to active duty until a few days prior to the Armistice in 1918. In 1919 while still on active duty, Young returned to Liberia and in 1922 while on an inspection trip to Nigeria, he died in Lagos of nephritis.

Selected Reading List

As was the case in the antebellum period, much of the literature in the postwar period continues to be concerned with operations of army and navy units. For the army this meant participation in Reconstruction, continued conflicts with the Native Americans in the process of westward expansion, and overseas conflicts. For the navy this meant participation in diplomacy and oceanographic research. The only major change in this area of concern over the past two decades has been in the treatment of the wars with the Native Americans, with recent works expressing more interest in, and sympathy for, the vanquished. These wars are now portrayed more as an embarrassing tragedy than as an exciting and colorful part of our national heritage.

There are two new major issues in the period, however, that are getting attention from historians. The first of these is linked with the change in the nation's image of itself and its legitimate role in world affairs toward the end of the century. This change allowed the armed forces to be seen less as means for continental pacification and security and more as instruments for the deployment of force in pursuit of expanding national interests. This change led both forces to participate in imperialist activities in the Caribbean and the Pacific, including the Hispano-American War and the Philippine-American War. More importantly, it led to an almost revolutionary modernization of the armed forces. Guided by the theoretical conceptions of Alfred Thayer Mahan in the navy and Emory Upton in the army, both forces were transformed in the decades immediately prior to World War I. The navy built steel battleships to contest control of the seas while the army prepared to fight wars of a European character and dimension. While historians were always aware of both changes, they are paying more attention to both. Finally, as is the case in other eras, there is a growing interest in the social history of soldiers and sailors.

Reference

Dawson, Joseph G., III. *The Late 19th Century U.S. Army, 1865–1898: A Research Guide* (1990). Dawson provides an annotated guide to over 1,200 books, articles, dissertations, and sources, topically organized and covering a variety of areas with an emphasis on operations.

Fletcher, Marvin. *The Peacetime Army, 1900–1941: A Research Guide* (1988). Fletcher compiled an annotated guide to nearly 1,000 books, articles and dissertations, organized topically, dealing with the army's activities outside of participation in the First World War.

Activities of Service Forces

The Army in Reconstruction

Dawson, Joseph G., III. *Army Generals and Reconstruction: Louisiana, 1862–1877* (1982). This is a sympathetic study of efforts by generals responsible for occupation to execute the changing programs developed by political leaders in both Washington and Louisiana.

Richter, William L. *The Army in Texas During Reconstruction: 1865–1870* (1987). Richter argues that despite its small size, the army played a major political role in Texas during reconstruction. While it sought to carry out its mission fairly, it often became dictatorial.

Sefton, James E. *The United States Army and Reconstruction, 1865–1877* (1967). This is the leading overall study of the question. Sefton sees the army as having adapted successfully to the requirements of a unique task.

Singletary, Otis A. *Negro Militia and Reconstruction* (1957). Singletary provides a survey of how African American militia units were raised, organized, armed and trained.

The Navy and Diplomacy

Challener, Richard D. *Admirals, Generals, and American Foreign Policy, 1898–1914* (1973). Challener surveys the interests and the impact of the services on the formulation of American foreign policy in this period.

Hagan, Kenneth J. *American Gunboat Diplomacy and the Old Navy, 1877–1889* (1973). Hagan argues that American naval strategy in this period was heavily influenced by the forces and needs of mercantilistic expansionism.

Healy, David. *Gunboat Diplomacy in the Wilson Era: The U.S. Navy in Haiti, 1915–1916* (1976). This is a study of the American intervention in Haiti and the role of naval officers in shaping the policies of that intervention.

Johnson, Robert E. *Far China Station: The U.S. Navy in Asian Waters, 1800–1898* (1979). This is a survey of the operations of the ships on station in the far Pacific from the Opium War to the battle of Manila Bay.

Long, David F. *Gold Braid and Foreign Relations: Diplomatic Activities of U.S. Naval Officers, 1798–1883* (1988). Long presents the stories of a number of instances where naval officers were involved in diplomatic activities in the nineteenth century arranged geographically and chronologically.

O'Connell, Robert L. *Sacred Vessels: The Cult of the Battleship and the Rise of the U.S. Navy* (1991). O'Connell argues in this controversial work that American naval leaders emphasized the development of the modern battleship more because they saw it as a symbol of the traditional structure and values of their profession than for its intrinsic technological superiority as a weapons system.

Still, William N., Jr. *American Sea Power in the Old World: The United States Navy in European and Near Eastern Waters, 1865–1917* (1980). This is a study of the operations of naval units on station in Europe and particularly in the Eastern Mediterranean. As with the case of Johnson above, Still has little interest in policy or the Navy's intervention in diplomacy.

Yerxa, Donald A. *Admirals and Empire: The United States Navy and the Caribbean, 1898–1945* (1991). This is a study of the changing role of the Caribbean in American naval strategic thinking during the first half of the twentieth century.

Native American Wars: Reference and General

Delo, David M. *Peddlers and Post Traders: The Army Sutler on the Frontier* (1992). In his survey of the activities of sutlers, Delo argues that while these entrepreneurs clearly had a corrupting and disruptive impact on the frontier community, their overall contribution was positive in terms of providing services needed to stabilize both military and civilian life on the frontier.

Miller, Darlis A. *Soldiers and Settlers: Military Supply in the Southwest, 1861–1885* (1989). Following recent interest in economic aspects of the army's garrison role in the west, Miller studies its economic impact in the southwest in terms of purchases of supplies.

Selby, John M. *The Conquest of the American West* (1976). This is a popular account from a British perspective of selected aspects of American penetration of the west including explorations, settlements, and military conflicts.

Utley, Robert M. *Frontier Regulars: The United States Army and the Indian, 1866–1890* (1973). This is the leading survey on the subject. Utley is objective, yet sympathetic to the army.

Utley, Robert M. *The Indian Frontier of the American West, 1846–1890* (1984). Utley places army-Native American relations into the broader context of Native American policy and cultural contact and misunderstanding.

Wooster, Robert A. *The Military and United States Indian Policy, 1865–1903* (1988). Wooster argues that the War Department had no coherent system of policies for dealing with the Native Americans nor the institutional mechanism for creating a line of policy.

Native American Wars: The Southwest

Altschuler, Constance W. *Chains of Command: Arizona and the Army, 1856–1875* (1981). This is a descriptive study of the development of the army's organizational structure in the southwest.

Faulk, Odie B. *Crimson Desert: Indian Wars of the American Southwest* (1974). Faulk provides surveys of the tribes of the southwest, the topography of the area, and the organization of the army, followed by narratives of conflicts with the Navaho, Comanche, and Apache.

Faulk, Odie B. *The Geronimo Campaign* (1969). This is an objective narrative of the campaign that led to the surrender of Geronimo.

Haley, James L. *The Buffalo War: The History of the Red River Indian Uprising of 1874* (1976). Haley provides a detailed narrative of the military operations in a war against the Comanche, Kiowa, and Arapaho that led to the clearing of the area for white settlement.

Hoig, Stan. *The Battle of Washita: The Sheridan-Custer Indian Campaign of 1867–69* (1976). Washita was a massacre rather than a battle. Hoig analyzes the campaign that preceded the massacre and attempts to explain the reasons for the army action.

Leckie, William H. *The Military Conquest of the Southern Plains* (1963). Leckie's account represents an earlier view of the wars with the Plains tribes. He examines nine incidents from the period 1867–1874 to provide a sense of the character of the wars.

McNitt, Frank. *Navajo Wars: Military Campaigns, Slave Raids and Reprisals* (1972). McNitt provides a largely military narrative of the maneuvers and engagements in the Navaho wars, which he sees resulting from white encroachment on Navaho lands.

Thrapp, Dan L. *The Conquest of Apacheria* (1967). This is a survey of Apache resistance to Spanish and American encroachments for two centuries with emphasis on the final struggle against the American army.

Trafzer, Clifford E. *The Kit Carson Campaign: The Last Great Navaho War* (1982). This is a study of the military campaigns against the Navaho in the late 1860s with some attention and sympathy given to the Navaho.

Native American Wars: The Central Plains and Far West

Marshall, S. L. A. *Crimsoned Prairie: The Wars Between The United States and the Plains Indians During the Winning of the West* (1972). This is a military history of the operations taken against the tribes on the plains, with emphasis on command on both sides.

Thompson, Erwin M. *Modoc War: Its Military History and Topography* (1971). Thompson provides a detailed chronological narrative of the military operations of the war which he portrays as the result of a tragic clash of cultures.

Native American Wars: Northern Plains

Bailey, John W. *Pacifying the Plains: General Alfred Terry and the Decline of the Sioux, 1866–1890* (1979). Terry is portrayed as a humanitarian officer as concerned with keeping the Sioux safe from white exploitation as in keeping them on the reservations.

Brown, Dee. *Bury my Heart at Wounded Knee: An Indian History of the American West* (1970). Using a large number of direct quotations, Brown presents the Native American perspective of the American conquest of the west.

Gray, John S. *Centennial Campaign: The Sioux War of 1876* (1976). Gray places Custer and the battle of the Little Big Horn in the broader context of the entire campaign.

Hedren, Paul L. *Fort Laramie in 1876: Chronicle of a Frontier Post at War* (1988). This is one of the most recent "fort histories." Hedren uses Laramie's activities during the symbolic year of 1876 to illustrate the wide range of functions served by western forts.

Josephy, Alvin M., Jr. *The Nez Perce Indians and the Opening of the Northwest* (1965). This is a narrative military history of the campaign against Chief Joseph in 1877. Josephy is strongly sympathetic with the Nez Perce and sets the campaign in the context of four decades of white relations with the Native Americans.

Utley, Robert M. *Custer and the Great Controversy: The Origin and the Development of a Legend* (1962). The literature on Custer and the Little Big Horn is massive. This is the best place to start to thread one's way through it.

Utley, Robert M. *The Last Days of the Sioux Nation* (1963). This is an account of Wounded Knee and the end of Sioux resistance against the army placed within a largely Sioux context though not without sympathy for the army.

The Hispano-American War and the Philippine-American War

Cosmas, Graham A. *An Army for Empire: The United States Army in the Spanish-American War* (1969). Cosmas provides a study of the organizational as well as military effort by the army, and argues that the army was more efficient than has commonly been thought.

Dierks, Jack C. *A Leap to Arms: The Cuban Campaign of 1898* (1970). This is a description of the battle of Santiago Bay placed within the context of the entire Cuban campaign.

Foner, Philip S. *The Spanish-Cuban-American War and the Birth of American Imperialism, 1895–1902* (1972). Foner offers a revisionist account of the war pointing to its economic origins and its causal links to the rise of American imperialism.

Gates, John M. *Schoolbooks and Krags: The United States Army in the Philippines, 1898–1902* (1973). Gates argues that the American military pacification of the Philippines was basically benevolent in its outlooks and methods.

Linderman, Gerald F. *The Mirror of War: American Society and the Spanish-American War* (1974). Linderman presents six case studies showing the impact of the war on American society and American response to it.

Linn, Brian M. *The U.S. Army and Counterinsurgency in the Philippine War, 1899–1902* (1989). Linn analyzes the army's counterinsurgency tactics in Luzon and credits the initiative of local American commanders for the overall success of the campaign.

May, Glenn A. *Battle for Batangas: A Philippine Province at War* (1991). May is interested in the impact of the war on American soldiers and Philippine civilians. While he is more interested in the latter, he remains positive toward American soldiers whom he credits with maintaining basically civil relations with the Filipinos.

Miller, Stuart C. *"Benevolent Assimilation:" The American Conquest of the Philippines, 1899–1903* (1982). This is a critical study of the campaign, with conclusions very much in opposition to those of Gates, Linn, and May, although Miller's emphasis is on the American public response to the war.

O'Toole, G. J. A. *The Spanish War: An American Epic, 1898* (1984). This is a popular history of the war that stresses its origins and provides highly detailed descriptions of combat.

Trask, David F. *The War with Spain in 1898* (1981). This is currently considered to be the best scholarly military history of the war. Trask also gives some attention to political events.

Venzon, Anne C. *The Spanish-American War: An Annotated Bibliography* (1990). This is a guide to nearly 1,200 entries including books, articles, dissertations, fiction, and sources, organized by subject.

Welch, Richard E. *Response to Imperialism: The United States and the Philippine-American War, 1899–1902* (1979). This is an analysis of American popular response to and support for the military effort to pacify the Philippines.

The Pacification of Mexico, the Caribbean, and Central America

Healy, David F. *The United States in Cuba, 1898–1902: Generals, Politicians, and the Search for Policy* (1963). In describing the politics of military occupation of Cuba, Healy argues that policy tended to develop more out of circumstances than design.

Millett, Allan R. *The Politics of Intervention: The Military Occupation of Cuba, 1906–1909* (1968). Millett provides a sympathetic analysis of the problems facing American military officers in the occupation and the policies adopted to meet them.

Other Activities and Relationships

Cooling, B. Franklin. *Grey Steel and Blue Water Navy: The Formative Years of the American Military-Industrial Complex, 1881–1917* (1979). Cooling places the birth of the military-industrial complex in the development of a symbiotic relationship between the navy and the American steel industry.

Cooper, Jerry M. *The Army and Civil Disorder: Federal Military Intervention in Labor Disputes, 1877–1890* (1971). Cooper provides an overview of the use of army in labor disputes, arguing that although officers possessed middle-class attitudes towards labor, they minimized violence used.

Ponko, Vincent, Jr. *Ships, Seas, and Scientists: U.S. Naval Exploration and Discovery in the Nineteenth Century* (1974). There have been a number of books written about naval contributions to exploration and scientific research in the nineteenth century. This book provides a survey introduction to the entire area.

Institutional Reorganization and Modernization

Abrahamson, James L. *America Arms for a New Century: The Making of a Great Military Power* (1981). Abrahamson traces the modernization of both the army and the navy in the first two decades of the twentieth century as a response to new perceptions of their role as America became a great industrial power.

Armstrong, David A. *Bullets and Bureaucrats: The Machine Gun and the United States Army, 1861–1916* (1982). Armstrong analyzes the process by which the army adopted the machine gun and the reluctance of the traditionalist bureaus to do so.

Browning, Robert S., III. *Two if by Sea: The Development of American Coastal Defense Policy* (1987). This is a detailed history of the development of American coastal defense policy in the nineteenth century and of the forts upon which it was based.

Chambers, John W. *To Raise an Army: The Draft Comes to Modern America* (1987). Most historians see the modernization of the army to be primarily the work of civilians. Chambers supports this by providing an interpretive study of the intellectual and social origins of the movement that led to the draft legislation of 1917.

Crossland, Richard B. and James T. Currie. *Twice the Citizen: A History of the United States Army Reserve* (1984). This is an official survey of the institutional development of the army reserve organization from 1908 to the present.

Dorwart, Jeffery M. *The Office of Naval Intelligence: The Birth of America's First Intelligence Agency, 1865–1918* (1977). Dorwart surveys the development of ONI noting the slow early development of the agency and its forerunners and emphasizing its rapid growth during the First World War.

Finnegan, John P. *Against the Specter of a Dragon: The Campaign for American Military Preparedness, 1914–1917* (1975). Following the same line as Chambers, Finnegan argues that the preparedness movement was largely inspired by civilians as an outgrowth of progressivism.

Hammond, Paul Y. *Organizing for Defense: The American Military Establishment in the Twentieth Century* (1961). This is an interpretative study of army and navy organizational development in the first half of the twentieth century.

Herrick, Walter R., Jr. *The American Naval Revolution* (1961). Herrick explains the revolution in terms of greater imperialist and commercial interest on the part of the nation as well as the leadership of Benjamin Tracy as Secretary of the Navy.

Logan, John A. *The Volunteer Soldiers of America* (1887). Logan provided the classic case for the idea of the citizen-soldier in America. This idea contrasts sharply with Emory Upton's idea of an army based on professional regulars.

Mahan, Alfred T. *The Influence of Sea Power upon History: 1660–1783* (1890). This is Mahan's classic exposition of the idea of a "Blue Water" navy that became the ideological basis for the modernization of the American navy.

Nelson, Otto L. *National Security and the General Staff* (1946). Nelson provides a detailed survey of the development of overall army organization from the point of view of the general staff since the beginning of the twentieth century.

Pearlman, Michael. *To Make Democracy Safe for America: Patricians and Preparedness in the Progressive Era* (1984). Following the argument that it was civilians who modernized the army, Pearlman analyzes the civilian social movement advocating universal military training in the first two decades of the twentieth century as a counter to growing radicalism and materialism.

Reardon, Carol. *Soldiers and Scholars: The U.S. Army and the Uses of Military History, 1865–1920* (1990). Reardon analyzes the way in which military history was used to educate army officers and conflicts that grew between the army and the historians on the issue.

Shulimson, Jack. *The Marine Corps' Search for a Mission, 1880–1898* (1993). Shulimson's book is a study of the efforts of a small group of Marine officers to find a new role for the corps that would guarantee its continued institutional existence as well as provide a focus for rising military professionalism among marines.

Spector, Ronald H. *Professors of War: The Naval War College and the Development of the Naval Profession* (1977). This is a study of the early decades of the War College and its contribution to the development of the rise of modern professionalism in the service.

Upton, Emory. *The Armies of Asia and Europe* (1878) and *The Military Policy of the United States* (1904). Both books present Upton's arguments in favor of an army based on regulars that became the ideological basis upon which the army modernized itself in subsequent decades.

Social Histories of Soldiers and Others

Billington, Monroe L. *New Mexico's Buffalo Soldiers, 1866–1900* (1991). This is a social history of the life and activities of African American soldiers in New Mexico together with the special problems of racial prejudice these soldiers faced both inside the army and out.

Dunlay, Thomas W. *Wolves for the Blue Soldiers: Indian Scouts and Auxiliaries with the United States Army, 1860–1890* (1982). Dunlay provides an analysis of the motivations for Native Americans joining army units and of their use by the army.

Fletcher, Marvin. *The Black Soldier and Officer in the United States Army, 1891–1917* (1974). Fletcher's social history of African American officers and men in the army emphasizes the problems of dealing with racial prejudice.

Foner, Jack D. *The United States Soldier Between Two Wars: Army Life and Reforms, 1865–1898* (1970). This is a social history of soldiers with special attention given to African Americans and Native Americans in the army.

Fowler, Arlen F. *The Black Infantry in the West, 1869–1891* (1971). Fowler provides an account of the varied activities of the 24th and 25th Colored Infantry regiments.

Jones, Virgil C. *Roosevelt's Rough Riders* (1971). This is a study of the formation and military activities of this famous volunteer unit organized by Theodore Roosevelt and drawing its recruits from all classes and sections of the country.

Leckie, William H. *The Buffalo Soldiers: A Narrative of the Negro Cavalry in the West* (1967). Leckie provides a sympathetic account of the 9th and 10th Cavalry regiments whom he sees as effective despite the many disadvantages they faced.

Rickey, Don. *Forty Miles a Day on Beans and Hay: The Enlisted Soldier Fighting the Indian Wars* (1963). Rickey provides a social history of soldiers in the west in the period 1865–1890. He sees the special sense of physical and social isolation as having a demoralizing impact on them.

Smith, Sherry L. *The View from Officers' Row: Army Perceptions of Western Indians* (1990). Smith argues that officers ameliorated their racist views of Native Americans after personal contact to the point that a certain measure of respect emerged.

Whitman, Sidney E. *The Troopers: An Informal History of the Plains Cavalry, 1865–1890* (1962). This is a popular social history concerned more with the men and organization of the cavalry than with its military engagements.

Wooster, Robert. *Soldiers, Suttlers, and Settlers: Garrison Life on the Texas Frontier* (1987). Wooster provides a topical analysis of soldier life on army posts in Texas between 1848 and 1890.

4

The Unsettled Period: 1915–1941

Uncertainty marked American military and foreign affairs during this period. Events outside the Western Hemisphere drew a reluctant United States into two world wars and in the process altered the place of the armed services in American society. When war broke out in Europe in 1914, the nation had neither the intent nor the military means to intervene. Nonetheless, although largely indifferent to military matters, President Woodrow Wilson confronted a growing demand for military reform and naval expansion. A preparedness movement, led by the likes of Theodore Roosevelt, Elihu Root, and Major General Leonard Wood, clamored for universal military training and an expanded navy. Preparedness supporters did not call for intervention in World War I, but argued that in a world at war an unprepared United States lay at the mercy of the victor. Wilson ultimately responded to the demands for change. He supported congressional leaders in shaping the National Defense Act of 1916, which extended greater federal control over the National Guard, created an Organized Reserve Corps for the army, and increased the regular forces. Wilson also signed the Naval Act of 1916 which committed the nation to creating a navy "second to none."

Meanwhile, Wilsonian diplomacy led to the dispatch of a punitive expedition into Mexico, to catch and punish revolutionary hero and bandit Francisco "Pancho" Villa and to impose order on the revolution. The expedition and further disorders along the border severely taxed the army. Wilson called the National Guard to federal service in June 1916 to reinforce the army along the border. The mobilization went badly and raised further doubts within the army general staff about the value of the guard.

In early 1917, as the last regulars left Mexico and Guardsmen went home, Wilsonian criticism of Germany's submarine warfare led to a break in diplomatic relations and then an American declaration of war in April. Wilson discovered belatedly that the army was ill-prepared to take a place on the Western Front. War with Germany forced the United States to raise a mass army by conscription and organize the home front through large federal agencies to feed and equip that army. Unlike previous wars, military professionals dominated the American Expeditionary Force sent to France. The AEF held no volunteer political generals as the army adopted a thorough training program to shape citizen soldiers in their own image. While American forces did not enter combat in a substantive way until June 1918 their numbers made the final difference in Allied victory. Divisions from the AEF helped stem the tide of the furious German offensives of June and July, and contributed significantly to the successful Allied counteroffensives of late summer and autumn.

At first glance it would appear that American participation in World War I did not affect military policy greatly. The National Defense Act of 1920, an amendment to the 1916 act, rejected general staff requests for a 500,000 man army and universal military training. Instead, the law confirmed the National Guard as the first line reserve, provided for an enlarged army, and established an army reserve of twenty-seven divisions. In the ensuing two decades, however, a fiscally conservative Congress and economic depression denied the War Department the funds necessary to maintain the army and guard at even half the authorized strengths or to organize even one skeleton reserve division.

The navy also suffered postwar reductions. Although authorized by the 1916 Naval Act to create a two-ocean fleet of sixty battleships, the navy saw its dreams dashed at the Washington Naval Conference in 1922. Agreements at the conference set a moratorium on capital ship construction and established ratios of naval strength among the United States, Britain, Japan, France, and Italy. But, in the ensuing years of fiscal conservatism and depression, the navy was denied funds to build ships up to agreed treaty levels. Meanwhile, other conference agreements prevented the United States from building fortified bases on Guam and in the Philippines.

Although many historians see interwar military and naval policies as short-sighted, the armed services were sufficient to serve American foreign policy goals until the mid-1930s. Admittedly, the army lacked the personnel to carry out an effective training program and the money to acquire new weapons or to mechanize its forces. On the other hand, the general staff had learned a great deal during World War I about how to mobilize an army. The staff spent much of its time in the 1920s and 1930s planning for manpower and industrial mobilization, planning which proved of great value in 1940 and 1941. If money was always lacking, nonetheless War Department appropriations in the interwar years were twice that of the prewar era. The National Guard was now permanently established and if it failed to meet army training standards it still provided the outlines of eighteen combat divisions the army otherwise lacked.

Perhaps most importantly, the interwar army offered excellent educational opportunities to a generation of officers who would meet the challenge of the next war. From the branch schools for infantry and artillery, to the Army Air Corps Tactical School, to the Command and General Staff College, to the Army War College, captains, majors, and lieutenant-colonels served as students and instructors. These men developed new tactical ideas and doctrine for weapons and technology which would only become available to them at the end of the period. Their studies at the Army War College taught them to think strategically and to plan operations. If these soldiers were uncertain when and where they might serve their nation next, they were at least intellectually prepared for the event.

The navy managed to cope with its restrictions as well. Limits set by the Washington Conference compelled them to modernize the fleet left to them. Conversion from coal to oil improved ship speed and efficiency. Reliance on plastics and aluminum allowed ship construction improvements under the weight limits set by treaty. Naval research in electronics contributed greatly to advances in radar and radio communications. Although battleship admirals dominated the service, the navy found a place for aircraft carriers within a "balanced fleet" concept which sought to keep as many types of ships active as possible. Throughout the interwar years naval planners focused on the Orange Plan, a longstanding contingency plan which anticipated war with Japan. The Marine Corps, too, considered the probabilities of oceanic warfare. Marines in the 1930s developed theories of amphibious warfare without the benefit of landing craft or much support from their brother sailors. If the Leathernecks lacked the equipment or institutional support to test their theories the ideas were there nonetheless.

The test for American military and foreign policy came after 1937, when first Japan, then Germany challenged the international status quo. Greater uncertainty plagued military and naval planners from 1937 through 1941 than had been the case in 1917. They confronted the dangers of a two-front war yet received little guidance from President Franklin D. Roosevelt on how to plan for such a war. The United States began a gradual buildup with increased naval appropriations in 1937 and 1938, but did not undertake serious mobilization efforts until after war broke out in Europe in 1939.

Even then, the military was compelled to march behind a president who preferred to move to a war footing one step at a time. Still, Congress authorized Roosevelt to federalize the National Guard in late August 1940 and approved peacetime conscription for training purposes a month later. It was then that the effects of two decades of limited defense spending emerged. Navy and army leaders might have a sound grasp of what was needed to be done, but they lacked personnel, training facilities, weapons, and equipment to implement full mobilization immediately. Despite the increasing flow of defense dollars in 1940 and 1941, when the Japanese bombed Pearl Harbor, the United States was only partially mobilized and far from ready to fight a global war. Yet the declaration of war ended the unsettled issue of American involvement in world affairs. A full year would pass before American forces began to contribute to Allied efforts in a substantive way, but the foundations upon which that mighty force was built were developed and maintained during the interwar years.

Chronology

1915

Jan	28	Congress creates a coast guard (merges the Life-Saving Service and the Revenue-Cutter Service)
Mar	3	Congress authorizes a Chief of Naval Operations
Mar	3	Naval Reserve established
Mar	25	F-4 (first submarine to sink)
May	11	William Benson (Chief of Naval Operations)
Jul	28	U.S. forces land Haiti—ends Aug 15, 1934
Aug	10	First Plattsburg (NY) Citizens Camp—ends Sep 16
Aug	15	*Gendarmerie d'Haiti* (Haitian intervention)
Nov	1	First National Guard aviation unit (New York)
Nov	5	First aircraft launched by a catapult from a ship while underway (Henry C. Mustin, USN)

1916

Jan	6	U.S. forces land Cuba—ends Feb 6, 1922
Mar	9	Columbus, NM raided by Mexican nationals
Mar	9	Newton D. Baker (Secretary of War)
Mar	14	Pershing Expedition enters Mexico—ends Feb 7, 1917
Mar	15	Air action—Columbus, NM (Mexican Intervention)
Mar	29	Battle of Guerreo (Mexican Intervention)
Apr	10	Battle of La Joya (Mexican Intervention)
Apr	12	Battle of Parral (Mexican Intervention)
Apr	22	Battle of Tomochic (Mexican Intervention)
May	5	Glen Springs and Boquillas, TX raided by Mexican nationals
May	5	U.S. forces land Dominican Republic—ends Sep 16, 1924
May	9	National Guard units mobilized (AZ, NM & TX)
May	25	Battle of Alamillo (Mexican Intervention)
Jun	3	Army Reserve Officers Training Corps established (Navy, 1926; Air Force, 1946)
Jun	18	Remaining National Guard units mobilized
Jun	21	Battle of Carrizal (Mexican Intervention)

Jun   28   Army Reserve units mobilized
Jul   12   First ship to carry and operate an aircraft completes test
           program (USS *North Carolina*)
Jul   13   First National Guard air unit mobilized (New York)
Aug   15   Naval civilian training cruise—ends Sep 9
Aug   19   Naval Militia mobilized as National Naval Volunteers
Aug   29   Naval Flying Corps & Naval Reserve Flying Corps established
Sep   2   First inter-aircraft radio-telegraphy
Oct   20   USS *Maumee* commissioned (first diesel-powered surface ship)

1917

Feb   28   First aircraft-ground station voice transmission
Mar   19   Navy and Coast Guard women reserves established
Mar   21   First woman non-medical staff in a military service (Loretta
           Walsh, USN)
Mar   22   First Coast Guard aviator (Elmer Stone)
Apr   6   United States declares war on Germany
Apr   19   U.S. forces dispatched to Eureka & Helena, MT (labor unrest)
Apr   20   First flight USN non-rigid airship (DN-1)
Apr   27   1st Marine Aeronautic Company activated
May   1   *Guardia Nacional Dominica* created (Dominican Intervention)
May   4   Destroyer Division Eight arrives Queenstown/Cobh, Ireland
May   8   First anti-submarine operation European Theater (Destroyer
           Division Eight)
May   12   Congress passes Chief of Staff Act
May   18   Congress passes Selective Service Act
May   26   John J. Pershing (Commander in Chief, American
           Expeditionary Forces)
May   28   First operational oil refueling while underway (USS *Maumee*
           and Destroyer Division 5)
Jun   5   First naval aviation unit arrives in France (1st Aeronautical
           Detachment)
Jun   11   U.S. forces dispatched to Butte, MT (labor unrest)
Jun   15   First USA officers' training camps—ends Aug 15
Jun   26   1st Division arrives in France
Jul   12   U.S. forces dispatched to Kingman, Humboldt, Morenci,
           Bisbee, Jerome, Ajo, Ray & Globe, AZ (labor unrest)
Jul   30   Charles Young, USA retires for "medical" reasons
Aug   13   Marine women reserves established
Aug   14   First aerial torpedo launch test
Aug   23   Racial incident in Houston, TX involving 24th U.S. Infantry
Aug   25   Liberty 12-cylinder aircraft engine completes 50-hour endur-
           ance test

Sep 11 U.S. forces dispatched to Chattanooga, TN (labor unrest)
Sep 22 Tasker Bliss (Chief of Staff, USA)
Oct 10 U.S. forces dispatched to Astoria, OR (labor unrest)
Oct 21 1st Division enters front lines
Oct 27 First submarines (K 1, 2, 5, 6) arrive European theater—Ponta
         Delgaga, Azores
Oct 31 U.S. forces dispatched to Damonmound, Sourlake, Goosecreek,
         Humble & Englewood, TX (labor unrest)
Nov   2 U.S. forces dispatched to Vivian, Lewis, Oil City, Mansfield,
         Vinton, Shrevesport, Crichton, Edgerly & Mooringsport, LA
         (labor unrest)
Nov   5 USS *Alcedo* (first warship sunk by German submarine, UC-71)
Nov 17 USS *Nicholson* and USS *Fanning* sink German submarine (U-58)
Nov 18 First naval aviation coastal patrol in European theater
Nov 20 First major campaign involving U.S. forces—ends Dec 4—
         Cambrai
Nov 29 USN Battleship Division Nine arrives at Scapa Flow, UK
Dec   7 U.S. declares war on Austria-Hungary
Dec 11 Execution of alleged participants in Houston racial incident
         (24th Infantry)
Dec 27 First African American regiment lands in France (369th
         Infantry, New York National Guard)

1918

Jan 14 Curtiss HS-1 enters operational service (first USN flying boat)
Jan 21 1st Marine Aeronautical Company arrives Ponta Delgada,
         Azores to undertake anti-submarine operations
Jan 27 American submarines arrive Queenstown (Cobh), Ireland
Feb 18 First operational Air Service unit in the European theater
         (103rd Aero Pursuit Squadron)
Feb 19 Naval Railway Batteries activated (Nos. 1-5)
Mar 16 U.S. forces dispatched to St. Maries, ID (labor unrest)
Mar 19 First naval air victory (Stephen Potter)
Mar 21 Somme Campaign—ends Apr 6
Apr   8 369th Infantry affiliated with French 16th Division
Apr   9 Lys Campaign—ends Apr 27
Apr 14 First air victories (Alan F. Winslow & Douglas Campbell, USA)
Apr 23 First submarine sunk by U.S. aircraft (K.R. Smith & O.E.
         Williams, USN)
May 11 American Expeditionary Force receives U.S. built aircraft
         (DH-4 Liberty)
May 19 Peyton March (Chief of Staff, USA)
May 20 Army aviation separated from Signal Corps

May 24 U.S. forces (USS *Olympia*) land at Murmansk (Russian Intervention)
May 27 Aisne Campaign—ends Jun 5
May 28 Battle of Cantigny—ends May 31
May 31 First air ace (Douglas Campbell, USA)
May 31 Battle of Chateau-Thierry—ends Jun 4
Jun   4 Battle of Belleau Wood—ends Jun 26
Jun   8 Operation to establish North Sea Mine Barrage begins—ends Oct 26
Jun   9 Montdidier-Noyon Campaign—ends Jun 13
Jun 12 First day-bombing raid (96th Bombing Squadron)
Jun 18 First independent operation by lst Gas Regiment, USA
Jul   1 Battle of Vaux
Jul   4 Battle of Hamel
Jul 15 Champagne-Marne Campaign—ends Jul 18
Jul 15 U.S. forces dispatched to Alameda, CA (labor unrest)
Jul 18 Aisne-Marne Campaign—ends Aug 6
Aug   3 U.S. forces land Archangel—ends Jun 27, 1919 (Russian Intervention)
Aug   8 Somme Campaign—ends Nov 11
Aug   8 Battles of Gressaire Wood and Chilpilly Ridge
Aug 15 First night-bombing raid (Night Wing, Northern Bombing Group)
Aug 15 U.S. forces dispatched to Columbus, GA (labor unrest)
Aug 15 U.S. forces land Vladivostok—ends Apr 1, 1920 (Russian Intervention)
Aug 18 Oise-Aisne Campaign—ends Nov 11
Aug 19 Ypres-Lys Campaign—ends Nov 11
Aug 26 War Department General Order (#80) grants Chief of Staff "rank and precedence over all other officers"
Aug 27 Battle of Nogales, TX (border incident)
Aug 28 U.S. Air Service created
Sep   6 Naval Railway Battery fires first barrage—Soissons
Sep 12 St. Mihiel Campaign—ends Sep 16
Sep 12 Dismounted cavalry action—Nonsard (2nd Cavalry)
Sep 12 First combat by armor unit (304th Tank Brigade)
Sep 12 Air action—ends Sep 15—St. Mihiel
Sep 24 First naval aviation ace (David S. Ingalls)
Sep 26 Meuse-Argonne Campaign—ends Nov 11
Sep 26 USCGC *Tampa* sunk by UB 91 (convoy escort)
Oct   1 First aerial combat use electrical bomb release
Oct   2 First use of phosgene gas in support of an American offensive—Bois La Ville
Oct   3 Naval action—Durazzo, Albania

Oct 12   Oxygen tanks authorized for all combat aircraft
Oct 14   First "organized" raid Day Squadron, Northern Bombing
          Group—Thielt Rivy, Belgium
Oct 24   Vittorio Veneto Campaign—ends Nov 4
Nov   3   Battle of Ponte della Delizia, Italy
Nov   6   Last strategic bombing action—Mouzon & Raucourt, France
Nov 11   Armistice signed between Allied/Associated Powers and
          Germany
Nov 11   Battle of Tulgas—ends Nov 14 (Russian Intervention)
Nov 17   U.S. forces dispatched to Winston-Salem, NC (racial unrest)
Dec 30   Battle of Kodish—ends Jan 7 (Russian Intervention)

1919

Jan 19   Battle of Shenkursh—ends Jan 24 (Russian Intervention)
Feb   6   U.S. forces dispatched to Seattle & Tacoma, WA (labor unrest)
Feb   7   U.S. forces dispatched to Butte, MT (labor unrest)
Mar   3   U.S. forces dispatched to Gerard, GA (labor unrest)
Mar 25   U.S. forces land Murmansk—ends Jul 28, 1919 (Russian
          Intervention)
Apr 28   First use free-type back-pack parachute
May   8   First air transit Atlantic Ocean—arrives Lisbon, Portugal May
          27 (Seaplane Division One, USN)
Jul 21   U.S. forces dispatched to Washington, DC (racial unrest)
Jul 22   U.S. forces dispatched to Norfolk, VA (racial unrest)
Sep   3   John J. Pershing (General of the Armies)
Sep 28   U.S. forces dispatched to Omaha, NE (racial unrest)
Oct   2   U.S. forces dispatched to Elaine, AR (racial unrest)
Oct   2   William Reynolds (Captain-Commandant, USCG)
Oct   6   U.S. forces dispatched to Gary, IN (labor unrest)
Oct   6   First radio-telegraph message received from a submarine
          while submerged (H-2)
Oct 26   U.S. forces dispatched to Knoxville, TN (labor unrest)
Oct 27   U.S. forces dispatched to Rock Springs, WY (labor unrest)
Oct 28   U.S. forces dispatched to Knoxville, TN (labor unrest)
Oct 30   U.S. forces dispatched to Helper, UT (labor unrest)
Oct 31   U.S. forces dispatched to Charleston, Beckley & Clothier, WV
          (labor unrest)
Nov   1   Robert Coontz (Chief of Naval Operations)
Nov   1   U.S. forces dispatched to Brownsville, PA (labor unrest)
Nov   3   U.S. forces dispatched to Gallup & Raton, NM (labor unrest)
Nov 20   U.S. forces dispatched to Bayne, WA (labor unrest)
Nov 25   U.S. forces dispatched to Bogalusa, LA (labor/racial unrest)
Nov 30   U.S. forces dispatched to Pittsburg, KS (labor unrest)

Dec 6   U.S. forces dispatched to Sandcoulee, Red Lodge, Roundup &
            Bear Creek, MN (labor unrest)
Dec 7   U.S. forces dispatched to McAlester, OK (labor unrest)

1920

Jan 21   U.S. forces dispatched to Dumas, AR (racial unrest)
Feb 9   U.S. forces dispatched to Lexington, KY (racial unrest)
Feb 25   U.S. forces dispatched to Montessano, WA (civil unrest)
Jun 4   Army Air Service replaces Air Service
Jun 20   John Lejeune (Commandant, Marine Corps)
Jul 26   Vought VE-7 (first American fighter enters operational service,
            USN)
Aug 7   U.S. forces dispatched to Denver, CO (labor unrest)
Aug 28   U.S. forces dispatched to Williamson & Thacker, WV (labor
            unrest)
Nov 28   U.S. forces dispatched to Mingo County, WV (labor unrest)

1921

Feb **   Martin MB-2 (first *American* bomber enters operational service,
            Army Air Service)
Mar **   Orenco D (first *American* fighter enters operational service,
            Army Air Service)
Mar 5   John Weeks (Secretary of War)
Mar 6   Edwin Denby (Secretary of the Navy)
Jul 1   John J. Pershing (Chief of Staff, USA)
Jul 21   German battleship (*Ostfriesland*) sunk with aerial bombs
Aug 25   Treaty ends U.S. participation in World War One
Aug 30   U.S. forces dispatched to Logan, Mingo & Boone Counties, WV
            (labor unrest)
Sep 1   U.S. forces dispatched to St. Albans, WV (labor unrest)
Oct 4   Naval Aircraft Factory PT-1 (first torpedo-attack aircraft enters
            operational service, USN)
Nov 8   U.S. forces assigned to guard mail—ends Mar 16, 1922
Dec 16   USS *Wright* commissioned (first airship tender)

1922

Feb 6   Naval arms limitation treaty signed (Five-Power)
Mar 20   USS *Langley* commissioned (first aircraft carrier)
Jun 19   Army Air Service establishes Model Airways to promote long
            distance flight
Sep 27   First mass aerial torpedo attack on a ship while underway
            (USS *Arkansas*)

Oct   2   Air Service Balloon and Airship School activated Scott Field—
            inactivated Sep 17, 1928
Oct   17   First carrier takeoff (V.C. Griffin, USN)
Oct   26   First carrier landing while underway (G. de C. Chevalier,
            USN)
Nov   18   First catapult launch of an aircraft from a carrier (Kenneth
            Whiting, USN)
Dec   **   Curtiss/Naval Aircraft Factory TS-1 (first purpose designed
            fighter enters operational service, USN)

1923

Jan   15   Army Air Service requires in-flight availability of parachutes
Jan   24   U.S. forces withdraw from Germany
May   2   First non-stop trans-continental flight—ends May 3 (Oakley
            Kelly & John Macready, USAAS)
Jun   27   Army Air Service aircraft uses pipeline in-flight refueling—San
            Diego, CA
Jul   21   Edward Eberle (Chief of Naval Operations)
Oct   10   USS *Shenandoah* commissioned (first rigid airship designed
            and built by USN)

1924

Jan   11   Frederick Billard (Commandant, USCG)
Mar   19   Curtis Wilbur (Secretary of the Navy)
Apr   6   Round-the-world flight—ends Sep 28 (Army Air Service)
Sep   14   John Hines (Chief of Staff, USA)
Nov   11   First night catapult launch of aircraft (D. Kiefer, USN)
Nov   17   First operational carrier joins Battle Fleet (USS *Langley*)

1925

Feb   5   First night carrier landing while underway (H. J. Brow, USN)
Apr   8   First intentional night carrier landing while underway (J. D.
            Price, USN)
Sep   21   President's Aircraft Board (Dwight Morrow) investigates
            military aviation—ends Oct 16
Oct   14   Dwight Davis (Secretary of War)
Oct   28   W. Mitchell court-martial—found guilty Dec 17
Dec   25   Boeing FB-1 (first carrier fighter enters operational service,
            USN)

1926

Jan   8   First flight only U.S. built semi-rigid military airship (RS-1)

May	6	U.S. forces land Bluefields, Nicaragua—ends Jun 5 (USS *Cleveland*)
Jul	2	Army Air Corps replaces Army Air Service
Jul	2	Naval aviators accepted as line officers
Nov	21	Charles Summerall (Chief of Staff, USA)

1927

Jan	6	U.S. forces land Nicaragua—ends May 3, 1933
May	12	*Guardia Nacional* created (Nicaraguan Intervention)
Jul	17	First organized combat dive bombing attack (Nicaraguan Intervention)
Nov	14	Charles Hughes (Chief of Naval Operations)
Dec	19	Army Air Corps Pee Dee River, NC bomb test—ends Dec 24

1928

Jan	6	First combat aerial resupply (Nicaraguan Intervention)

1929

Mar	5	Charles Adams (Secretary of the Navy)
Mar	5	Wendell Neville (Commandant, Marine Corps)
Mar	6	James Good (Secretary of War)
May	8	First test submarine escape device (Momsen lung)
Dec	9	Patrick Hurley (Secretary of War)

1930

Jul	9	Ben Fuller (Commandant, Marine Corps)
Sep	17	William Pratt (Chief of Naval Operations)
Nov	21	Douglas MacArthur (Chief of Staff, USA)

1931

May	27	First full-scale aircraft wind tunnel functional

1932

May	9	First solo aircraft instrument flight (Albert F. Hegenberger, USAAC)
Jun	14	Harry Hamlet (Commandant, USCG)
Jul	28	U.S. forces dispatched to Washington, DC (civil unrest)
Dec	27	Douglas B-7 (first monoplane bomber enters operational service, Army Air Corps)

1933

Mar	4	George Dern (Secretary of War)

Mar   4   Claude Swanson (Secretary of the Navy)
Apr 10   USA assumes control of Civilian Conservation Corps
Jun 15   National Guard constituted army reserve component
Jun 21   Grumman FF-1 (first retractable-undercarriage fighter enters
          operational service, USN)
Jul   1   William Standley (Chief of Naval Operations)

1934

Jan 17   Fleet Marine Force established
Jan 17   Boeing P-26 (first all-metal monoplane fighter enters opera-
          tional service, Army Air Corps)
Feb 19   Army Air Corps authorized to carry mail—ends Mar 10;
          resumes Mar 19—ends Jun 1
Feb 22   Martin B-10 (first all-metal monoplane bomber enters opera-
          tional service, Army Air Corps)
Mar   1   John Russell (Commandant, Marine Corps)
Jun   4   USS *Ranger* commissioned (first purpose designed carrier)

1935

Mar   1   General Headquarters Air Force activated
Oct   2   Malin Craig (Chief of Staff, USA)

1936

Jun 12   First African American USMA graduate since 1889 (Benjamin
          O. Davis, Jr.)
Jun 14   Russell Waesche (Commandant, USCG)
Jun 22   Congress designates Coast Guard as the enforcement arm of
          U.S. laws on the high seas & inland waters
Sep 25   Harry Woodring (Secretary of War)
Dec   1   Thomas Holcomb (Commandant, Marine Corps)

1937

Jan   2   William Leahy (Chief of Naval Operations)
Jun   1   Army Air Corps ends lighter-than-air operations
Aug   2   Republic P-35 (first retractable-undercarriage, enclosed cock-
          pit, single-seat fighter enters operational service, Army Air
          Corps)
Oct   5   Douglas TBD (first all-metal monoplane torpedo plane enters
          operational service, USN)
Dec 12   USS *Panay* sunk by Japanese aircraft—(Nanking) Nanjing,
          China

1939

Jun 23 Coast Guard Reserve established
Aug 1   Harold Stark (Chief of Naval Operations)
Sep 1   George C. Marshall (Chief of Staff, USA)
Sep 6   Neutrality Patrol established in Atlantic Ocean (USN)
Dec 8   Brewster F2A (first monoplane fighter enters operational service, USN)

1940

Jan 2   Charles Edison (Secretary of the Navy)
Jan 23 U.S. Army battalion moved into "combat" solely by aircraft (exercise)
May 14 Congress provides that wartime service will be for "the duration" plus six months
Jul 10 Henry Stimson (Secretary of War)
Jul 11 William Knox (Secretary of the Navy)
Jul 18 First army parachute platoon organized—first battalion activated Oct 2
Aug 27 Congress authorizes president to activate reserves
Sep 5   First military flight Hawaii to Philippines—ends Sep 12
Sep 16 Congress authorizes peacetime conscription (Burke-Wadsworth Act)
Sep 25 U.S. cryptographic group "breaks" code produced by Japanese enciphering machine
Oct 1   First Native American general in USA (Clarence L. Tinker)
Oct 15 Marine Corps Reserve mobilized
Oct 25 First African American general (Benjamin O. Davis)

1941

Mar 22 First African American flying unit operational (99th Pursuit Squadron)
Apr 9   USS *North Carolina* commissioned (first battleship since 1922)
May 21 *Robin Moor* attacked by U-69 (Ger.)
May 22 President F. Roosevelt directs War Department to prepare for an invasion of the Portuguese Azores (Plan GREY)
May 25 USCGC *Modoc* reports location of *Bismarck* (Ger.)
Jun 2   USS *Long Island* commissioned (first escort carrier)
Jun 9   U.S. forces dispatched to Inglewood, CA (labor unrest)
Jun 20 Army Air Forces replaces Army Air Corps
Jul 7   U.S. forces land Iceland
Jul 12 William J. Donovan (Coordinator of Information)

Jul   15   USN authorized to attack any Axis ship approaching a convoy
Jul   19   Tuskegee Institute pilot program established
Jul   26   Philippine armed forces placed under USA command
Aug 18   Congress removes 12-month limitation draftee service
Sep   1   USN authorized to attack Axis ships anywhere in Atlantic
Sep   4   USS *Greer* attacked by U-652 (Ger.)
Sep   27   SS *Patrick Henry* launched (first Liberty ship)
Oct   17   USS *Kearny* attacked by German submarine (U-568)
Oct   31   U.S. forces dispatched to Bendix, NJ (labor unrest)
Oct   31   USS *Reuben James* sunk by German submarine (U-562)
Nov   1   Coast Guard placed under USN control
Nov 10   USCGC *Campbell* assigned convoy escort (first of many such
            operations by USCG)
Nov 21   U.S. forces occupy Dutch Guiana
Dec   1   Communications Security Unit (USN) unable to read Japanese
            naval code (JN-25)
Dec   7   Japanese naval air operation—Pearl Harbor, HI
Dec   7   First Japanese aircraft destroyed—Hawaiian Islands (George S.
            Welch, USAAF)
Dec   8   U.S. declares war on Japan
Dec   8   USS *Wake* boarded by Japanese forces in Shanghai, China (only
            U.S. warship captured intact during WW II)
Dec   8   Japanese aircraft attack Nichols Field—Manila, Philippine
            Islands
Dec   8   First Japanese aircraft destroyed—Philippines (Randall Keator,
            USAAF)
Dec 10   Japanese forces land Philippine Islands—Northern Luzon
Dec 10   First Japanese submarine (I-70) sunk by naval air action (USS
            Enterprise)
Dec 10   Japanese capture Guam
Dec 11   State of war—Germany, Italy, and U.S.
Dec 11   Battle of Wake Island—ends Dec 23
Dec 16   Air ace (Boyd Wagner, USAAF)
Dec 17   Chester Nimitz (Commander in Chief, U.S. Pacific Fleet)
Dec 20   Communications Security Unit (USN) breaks Japanese naval
            code (JN-25)
Dec 20   Ernest J. King (Commander in Chief, U.S. Fleet)
Dec 22   Japanese forces land Philippine Islands—Lingayen Gulf
Dec 22   ARCADIA Conference—ends Jan 14, 1942
Dec 23   U.S. forces move to Bataan Peninsula, Philippines—ends Jan 7,
            1942

Military Operations

PUNITIVE EXPEDITION TO MEXICO (Mar 14, 1916). Following Gen. Francisco "Pancho" Villa's raid on Columbus, New Mexico (March 9), President Woodrow Wilson authorized an expedition to punish the Mexican revolutionary leader. Gen. John J. Pershing's force fought several small engagements at Guerreo (March 29), La Joya (April 10), Parral (April 12), and Tomochic (April 22), but Villa escaped, withdrawing deeper into Mexico. President Venustiano Carranza, meanwhile, objected to the American presence, which numbered over 11,000 troops by June. Discussions by a Joint High Commission avoided a formal state of war, which loomed after clashes between American and Mexican regulars at Mazatlan (June 19) and Carrizal (June 21). Although talks broke down in January, Wilson ordered the withdrawal of the expedition, which was completed by February 7, 1917.

BATTLE OF CANTIGNY (May 28, 1918). This battle was the first offensive operation in the Great War involving American ground forces. Following a rolling barrage, troops of the First Division captured the heights around Cantigny. They then successfully withstood a 72-hour barrage and several German counterattacks. The victory lifted American and Allied morale just as the Germans opened a large offensive against the Chemin des Dames line.

BATTLE OF BELLEAU WOOD (Jun 4, 1918). The Germans' unexpectedly successful attack along the Chemin des Dames front (from Soissons to Reims) stalled in Belleau Wood, near Chateau Thierry, as marines from the fresh American Second Division marched into the line on June 4. The marines, making a frontal assault, fought gallantly but at tremendous cost. They lost more than 5,000 of the 8,000 troops engaged in the battle. Their action stopped the Germans, but fueled a controversy over the wisdom and necessity of a frontal infantry assault on entrenched troops.

BATTLE OF VAUX (Jul 1, 1918). Having stopped the Chemin des Dames offensive at Belleau Woods, American army troops from the Second Division advanced against German troops in the town of Vaux, outside Chateau-Thierry. Their assault worked to perfection. Artillery softened the enemy and units entered the city with clear maps and plans. The attack itself took twenty minutes, at a cost of 46 Americans killed. The incident stood in stark contrast to the costly tactics used by the marines in the Belleau Wood fight.

AISNE-MARNE OFFENSIVE (Jul 18–Aug 2, 1918). The offensive began after an American regiment under Colonel Ulysses Grant McAlexander held out against a German attack on July 15–16. On the 18th, American troops got into line just in time to begin the offensive, which went well the first day but settled into a slow, costly advance. As at Belleau Woods, American troops used frontal attacks to assault machine gun emplacements, with heavy losses. The battle ended in victory, however, when French troops took Soissons on August 2.

SIBERIAN EXPEDITION (Aug 16, 1918). President Woodrow Wilson, who originally protested the Allied invasion of eastern Siberia on April 9, reluctantly sent 10,000 troops to Vladivostok to assist in the evacuation of the Czech Legion. They began to arrive on August 15. Gen. William S. Graves was ordered to protect a stretch of the Trans-Siberian Railroad and scrupulously avoided entanglement in the civil war swirling around the troops. Thirty-six soldiers were killed, but all by bandits. Wilson did not recall the force until January 1920. By April 1, 1920 the evacuation was complete.

ARCHANGEL EXPEDITION (Sep 5, 1918). On September 5, about 4,500 American troops joined British and French troops who had occupied the port for a month. The mission was purportedly to aid Russia, now out of the war and convulsed by revolution. The Americans then joined an Allied expedition to the railroad link at Vyatka, about 600 miles away, to offer the embattled Czech Legion an alternative route out of Russia. Harassed by Bolshevik forces, the expedition halted in mid-October half way to its destination and took up defensive positions. The American troops fought small battles at Tulgas and Kodish, losing about 250 dead. They completed their withdrawal on June 27, 1919.

BATTLE OF ST. MIHIEL (Sep 12–16, 1918). The first independent action by the American army in the Great War occurred here. In four days, 500,000 or so American and 100,000 French troops successfully drove back the Germans, who were battle-weary and already in the process of evacuating the salient around St. Mihiel. Gen. John J. Pershing asserted the victory vindicated his insistence on a separate American force using mobile tactics, but, in fact, the rear support encountered great difficulty in supplying his quickly moving troops.

MEUSE-ARGONNE OFFENSIVE (Sep 26–Nov 11, 1918). Part of a large Allied offensive, Pershing's force overcame logistical difficulties and advanced between the Meuse River and the Argonne Forest. Although enjoying superior numbers, the American assault quickly bogged down against determined German resistance. Problems in supply, too, slowed the assault as they had at St. Mihiel. On October 14, the Americans finally breached the formidable defense-in-depth, the Kriemhilde, but seventeen days behind schedule. The attack then stalled before the Romagne heights. The armistice of November 11 ended the fighting.

BONUS ARMY INCIDENT (Jul 28, 1932). Gen. Douglas MacArthur ordered Gen. Perry L. Miles to assist Washington, DC police in removing "Bonus Army" marchers from condemned buildings along Pennsylvania

Avenue. The marchers sought to convince Congress to pay their World War I bonuses early. Accompanied by cavalry, machine guns, and tanks, the troops fired tear gas to clear the buildings, then herded the marchers towards their shanties on Anacostia Flats. The army cleared the Flats, burning the shanties. MacArthur, with considerable exaggeration, declared that the nation had narrowly averted a revolution.

ATTACK ON PEARL HARBOR (Dec 7, 1941). Admiral Isoroku Yamamoto's brilliant, controversial assault opened when carrier-launched planes attacked on Sunday morning, achieving complete surprise. Adm. Chuichi Nagumo sent two waves, first disabling the airfields, then destroying or damaging eleven warships. But he failed to order a third wave, sparing valuable oil reserves. American aircraft carriers, furthermore, were not in port. It was a great but incomplete victory, which unified American public opinion.

RETREAT TO BATAAN (Dec 22, 1941–Apr 9, 1942). Gen. Masaharu Homma's army landed on the west (December 22) and south (December 24) ends of Luzon. Gen. Jonathan M. Wainwright and Gen. Albert M. Jones slowly retreated from the invasions, moving their American and Filipino troops behind the defenses of the Bataan Peninsula, which they reached on January 7. Supplies ran dangerously low as the Japanese forced them further down the peninsula. Following orders, MacArthur escaped from Corregidor to Australia on March 11, leaving Wainwright to hold out on Corregidor, a small island at the mouth of Manila Bay. On April 9, without consulting Wainwright, Gen. Edward P. King, Jr. ordered his force to surrender, ending the ordeal.

Biographical Notes

ALLEN, HENRY TUREMAN (1859–1930). An 1882 graduate of West Point, Allen saw service in the American West, attache duty in Russia and Germany, and combat in Cuba and the Philippines. Returning to the United States in 1907, Allen took part in the Punitive Expedition in Mexico (1916–1917) before taking command of the 90th Division in August 1917. Allen then took the 90th Division to France in June 1918 where it fought extensively in the Meuse-Argonne offensive. Following the armistice, Allen served as commander of the U.S. occupation forces in Germany. From 1919 to 1923 he executed his responsibilities as military commander and diplomat with skill and success. Allen retired in 1923.

ANDREWS, FRANK MAXWELL (1884–1943). After routine tours of duty following graduation from West Point in 1906, Andrews transferred from the cavalry to the aviation section of the Signal Corps in 1917. Although Andrews went to Europe after the Armistice in 1918, he spent 1920–1923 with the occupation forces in Germany as the head of the air service. Returning to the United States, Andrews held successively more senior aviation posts in the 1920s and 1930s. Following the reorganization of the Army Air Corps in 1935, Andrews became the commander of the newly established General Headquarters Air Force at Langley Field. General Andrews provided the leadership necessary to ready the GHQ Air Force for offensive combat operations prior to World War II. He also played a major role in the development of the B-17 bomber. In 1941 Andrews subsequently became the first American airman to command a theater (Caribbean). From there he held command in the Middle East and in February 1943 served as commander of all U.S. forces in Europe. On May 3, 1943, General Andrews died in an aircraft accident in Iceland.

ANSELL, SAMUEL TILDEN (1875–1954). A graduate of West Point in 1899 and the law school at the University of North Carolina (1904), Ansell served in the Philippines and as attorney before the Federal courts of the U.S. for Puerto Rico and the Philippines. While serving in the Office of the Judge Advocate General in 1917, Ansell received promotion to the temporary rank of brigadier general as the Acting Judge Advocate General because Gen. Enoch H. Crowder was overseeing the draft as Provost Marshal General. For the next two years Ansell sought to address the shortcomings of the Articles of War when applied to an army of four million fighting in Europe. Because many courts-martial at home and overseas meted out excessive sentences and other injustices, Ansell established a board of review and sought other changes to provide soldiers with procedural safeguards similar to those found in civilian criminal law. Ansell resigned from the army in 1919 and publicly advocated Congressional reform of military justice. Some of Ansell's proposals relating to review of serious offenses were incorporated in the National Defense Act of 1920, but his greatest contribution to military jurisprudence was the influence his reform ideas had on the drafting of the Uniform Code of Military Justice after World War II.

BALLOU, CHARLES CLARENDON (1862–1928). A West Point graduate in 1886, Ballou served in the Philippines on four different tours of duty. Following routine duty assignments, Ballou took command of the 92nd Infantry Division, which was made up of African Americans. The 92nd went to France in July 1918 and fought with distinction in the Meuse-Argonne offensive in the Fall of 1918. Ballou briefly commanded the VI Corps along with the 92nd prior to the armistice. He then commanded the 89th Division on occupation duty until early 1919. Returning to the United States, Ballou was involved in the declaration of martial law in Denver following labor unrest in 1920.

BLISS, TASKER HOWARD (1853–1930). Bliss began his education at Bucknell University but graduated from West Point in 1875. He served in various artillery posts until the outbreak of the Hispano-American War. He fought in Puerto Rico and returned to Washington in 1902 to serve on the War College Board as an advisor to the Secretary of War, Elihu Root. There Bliss was involved in the establishment of the army's general staff system. In May 1917 Bliss was appointed assistant to Gen. Hugh L. Scott, the army Chief of Staff. In September Gen. Bliss became Chief of Staff despite being beyond the age of regular retirement. Bliss oversaw the rapid growth of the U.S. Army in World War I and functioned as an effective administrator. Gen. Peyton C. March succeeded Bliss as Chief of Staff in May 1918, but Bliss' service on the Supreme War Council of the Allies and his strong support for President Wilson's League of Nations earned him the assignment as a U.S. delegate to the Versailles Peace Conference in 1919.

BROWNING, JOHN MOSES (1855–1926). Son of a gunsmith, Browning began making guns at an early age. In 1884 he earned a patent for a repeating rifle that he invented. He subsequently designed various weapons for several firearms manufacturers as well as for his own company, which he organized with his brother. Browning designed a machine gun in 1890 that was later manufactured by the Colt company and adopted by the army. Another of his machine guns was used in the Hispano-American War. In World War I the army used his automatic pistol, which was made by Colt, his heavy water-cooled machine gun and his machine guns for airplanes. Browning's 1918 model .30-caliber automatic rifle, known as the BAR, quickly became an army standard. He also developed an air-cooled .30-caliber light machine gun used in World War II. Browning's weapons had an outstanding record for success in combat.

BULLARD, ROBERT LEE (1861–1947). Following graduation from West Point in 1885, Bullard entered the infantry and had a series of routine assignments in the Southwest. He took part in the campaign in Cuba during the Hispano-American War and served in the Philippines (1900–1904). Following additional service in the United States and Cuba, Bullard took command of National Guard forces along the U.S.-Mexican border (1916). From there he went to France in June 1917 as a brigade commander in the 1st Division. Bullard later took command of the 1st Division and on May 28, 1918, his forces mounted the first American divisional offensive of the war at Cantigny, which he captured and held. In July 1918 Bullard was assigned to command the U.S. III Corps, which fought very effectively in the Aisne-Marne (July–August) and Meuse-Argonne (September) offensives against the Germans. When Gen. John J. Pershing organized the Second Army in October, he placed Bullard in command with the temporary rank of lieutenant general. Bullard returned to the United States in May 1919 and retired from the army in 1925.

BUTLER, SMEDLEY DARLINGTON (1881–1940). At the outbreak of the
Hispano-American War, Butler attempted to enlist in the army, but he
later secured a commission in the Marine Corps as a second lieutenant
by misstating his age. He saw no service in Cuba, but Butler then went
to the Philippines and in 1900 took part in the relief of the foreign embassies in Beijing, China, where he twice rescued wounded comrades.
Assignments in Honduras, the Philippines again, Panama, and Nicaragua followed. Butler won his first Medal of Honor during the Mexican
Intervention (1914) and a second in the course of the Haitian Intervention (1915). Butler was acknowledged to be a fine leader of troops in
combat, but he saw no action in France in World War I, where he commanded a training camp. Promoted to brigadier general in 1921, Butler
served as a training-base commander at Quantico, Virginia, and San
Diego, California. When Chinese rebels threatened foreign national and
consular officials in Nanking, China in 1927, Butler led a marine expeditionary force (1927–1929) and tactfully defused a tense situation. Promoted to major general in 1929, Butler was a candidate for commandant
of marines, but he fell out of favor due to his strong personality. Butler
retired in 1931 and ran unsuccessfully for the U.S. Senate in 1932.

CHAFFEE, ADNA ROMANZA JR. (1884–1941). The son of Gen. Adna R.
Chaffee, the young Chaffee went to China with his father before entering West Point. Following graduation in 1906, Chaffee entered the cavalry and saw service in a variety of posts and schools including the Philippines (1914–1916). Chaffee served with distinction with the 81st Division in France during the fighting at St. Mihiel and on the Meuse-Argonne
offensive. After the war, Chaffee held a variety of assignments including a post on the general staff (1927) that involved him in the development of the mechanized striking force, which utilized the tank and other
mobile armor. Called by some the "father of the Armored Force" in the
U.S. Army, Chaffee earned the star of a brigadier general in 1938 and
went on to become Chief of the Armored Force (1940–1941).

CHRISTIE, JOHN WALTER (1865–1944). Christie got his start working with
machines building marine engines in New York City, but had some formal education at Cooper Union. Christie later turned his talents to building and testing automobiles of his own design, and by 1916 entered the
field of military ordnance. He also built a four-wheel-drive truck designed to operate in rugged terrain. During and after World War I,
Christie actively developed tanks and other armored vehicles for the
army. His greatest contribution was the development of a mechanism
that allowed travel with or without tracks by utilizing a single suspension system and larger rubber-tired wheels. Christie also experimented
with amphibious craft in the 1920s, but his tracked landing vehicle was
judged unsuccessful. In 1928 Christie built the M1928 tank, which had

an innovative design with an independent suspension system that permitted the tank to remain more nearly level as it passed over uneven ground. The result was a more stable gun platform and a tank that could go as fast as 43 mph. Christie's tank designs found more favor, however, outside the U.S. and the Soviets made his M1928 design the basis of the BT series of tanks, which evolved into the Soviet T-34 of World War II. The British also bought Christie-built tanks in the 1930s. Despite these successes, Christie died nearly penniless in 1944.

CRAIG, MALIN (1875–1945). Malin Craig went to West Point graduating in 1898. He then saw service in Cuba, China, the Philippines, and San Francisco during the earthquake of 1906. Craig went to France in 1917 as a staff officer in the 41st Division. In January 1918 he became Chief of Staff of the I Corps and held that post throughout the heavy fighting of that year. Following service in occupied Germany, Craig returned to the United States and soon became commandant of the Cavalry School at Ft. Riley, Kansas (1921–1923). By 1926 he was Chief of Cavalry. Craig held a series of posts in the U.S. and Panama before becoming Chief of Staff in 1935. General Craig did much in his nearly four-year term as the army's top officer to modernize its equipment and improve its training. He retired in 1939, but returned to active duty for additional service during World War II.

CROWDER, ENOCH HERBERT (1859–1932). An 1881 graduate of West Point, Crowder entered the cavalry, but began to study law shortly after reporting for active duty. He earned a license to practice in 1884. From 1885–1889 Crowder taught military science at the University of Missouri and received a law degree in 1886. Frontier duty in the Dakotas followed with service as a judge advocate in the Philippines in 1898. At the end of his tour in the Philippines, Crowder began his duties in the judge advocate general's department. He served as an observer in the Russo-Japanese War (1904–1905) and in Cuba (1906–1909) as a staff officer for the provisional governor. He was a delegate to the Fourth Pan-American Conference in 1910. In 1911 Crowder was promoted to brigadier general and made Judge Advocate General. He held that post until he retired in 1923. During those twelve years of service, Crowder oversaw the revision of the Articles of War (1916) and the *Manual for Courts-Martial* and the drafting of the Selective Service Act (1917). He also served as Provost Marshal General and was responsible for implementing the military draft during World War I. Promoted to major general in October 1917, Crowder resisted the efforts of his chief subordinate, Gen. Samuel T. Ansell, to establish review of serious courts-martial offenses in 1917–1919. Crowder subsequently agreed to some modest reforms in the Articles of War of 1920. After his retirement, Crowder served as ambassador to Cuba until 1927.

DAVIS, BENJAMIN OLIVER (1877–1970). Davis was the first African American to attain the rank of general in the U.S. Army. Educated at Howard University, Davis' military career began in 1898 when he received a temporary commission during the Hispano-American War. After the war Davis enlisted in the regular army as a private and subsequently passed an examination in 1901 to win a commission as a second lieutenant in the cavalry. Davis' duty assignments included a tour in the Philippines, teaching military science at Wilberforce and Tuskegee universities, a tour as military attaché in Liberia, and service as an instructor of the 372nd Infantry of the Ohio National Guard. Promoted to full colonel in 1930, Davis took command of a National Guard unit from Harlem in 1938. Davis finally won the star of a brigadier general in 1940. The following year he retired due to his age but was immediately called back to service. In 1942 Gen. Davis went to Europe to assist in easing social tensions in the army. Awarded the Distinguished Service medal, Davis served as an assistant to the Inspector General until he retired in 1948. His son, Benjamin O. Davis, Jr., became a general in the U.S. Air Force.

DE SEVERSKY, ALEXANDER PROCOFIEFF (1894–1974). Born in Russia, De Seversky graduated from the Imperial Naval Academy (1914) and went to aviation training. During World War I, he was one of Russia's air aces despite a crash in 1915 that cost him a leg. In 1917 just before the Russian Revolution, De Seversky left on a mission to the United States where he found a job as a test pilot and consulting engineer to the U.S. Air Service. He subsequently founded his own aviation company, became a naturalized U.S. citizen (1927), and joined the Army Air Corps Reserve. During the 1930s De Seversky developed an all-metal, cantilevered-wing trainer for the army and in 1938 a turbo-supercharged air-cooled fighter plane. This latter aircraft became the prototype for the P-47 Thunderbolt. De Seversky's aviation firm suffered financially despite his numerous contributions to military aviation and in 1939 he left the firm, which then became the Republic Aircraft Corp. De Seversky was always a popular advocate of air power and his comments on the subject did much to awaken the general public as to the wartime potential of the airplane.

DICKMAN, JOSEPH THEODORE (1857–1927). Dickman graduated from West Point in 1881. His early duty assignments were in the West where he took part in the army's effort to capture Geronimo. With the outbreak of the Hispano-American War, Dickman went to Cuba. From there he served in the Philippines, and China under Gen. Adna R. Chaffee. In May 1917 Dickman was promoted to brigadier general and in November he took over the 3rd Infantry Division which went to France in April 1918. Dickman's division fought at Chateau-Thierry and held the Marne crossing against fierce German attacks. This earned the division the nickname "The Rock of the Marne." Dickman subsequently commanded the IV Corps (1918) at St. Mihiel and I Corps in the Meuse-Argonne offensive, and the Third Army (1918–1919) in occupied Germany. He retired in 1921.

DOUGLAS, DONALD WILLS (1892–1981). Douglas attended the Naval Academy from 1909 to 1912, but he transferred to the Massachusetts Institute of Technology in order to study aeronautical engineering. He graduated in 1914 and became an assistant to Jerome C. Hunsaker in the MIT aerodynamics laboratory. Based on Hunsaker's recommendation, the Glenn L. Martin aircraft company hired Douglas as its chief engineer in 1915. In 1920 Douglas formed the Davis-Douglas Company to build aircraft. This firm became the Douglas Aircraft Company in 1928. Under Douglas' leadership, the company produced the streamlined "Cloudster" in 1921 for the Navy, the DWC aircraft for the army (1924), the DC-1 (1932), the DC-3 (1936), the DC-4 (1938), the A-20 Havoc light bomber (1939), the A-24 or SBD Dauntless (1939), the B-19 bomber (1941) the A-26 Invader (1944), DC-6 (1948), and the DC-8 (1959). In 1967 Douglas' company merged with the McDonnell company to form the McDonnell Douglas Corp. Two of Douglas' SWC aircraft made the first successful globe-circling flight in 1924 in 175 days and the DC-3 was the first sleeper-transport plane in commercial use. Modified for military use as the C-47 Skytrain, the DC-3 is one of the most reliable aircraft ever built.

ELLYSON, THEODORE GORDON (1885–1928). Born in Richmond, Virginia, Ellyson graduated from the Naval Academy in 1905. Following various assignments afloat, the navy ordered Ellyson to San Diego for instruction in aviation with Glenn H. Curtiss. As the first naval officer to undergo flight training, Ellyson earned the designation of Naval Aviator No. 1. He was also the first pilot of an airplane to be successfully launched from a catapult on November 12, 1912. Ellyson subsequently served as the executive officer of the naval air station at Hampton Roads, Virginia and was a member of the naval mission to Brazil (1922–1925). Ellyson died in an air accident on February 27, 1928. At the time of his death he held the rank of commander and was serving as the executive officer of the newly-built aircraft carrier USS *Lexington*.

FOULOIS, BENJAMIN DELAHAUF (1879–1967). A pioneer in military aviation, Foulois began his long career with the army in 1898 as a private in the engineers. He rose through the ranks during service in the Hispano-American war and the Philippines, where he earned a commission as a second lieutenant. Foulois then went to the Army Signal School (1906) and then worked with dirigibles (1908). In 1910, after taking a course in piloting by correspondence from Orville and Wilbur Wright, Foulois was able to solo after only about 90 minutes of in-flight training. From 1910 to 1914 he was involved in flight training in Texas and patrolling the Mexican border by air. There he experimented with the use of radio on aircraft. In 1917–1918 Foulois served as Chief of Air Services for the American Expeditionary Force in France. He regularly flew combat missions. In the 1920s Foulois was an air observer and a military attaché in Berlin. From 1931 to 1935 he was Chief of the Army Air Corps with the rank of major general. In that post Foulois sought the construction of a long-range high-speed bomber for the army. The Boeing Company design for what became the B-17 Flying Fortress grew out of Foulois' advocacy.

GRAVES, WILLIAM SIDNEY (1865–1940). An 1889 graduate of West Point, Graves served as an infantry officer at various western posts and in the Philippines. He took part in the relief of San Francisco following the earthquake in 1906 and served on the General Staff in Washington in 1911–1912 and 1914–1918. In August 1918 Secretary of War Newton D. Baker sent Graves to Vladivostok, Siberia in command of a force of about 10,000 U.S. troops whose mission was to protect Allied military stores in depots along the Trans-Siberian Railway. Although Graves was under some pressure to also take some form of action against the Bolsheviks in revolutionary Russia, he resisted this possibility and carefully adhered to his orders. Graves and his men withdrew from Siberia in April 1920. He retired from the army in 1928.

GRUMMAN, LEROY RANDLE (1895–1982). Grumman graduated from Cornell University in 1916, with a degree in engineering. With the outbreak of World War I, he joined the navy and learned to fly (1918). The navy then sent him to M.I.T. (1919) and subsequently assigned him to the Naval Aircraft Factory in Philadelphia as an engineer and test pilot. Grumman left active duty in 1920 and joined the Loening Aeronautical Engineering Corp. as an aeronautical engineer. In 1929 Grumman and two partners formed the Grumman Aircraft Engineering Corp. Aided by navy contracts and the approach of World War II, Grumman built his company into a giant aircraft corporation from a small beginning. The Grumman firm built the F4F Wildcat fighter (and the British version called Martlet), the F6F Hellcat fighter, and the TBF Avenger torpedo bomber. Technical innovations such as retractable landing gear, folding wings, and production efficiency characterized the Grumman firm's operations. In 1946 Grumman became chairman of the board. He retired in 1966.

HARBORD, JAMES GUTHRIE (1866–1947). Harbord graduated from Kansas State Agricultural College (Kansas State University) in 1886 and enlisted as a private in the army in 1889. Commissioned as a second lieutenant two years later, Harbord fought in the Hispano-American War and in the Philippines (1902–1914). Gen. John J. Pershing appointed

Harbord Chief of Staff of the American Expeditionary Force in May 1917. Gen. Harbord commanded the 4th Marine Brigade during the Battle of Belleau Wood (June 1918), the 2nd Division at Soissons, and later took charge of the Services of Supply. Harbord proved to be an aggressive combat commander and an exceptional staff and supply officer. In 1919 Harbord headed the American Military Mission to Armenia under the auspices of the League of Nations. Promoted to major general in 1919, Harbord retired from the army in 1922. The next year he became president of the Radio Corporation of America and in 1930 was appointed chairman of the board. He retired from RCA in 1947.

HINES, JOHN LEONARD (1868–1968). A 1891 West Point graduate, Hines fought in Cuba in the Hispano-American War and in the Philippines (1900–1901 and 1903–1905). Hines served as adjutant to Gen. John J. Pershing in 1916 in the Punitive Expedition to Mexico and as assistant adjutant general for Pershing's American Expeditionary Force in France in 1917. Hines successively commanded the 16th Infantry regiment, a brigade in the 1st Division, the 4th Division at St. Mihiel and Meuse-Argonne (1918), and the III Corps. Hines was the only American commander to lead successively a regiment, brigade, division, and corps in World War I. From 1924 to 1926 Hines served as Chief of Staff. He retired in 1932 and died at the age of one hundred.

KIMMEL, HUSBAND EDWARD (1882–1968). A 1904 graduate of the Naval Academy, Kimmel had various assignments at sea including duty on the battleship *Georgia* during the Battle Fleet's world cruise of 1907–1909. Kimmel was wounded in the occupation of Veracruz, Mexico (1914), served as executive officer of the *New York* in World War I, and moved up through the navy's senior ranks until he earned promotion to rear admiral in 1937. In February 1941 Kimmel became Commander in Chief, U.S. Fleet. The U.S. Fleet (later renamed the Pacific Fleet) was headquartered at Pearl Harbor, Hawaii. As the highest ranking naval officer afloat at the time of the Japanese attack on Pearl Harbor on December 7, 1941, Kimmel received considerable blame for the lack of preparedness and poor response of the naval forces there. A presidential board of inquiry subsequently accused Kimmel of dereliction of duty. Kimmel was suspended from command during the investigation and he subsequently retired in March 1942. A 1944 naval court of inquiry, however, found no mistakes in judgment and a congressional investigation (1945–1946) found mistakes in judgment but no dereliction of duty.

LEJEUNE, JOHN ARCHER (1867–1942). Educated at Louisiana State University and the U.S. Naval Academy (1888), Lejeune spent two years at sea before transferring to the Marine Corps. He participated in the occupation of Puerto Rico (1898–1899), served in Panama (1903–1909), and was the first Marine admitted to the Army War College (1910). Promoted to brigadier general in 1916, Lejeune commanded the only marine brigade in the American Expeditionary France. Lejeune became the first marine officer to command an army division with his appointment to the 2nd Infantry Division in 1918. He became Commandant of the Marine Corps in 1920 and worked vigorously to promote the technical doctrine and techniques of amphibious warfare. Lejeune retired from active service in 1929 to become Superintendent of the Virginia Military Institute (1929–1937).

LIGGETT, HUNTER (1857–1936). Graduating from West Point in 1879, Liggett entered the infantry and served for nearly twenty years in various posts in the American West and South. Service in Cuba and the Philippines during the Hispano-American War (1898–1901) preceded assignments at the Army War College (1910) and a second tour in the Philippines (1915–1917). Ordered to command the 41st Infantry Division (1917) in the American Expeditionary Force in France, Liggert subsequently commanded the I Corps, as part of the French Sixth Army, in a defensive position around Chateau-Thierry. In the summer of 1918 the I Corps was involved in heavy fighting with the German forces in that area and participated in the Second Battle of the Marne. As the Allied armies advanced in the fall of 1918, Liggett took command of Gen. Pershing's First Army along the Meuse River. Following the armistice in November 1918, Liggett's forces participated in occupation duty in France. Gen. Liggett subsequently retired in 1921.

McNAIR, LESLEY JAMES (1883–1944). A graduate of West Point (1904), McNair served in various artillery posts, and participated in the occupation of Veracruz, Mexico in 1914. During 1916–1917 McNair served with Gen. John J. Pershing in the Punitive Expedition in Mexico and on the staff of the General Headquarters, American Expeditionary Forces in France (1917–1919). During the 1920s and 1930s, McNair had a series of assignments involving officer training. In 1940 Gen. George C. Marshall appointed McNair chief of the General Headquarters (later Army Ground Forces). General McNair was responsible for the training of ground combat troops for the army during WW II. His most notable contribution was the introduction of simulated battle conditions as part of the training regime. While observing combat on July 25, 1944, near St. Lo, France, McNair was killed by an American bomb that fell short of its target.

MARCH, PEYTON CONWAY (1864–1955). A graduate of Lafayette College (1884), March entered West Point and was commissioned in the artillery in 1888. He served in a variety of posts in the East and California until 1898 when he took part in the capture of Manila. March participated in the combat operations in the Philippines until 1901. From 1903 to 1907 he served on the Army's General Staff which included duty as an observer with the Japanese army in the Russo-Japanese War. Service on the Mexican border (1916) preceded orders that sent March to France (1917) as commander of artillery in the American Expeditionary Force. In France March organized several field artillery training schools. Recalled to Washington in the spring of 1918, March took over the duties of Chief of Staff from Gen. Tasker H. Bliss. March held the rank of general, only the third U.S. army officer to hold that rank. As chief of staff, he greatly increased the flow of troops to France and oversaw a wide-ranging reorganization of the army. March retired in 1921.

MENOHER, CHARLES THOMAS (1862–1930). Following education at West Point (1886), Menoher served in various posts as an artillery officer. He went to Cuba during the Hispano-American War and then served three tours in the Philippines. From 1903 to 1907 he was a member of the original Army general staff. In World War I, Menoher commanded the School of Instruction for Field Artillery of the American Expeditionary Forces in France and in December 1917 took command of the 42nd (Rainbow) Division, which was involved in the fighting at St. Mihiel and the Meuse-Argonne offensive. In November 1918 Menoher received command of the VI Corps. A short time later, Menoher returned to the United States as Director of the Air Service. Reorganization of the army's air arm in June 1920 separated it from the Signal Corps and made the air service part of the line of the army. Menoher subsequently clashed with his assistant, Col. William Mitchell. Menoher was relieved, at his own request, in October 1921 and retired in 1926.

MITCHELLL, WILLIAM (1879–1936). An outspoken advocate of air power, he resigned from the army following a court-martial for his public criticism of the war and navy departments for what he perceived as their mismanagement of aviation in the national defense. Alfred F. Hurley, *Crusader for Air Power* (1975).

MOFFETT, WILLIAM ADGER (1869–1933). Graduating from the Naval Academy in 1890, Moffett served under Commodore George Dewey in the Battle of Manila Bay (1898). He took part in the occupation of Veracruz, Mexico in 1914, and won a Medal of Honor for his daring in landing a force of marines. Moffett went on to several commands ashore and captained the *Mississippi* (1918–1921). In March 1921 Moffett became chief of the newly formed Bureau of Aeronautics with the rank of rear admiral. During his tenure with the bureau (1921–1933), Moffett organized the naval aviation program, encouraged experimentation with aircraft, equipment, and procedures, and promoted the use of aircraft at sea. A strong supporter of rigid airships (dirigibles), Moffett was very effective in helping the navy to secure appropriations for three airships. On April 4, 1933, Moffett died in the crash of the airship *Akron* during a storm.

NORDEN, CARL LUKAS (1880–1965). Born of Dutch parents in Java, Norden grew up there and in the Netherlands, Germany, and Switzerland. He came to the United States in 1904 and held various engineering positions until 1911 when he joined the Sperry Gyroscope Company. Norden left the Sperry firm in 1915 and subsequently received several engineering contracts from the U.S. Navy. Among his achievements in the 1920s was his development of the arresting gear for the aircraft carriers *Lexington* and *Saratoga*. Throughout the 1920s Norden also worked on the development of a gyrostabilized bomb sight for the navy. In 1928 Norden formed his own engineering company and with the help of Capt. Federick I. Entwistle continued work on his bombsight. By 1931 Norden perfected a bombsight which combined an optical system, a gyro-stabilizing system, and a computer (Mark XV). Norden continued to improve his bombsight during the 1930s. As one of the most highly-kept secrets of World War II, the Norden bombsight was widely used by the U.S. during the war. The bombsight made possible the technique of high-altitude precision bombing and replaced the obsolete Sperry bomb-sight which was much less accurate.

NORTHROP, JOHN KNUDSEN (1895–1981). Northrop gained experience with aviation as a draftsman and mechanic prior to World War I. During the war he served in the Signal Corps in the aviation section. In 1923 Northrop went to work for the Douglas Company. He left the Douglas Company in 1927 and joined the Lockheed Aircraft Company for which he designed the Lockheed Vega. Northrop left Lockheed in 1928 and in early 1932 he formed the Northrop Corporation with backing from Douglas. In 1937 Douglas absorbed the Northrop firm; so two years later Northrop set up a new corporation. There Northrop designed and built a number of aircraft including the P-61 Black Widow which became the army's standard large all-weather fighter in World War II. Northrop is also well-known for his persistence in designing and building the B-35 and B-49 Flying Wings. A flying wing aircraft looked much like a boomerang and lacked a fuselage and tail. The theory behind this design was to minimize drag in the air and to maximize lift for carrying passengers or freight or bombs. Although none of Northrop's flying wings had a long operational life, largely due to technical problems, they laid the foundation for the later B-2 bomber.

O'RYAN, JOHN FRANCIS (1875–1961). Educated at City College of New York and New York Law School, O'Ryan was admitted to the bar in 1898. The year previously he enlisted in the New York National Guard and he rose through the ranks to command of the New York Division in 1912. In 1914 O'Ryan left the practice of law, attended the Army War College, and commanded the 6th New York Division on the Mexican border (1916). When war broke out for the United States in 1917, O'Ryan's division was mobilized as the 27th Division and sent to France in 1918. O'Ryan, at age 42, was not only the youngest general to command a U.S. division for an extended period in World War I, but also the only National Guard officer to remain in such a post throughout the war. O'Ryan's division fought as part of the British Fourth Army in operations along the heavily defended Hindenburg line near St. Quentin in late September and early October 1918. In 1919 O'Ryan returned to New York City and his law practice. He subsequently served as Police Commissioner of New York (1934) and Civilian Defense Director of the State (1941).

PALMER, JOHN MCAULEY (1870–1955). Palmer graduated from West Point in 1892 and began his career with the infantry. Palmer reached Cuba after the hostilities ended during the Hispano-American War, but he did see action with the China Relief Expedition in 1900. From 1901–1906 he taught chemistry at the Military Academy and then saw service in the Philippines (1906–1907). Beginning in 1908 he spent two years at the Army School of the Line and Staff College where he became good friends with George C. Marshall. Palmer then had two years (1911–1912) on the general staff, another tour in China, and then returned to the general staff in 1916 where he helped plan for the American Expeditionary Force that went to France in 1917. Palmer was a major contributor to the legislation that became the Draft Act of 1917. In June 1917 Gen. John J. Pershing selected Palmer as his assistant chief of staff for operations. While in France, Palmer suffered a serious breakdown and went on a diplomatic mission to Italy. In 1918 he returned to France to command the 58th Infantry Brigade of the 29th Division in the fighting around Verdun. In 1919–1920 Palmer was very involved in discussions over army reorganization. He was a principal author of the National Defense Act of 1920, a major piece of legislation for the postwar army. Palmer retired in 1926, but he subsequently returned to active duty and helped frame the Selective Service Act of 1940.

PERSHING, JOHN JOSEPH (1860–1948). He was the commanding general of the American Expeditionary Force (1917–1918) in France during World War I. In 1919 the U.S. Congress made him the first General of the Armies since George Washington. Frank E. Vandiver, *Black Jack: The Life and Times of John J. Pershing* (2 vols, 1977).

REEVES, JOSEPH MASON (1872–1948). An 1894 graduate of the Naval Academy, Reeves entered the navy's engineering corps. He served on the *Oregon* during its famous run from San Francisco to Key West in 1898. The next year Reeves transferred to the line corps and after several more assignments afloat received his first command, the experimental electric-drive collier *Jupiter*. Reeves commanded two different battleships in World War I and was also a naval attaché in Rome (1919–1921). In October 1925 Reeves completed training as an aviation observer and took command of Aircraft Squadrons, Battle Fleet. In that post he helped develop the Navy's carrier forces and to build a trained tactical naval air force. Reeves went on in 1931 to other commands, including commander of the Battle Fleet and Commander in Chief of the U.S. Fleet— the first aviation officer to hold this post. Following retirement, Reeves was recalled to active duty in 1940 and retired again as an admiral in 1946. During World War II he served as a member of the commission that investigated the 1941 disaster at Pearl Harbor.

SCOTT, HUGH LENOX (1853–1934). Scott graduated from West Point in 1876, entered the cavalry, and spent much of the next twenty years in the American West with the 7th Cavalry. He saw plenty of action on the frontier and became knowledgeable in practices and languages of several Native American tribes. In 1897 he was attached to the Bureau of American Ethnology of the Smithsonian Institution, where he prepared a study of Native American sign language. In the Hispano-American War Scott went to Cuba but saw no action. From 1903–1906 he was a military governor in the Philippines. In November 1914 Scott became Chief of Staff and continued to serve in a diplomatic role in dealing with Native Americans and Mexican officials, especially relating to the activities of Pancho Villa in 1916. Scott's involvement with the army's preparations for World War I led to his retention on active duty until 1919. He subsequently served for ten years on the Board of Indian Commissioners.

STARK, HAROLD RAYNSFORD (1880–1972). Educated at the U.S. Naval Academy (1903), Stark served in various assignments afloat and ashore until World War I. From 1917 to 1919 he was an aide to Adm. William S. Sims who was in command of U.S. naval operations in Europe. Following the war Stark progressed through various posts until August 1, 1939 when he became Chief of Naval Operations (CNO). In that post he worked closely with Gen. George C. Marshall in developing a strategy for U.S. forces in the event of war. In the reorganization that followed the Pearl Harbor disaster, Stark took command in early 1942 of the U.S. naval forces in Europe, a largely administrative post. Stark received much criticism for his supposed failure to better inform Adm. Husband E. Kimmel of intelligence data relating to a possible Japanese attack on Hawaii. Stark served out the war in his European post acting as a liaison between U.S. and British naval forces. He retired in 1946.

STIMSON, JULIA CATHERINE (1881–1948). Julia Stimson was educated at Vassar (B.A., 1901), Columbia University (1901–1903), and Washington University (M.A., 1917). She attended the New York Hospital Training School for Nurses (1904–1908), and subsequently served as superintendent of nurses at hospitals in New York and St. Louis. Stimson became a reserve Red Cross nurse in 1909. In 1917 she became chief nurse of American Red Cross Hospital Unit No. 21, which was subsequently attached to British forces in Rouen, France (1917–1918). She later enlisted in the Army Nurse Corps in 1917. Because of her exceptional organizational and administrative skills, Stimson became Chief Nurse of the American Red Cross in France (1918) and later director of the nursing service of the American Expeditionary Force (1918–1919). From 1919 to 1933 Stimson served as dean of the Army School of Nursing and from 1919 to 1937 as superintendent of the Army Nurse Corps. Congress granted nurses "relative" rank in 1920 and Stimson became a major, the first female major in the army. When Congress authorized full commissioned rank to army nurses in 1947, Stimson was promoted to colonel on the retired list (1948).

SUMMERALL, CHARLES PELOT (1867–1955). Summerall graduated from West Point (1892) and entered the infantry before switching to the artillery. Summerall saw action in the Philippines (1899–1900) and in China (1900–1901). Various assignments followed that took him to Alaska, Texas, Pennsylvania, California, and Alabama (1917) as well as the USMA (1905–1911). Summerall served with the American Expeditionary Force (1917–1919) as commander of the 1st Division (July–October 1918) during the Aisne-Marne, St. Mihiel, and Meuse-Argonne actions. In October 1918 Summerall took command of the V Corps. Successive command of the IX and IV Corps followed in 1919 while Summerall was on occupation duty. He also was an adviser to the American delegation at the Versailles peace conference. Summerall later served as Chief of Staff (1926–1930) until he retired in early 1931. From 1931 to 1953 Summerall served as President of The Citadel.

THOMPSON, JOHN TALIAFERRO (1860–1940). Educated at Indiana University and West Point (1882), Thompson served in a succession of artillery posts following graduation. He was chief ordnance officer of the IV corps at Tampa, Florida and in Cuba during the Hispano-American War. Thompson went on to assignments at the arsenals at Rock Island, Illinois and Springfield, Massachusetts (1899–1907) and chief assistant to the chief of ordnance in Washington, DC (1907–1914). In 1914 Thompson retired and became a consultant to the Remington Arms-Union Metallic Cartridge Company. When the United States entered World War I, Thompson returned to active service to supervise the design and manufacture of small arms and ammunition for the army. He redesigned the model 1903 Enfield rifle to take standard .30-caliber ammunition and by the end of the war 2.5 million American Enfields were produced. In 1919 Thompson went back to his consulting business. With the help of John N. Blish, Thompson invented and patented (1920) the Thompson submachine gun, a light, fully automatic weapon firing .45 caliber ammunition with a high degree of reliability. The "tommy gun," as it was called, quickly became a standard weapon for military forces, police, the Federal Bureau of Investigation, and gangsters.

Selected Reading List

The period between 1914 and 1941 in American military history is generally divided into three parts, each of which has its own distinct character. The first of these is the period between 1914 and 1919. This interval is dominated by American concerns with respect to World War I and those conflicts which erupted immediately afterwards. The second, the interwar period between 1919 and 1939, is dominated by the introduction of industrial technology into warfare, especially in the air force and the navy. The third is the prewar period from 1939 to the American entrance into World War II, which is dominated by diplomacy, contingency planning, and Pearl Harbor.

World War I

While Americans remained excited about their experience in the Great War throughout much of the 1920s, this enthusiasm diminished in the 1930s under the impact of rising pacifism and growing skepticism as to the validity of earlier perceptions of the war. Since then, outside of the publication of occasional general histories, there is relatively little interest among American historians about the United States' participation in the war. Moreover, while European historians developed renewed interest in the operational side of the war, the more recent American work deals largely with its social side, particularly its impact on combatants and on the home front. In the latter area, there is some interest in the war as a "modernizing" force in America, as seen in the efforts to mobilize both the economy and the society to meet the needs of a "total war."

Finally, Americans were also involved in several military operations subsequent to the armistice in 1918. Of these, the one attracting the greatest historical interest is the intervention in the Russian Civil War in 1919–1920. However, the books that appear periodically on this topic are often more concerned with the diplomatic side of the intervention than with the military.

Reference and General

Asprey, Robert. *At Belleau Wood* (1965). This is a highly detailed tactical narrative of the stand and final counterattack of the Marines of the 2nd Division. Asprey sees the action playing a major role in halting the Ludendorf offensive.

Coffman, Edward M. *The War to End All Wars: The American Military Experience in World War I* (1968). Coffman describes military planning, organization, and operations as well as the impact of combat on the soldiers, making this the best operational history of American participation in the war.

Cornebise, Alfred E. *Typhus and Doughboys: The American Polish Typhus Relief Expedition, 1919–1921* (1982). Cornebise presents a highly detailed and descriptive survey of the operations of American sanitary units sent to Poland to combat the typhus epidemic raging there as a result of the World War and later Russian Civil War.

Goldhurst, Richard. *The Midnight War: The American Intervention in Russia, 1918–1920* (1978). Goldhurst uses a significant amount of anecdotal material to provide vivid descriptions of all aspects of American participation in the diplomacy and military operations of the intervention.

Halliday, E. M. *The Ignorant Armies* (1960). While critical of the goals of the interventions in Northern Russia in 1918–1919 and of the leadership from Washington, Halliday remains sympathetic to the soldiers as he portrays their military and social activities.

Maddox, Robert. *The Unknown War with Russia: Wilson's Siberian Intervention* (1977). Maddox's work is focused on the diplomatic side of the conflict which he, along with others, assesses critically as providing the seeds of the Cold War.

Marrin, Albert. *The Yanks Are Coming: The United States in the First World War* (1986). Marrin offers a popular and anecdotal combat history of the war with an emphasis on personalities at both the command and enlisted level.

Paxson, Frederic L. *American Democracy and the World War* (3 Vols., 1936–1948). Although Paxson's work is now clearly dated, it is still considered the best multi-volume history of American participation in the war and its impact on society.

Woodward, David and Robert F. Maddox. *America and World War I: A Selected Bibliography of English-Language Sources* (1985). The authors provide a wide-ranging annotated bibliography of over 2,000 books, articles, dissertations, documents, private papers, films, and oral histories topically organized and indexed.

Social Histories

Barbeau, Arthur E., and Florette Henri. *The Unknown Soldiers: Black American Troops in World War I* (1974). The authors' history of the recruitment, training, and combat operations of African American units is focused both on the severe discrimination suffered by the men in those units and on their later admirable performance under fire.

Hewitt, Linda L. *Women Marines in World War I* (1974). This is a brief, topically organized social and pictorial history of those women who became marines in the war.

Patton, Gerald W. *War and Race: The Black Officer in the American Military, 1915–1941* (1981). Despite the dates given in the title, this book deals mostly with the experience of African American officers in World War I and their efforts to win respect and a satisfactory position within the army.

Schneider, Dorothy and Carl. *Into the Breach: American Women Overseas in World War I* (1991). In this survey of the range of activities of the over 25,000 American women who went overseas in World War I, the Schneiders argue that the women were motivated chiefly by idealism and by the desire to be "new women" who used volunteer activities to create a role for themselves in the public sphere.

The Home Front: Industrial and Popular Mobilization

Breen, W. J. *Uncle Sam at Home: Civilian Mobilization, Wartime Federalism, and the Council of National Defense, 1917–1919* (1984). Claiming that voluntarism was still a vital force in America at this time, Breen analyzes the power, composition, and scope of action of the state Councils of National Defense in mobilizing society for war.

Conner, Valerie J. *The National War Labor Board: Stability, Social Justice, and the Voluntary State in World War I* (1983). In a topical analysis of the policies and actions of the board in selected cases, Conner argues that its effectiveness was limited by Wilson's restraint and emphasis on voluntarism.

Cuff, Robert D. *The War Industries Board: Business-Government Relations During World War I* (1973). Cuff analyzes the operations of the War Industries Board in terms of the formulation of its policies and its negotiations with various industries.

Gilbert, Charles. *American Financing of World War I* (1970). Gilbert's book, written for a general audience, provides a detailed and critical analysis of American efforts to raise money for the war.

Gruber, Carol S. *Mars and Minerva: World War I and the Uses of Higher Learning in America* (1975). Gruber analyzes how the government made use of academics in its propaganda efforts and the willingness of those academics to be so used.

Kennedy, David M. *Over Here: The First World War and American Society* (1980). Kennedy makes the most explicit exposition of the argument that the war was a major modernizing force on American society.

Schaffer, Ronald. *America in the Great War: The Rise of the War Welfare State* (1991). Schaffer extends the modernization argument made by others by exploring the impact the sudden extension of government control over many aspects of life had on individuals.

Zimmerman, Phyllis. *The Neck of the Bottle: George W. Goethals and the Reorganization of the U.S. Army Supply System, 1917–1918* (1993). Zimmerman argues that due to internal political struggles in the army, Goethals was never given the authority necessary to make his reorganization of the supply system in World War I a success in terms of actually creating a rational procurement system.

The Interwar Period: 1919–1939

Whether or not modernization is relevant to the study of America's participation in World War I, it is clearly the major force shaping American military development in the interwar period. In all of the armed services the period is dominated by revolutionary developments that were the immediate product of technological change, especially the adaptation of gasoline and diesel engines to military use, and, in the longer term, the result of the increased integration of the military realm of activity into the industrial patterns coming to dominate society. In the navy this led to two revolutions: the introduction of the carrier and naval air power that lifted warfare above the surface of the water, and the rapid further development of submarines which carried it beneath the surface. In the army there were also two revolutions: the development of an air arm that was nearly consumed with the ambition to become an independent service force, and the introduction of the concept of mechanized warfare based on the use of the newly introduced tank. The revolutionary character of these new weapons created enormous tensions within the services as radical proponents of new systems fought conservatives in an effort to reorganize armed forces and reconceptualize traditional approaches to warfare around the new mechanized weapons.

Historical treatment of this period is still quite fragmented with major interest focused on the development of the individual new systems. Air Force history is centered on the development of the air arm as a new service with its own doctrines, while the conflict between the air force's tactical support role and its ambitions to become a strategic force is reflected in histories of the development of each of these divergent portions of the air program. In a similar way, while there is still some interest in naval operations and participation in diplomacy in this period, many naval historians of the interwar period are attracted to the development of carriers and submarines. In regard to the army, on the other hand, historians largely ignore the tank and focus their interest on the issues of concern to army conservatives, such as manpower mobilization and even nostalgic looks at the "Old Army."

The Rise of the Air Force

Copp, DeWitt S. *A Few Great Captains: The Men and Events that Shaped the Development of U.S. Air Power* (1980). Seeing the actions of leaders as critical in the inter- and intra-service fighting that characterized the development of the air force from its earliest days to the beginning of World War II, Copp provides a group biography of those leaders.

Flammer, Phillip M. *The Vivid Air: The Lafayette Escadrille* (1981). With an emphasis on the flyers, and especially the "aces," Flammer provides a history of the squadron from its formation until it was absorbed into the American air service.

Frisbee, John L., ed. *Makers of the U.S. Air Force* (1989). This is a collection of brief biographies of officers who played leading roles in the development of the air force with an emphasis on their success in overcoming obstacles to that development.

Futrell, Robert F. *Ideas, Concepts, Doctrine: A History of the Basic Thinking in the United States Air Force, 1907–1964* (1971). Arguing that air force officers were more situational than theoretical in their way of thinking, Futrell analyzes the evolution of institutional thought within the force as to the appropriate role of air power in warfare.

Greer, Thomas H. *The Development of Air Doctrine in the Army Air Force, 1917–1941* (1955). In contrast to Futrell, Greer sees air force thought as the revolutionary product of a few officers who then struggled against institutional conservatism to get their ideas accepted.

Hallion, Richard P. *Strike from the Sky: The Story of Battlefield Air Attack, 1911–1945* (1989). While Hallion's book deals with the historical development of tactical ground support air operations carried out by the air forces of all major industrial powers, it is still the best book available on American operations in this area.

Holley, Irving B. *Ideas and Weapons: Exploration of the Aerial Weapon by the United States During World War I* (1953). Holley uses the growth of American air power as a case study of the complex interaction of weapons and doctrine. He argues that the pace of the development of weapons is governed by the development of doctrine as to their appropriate application in war.

Hudson, James J. *Hostile Skies: A Combat History of the American Air Service in World War I* (1968). While Hudson gives some attention to the organization and training of the American Air Service, the bulk of his history is devoted to the pilots, the planes, and the activities of both.

Hurley, Alfred F. *Billy Mitchell: Crusader for Air Power* (1964). Hurley's biography focuses on Mitchell's ideas about air power and, especially, on his use of sensationalist tactics to get them accepted.

Jakeman, Robert J. *The Divided Skies: Establishing Segregated Flight Training at Tuskegee, Alabama, 1934–1942* (1992). This is a narrative history of the establishment of the single black air force training unit, the 99th Pursuit Squadron, at Tuskeegee from its founding to the graduation of its first class in 1942. The narrative is set in the context of the larger civil rights struggle in the 1930s and focuses on African American efforts to overcome discrimination in the Army Air Force.

Kelsey, Benjamin S. *The Dragon's Teeth? The Creation of United States Air Power for World War II* (1982). Kelsey offers a highly detailed and episodic analysis of the development of the technological and industrial base in the United States that allowed for the rapid expansion of American air power in World War II.

Maurer, Maurer. *Aviation in the U.S. Army, 1919–1939* (1987). While Maurer's highly detailed descriptive survey of the institutional development of the air force in this period concentrates on the issue of autonomy, it also provides lively portraits of major operations such as carrying the air mail.

Sherry, Michael S. *The Rise of American Air Power: The Creation of Armageddon* (1987). In this history of American strategic bombing from the beginning of the century to the advent of the atomic bomb, Sherry argues that attitudes, and especially what he calls the "armageddon mentality," played a critical role in the development of aerial bombardment.

Sims, Edward H. *Fighter Tactics and Strategy, 1914–1970* (1972). In this survey of American fighter tactics employed in the wars of the twentieth century through Vietnam, Sims places his emphasis on the actions of selected individual aces.

The Navy: Operations—Carriers and Submarines

Caras, Roger A. *Wings of Gold: The Story of United States Naval Aviation* (1965). Caras presents a popular survey of the development of naval aviation, focussing on men, planes, and operations. Nearly half of the book is devoted to the years prior to World War II.

Cole, Bernard D. *Gunboats and Marines: The United States Navy in China, 1925–1928* (1983). Cole describes the efforts of American naval gunboats to protect the lives of Americans in China in the face of policy differences between the State Department and the Asiatic Fleet and the anti-imperialist movement sponsored by the Kuomintang.

Dorwart, Jeffery M. *Conflict of Duty: The U.S. Navy's Intelligence Dilemma, 1919–1945* (1983). This volume continues Dorwart's history of the ONI noted earlier, arguing that the effort to carry on counterespionage alongside traditional intelligence-gathering activities seriously hampered the effectiveness of the Office in both.

Harrod, Frederick S. *The Manning of the New Navy: The Development of a Modern Naval Enlisted Force, 1899–1940* (1978). Harrod argues that by the end of the 1920s the navy successfully recruited and trained a nearly permanent force of technically skilled seamen, a large number of whom were willing to make the navy a career.

Hoyt, Edwin P. *Submarines at War: The History of the American Silent Service* (1983). This popular history emphasizes men, boats, and operations more than institutional development.

Melhorn, Charles M. *Two-Block Fox: The Rise of the Aircraft Carrier, 1911–
    1929* (1974). Melhorn argues that the American carrier program devel-
    oped in the 1920s as a response to America's deteriorating strategic po-
    sition in the Pacific in regard to battleships and cruisers, especially after
    the Washington Conference.

Polmar, Norman. *The American Submarine* (1981). This is a popular history
    of the development of submarines from the earliest developments to
    nuclear-powered boats with the narrative enhanced by over two hun-
    dred photographs.

Reynolds, Clark G. *The Fast Carriers: Forging of an Air Navy* (1968). Reynolds
    provides a descriptive study of the development of the carrier arm of
    the navy with his focus on leadership and the struggle between the battle-
    ship and carrier factions.

Smith, Myron J. *The American Navy, 1918–1941: A Bibliography* (1974). Smith
    compiled over 3,000 entries including books, articles, dissertations, and
    documents in English chronologically organized with occasional anno-
    tation.

Turnbull, Archibald D. and Clifford L. Lord. *History of United States Naval
    Aviation* (1949). While dated, this is still the basic history of the early
    development of naval aviation. The focus of the book is on institutional
    development, with discussion of inter- and intra-service quarrels as well
    as debates within congress.

Vlahos, Michael. *The Blue Sword: The Naval War College and the American
    Mission, 1919–1941* (1980). Vlahos' essay is a complex study of the role
    of the Naval War College in structuring the mentalité of naval officers in
    the interwar period. Vlahos argues that the officers' outlook was a com-
    pound of the existing American ethos and the professional values handed
    down, in part, through the College.

The Army

Bauer, Theodore. *History of the Industrial College of the Armed Forces, 1924–
    1983* (1983). This sixty-year anniversary history of the College focusses
    on the evolution of its mission and institutional program.

Gillie, Mildred H. *Forging the Thunderbolt: A History of the Development of the
    Armored Force* (1947). Despite its age, this is still the only published his-
    tory of the development of American armor during the entire interwar
    period. Gillie sees this development as the result of the efforts of a few
    farsighted pioneers struggling against the conservatives who controlled
    the army.

Griffith, Robert K. Jr. *Men Wanted for the U.S. Army: American Experience
    with an All-Volunteer Army Between the Wars* (1982). Griffith provides an
    examination of the Army's manpower policies in the interwar period
    within the far broader framework of national priorities and defense poli-
    cies.

Holley, Irving B. *General John M. Palmer: Citizen Soldiers and the Army of Democracy* (1982). In this biography, Holley focuses on Palmer's role in developing the army between 1911 and 1925 along democratic "citizen-soldier" lines rather than along the more Uptonian lines of a standing army favored by most army professionals.

Killigrew, John W. *The Impact of the Great Depression on the Army* (1979). Killigrew argues that, as a conservative institution, the army accepted the government's need to reduce expenditures in time of depression, and responded by trying to find ways to save all of its programs rather than remodel itself to optimize defense capability within the limit of resources available.

Kreidburg, Marvin A., and Merton G. Henry. *History of Military Mobilization in the United States Army, 1775–1945* (1955). This is an official history of how ground forces were mobilized in the United States, with the larger part of the book devoted to the development of personnel and industrial mobilization plans during the interwar period.

Lindley, John M. *"A Soldier Is Also a Citizen:" The Controversy over Military Justice in the U.S. Army, 1917–1920* (1990). Lindley examines the largely unsuccessful efforts by General Samuel Ansell to reform the American military justice system by basing it on a citizen's rights rather than on the need to maintain military discipline.

Lisio, Donald J. *The President and Protest: Hoover, Conspiracy, and the Bonus Riot* (1974). Lisio offers a revisionist account of Hoover's role in the march, claiming the president's response to the episode was basically humanitarian and that the violent dispersal of the Bonus Army was carried out by MacArthur in a manner far exceeding Hoover's instructions.

Noble, Dennis L. *The Eagle and the Dragon: The United States Military in China, 1901–1937* (1990). Noble provides a study of the officers and men of all branches who served in China in this period, noting why they applied for such service as well as official duties and extracurricular life.

Truscott, Lucian K. Jr. *The Twilight of the U.S. Cavalry: Life in the Old Army, 1917–1942* (1989). With some attention given to operations, this is basically a social history of the cavalry as it stood recognizably on the eve of a revolutionary modernization.

Vogel, Victor. *Soldiers of the Old Army* (1990). Using a topical organization and drawing to some degree on his own experience, Vogel paints a picture of the training, activities, and social life of the soldiers of the interwar army.

Wilson, Dale E. *Treat 'Em Rough: The Birth of American Armor, 1917–1920* (1989). Wilson provides a history of American tank forces from their birth in World War I until the dissolution of the Tank Corps by the National Defense Act of 1920 with a focus on the critical role played by Patton in the development of organization and doctrine.

The Marine Corps

Mersky, Peter B. *U.S. Marine Corps Aviation: 1912 to the Present* (1983). Mersky offers a narrative of both the institutional development and operational history of the marines' air wing with an emphasis on pilots and planes.

Williams, Robert H. *The Old Corps: A Portrait of the U.S. Marine Corps Between the Wars* (1982). Basing his work substantially on personal experience, Williams presents a social history of the marine corps as it was passing through the difficult transition from a ship security force to an amphibious assault force.

The Prewar Period: 1939–1941

General military histories of the prewar period are concerned with strategic, logistic, and manpower planning, as well as the role of the military in the diplomacy that led up to American intervention in the war. The issue that dominates interest in this period, however, is the attack on Pearl Harbor. There is possibly more written about Pearl Harbor than any other single-day encounter in American military history. As is noted below, the attack now has its own published bibliography of over 1,500 items. The general histories of Pearl Harbor now seem to fall into three categories. Some authors such as Prange and Slackman below treat the attack within the framework of traditional military history, presenting and analyzing events from a largely military point of view. However, American shock at the attack has generated an unsatiated search for villains. As a result, there is also a large corpus of books such as those by Barnes, Toland, and Rusbridger and Nave which treat the attack within the framework of conspiracy theory. These books generally follow the lead of Charles Tansill's diplomatic history, *Back Door to War* (1952), which argues that Roosevelt deliberately provoked the attack to get the country to follow him into a war with Germany. Finally, a few historians such as Albright and Barker have examined Pearl Harbor from the Japanese point of view, arguing that the success of the attack should be seen as the result of intelligent Japanese planning rather than American duplicity or ineptness.

Prewar Military Diplomacy, Planning and Operations

Abbazia, Patrick. *Mr. Roosevelt's Navy: The Private War of the U.S. Atlantic Fleet, 1939–1942* (1975). Abbazia describes the belligerent activities of the Navy in the Atlantic before the declaration of war, claiming that they were intentionally ordered by Roosevelt who tried to develop forms of force without recourse to a formal war that American public opinion would not sustain.

Bailey, Thomas A. and Paul B. Ryan. *Hitler vs Roosevelt: The Undeclared Naval War* (1979). The authors survey all aspects of American prewar naval belligerency in the Atlantic including the destroyers-for-bases deal and Lend-lease arguing that these actions, in part, arose from a personal feud between Roosevelt and Hitler.

Clifford, J. Garry and Samuel R. Spencer, Jr. *The First Peacetime Draft* (1986). This is a study of the efforts of the civilian veterans of the Plattsburg movement to mobilize political support for the draft on the eve of America's entry into World War II.

Fehrenbach, T. R. *F.D.R's Undeclared War, 1939–1941* (1967). Fehrenbach offers a variant of the Roosevelt conspiracy theory, arguing that the president ordered American prewar belligerent activities to draw a reluctant public into a war that he wisely understood was inevitable and in the national interest.

Flynn, George Q. *Lewis B. Hershey: Mr. Selective Service* (1985). While Flynn's biography covers Hershey's entire life, it focuses on his role in the development of selective service prior to and during World War II.

Leutze, James R. *Bargaining for Supremacy: Anglo-American Naval Collaboration, 1937–1941* (1977). This is a study of American and British naval diplomacy at the cabinet and staff level that argues that the relationship between the prospective allies in this area was strained by the primacy each placed on the pursuit of its own national interest.

Watson, Mark S. *Pre-War Plans and Preparations* (1950). While dated, Watson is still the best source on the functioning of the War Department and the Army General Staff and on the preparations and planning carried out by both prior to the war.

Pearl Harbor

Albright, Harry. *Pearl Harbor: Japan's Fatal Blunder* (1988). Albright analyzes the Japanese approach to war, the strategic concepts behind their decision to attack, the planning of the attack and the attack itself, concluding that the Japanese blundered in not following through on their tactical victory to make it strategically decisive.

Barker, A. J. *Pearl Harbor* (1969). This is a narrative of the attack from the Japanese perspective written at a popular level with numerous photographs. The attack is seen as well-planned and well-executed, but a failure since it missed the American carriers.

Barnes, Harry E. *Pearl Harbor After a Quarter of a Century* (1972). This is an extension of Tansill's conspiracy theory that attempts to place the use of Pearl Harbor as a provocation into the larger stream of military planning and diplomacy being developed to carry the United States into a war with Germany.

Bartlett, Bruce R. *Cover Up: The Politics of Pearl Harbor, 1941–1946* (1978). Accepting the Roosevelt conspiracy theory, Bartlett traces what he sees to be the political efforts to cover Roosevelt's action by concerted efforts to place the blame for the attack on the local military commanders, General Short and Admiral Kimmel.

Prange, Gordon. *At Dawn We Slept: The Untold Story of Pearl Harbor* (1981). This is now the best military history of the attack available. It is told from both sides, with an emphasis on personalities, and sees the success of the attack as more of a product of Japanese skill than American ineptness.

Rusbridger, James and Eric Nave. *Betrayal at Pearl Harbor: How Churchill Lured Roosevelt into World War II* (1991). This is a variant of the conspiracy theory with a new devil. Following the lead of Toland and others who see the key to the conspiracy in foreknowledge of the attack based on coded message intercepts, the authors argue that while Roosevelt had no knowledge of the impending attack, Churchill did, since the British were reading the Japanese diplomatic traffic.

Slackman, Michael. *Target Pearl Harbor* (1990). This is a popular history of the attack with emphasis on individual responses and actions at the command and enlisted level.

Smith, Myron J. *Pearl Harbor: A Bibliography* (1991). Smith's bibliography contains over 1,500 entries including books, articles, and sources in ten languages with some degree of topical organization. There is little annotation, but some historiographic introduction as well as a chronology of the attack and the events leading up to it.

Toland, John. *Infamy: Pearl Harbor and Its Aftermath* (1982). Toland offers a newer version of the conspiracy theory in which he argues that the MAGIC intercepts provided leaders in Washington with advanced knowledge of the attack which was kept from the local commanders to allow the Japanese a success that would drive the country to war.

5

The Global Period:
1942–1963

World War II is a defining moment in American military history. Victory over Germany and Japan in 1945 left the United States the greatest military and economic power in the world. However, the war also enhanced the power of the Soviet Union. The inability of Americans and Russians to agree on postwar settlements in Europe and Asia, plus a Communist triumph in the Chinese civil war in 1949, generated a Cold War which persisted for decades. Cold War policies led the nation to adopt military practices unlike any followed during the previous century and a half.

In early 1942, the United States found itself at war in the Pacific Ocean and Europe yet lacking the means to bring its armed power to bear in either theater. In prewar planning and consultations with the British, American strategists concluded that Germany must be defeated first. A strategic defense would prevail toward the Japanese home islands. The Pearl Harbor attack forced a change in the strategy. Unless the Japanese were halted, the United States might well have to withdraw to the North American continent before initiating an offense against Japan.

Still, an operational strategy in either theater could not begin without national mobilization. Until America committed itself to a complete war effort the best it could do was hold the line in the eastern Pacific. The need to mobilize and coordinate efforts with its allies necessitated the creation of agencies to allocate resources, determine material needs, and shape strategic plans. President Franklin Roosevelt oversaw home front mobilization through a myriad of civilian agencies which altered the power of the federal government permanently.

The enormous expansion of American armed forces, coupled with the global expanse of the war, required highly complex and bureaucratic military agencies. British and Americans established the Combined Chiefs of Staff (CCS) in early 1942, composed of military men from ground, sea, and air services of both nations. The CCS planned and directed grand strategy for the two western allies. In the meantime, Roosevelt created the Joint

Chiefs of Staff (JCS), which included the army and navy, and granted the Army Air Force equality with the older services, to direct American planning efforts.

America's industrial might and its geographic location gave it a strategic flexibility none of the other belligerents possessed. It was the only combatant nation to contribute substantively to allied efforts in all the major theaters. While it was impossible for the United States to place substantial units in the China-Burma-India theater, Lend-Lease and air transport were of inestimable value—particularly to the Chinese. Lend-Lease goods, especially trucks and locomotives, also went to aid the Russians on the Eastern front. However, American ground, air, and sea forces dominated in Western Europe after the Normandy landings in June 1944, while the war against Japan in the Western Pacific was largely an American effort.

In the Pacific, the American ability to repair and replace ships, especially the deployment of new carriers, caught the Japanese by surprise. While not discounting the desperate fighting into 1945, in retrospect it can be seen that by late 1943 the United States had gained the initiative against Japan and was advancing towards the home islands in a two-pronged attack led by attack carriers and a remarkable fleet train of logistical and repair ships which revolutionized naval warfare. At the same time, the navy's submarine force decimated Japanese merchant shipping. From late 1944, the United States carried out an increasingly devastating strategic bombing campaign against Japan. Use of the atomic bomb on Hiroshima and Nagasaki in August 1945 at last compelled the Japanese to surrender.

The complexities of allied relations shaped the American effort in the European theater. Controversies surrounding the establishment of a second front tested the coalition from early 1942 through the Normandy landings. From the time the United States entered the war, the Soviets requested that the British and Americans place a ground army in western Europe to fight the Germans as soon as possible. American military planners, notably Army Chief of Staff George C. Marshall, agreed with the Soviet demand for a second front. Unfortunately, the need to divert men and resources to the Pacific early in the war delayed an immediate second front. Disagreements between American and British strategists also affected strategic planning. The British preferred to operate on the periphery, wearing out the Germans with limited ground campaigns and strategic bombing. U.S. Army Air Force leaders endorsed the bombing campaign as well.

In the short run, the British view prevailed, leading to American participation in landings in North Africa in late 1942 and then to indecisive invasions of Sicily and Italy. Only in 1944, as American soldiers and equipment came to dominate the Anglo-American forces, did the general American preference for a direct invasion of France win out. By that time, the Soviets had spent two desperate years fighting the best of the German Army largely on its own.

As in the Pacific, American war production and technological innovation shaped the war. America's ability to produce aircraft for both tactical and strategic purposes, for example, led to the destruction of the Luftwaffe and an unrelenting strategic bombing offensive against Germany. While the part the United States played in the European war did not match its predominance in the Pacific, its role was significant. More importantly, the Anglo-American alliance, despite sharp disagreements over strategy, represented one of the most successful military coalitions ever. British-American relations with the Soviet Union were, however, less successful.

Postwar relations between the Soviet Union and the United States and its Western European allies deteriorated rapidly after 1945. In response to a perceived Soviet threat to American interests, in Europe particularly, and around the world generally, the United States formulated the doctrine of containment. Containment soon took on a strong military element. From the earliest days of the Cold War, the United States based its contingency plans for a possible war with the Soviet Union on the use of atomic weapons. Strategic warfare evolved into the concept of deterrence, that is the assumption that if the enemy knew it faced nuclear devastation it would not initiate general warfare. Once the Soviet Union acquired nuclear weapons in 1949 it too sought to deter its opponent. In the ensuing decades, the two nations competed to develop more destructive nuclear weapons and more effective delivery systems. The shadow of nuclear holocaust haunted Cold War relations for its duration.

Fear of Soviet Communism prompted the United States to abandon its traditional military practices. Although the new policies developed haltingly, by 1950 the break with the past was clear. Approval of the National Security Act of 1947 gave the nation a large, permanent national security apparatus to guide military and security policy. The law made the wartime Joint Chiefs of Staff permanent and created an independent air force. Later modifications established the Department of Defense, and ensured the Secretary of Defense would function as the chief civilian military advisor to the president. In 1948, Congress instituted a peacetime selective service which would endure for a quarter of a century. With the creation of the North Atlantic Treaty Organization in 1949, the United States committed itself to the military defense of Western Europe. Military spending escalated during the Cold War on a scale unthinkable a decade earlier.

But possession of the atomic bomb and a highly productive economy did not give the United States undisputed sway on the international scene. Containment through deterrence did not force the Soviets to abandon their control of the Eastern European nations nor save the Nationalist Government of Jiang Jieshi in China. Neither did it prevent the Communist government of North Korea from invading South Korea in 1950. President Harry Truman's decision to use American military power to preserve South Korea, under the auspices of the United Nations, illustrated both the American capacity to respond to a perceived threat in Asia and the constraints imposed by a policy designed to halt Communist expansion short of general war.

After initial setbacks following American intervention, General Douglas MacArthur's forces virtually destroyed the North Korean army. MacArthur's success, however, prompted China to enter the war. The Truman administration then had to reevaluate its policy in Korea. Fearing a Soviet move into Western Europe while the United States spilled its blood in Asia, Truman and the JCS decided to restrict the conflict to the Korean peninsula and fight a conventional war until the Chinese accepted an armistice. Although the Korean War led to substantial mobilization efforts, a major rearmament program, and a major troop commitment to NATO, the fact that Truman refused to fight to win generated protest at home. In the end, the Korean conflict stumbled to an armistice which left the peninsula, and the U.S., divided.

President Dwight D. Eisenhower came to office in 1953 with the promise to confront Communist aggression more forcefully than had Truman. The potential for mass warfare and Eisenhower's own good sense, however, led to continuity not change. Indeed, Eisenhower reduced defense spending, cut conventional Army forces, and made deterrence the centerpiece of his defense policy. Eisenhower's "New Look," though, fueled an arms race. As the United States created a nuclear triad, with warheads to be delivered from submarines, bombers, and land-based ballistic missiles, the Soviets made every effort to match American strategic weaponry.

At the same time, criticism of the New Look by disgruntled Army leaders, academic policy specialists, and Democratic politicians emerged. These critics depicted massive retaliation as a hollow strategy based on an all-or-nothing approach. Nuclear warfare, in the critic's view, could only be justified if the Soviets directly and immediately threatened America's fundamental well-being. Thus, if confronted by indirect threats from subversion, guerilla war, or military aggression of a regional nature, the United States lacked the means to respond.

Therefore, Eisenhower's critics called for a military policy that embodied a "flexible response." Some suggested that theater and tactical nuclear weapons could be used on a limited basis to match Soviet and Warsaw Pact advantages in conventional forces in Europe and yet avoid all-out nuclear warfare. Others believed larger American conventional ground forces could enforce containment but keep war below the nuclear threshold. Finally, some defense intellectuals contended that Communist subversion and guerilla warfare could be matched by specially trained special forces adept at unconventional, low intensity war.

John F. Kennedy advocated flexible response during the 1960 presidential campaign. Once elected, Kennedy implemented the policy by increasing defense spending, upgrading the intercontinental ballistic missile force, and expanding the Army. Deterrence remained at the heart of American policy, but flexible response appeared to give the United States options to ensure containment along a continuum of violence but remain below the threshold of general or nuclear war.

Kennedy quickly encountered the complexities of great power conflict. His first lesson came in April 1961, when the CIA sponsored Bay of Pigs invasion of Cuba, involving Cuban exiles hoping to oust Fidel Castro, failed miserably. America could not, so it seemed, contain Communism in its own backyard. Nuclear weapons were no option in dealing with Castro and neither was Theodore Roosevelt-style gunboat diplomacy. The Bay of Pigs failure suggested that a none-too-subtle covert operation did not provide the answer either. Kennedy had little choice but to accept defeat and soldier bravely on.

Confrontations with the Soviet Union and its leader Nikita Khrushchev over Berlin, then Cuba, illustrated simultaneously the limits of America's burgeoning power under the Kennedy defense build-up and the possibility that Soviet-American disputes could escalate perilously close to nuclear war. The Berlin crisis of 1961–1962 led Kennedy to institute a partial reserve mobilization to demonstrate American firmness as the Soviets constructed a wall through the divided city. Next, the installation of medium-range Soviet missiles armed with nuclear warheads in Cuba in 1962 precipitated a crisis which genuinely threatened nuclear war. A naval quarantine and last minute personal communications between Kennedy and Khrushchev defused the confrontation. But if the Cuban Missile Crisis tempered Kennedy's confrontational impulses, his administration remained committed to stopping perceived Communist subversion and unconventional war in the Third World.

Unlike its effort in World War II, American military policy during the Cold War years failed to produce total victory. In part that was due to a key element of policy, the avoidance of general war with the Soviet Union. The incessant advances in military technology, from missiles to shoulder weapons, and the multiple defense alliances within the two Cold War power blocs, however, suggested that even conventional warfare offered few promising uses of armed force as an instrument of national policy. The so-called limited war in Korea, for example, generated more than one million military and civilian deaths. Cold War containment fundamentally altered military policy and the place of the military in American society, but an enlarged military did not necessarily ensure American security or allow the nation to freely impose its will in the international arena.

Chronology

1942

Jan   7   Siege of Bataan—ends Apr 9

Jan   9   Combined Chiefs of Staff (U.K. & U.S.) created

Jan   9   U.S. Joint Chiefs of Staff created

Jan 14 First flight Sikorsky R-4 (first helicopter outside Germany placed in series production)

Jan 24 Naval action—Makassar Strait/Balikpapan

Jan 26 U.S. forces land Northern Ireland

Jan 27 USS *Gudgeon* (first submarine to sink a Japanese warship)

Jan 29 USCGC *Alexander Hamilton* torpedoed by U-132

Feb   1   Naval air operation—Marshall/Gilbert Islands

Feb   2   Joseph W. Stilwell designated Chief of Staff to Supreme Commander, China Theater—Jiang Jieshi (Chiang Kai-shek)

Feb 20 First naval aviation ace (Edward O'Hare)

Feb 21 USCGC *Spencer* sinks U-225 (The first of several such engagements.)

Feb 22 Douglas MacArthur ordered to Australia—arrives Mar 17

Feb 27 Naval action—ends Feb 28—Java Sea

Feb 28 Naval action—ends Mar 1—Sunda Straits

Mar   7   Japanese forces land New Guinea

Mar 16 U.S. forces land Australia

Mar 26 Ernest King (Chief of Naval Operations)

Mar 30 Douglas MacArthur (Allied Supreme Commander, Southwest Pacific Area)

Mar 30 Chester Nimitz (Commander in Chief, Pacific Ocean Areas)

Apr 14 COI/OSS Detachment 101 activated (Burma Theater)

Apr 18 Air action—Tokyo

Apr 24 Cryptoanalysis establishes Japanese naval intentions in the South Pacific

May   4   Naval action—ends May 8—Coral Sea/Solomon Sea

May   6   U.S. forces in the Philippines surrender

May 14 Women's Army Auxiliary Corps established

May 16 Oveta Culp Hobby (Director, Women's Army Auxiliary Corps)

May 27 Americal Division activated (only WW II division to bear a name instead number)

Jun   3   Naval action—ends Jun 6—Midway Island

Jun   6   Artillery units authorized attached aircraft (origin of army aviation branch)

Jun   7   Japanese forces land Attu and Kiska—Aleutian Islands

Jun 10 First air & naval anti-submarine operation—ends Jun 13 (U-157 sunk)

Jun 12 Air action—Ploesti, Rumania (also Aug 1, 1943 & Apr 5, 1944)
Jun 22 Joseph Stilwell (Commander U.S. Forces in China, Burma & India Theater)
Jun 22 Japanese naval bombardment—Ft. Stevens, OR
Jun 28 Dwight D. Eisenhower assumes command U.S. forces, Europe
Jul   3 First flight test of a retro-firing aircraft rocket
Jul   6 First flight test of a forward-firing aircraft rocket
Jul   7 First German submarine (U-701) sunk solely by air action (Harry Kane, USAAF)
Jul 13 Office of Strategic Services created (OSS)
Jul 21 Women's Reserve of the Navy established—ends Sep 1, 1946
Aug   3 Mildred H. McAfee (Director, Women's Reserve of the Navy)
Aug   7 U.S. forces land Florida, Gavutu, Guadalcanal, Tanambogo and Tulagi (Solomon Islands Campaign)
Aug   8 Naval action—ends Aug 9—Savo Island
Aug 14 First German aircraft destroyed (Joseph Shaffer & Elza Shahan, USAAF)
Aug 17 Air action—Rouen & Sotteville (Eighth Air Force attacks first European target)
Aug 17 U.S. forces land Butaritari—ends Aug 18—Makin Atoll
Aug 19 U.S. forces land Dieppe
Aug 19 First German fighter aircraft destroyed (Samuel Junkin, Jr., USAAF)
Aug 23 Naval action—ends Aug 25—Eastern Solomons
Aug 26 First marine aviation ace (Marion Carl, USMC)
Aug 30 U.S. forces land Adak—Aleutian Islands
Aug   1 First German submarine destroyed by USCG air action (Henry White, USCG)
Sep   1 First use Naval Construction Battalions (Seabees) in a combat zone
Sep   5 Women's Auxiliary Ferrying Squadron established
Sep   6 Air action—Meaulte (first aircraft losses Eighth Air Force)
Sep 12 Dwight D. Eisenhower (Allied Expeditionary Force, Northwest Africa)
Sep 15 Women's Flying Training Detachment established
Oct 11 Naval action—ends Oct 12—Cape Esperance
Oct 26 Naval action—ends Oct 27—Santa Cruz Islands
Oct 29 Alaska Military Highway opened to traffic
Oct 31 Marine Corps Women's Reserve established—ends Sep 1, 1946
Nov   6 U.S. forces dispatched to Fairport Harbor & Perry, OH (labor unrest)
Nov   8 U.S. forces land Northwest Africa (Operation Torch)
Nov   8 First combat use airborne troops—Oran, Algeria

Nov 12 Naval action—ends Nov 15—Guadalcanal
Nov 19 Battle of Buna—Jan 2, 1943 (New Guinea Campaign)
Nov 23 Coast Guard Women's Reserve established—ends Jun 30, 1946
Nov 24 Dorothy C. Stratton (Director, Coast Guard Women's Reserve)
Nov 30 Naval action—Tassafaronga
Dec 14 First Landing Ship, Tank (LST) commissioned

1943

Jan 5 First aircraft destroyed by proximity fused projectile in combat (USS *Helena*)
Jan 15 Construction of the Pentagon completed
Jan 14 Casablanca conference—ends Jan 23
Jan 27 Air action—Wilhelmshaven (Eighth Air Force attacks first German target)
Jan 29 Naval action—ends Jan 30—Rennell Island
Jan 29 Ruth C. Streeter (Director, Marine Corps Women's Reserve)
Feb 19 Battle of Kasserine Pass—ends Feb 20
Feb 21 U.S. forces land Russell Islands (Solomon Island Campaign)
Mar 1 Air action—ends Mar 4—Bismarck Sea
Mar 21 First woman pilot to die on active duty (Cornellia Fort, WAFS)
Mar 26 Naval action—Komandorski Islands
Apr 15 Sino-American Cooperative Organization activated
Apr 23 First Native American Admiral (Joseph J. Clark)
May 11 U.S. forces land Attu (Aleutian Campaign)
May 12 TRIDENT Conference—ends May 25
May 22 First escort carrier to destroy German submarine (USS *Bogue* sinks U-569)
May 25 U.S. forces dispatched to Mobile, AL (racial unrest)
Jun 21 U.S. forces dispatched to Detroit, MI (racial unrest)
Jun 28 Women's Army Corps established—ends Oct 20, 1978
Jun 30 U.S. forces land Rendova and New Georgia (Solomon Islands Campaign)
Jul 1 Jacqueline Cochran (Director, Women's Airforce Service Pilots)
Jul 5 Women's Airforce Service Pilots established—ends Dec 20, 1944
Jul 6 Naval action—Kula Gulf
Jul 10 U.S. forces land Sicily (Operation Husky)
Jul 10 First combat use amphibious (DUKW) truck—Sicily
Jul 13 Naval action—Kolombangara
Jul 18 Only nonrigid airship (K-74) lost to enemy action (U-134)
Jul 21 *Command and Employment of Air Power* published (FM 100-20)
Aug 6 Naval action—ends Aug 7—Vella Gulf
Aug 14 QUADRANT Conference—ends Aug 24

Aug 15   U.S. forces land Vella Lavella (Solomon Islands Campaign)
Aug 15   U.S. forces land Kiska (Aleutian Campaign)
Aug 17   Air action—Schweinfurt & Regensburg, Germany
Sep   8   Italy surrenders
Sep   9   U.S. forces land Salerno (Italian Campaign)
Oct   6   Naval action—Vella Lavella
Oct 13   Battle of the Winter Line—ends May 23, 1944 (Italian Campaign)
Oct 14   Air action—Schweinfurt, Germany
Oct 27   U.S. forces land Treasury and Choiseul Islands (Solomon Islands Campaign)
Nov   1   U.S. forces land Bougainville (Solomon Islands Campaign)
Nov   2   Naval action—Empress Augusta Bay
Nov 20   U.S. forces land Makin & Tarawa (Gilbert Islands Campaign)
Nov 22   SEXTANT Conference I—ends Nov 26
Nov 25   Naval action—Cape St. George
Nov 28   EUREKA Conference—ends Dec 1
Dec   3   SEXTANT Conference II—ends Dec 7
Dec   5   Air action—Ligescourt, Champagne-les-Hesdin & Saint-Josse (first use North American P-51 as bomber escort)
Dec   8   Battle of San Pietro—ends Dec 21 (Italian Campaign)
Dec 26   U.S. forces land Cape Gloucester—New Britain
Dec 27   USA assumes control of U.S. railroads—ends Jan 18, 1944

1944

Jan   1   Alexander Vandergrift (Commandant, Marine Corps)
Jan   2   U.S. forces land Saidor—New Guinea
Jan 11   Air action—German aircraft industry & air force begins (Operation Pointblank)
Jan 16   Dwight D. Eisenhower (Supreme Commander of the Allied Expeditionary Force)
Jan 22   U.S. forces land Anzio (Italian Campaign)
Jan 31   U.S. forces land Kwajalein (Marshalls Campaign)
Feb 15   Air action—Monte Cassino, Italy
Feb 17   U.S. forces land Eniwetok (Marshalls Campaign)
Feb 18   Naval air action—Truk (first night operation by carrier aircraft)
Feb 24   First use of magnetic airborne detection (MAD) to locate a submerged enemy submarine (U-761)
Feb 26   Navy Nurse Corps accorded temporary commissions
Feb 29   U.S. forces land Admiralty Islands (New Guinea Campaign)
Mar   4   Air action—Berlin
Mar 20   USS *Mason* commissioned (first ship predominantly African American crew)

Apr 22 U.S. forces land Aitape, Tanahmerah Bay & Humboldt Bay (New Guinea Campaign)
Apr 23 First helicopter (YR-4) rescue combat—Burma
Apr 28 Naval action—Slapton Sands (German forces disrupt a practice invasion exercise off British coast)
May 17 U.S. forces land Toem (New Guinea Campaign)
May 18 U.S. forces land Wakde Island (New Guinea Campaign)
May 19 James Forrestal (Secretary of the Navy)
May 21 Air action—French transportation facilities begins (Transportation Plan)
May 27 U.S. forces land Biak (New Guinea Campaign)
May 29 First transatlantic crossing by USN nonrigid airship—ends Jun 1
Jun   4 USS *Pillsbury* seizes U-505 (First enemy vessel captured by boarding since 1815)
Jun   4 U.S. forces occupy Rome
Jun   6 U.S. forces land Normandy (Operation Overlord)
Jun 15 First B-29 attack on Japan from Chinese bases
Jun 15 U.S. forces land Saipan (Mariana Islands Campaign)
Jun 19 Naval air action—ends Jun20—Philippine Sea
Jun 22 Army Nurse Corps accorded temporary commissions
Jun 22 President F. Roosevelt signs Servicemen's Readjustment Act (GI Bill)
Jul   2 U.S. forces land Woemfoor Island (New Guinea Campaign)
Jul 21 U.S. forces land Guam (Mariana Islands Campaign)
Jul 24 U.S. forces land Tinian (Mariana Islands Campaign)
Jul 25 U.S. forces break out from Normandy beachhead (Operation Cobra)
Aug   3 U.S. forces occupy Myitkina (Burma Campaign)
Aug   3 U.S. forces dispatched to Philadelphia, PA (racial/labor unrest)
Aug 13 Battle of the Falaise Pocket—ends Aug 20
Aug 15 U.S. forces land Southern France (Operation Dragoon)
Aug 20 U.S. forces cross Seine River
Aug 23 Battle of Montelimar—ends Aug 28
Aug 25 U.S. forces occupy Paris
Aug 28 First German jet (Me 262) destroyed (Joseph Myers & M. D. Croy, USAAF)
Sep 11 U.S. forces enter Germany
Sep 12 OCTAGON Conference—ends Sep 16
Sep 15 U.S. forces land Morotai (Halmahera Islands Campaign)
Sep 15 U.S. forces land Peleliu (Palau Islands Campaign)
Sep 17 Airborne operation—Holland (Operation Market)
Oct 15 Only German surface ship captured (USCGC *Eastwind* & USCGC *Southwind* seize *Externsteine*, Ger.)

Oct 20   U.S. forces land Leyte (Philippine Campaign)
Oct 23   Naval action—ends Oct 26—Leyte Gulf
Oct 25   First planned suicide attacks by Japanese aircraft on U.S. naval vessels—Leyte Gulf
Nov 24   First B-29 attack Japan from Marianas Islands
Dec 1   First ballistic missile test (Private A)
Dec 15   U.S. forces land Mindoro (Philippine Campaign)
Dec 16   Battle of the Ardennes—ends Jan 28, 1945
Dec 21   Siege of Bastogne—ends Dec 27

1945

Jan 9   U.S. forces land Lingayen Gulf (Philippine Campaign)
Jan 30   ARGONAUT Conference—ends Feb 12
Feb 3   Battle of Manila—ends Mar 3 (Philippine Campaign)
Feb 14   Air action—Dresden, Germany
Feb 19   U.S. forces land Iwo Jima (Bonin Islands Campaign)
Mar 5   Battle of the Rhineland—ends Mar 25
Mar 7   U.S. forces cross Rhine River—Remagen
Mar 9   USAAF initiates incendiary bombing campaign against Japanese home islands
Mar 22   U.S. forces cross Rhine River—Oppenheim
Apr 1   U.S. forces land Okinawa—Ryukyu Islands
Apr 5   Freeman Field, USAAF Incident (racial unrest)
Apr 7   Naval air action sinks *Yamato* (Japan)
Apr 11   U.S. forces reach Elbe River
Apr 23   First combat use of an automatic homing missile (SWOD Mark 9, BAT)
Apr 25   U.S. & U.S.S.R. forces make contact—Torgau, Germany
May 2   German forces in Italy surrender
May 7   Remaining German forces surrender—Reims, France
May 25   Joint Chiefs of Staff approve the Nov 1 invasion of Kyushu Island, Japan (Operation Olympic)
Jun 16   U.S. forces dispatched to Chicago, Illinois (labor unrest)
Jul 16   TERMINAL Conference—ends Aug 2
Jul 30   Largest warship sunk solely by submarine action (USS *Indianapolis*)
Aug 6   Atomic bomb dropped on Hiroshima, Japan (*Enola Gay*)
Aug 9   Atomic bomb dropped on Nagasaki, Japan (*Bock's Car*)
Aug 14   Douglas MacArthur (Supreme Commander, Allied Powers, Japan)
Aug 15   Japanese government announces surrender
Sep 3   Japanese forces in the Philippine Islands surrender
Sep 8   U.S. occupation forces enter Korea

Sep   9   U.S. Military Government, Korea—ends Aug 15, 1948
Sep 27   Robert Patterson (Secretary of War)
Sep 30   U.S. forces land (Tangku) Tanggu (Chinese Civil War)
Sep 30   U.S. forces land (Chinwangtao) Qinhuangdao (Chinese Civil War)
Oct   1   U.S. Military Government, Germany—ends Sep 21, 1949
Oct   6   U.S. forces engage People's Liberation Army (Tientsin) Tianjin
          (Chinese Civil War)
Oct 11   U.S. forces land (Tsingtao) Qingdao (Chinese Civil War)
Oct 18   Intermittent combat U.S. forces and People's Liberation Army—
          ends May 26, 1949 (Chinese Civil War)
Nov   6   Ryan FR-1 (first "all-jet" carrier landing)
Nov 15   Gillem Board Report: *Utilization of Negro Manpower in the Post
          War Army* submitted to the Secretary of War
Nov 19   Dwight Eisenhower (Chief of Staff, USA)
Dec   3   Lockheed F-80 (first jet fighter enters operational service, USAAF)
Dec 15   Chester Nimitz (Chief of Naval Operations)

1946

Jan   1   Joseph Farley (Commandant, USCG)
Apr 25   Air National Guard established
Apr 27   War Department Circular #124 (Gillem Board) issued
May 22   First guided ballistic missile test (WAC Corporal)
Jul   1   Bikini Atoll atomic bomb test (second test Jul 25)
Jul 21   McDonnell FD-1 (first pure-jet carrier landing & takeoff)
Oct 27   MacDill Army Airfield Incident (racial unrest)
Dec 19   Presidential Advisory Commission on Universal Military Train-
          ing

1947

Feb 12   First test of a submarine-launched guided missile (USS *Cusk*)
Mar 31   Selective service ends
Apr 16   Army & Navy Nurse Corps accorded permanent commissions
          in USA/USN
Jul 19   Kenneth Royall (Secretary of War)
Jul 23   McDonnell FH-1 (first jet carrier fighter enters operational ser-
          vice)
Sep 17   Congress creates an air force
Sep 17   Kenneth Royall (Secretary of the Army)
Sep 17   James Forrestal (Secretary of Defense)
Sep 18   W. Stuart Symington (Secretary of the Air Force)
Sep 18   John Sullivan (Secretary of the Navy)
Sep 26   Carl Spaatz (Chief of Staff, USAF)

Oct 14   First faster-than-sound flight (Charles Yeager)
Dec 15   Louis Denfeld (Chief of Naval Operations)

1948

Jan   1   Clifton Cates (Commandant, Marine Corps)
Feb   7   Omar Bradley (Chief of Staff, USA)
Mar 25   Congress authorizes inactive duty pay for USA Organized
          Reserve Corps
Mar 27   Assignment of mission responsibility for Army, Navy and Air
          Force (Key West Conference)
Apr   1   First USN helicopter squadron activated
Apr 26   First USAF fighter exceeds Mach 1 and lands safely (North Ameri-
          can F-86)
Apr 30   Hoyt Vandenburg (Chief of Staff, USAF)
May   5   First carrier-qualified jet squadron activated (VF 17-A)
May 10   USA assumes control of U.S. railroads—ends Jul 9
Jun   2   Women denied duty combat aircraft or any vessel other than
          hospital ship or transport (Women's Armed Services Act)
Jun 12   Congress passes Women's Armed Services Integration Act
Jun 12   Women in the Air Force (WAF) established
Jun 22   Selective service re-established
Jun 26   Berlin Air Lift—ends Sep 30, 1949
Jul 20   First jet transit of the Atlantic
Jul 26   Executive Order 9981 issued (equality of treatment & opportu-
          nity guaranteed for all members of armed services)
Sep 18   Committee on Equality of Treatment and Opportunity in the
          Armed Forces (Fahy Committee) selected
Oct   1   Congress authorizes inactive duty pay Air Force Reserve
Nov **   North American B-45 (first jet bomber enters operational service,
          USAF)

1949

Mar 28   Louis Johnson (Secretary of Defense)
Apr 23   Secretary of Defense cancels construction USS *United States*
          (CVA-58)
May 25   Francis Matthews (Secretary of the Navy)
Jun   3   First African American graduate USNA (Wesley Brown)
Jun 20   Gordon Gray (Secretary of the Army)
Jun 29   U.S. occupation forces withdraw from South Korea
Jul   1   Military Advisory Group, South Korea established
Aug   9   First emergency use of a pilot-ejection seat (J. L. Furin, USN)
Aug 15   Omar Bradley (Chairman, Joint Chiefs of Staff)

Aug 16 J. Lawton Collins (Chief of Staff, USA)
Sep 13 North American AJ-1 (first nuclear-capable carrier aircraft enters operational service)
Sep 21 U.S. High Commissioner for Germany created
Oct   5 Hearings: House Armed Services Committee—ends Oct 21 (revolt of the admirals)
Oct   6 Congress passes Mutual Defense Assistance Act
Nov   1 Forrest Sherman (Chief of Naval Operations)

1950

Jan   1 Merlin O'Neill (Commandant, USCG)
Mar 15 Joint Chiefs of Staff assign USAF responsibility for strategic missile operation/development
Apr 12 Frank Pace, Jr. (Secretary of the Army)
Apr 14 National Security Council Document 68 presented to National Security Council
Apr 24 Thomas Finletter (Secretary of the Air Force)
May   5 Uniform Code of Military Justice established
Jun   1 Ground Observer Corps created (24-hour operation Jul 14, 1952)
Jun 25 North Korea invades South Korea
Jun 25 President H. Truman approves limited air and naval operations in Korea
Jun 26 President H. Truman approves unrestricted air and naval operations in Korea
Jun 27 U.N. Security Council imposes military sanctions against North Korea
Jun 27 First air victory (William G. Hudson, USAF)
Jun 28 First reconnaissance mission by jet aircraft (Bryce Poe II, USAF)
Jun 29 Naval bombardment—Sanchock, Korea (first of many such operations)
Jun 29 Washington press corps labels Korean conflict a "police action"
Jun 30 President H. Truman commits ground forces to the Korean theater
Jul   2 Naval action—Chumunjin
Jul   3 Naval air action—Pyongyang (USS *Valley Forge*)
Jul   3 First naval air victory (L. H. Plog & E. W. Brown)
Jul   5 Battle of Osan
Jul   6 First Mobile Army Surgical Hospital (8055th MASH) arrives in South Korea
Jul   7 Battle of Chonan—ends Jul 8
Jul   8 Douglas MacArthur (Commander in Chief, U.S. Far East and United Nations Command, Korea)

Jul   9   Battle of Choui
Jul 11   Battle of Chochiwon
Jul 13   Air action—Wonson (first strategic air operation)
Jul 13   Walton H. Walker (U.S. 8th Army)
Jul 14   Battle of Kum River & Taejn—ends Jul 20
Jul 26   Battle of Hadong
Aug   2   Battle of Chindong-ni—ends Aug 3
Aug   4   First helicopter medical evacuation—Chindong-ni
Aug   5   Battle of Naktong Bulge—ends Aug 26
Aug 10   Air operation—Rashin (Najin)
Aug 15   Korean Augmentation of the U.S. Army (KATUSA) program
Aug 16   Air operation—Taegu (carpet bombing)
Aug 25   USA assumes control U.S. railroads—ends May 21, 1952
Aug 26   Battle of Pusan Perimeter—ends Sep 10
Sep   1   President H. Truman mobilizes selected National Guard units
Sep   3   Second Battle of Naktong Bulge—ends Sep 5
Sep   5   Battle of Yongchon—ends Sep 13
Sep 13   Naval bombardment—Wolmi-do Island (also Sep 14)
Sep 15   Amphibious assault Inchon (Operation Chromite)
Sep 19   Pusan Breakout Offensive—ends Sep 23
Sep 21   George Marshall (Secretary of Defense)
Sep 26   Inchon force and Pusan force link-up
Sep 29   U.N. forces occupy Seoul
Oct   7   U.N. General Assembly authorizes unification of the two Koreas
Oct 15   Wake Island Conference (MacArthur & Truman)
Oct 19   U.N. forces capture Pyongyang
Oct 20   Airborne assault—Sukchon and Sunchon
Oct 25   U.S. forces land Wonsan
Oct 25   Chinese First Phase Offensive—ends Nov 6
Oct 29   U.S. forces land Iwon
Oct 29   U.S. forces land Chinnampo
Nov   1   First appearance MiG-15 Korean Theater Operations
Nov   2   People's Republic of China acknowledges presence in Korea of
          the *Volunteer Corps for the Protection of the Hydroelectric Zone*
Nov   8   First all-jet aerial combat (Russell Brown, USAF)
Nov   8   Air action—Yalu River bridges
Nov 21   U.S. forces reach Yalu River (Hyesanjin)
Nov 24   U.N. offensive operations resume
Nov 25   Chinese Second Phase Offensive
Dec   1   U.N. forces at Changjin (Chosin) & Pujon (Fusen) Reservoirs
          withdraw to Hungnam—ends Dec 11
Dec   1   MASH units receive helicopters equipped to carry casualties
          (Bell 47)

Dec 3   Wonson evacuation—ends Dec 10
Dec 4   Chinnampo evacuation—ends Dec 6
Dec 5   U.N. forces leave Pyongyang
Dec 5   Largest aeromedical airlift of war (3,925 patients)
Dec 7   Inchon evacuation—ends Jan 5, 1951
Dec 15 Hungnam evacuation—ends Dec 24
Dec 23 Walton Walker killed (U.S. 8th Army)
Dec 26 Matthew Ridgway (U.S. 8th Army)
Dec 31 Chinese Third Phase Offensive

1951

Jan 4   U.N. forces leave Seoul
Jan 15 U.N. offensive (Operation Wolfhound)
Jan 25 U.N. offensive (Operation Thunderbolt)
Feb 5   U.N. offensives (Operations Roundup and Punch)
Feb 11 Chinese Fourth Phase Offensive
Feb 13 Battle of Chipyong—ends Feb 15
Feb 16 Naval siege—Wonson—ends Jun 27, 1953
Feb 21 U.N. offensive (Operation Killer)
Mar 7   U.N. offensive (Operation Ripper)
Mar 14 U.N. forces occupy Seoul
Mar 22 U.N. offensive (Operation Courageous)
Apr 3   U.N. offensive (Operation Rugged)
Apr 6   President H. Truman transfers control of atomic bombs from AEC
         to USAF
Apr 6   U.N. offensive (Operation Dauntless)
Apr 11 Douglas MacArthur relieved of command
Apr 11 Matthew Ridgway (Commander in Chief, U.S. Far East and
         United Nations Command, Korea)
Apr 14 James Van Fleet (U.S. 8th Army)
Apr 22 Chinese Fifth Phase Offensive
May 1   Naval air action—Hwachon Dam (only use of aerial torpedoes
         in Korean War)
May 3   Hearings: Senate Foreign Relations & Armed Services
         Committees—ends Jun 25 (MacArthur Hearings)
May 15 Chinese Fifth Phase Offensive renewed
May 18 Initial deployment to Japan of the 136th Fighter Bomber Wing
         (first participation of an air guard unit in the Korean War)
May 20 First jet ace (James Jabara, USAF)
May 22 U.N. offensive
May 31 Air interdiction campaign (Operation Strangle)
Jul 10 Armistice negotiations begin—Kaesong

Jul   14   Boeing KC-97 (first aerial tanker enters operational service, USAF)
Jul   31   Dan Kimball (Secretary of the Navy)
Aug 16   William Fechteler (Chief of Naval Operations)
Aug 18   Battle of Bloody Ridge—ends Sep 5
Aug 23   Armistice negotiations suspended—Kaesong
Aug 25   Air operation—Rashin (Najin)
Sep   13   Battle of Heartbreak Ridge—ends Oct 15
Sep   17   Robert Lovett (Secretary of Defense)
Sep   18   First meeting Defense Advisory Committee on Women in the Services
Sep   21   First helicopter lift of a combat unit (Operation Summit)
Oct   3   First USN helicopter anti-submarine squadron activated
Oct   24   Air operation—Namsi (largest air engagement of the Korean War)
Oct   25   Armistice negotiations resume—Panmunjom
Nov 12   U.N. forces cease offensive operations
Dec   15   Civil Reserve Air Fleet authorized (Depts of Commerce & Defense)

1952

Jan   1   Lemuel Shepherd (Commandant, Marine Corps)
Feb   18   Battle of Koje-do Island (dissident Korean POWs)
Mar   3   Air interdiction campaign (Operation Saturate)
May   1   Atomic-capable B-45A's arrive U.K.—deployment complete Jun 12
May   6   Germ warfare "confessions" by U.S. pilots appear in *Pravda* (Moscow, U.S.S.R.)
May   7   Second Battle of Koje-do Island—ends Jun 10 (dissident Korean POWs)
May   12   Mark Clark (Commander in Chief, U.S. Far East and United Nations Command, Korea)
Jun   20   Congress establishes force limits for the USMC (Douglas-Mansfield Act)
Jun   23   Air operation—Suiho
Jun   26   Battle of Old Baldy—ends Mar 26, 1953
Jul   9   Congress passes Armed Forces Reserve Act
Aug 27   Air operation—Pyongyang
Oct   14   Battle of Triangle Hill—ends Nov 5
Oct   26   Battle of the Hook—ends Oct 27
Nov   1   First hydrogen bomb test—Eniwetok
Dec   **   USS *Antietam* completes conversion (first angled flight deck carrier)

Dec   9   Air operation—Rashin (Najin)
Dec 16   First USAF helicopter squadron activated

1953

Jan 12   First landing on a carrier with an angled flight deck
          (S. G. Mitchell, USN)
Jan 28   Charles Wilson (Secretary of Defense)
Feb   4   Robert Anderson (Secretary of the Navy)
Feb   4   Robert Stevens (Secretary of the Army)
Feb   5   Harold Talbott (Secretary of the Air Force)
Feb 22   Maxwell D. Taylor (U.S. 8th Army)
Mar 21   Second Battle of the Hook
Mar 23   Battle of Pork Chop Hill—ends Jul 11
Apr 20   Exchange of sick/wounded POWs—ends May 3
May 20   First woman to undertake faster-than-sound flight (Jacqueline
          Cochran)
May 25   First artillery shell with nuclear warhead fired
Jun 30   Nathan Twining (Chief of Staff, USAF)
Jul 11   First marine aviation ace (John Bolt)
Jul 13   Battle of the Kumsong Salient—ends Jul 20
Jul 16   First naval aviation ace (Guy Bordelon)
Jul 27   Korean Armistice Agreement signed
Aug   5   POW exchange—ends Sep 24
Aug 17   Robert Carney (Chief of Naval Operations)
Aug 14   Arthur Radford (Chairman, Joint Chiefs of Staff)
Aug 16   Matthew Ridgway (Chief of Staff, USA)
Sep   1   First-jet-to-jet aerial refueling (KB-47G to YB-47F)

1954

Jan 12   Department of Defense desegregates military dependent schools
Apr   1   U.S. Air Force Academy established—opens Jul 11, 1955
May   3   Charles Thomas (Secretary of the Navy)
Jun   1   Alfred Richmond (Commandant, USCG)
Jun   1   First shipboard test of a carrier steam catapult (H. J. Jackson, USN)
Jul 26   USN aircraft (USS *Philippine Sea*) engage Chinese People's Re-
          public aircraft (Hainan Incident)
Aug 15   Air National Guard assigned first peacetime mission
          (Air Defense Alert)
Sep 30   USS *Nautilus* commissioned (first nuclear-powered submarine)

1955

Jan 17   USS *Nautilus* underway by nuclear power

Jun 30 Maxwell Taylor (Chief of Staff, USA)
Jul 21 Wilber Brucker (Secretary of the Army)
Aug   9 Congress passes Reserve Forces Act
Aug 15 Donald Quarles (Secretary of the Air Force)
Aug 17 Military Code of Conduct established
Aug 17 Arleigh Burke (Chief of Naval Operations)
Aug 22 First shipboard use of a carrier mirror landing system (R. G. Dose, USN)
Nov   1 USS *Boston* commissioned (first guided missile cruiser)
Nov   1 Military Assistance Advisory Group, Vietnam established

1956

Jan   1 Randolph Pate (Commandant, Marine Corps)
Mar 31 Douglas A-3 (first carrier jet bomber enters operational service)
Apr   8 Ribbon Creek "death march" occurs—Parris Island, SC
Jul 20 USS *Thetis Bay* commissioned (first helicopter assault carrier)
Nov 26 Secretary of Defense of restricts the range of USA missiles to 200 miles
Dec   1 USA inactivates the last combat mule unit
Dec   4 USA discontinues the use of carrier pigeons
Dec   9 Lockheed C-130 enters operational service

1957

Apr   1 Thomas Gates (Secretary of the Navy)
May   1 James Douglas (Secretary of the Air Force)
Jun 28 Boeing KC-135 (first jet tanker enters operational service)
Jul   1 Thomas White (Chief of Staff, USAF)
Aug 12 First shipboard test of an automatic carrier landing system (Don Walker, USN)
Aug 15 Nathan Twining (Chairman, Joint Chiefs of Staff)
Sep 24 U.S. troops dispatched to Little Rock, AR (civil unrest)
Oct   9 Neil McElroy (Secretary of Defense)

1958

Jul 15 U.S. forces land Lebanon—ends Oct 19 (Operation Bluebat)

1959

Feb 12 Last Convair B-36 leaves operational service (SAC all-jet)
Mar 17 First submarine to surface at the North Pole (USS *Skate*)
Jun   8 William Franke (Secretary of the Navy)
Jun 30 Lyman Lemnitzer (Chief of Staff, USA)

Jul   8   First advisors KIA South Vietnam—Bien Hoa
Oct   31   First ICBM (Atlas D) on alert status (full deployment Mar 30,
           1961—operational phase-out Apr 20, 1965)
Dec   2   Thomas Gates (Secretary of Defense)
Dec   11   Dudley Sharp (Secretary of the Air Force)
Dec   30   USS *George Washington* commissioned (first fleet ballistic missile
           submarine)

1960

Jan   1   David Shoup (Commandant, Marine Corps)
Feb   24   First submerged circumnavigation of globe—ends Apr 10 (USS
           Triton)
Apr   13   First maritime navigational satellite placed in orbit (USN Transit
           IB)
May   1   Francis Gary Powers shot down whilst flying covert espionage
           mission (Sverdlovsk, U.S.S.R.)
May   6   USS *Sea Poacher* vs. *Oriente* (Cuba)
Jul   20   First launch of a ballistic missile by a submerged submarine (USS
           George Washington)
Sep   31   George Decker (Chief of Staff, USA)
Oct   1   Lyman Lemnitzer (Chairman, Joint Chiefs of Staff)
Nov   15   First operational patrol by a ballistic missile submarine (USS
           George Washington)

1961

Jan   1   Very Low Frequency Radio Station—Cutler, ME—operational
           (USN)
Jan   20   John Connally (Secretary of the Navy)
Jan   21   Robert S. McNamara (Secretary of Defense)
Jan   23   Elvis Stahr (Secretary of the Army)
Jan   23   Eugene Zuckert (Secretary of the Air Force)
Apr   14   USAF 4400th Combat Crew Training Squadron (Jungle Jim) acti-
           vated
Jun   30   Curtis LeMay (Chief of Staff, USAF)
Aug   1   George Anderson (Chief of Naval Operations)
Sep   9   USS *Long Beach* commissioned (first nuclear-powered surface
           warship)
Oct   11   President J. Kennedy authorizes USAF training unit South Viet-
           namese Air Force (Operation Farmgate)
Nov   25   USS *Enterprise* commissioned (first nuclear-powered carrier)
Nov   30   USN terminates lighter-than-air program
Dec   26   Operation Farmgate aircraft prohibited from engaging in com-
           bat save in specific circumstances

1962

Jan   4   Fred Korth (Secretary of the Navy)
Jan 13   Operation Ranch Hand—ends Jan 7, 1971 (defoliation project)
Feb   6   Military Assistance Command, Vietnam established
Feb   8   Paul Harkins (Military Assistance Command, Vietnam)
Feb 14   U.S. advisors in South Vietnam authorized to return hostile fire
Mar 22   First deliberate rural pacification program South Vietnam
          (strategic hamlet) established
May 15   U.S. forces land Bangkok, Thailand—ends Aug 7
Jun   1   Edwin Roland (Commandant, USCG)
Jul   5   Cyrus Vance (Secretary of the Army)
Jul 25   Utility Tactical Transport Company activated (first USA armed
          helicopter company)
Aug 31   Last airship flight from Lakehurst Naval Air Station
Sep 30   U.S. troops dispatched to Oxford, MS (civil unrest)
Oct   1   Maxwell Taylor (Chairman, Joint Chiefs of Staff)
Oct   1   Earle Wheeler (Chief of Staff, USA)
Oct 24   Naval blockade—Cuba—ends Nov 20
Oct 26   Last B-52 delivered to USAF
Oct 27   First solid fueled ICBM (Minuteman I) on alert status—full
          deployment Jun 15, 1965; operational phase-out Sep 3, 1974

1963

Feb 14   11th Air Assault (Test) activated
May 12   U.S. forces dispatched to Birmingham, Mobile, & Tuskegee, AL
          (civil unrest)
Jun   5   Charles Bush (first African American graduate USAFA)
Jun 11   U.S. troops dispatched to Tuscaloosa, AL (civil unrest)
Jun 13   First fully automatic carrier landing with production equipment
          (R. K. Billings and R. S. Chew, Jr., USN)
Aug   1   David McDonald (Chief of Naval Operations)
Nov 29   Paul Nitze (Secretary of the Navy)

Military Operations

RAID ON TOKYO (Apr 18, 1942). Col. James Doolittle trained army air
   crews to launch sixteen B-25's from a carrier deck, their mission being to
   bomb Japanese cities. Taking off from the USS *Hornet* in heavy seas,
   Doolittle's squadron achieved surprise, bombed Tokyo and two other
   cities, and flew on to China. Fifteen planes crash-landed there, one in
   Russia. The raid lifted American spirits and convinced the Japanese to
   attack at Midway.

BATTLE OF THE CORAL SEA (May 4–8, 1942). The Coral Sea was the first sea battle fought entirely by aircraft. Adm. Frank Jack Fletcher's task force bombed the new base on Tulagi on May 4 and searched for Adm. Takeo Takagi's carriers. Both fleets dispersed; each suffered damage on the 7th. The next day the main forces engaged. In all, the Americans sank one small carrier and damaged another, but lost two ships and the carrier USS *Lexington*. While a tactical victory for Takagi, the battle halted the Japanese invasion of Port Moresby and weakened the Midway attack.

BATTLE OF MIDWAY (Jun 3–4, 1942). Adm. Isoroku Yamamoto used almost 200 ships and 600 aircraft, planning to capture Midway and destroy the oncoming, smaller American fleet. Warned by American codebreakers, however, Adm. Raymond Spruance sprung a trap. A diversionary Japanese force attacked the Aleutians on June 3, but American planes spotted the invasion fleet approaching Midway. By the next day, all four Japanese carriers were sunk or sinking and half their aircraft destroyed, the Americans losing the USS *Yorktown* in the process. The Japanese lost naval air superiority and suffered one of the most decisive defeats of the war.

BATTLE OF GUADALCANAL (Aug 7, 1942–Feb 7, 1943). Guadalcanal provided the Americans with their first major ground victory against Japan. American Marines landed on August 7 and captured the airfield. Japanese reinforcements attacked the perimeter at Bloody Ridge between September 12–14, with heavy losses. On October 26, Gen. Alexander Vandegrift launched a successful offensive against the burgeoning Japanese force. In January, combined American Army and Marine units pushed the enemy back to Cape Esperance, where the Japanese evacuated about 10,000 soldiers by February 7. The Japanese suffered 14,000 killed; the Americans, 1,600.

BATTLE OF SAVO ISLAND (Aug 8–9, 1942). The battle was "the worst American naval defeat since 1812." Adm. Gunichi Mikawa's cruisers used superior night tactics to achieve surprise against the American/ Australian force covering the landing on Guadalcanal. During the night, the Japanese sank four cruisers and badly damaged a fifth. Mikawa's only mistake was withdrawing at daylight, believing air attack imminent, thus leaving the defenseless American transports untouched.

NAVAL BATTLES OF GUADALCANAL (Nov 12–15, 1942). Adm. Daniel Callaghan's force met Adm. Hiroaki Abe's fleet, sent to support a Japanese reinforcement effort, on the 12th. The Japanese sank seven ships and damaged another but lost three and postponed the landing. American aircraft sank or damaged four ships the next day. Adm. Nobutaki Kondo's force engaged Adm. Willis Lee's task force in night battle on the 14th. The Japanese sank three ships and damaged two others, but lost a battleship, a destroyer, and several transports. The landing was a failure, and Admiral Isoroku Yamamoto halted his effort to regain Guadalcanal.

BATTLE OF THE KASSERINE PASS (Feb 19–25, 1943). Gen. Lloyd Fredendall's corps retreated as Gen. Jurgen von Arnim's tanks attacked at Faid on February 14. Gen. Erwin Rommel's Afrika Korps drove north to the Kasserine Pass, which he assaulted on the 19th. Breaking through the next day, the Germans captured large amounts of equipment. But Rommel stopped, expecting a counterattack, while the Allies reinforced their position. On the 22nd, Rommel skillfully retreated. Fredendall's cautious counterattack three days later cost him his command; he was replaced by Gen. George S. Patton.

BATTLE OF THE BISMARCK SEA (Mar 2–3, 1943). Having modified B-25s and retrained their crews to attack shipping at low altitudes, Gen. George C. Kenney's Fifth Air Force displayed its prowess in the Bismarck Sea. After B-17 attacks on March 2 sank two transports heading for New Guinea, B-25s and Australian Beauforts sank six remaining transports and four destroyers the next day. The Japanese lost 3,000 troops.

INVASION OF SICILY (Jul 10–Aug 17, 1943). Gen. George S. Patton's American troops and Gen. Bernard Montgomery's British force invaded Sicily's southern coast on July 10. Twelve days later the Americans took Palermo at the island's western end, then both forces converged on Messina, which Patton entered on August 17 while British troops controlled the city's outskirts. The Germans resisted stoutly and managed to extract 100,000 Axis troops before Sicily fell.

SALERNO INVASION (Sep 9, 1943). Following Gen. Bernard Montgomery's invasion of southern Italy and the surrender of the Italian government, Gen. Mark Clark was to land an Allied force and proceed to Naples. The invasion failed to achieve surprise and met unexpectedly stiff resistance while establishing two narrow beachheads on the 9th. By the 13th, German counterattacks threatened the entire plan, but timely reinforcements and heavy air and naval bombardment turned the tide on the 14th. Two days later, Field-Marshal Albrecht Kesselring ordered a retreat to the Gustav Line.

SOLOMON ISLANDS CAMPAIGN (Oct 27–Nov 2, 1943). After American and New Zealand troops seized the Treasury Islands (October 27), American Marines secured a beachhead on Bougainville, at Empress Augusta Bay, on November 1. Ground fighting continued for several months. Meanwhile, during the early hours of the 2nd, an American task force defeated a Japanese fleet sent to disrupt the invasion. Adm. William "Bull" Halsey subsequently ordered two risky carrier raids on a Japanese fleet at Rabaul; his luck held, and the Japanese were dealt a costly defeat.

BATTLE OF TARAWA (Nov 20–22, 1943). Reports of the bloody landing at Tarawa shocked the American public. Naval and air bombardments failed to destroy the Japanese defenses. Miscalculation also hampered the Marine assault on November 20; amphibious vehicles often could not cross the coral reef, leaving troops to wade ashore. The Marines took the island after two days of heavy fighting. Only 146 of 4,800 Japanese troops survived; American losses totaled 1,000 dead and 2,000 wounded.

ANZIO INVASION (Jan 22, 1944). Having opened an offensive against the Gustav Line, the Allies invaded Anzio, behind the German defenses, four days later. Surprised, Field-Marshal Albrecht Kesselring nevertheless responded brilliantly. Gen. John P. Lucas moved cautiously (he was replaced by Gen. Lucian K. Truscott on February 23), consolidating a beachhead; the Germans launched furious counterattacks on February 3, 16, and 28, the last halted by Allied air and artillery bombardment on March 4. German defenses held until mid-May. Both sides lost about 30,000 troops.

SIEGE OF MYITKYINA (May 17–Aug 3, 1944). To capture this key communications center in Northern Burma, Gen. Joseph "Vinegar Joe" Stilwell sent Chinese troops and Gen. Frank Merrill's exhausted GALAHAD force of American volunteers ("Merrill's Marauders") on a dangerous trek over the Kuman Mountains. On May 17, they surprised the Japanese defending the air strip at Myitkyina, but the Japanese rushed reinforcements to the city, which held out until August 3; its fall opened a crucial supply line to China.

NORMANDY INVASION (Jun 6, 1944). The long-awaited Allied invasion of Western Europe began on June 6. The Allies profited from air superiority and German disagreement as to how to defeat an invasion force. The invasion, however, was slowed by confusion, caution, and then determined resistance. The British Second Army was repulsed near Caen on July 18; after a successful offensive by the U.S. 1st Army on July 25, Gen. George S. Patton's Third Army broke through into open country at Avranches on July 31. A large number of Germans were captured in the "Falaise Pocket" (August 13–20) as the Allies exploited their victory.

BATTLE OF SAIPAN (Jun 15, 1944). After bombarding Saipan for several days, the Americans invaded this Marianas island on June 15 to face rugged terrain and fierce resistance; they advanced slowly. On July 7, the Japanese made a suicidal attack, losing almost 30,000 men. Thousands of civilians also chose suicide. American casualties were about 15,000. On July 21, American forces landed on Guam, and three days later another force stormed Tinian. By mid-August, the Marianas were in American hands, bringing Japan within striking distance of American B-29s.

BATTLE OF THE PHILIPPINE SEA (Jun 19–20, 1944). Adm. Jisaburo Ozawa planned to trap Adm. Raymond Spruance between the Japanese fleet and land-based planes, but aircraft from Adm. Marc Mitscher's carriers decimated the latter. Although Spruance refused to advance toward the enemy, radar as well as experienced pilots and superior aircraft produced American victory; the 19th became "The Great Marianas Turkey Shoot." On the 20th, Mitscher rediscovered the enemy carriers and launched a risky but successful night attack. In all, the Americans sank three carriers, damaged three others, and destroyed numerous Japanese aircraft, with light losses.

BATTLE OF LEYTE GULF (Oct 23–25, 1944). This engagement was the largest sea battle in history. Three Japanese fleets converged on American vessels covering Gen. Douglas MacArthur's Philippine landing. Submarine and aircraft attacks stopped Adm. Takeo Kurita's advance on the 24th, but Adm. William "Bull" Halsey, unannounced, sailed away to meet Adm. Jisaburo Ozawa's decoy fleet. Although Adm. J.B. Oldendorf's force wiped out Adm. Shoji Nishimura's ships in the Surigao Strait (October 25), Kurita's return that day caught Adm. Thomas Kinkaid off guard. Then Kurita disengaged, mistakenly believing he faced a larger force. Admiral Marc Mitscher's planes destroyed much of Ozawa's fleet that same day. The Japanese navy lost twenty-eight warships and 500 aircraft in the engagement.

BATTLE OF THE ARDENNES (Dec 16, 1944–Jan 16, 1945). On Hitler's orders, three German armies surprised the Allies along a seventy-mile front in the Ardennes on December 16. In the course of the "Battle of the Bulge" the Germans took almost 9,000 prisoners but failed to capture important fuel dumps. Montgomery constructed a strong defensive line to the north, and Allied armored divisions blunted the spearhead on December 24–25. Gen. George S. Patton's tanks, meanwhile, relieved an entrapped force at Bastogne (December 26). As foul weather cleared, Allied air forces joined the fray. On January 3, the Allies opened an offensive and eliminated the salient by the 16th.

BATTLE OF IWO JIMA (Feb 19–Mar 16, 1945). Gen. Harry Schmidt's large force of Marines assaulted the heavily fortified defenses of Iwo Jima on February 19 after only three days of bombardment. In fierce fighting, the Americans scaled Mount Suribachi at the southern tip by the 23rd (the photo of the flag raising was "the most famous of the Pacific war"), then slowly moved north against an enemy ensconced in bunkers, caves, and miles of tunnels. Resistance ended on March 16. About 200 of Japan's 22,000 troops survived; more than 6,800 Marines were killed and 20,000 wounded.

BATTLE OF OKINAWA (Apr 1–Jun 21, 1945). Supported by 1,200 ships, American troops landed on April 1. Resistance was light until April 4, when they encountered Gen. Mitsuru Ushijima's defensive lines of fortified caves and tunnels. Kamikaze (suicide) attacks against the warships, meanwhile, began on the 6th. Intense ground fighting lasted several weeks. When resistance ended on June 21, more than 12,000 American soldiers (including Gen. Simon Bolivar Buckner, Jr.), Marines, and sailors were killed, the heaviest toll of any Pacific campaign. Japanese losses totaled 70,000 troops and 80,000 Okinawans.

BATTLE OF THE PUSAN PERIMETER (Aug 5–Sep 10, 1950). As invading North Korean troops pushed South Korean and American armies into the southeast corner of Korea, Gen. Walton Walker established a defensive line (called the Pusan Perimeter), about 170 miles long and loosely defended. His United Nations force repulsed several bloody efforts to penetrate the perimeter, the last launched on September 1. The defenders outnumbered their attackers, and air power also proved vital for the defense.

INCHON INVASION (Sep 15, 1950). Gen. Douglas MacArthur conceived this highly risky landing on the west coast of Korea, far behind the lines at Pusan. Defying the odds, American naval and Marine forces succeeded, suffering light casualties and capturing Kimpo airfield. On the 16th, Gen. Walton Walker's United Nations command began an offensive against the Pusan Perimeter, breaking out on the 19th and catching the North Koreans between the two armies. Seoul, defended by 20,000 North Korean troops, "became an inferno" but was recaptured at month's end in hard fighting.

CHINESE FIRST PHASE OFFENSIVE (Oct 25–Nov 6, 1950). Gen. Douglas MacArthur divided his force, sending Gen. Edward Almond up the east coast to the Yalu River. Near Unsan on October 25, Chinese soldiers, aiding the North Koreans, attacked part of Gen. Walton Walker's combined force pursuing the enemy up the west coast towards the Yalu. The 8th Cavalry, sent to relieve the embattled force, lost about 600 men and the South Koreans an entire regiment between November 1 and 3 before the Chinese disengaged.

BATTLE OF THE CHONGCHON VALLEY (Nov 26–30, 1950). Gen. Douglas MacArthur's "final offensive" to the Yalu began on the 24th, but the Chinese in turn launched their Second Phase offensive against its western pincer. After inconclusive fighting on the 25th, the Chinese began to maul the U.N. forces, smashing Gen. Walton Walker's front lines. On the 30th, American troops retreating from Kunu-ri were ambushed at "the pass," losing 3,000 men and all equipment. Only a timely retreat to Pyongyang (subsequently evacuated on December 5) saved Walker's Eighth Army from annihilation. The defeat signified that the United Nations force would not win control of North Korea; "Inchon had been cancelled out by the Chongchon."

BATTLE OF THE CHANGJIN/CHOSIN RESERVOIR (Nov 27–Dec 11, 1950). Gen. Oliver Smith's 1st Marine Division (Gen. Douglas

MacArthur's planned eastern pincer in his "final offensive" to the Yalu) met Chinese frontal and flank attacks west of the reservoir on the 27th/28th. The column fought for three days in zero-degree temperatures while retreating to Hakawoo-ri (December 1–4). Task Force Drysdale, meanwhile, was decimated (November 29) trying to reach Hakawoo-ri from the south. Task Force Faith was destroyed while returning from east of the reservoir on the 1st. The retreat was completed by the 11th, and the division was evacuated by sea; it sustained 4,400 battle casualties. The United Nation's offensive was stopped in its tracks.

CHINESE FIFTH PHASE OFFENSIVE I (Apr 22–30, 1951). Beginning on the 22nd, the Chinese assaulted the Eighth Army with artillery and massed infantry attacks, often at night. Taking heavy losses in intense fighting, the Chinese broke through in two places, forcing a slow retreat by U.N. troops to the NO NAME line. The offensive climaxed on the 27th, as the western advance was stopped by ground and air forces just short of Seoul. The offensive petered out by the 30th. The Chinese failed to destroy the Eighth Army, sustaining 70,000 casualties while inflicting 7,000.

CHINESE FIFTH PHASE OFFENSIVE II (May 15–19, 1951). The second step of the offensive opened on May 15 with an attack on the eastern half of the U.N. line. Chinese troops threatened to envelope American Marine and Army units in hard combat. Gen. James Van Fleet allowed the eastern end of the offensive to advance 30 miles as he redeployed troops. He also ordered extraordinarily heavy artillery bombardments (the "Van Fleet load") which cost the Chinese dearly. The offensive collapsed on the 19th, Chinese casualties estimated to have reached 90,000.

U.N. OFFENSIVE (May 20–Jun 13, 1951). As the Chinese Fifth Phase Offensive collapsed, Gen. Matthew Ridgway, who replaced Gen. Douglas MacArthur as overall commander, allowed Gen. James Van Fleet to initiate a counteroffensive. With excellent artillery and close air support, Eighth Army troops moved north against the retreating Chinese, capturing thousands of prisoners and much materiel, inflicting heavy casualties and even reoccupying Pyongyang on the 13th. The offensive was halted there, however, for political and diplomatic reasons, much to Van Fleet's chagrin.

BATTLE OF BLOODY RIDGE (Aug 18–Sep 5, 1951). Republic of Korea forces attacked North Korean positions on Bloody Ridge and J-Ridge simultaneously on August 18, advancing and retreating over several days. American troops joined in a counterattack on Bloody Ridge in late August, but were pushed back on the 27th. Gen. Clovis E. Beyers ordered a broader assault on the 31st, eventually capturing the ridges on September 5 in a double envelopment as the exhausted North Koreans withdrew. U.N. casualties totaled 2,700.

BATTLE OF HEARTBREAK RIDGE (Sep 13–Oct 15, 1951). U.N. troops advanced against the North Korean stronghold on Heartbreak Ridge beginning on the 13th, but met heavy resistance. The attack halted on September 27, when Gen. Clovis E. Beyer's 2nd Division stopped to regroup, having failed to dislodge the defenders. On October 5 a second assault opened, moving up the valleys flanking the ridge, employing close air support, artillery, and tanks. The assault succeeded, but only with heavy fighting, using bayonets and flamethrowers to clear the ridge.

BATTLE OF PORKCHOP HILL (Mar 23–Jul 11, 1953). Chinese forces attacked U.N. positions on Old Baldy and Porkchop Hill on March 23. Assaults and counterattacks on Old Baldy dominated the early action, until Gen. Maxwell D. Taylor conceded the hill. On April 16, American troops fended off another effort to capture Porkchop; three days of hand-to-hand combat ensued and Eighth Army artillery fired a record 77,000 rounds in a single day. After harassing South Korean units for two months, the Chinese launched a massive assault on July 6. They slowly overcame the Americans' determined resistance, and Taylor withdrew his forces on July 11.

Biographical Notes

ALMOND, EDWARD MALLORY (1892–1979). Following graduation from Virginia Military Institute (1915), Almond took a commission in the infantry. He then served in France in World War I, taught military science (1919–1923), and graduated from the Command and General Staff School (1930) and the Army War College (1934). From 1934 to 1938 Almond served on the general staff and graduated from the Naval War College in 1940. With the entry of the United States into World War II, Almond took command of the then all-African American 92nd Division in July 1942. Following training in Alabama and Arizona, Almond and his division went to Italy (August 1944). The 92nd fought the Germans in Northern Italy and in April 1945 the celebrated 442nd Regiment (Nisei), a unit of the 92nd, took on the Germans' Gothic Line to open up the Po River Valley. Following the war Almond returned to the United States and then went to the Far East Command as a member of Gen. Douglas MacArthur's staff. In September 1950 Gen. Almond took command of the newly organized X Corps, which participated in the amphibious landing at Inchon on the west coast of Korea. The X Corps quickly captured Seoul, South Korea, and by November had reached the Yalu River in North Korea. After a massive Chinese counterattack, the X Corps withdrew to east-central Korea. There it was a major part of the U.N. defense line. Gen. Almond relinquished command of the X Corps in July 1951.

ARNOLD, HENRY HARLEY (1886–1950). As commanding general of the Army Air Force (1942–1946) Arnold supervised the prosecution of the air war during World War II. Thomas M. Coffey, *HAP: The Story of the U.S. Air Force and the Man Who Built It; General Henry H. (Hap) Arnold* (1982).

BRADLEY, OMAR NELSON (1893–1981). He commanded the First Army at Utah and Omaha beaches during Normandy invasion (June 6, 1944) and later the 12th Army Group—the largest force ever controlled by an American commander in the field. Charles Whiting, *Bradley* (1971).

BRERETON, LEWIS HYDE (1890–1967). A graduate of the U.S. Naval Academy (1911), Brereton transferred to the aviation section of the Signal Corps in 1912. He served in the Philippines (1916), France in World War I, and is jointly credited with Col. William Mitchell for developing the technique of dive bombing (1924–1927). In November 1941 Brereton took command of the Far Eastern Air Force in the Philippines, under the overall command of Gen. Douglas MacArthur. Following the Japanese attack in early December that destroyed most of his aircraft on the ground, Brereton withdrew to Java and carried on the air war with Japan. From there Brereton went to command of the Middle East Air Force (1942), which was later redesignated the Ninth Air Force. Gen. Brereton's aircraft flew missions against German Gen. Erwin Rommel in North Africa and the famous raid on the oil fields at Ploesti, Romania (August 1, 1943). A year later Gen. Brereton took over the First Allied Airborne Army to provide centralized control over training for allied airborne and glider troops in the European theater of operations. First Army had no supply function and no facilities for operation in the field inasmuch as it was a planning and coordinating headquarters. Brereton's war memoirs, *The Brereton Diaries*, were published in 1946.

CHENNAULT, CLAIRE LEE (1890–1958). Chennault formed the American Volunteer Group, or "Flying Tigers," to aid the Chinese and protect the Burma Road from Japanese air attacks (1941–1942). He also served as adviser to Jiang Jieshi (Chiang Kai-Shek) and subsequently commanded the Fourteenth Air Force in China. Martha Byrd, *Chennault: Giving Wings to the Tiger* (1987).

CLARK, MARK WAYNE (1896–1984). He commanded the allied Fifth Army in the Italian campaign (1943–1944) in World War II. He also held command of United Nations forces in Korea (1952–1953). Martin Blumenson, *Mark Clark* (1984).

COCHRAN, JACQUELINE (1910?–1980). Born in Pensacola, Florida, Cochran grew up in a foster home. She worked at various jobs, including beautician, and in 1934 she founded a cosmetics firm that she directed until 1963. In 1932 Cochran learned to fly. Six years later she won the Bendix Transcontinental Air Race. After war broke out in 1939, Cochran organized a group of American women to ferry aircraft from factory to operational units as part of Britain's Air Transport Auxiliary.

Cochran then returned to the United States and began a similar program for the Army Air Force. In July 1943, Cochran was made director of the Women's Airforce Service Pilots (WASP's), who flew noncombat missions. In 1945 Cochran received the Distinguished Service Medal— the first female civilian to receive that award. In 1948 she was commissioned a lieutenant colonel in the Air Force reserve and she continued her flying as a jet test pilot. Cochran was the first woman to break the sound barrier (1953) and set several speed records. In 1961 she set an altitude mark of 55,253 feet. Cochran also served as the first woman president of the Federation Aeronautic International (1959–1963). She retired in 1970.

DAVIS, BENJAMIN OLIVER, JR. (1912–). The son of the first African American general in the U.S. Army, the younger Davis attended Western Reserve University and the University of Chicago before graduating 35th in a class of 276 at the U.S. Military Academy (1936). Davis then served for five years in the infantry before transferring to the Army Air Corps in 1941. He took his flight training at Tuskegee Army Air Field earning his wings in March 1942, one of the first African Americans to become an army pilot. Appointed Commander of the 99th Fighter Squadron, which was made up entirely of African Americans, in September 1942 Davis took his squadron overseas. There the squadron flew tactical support missions over North Africa, Sicily, and Italy. Davis then served as group commander of the 332nd Fighter Group, which was also made up entirely of African Americans, from November 1943 to June 1945. Davis flew a total of sixty missions in 224 combat hours in World War II. Following his return to the United States, Davis held various command, staff, and training posts basically involved in social matters. He qualified as a jet pilot in 1954. He then held a series of posts in the Far East Air Forces and the 12th Air Force in Germany. He was appointed brigadier general in 1954, the Air Force's first African American general. Promotions to major general (1959) and lieutenant general (1965) followed. General Davis closed out his career as Deputy Commander of the U.S. Strike Command in Florida. He subsequently published his autobiography, *Benjamin O. Davis, Jr., American* in 1991.

DEAN, WILLIAM FRISHE (1899–1981). A graduate of the University of California (1922), Dean had joined the army reserve in 1921. Two years later he was commissioned a second lieutenant of the infantry in the regular army. In addition to assignments at various posts, Dean graduated from the Command and General Staff School (1936), the Army Industrial College (1939), and the Army War College (1940). During World War II, he initially served as a staff officer in Washington, D.C., but in mid-1944 he took over as deputy commander of the 44th Infantry Division, which was part of the Seventh Army in Europe. The 44th fought in the Vosges Mountains, captured Strasbourg, and crossed the Rhine in March 1945. By this time Dean was in full command of the 44th, which crossed the Danube in April 1945 and finished the war in Austria. In October 1947 Dean became military governor of South Korea. He subsequently assumed command of the 24th Infantry Division in June 1950 when it was sent to Korea to oppose the attacks of the North Koreans. At Taejon on July 20–21 Dean organized a rearguard action, but he was separated from his forces and taken prisoner 36 days later (August 25). Dean was awarded the Medal of Honor in September 1950, but his status as a prisoner was not known until December 19, 1951. Liberated on September 4, 1953, General Dean continued to serve until his retirement in 1955. He published *General Dean's Story* (with W. L. Worden) about his experiences as a prisoner in 1954.

DONOVAN, WILLIAM JOSEPH (1883–1959). He is best known for commanding the Office of Strategic Services (1942–1945) in World War II. The Central Intelligence Agency is the modern successor to the O.S.S. Corey Ford, *Donovan Of OSS* (1970).

DOOLITTLE, JAMES HAROLD (1896–1993). Doolittle led the famous raid by a force of sixteen B-25's that hit targets in Tokyo and other Japanese cities on April 18, 1942. He served in the North African and European theaters in World War II. Lowell Thomas and Edward Jablonski, *Doolittle: A Biography* (1976).

EAKER, IRA CLARENCE (1896–1987). He was the commanding general of the U.S. Eight Air Force (1942–1943) in World War II which carried out a sustained strategic bombing campaign against Nazi targets in Europe. James Parton, *Air Force Spoken Here: General Ira Eaker and the Command of the Air* (1986).

EICHELBERGER, ROBERT LAWRENCE (1886–1961). He was the commanding general of I Corps on New Guinea and New Britain (1942–1944). He commanded the Eighth Army (1944–1948) during the Philippine campaign and later during the occupation of Japan. Robert L. Eichelberger, *Our Jungle Road to Tokyo* (1950).

EISENHOWER, DWIGHT DAVID (1890–1969). As commander in chief of the allied forces in North Africa and Western Europe (1943–1945) he gained international renown. He was elected President of the United States in 1952. Stephen Ambrose, *Eisenhower: Soldier, General of the Army, President Elect, 1890–1952* (1983).

FLETCHER, FRANK JACK (1885–1973). After graduating from the Naval Academy (1906), Fletcher held various posts afloat. In April 1914 he won the Medal of Honor for rescuing refugees during the fighting at Veracruz, Mexico. Following submarine patrol duty in World War I, combat in the Philippines (1924), and training at the Naval War College (1930) and Army War College (1931), Fletcher took command of the carrier *Yorktown* in January 1943. He subsequently participated in the navy's raid on the Japanese-held Gilbert and Marshall Islands under Adm. William F. Halsey in February, 1942, the first U.S. naval offensive against Japan. Promoted to vice admiral, Fletcher commanded the combined *Yorktown-Lexington* carrier task forces in the battle of the Coral Sea (May 7–8, 1942). This was the first sea battle in which the vessels involved did not make direct contact. Fletcher's forces lost heavily—the *Lexington* was sunk—but they prevented the Japanese from threatening an invasion of Port Moresby in Australia. Following repairs at Pearl Harbor, Fletcher and the *Yorktown* steamed west to Midway Island where they joined the carrier forces commanded by Adm. Raymond A. Spruance. Although *Yorktown* was damaged in the ensuing battle (June 3–6, 1942), the Japanese lost four carriers and the war began to turn in favor of the United States. In August 1942 Fletcher commanded the expeditionary forces sent to Guadalcanal. Heavy fighting, especially in the battle of the Eastern Solomons, again damaged Fletcher's forces and wounded him. From December 1943 to 1945 Fletcher commanded the naval forces of the North Pacific area. He retired in 1947.

GALLERY, DANIEL VINCENT (1901–1977). Gallery graduated from the U.S. Naval Academy in 1920. Following various assignments afloat, Gallery went to flight school in 1926–1927 to earn his wings. In the 1930s Gallery served as an aviation squadron commander and chief of the aviator section of the Bureau of Ordnance. In December 1941 he took command of Fleet Air Base, Reykjavik, Iceland and oversaw naval aircraft engaged in convoy and antisubmarine service. Promoted to captain, Gallery received command of the escort carrier *Guadalcanal* in August 1943. While operating with five destroyer escorts in the area of the Cape Verde Islands on June 4, 1944, the *Guadalcanal* and her escorts forced the German submarine U-505 to surface. As the German crew abandoned their boat, Gallery ordered "away borders" and a boarding crew from one of the destroyers captured U-505 before it sank. The captured sub yielded valuable information on German torpedoes and naval codes, but it is chiefly remembered as the first enemy vessel captured on the high seas by the U.S. Navy since 1815. Gallery went on to have a distinguished career involving assignments ashore and afloat dealing with antisubmarine warfare. He was also the author of four books, including *Clear the Decks!* (1951), which tells the story of the capture of U-505.

GEIGER, RAY STANLEY (1885–1947). Educated at Florida State Normal School and Stetson University (graduated 1907), Geiger enlisted in the Marine Corps in 1907 and won a commission in 1909. He subsequently served in Nicaragua, Panama, China, and elsewhere. In 1917 he completed aviation training and became a pilot. In World War I he commanded a squadron in the 1st Marine Aviation Force in France and flew many bombing missions. During the 1920s and 1930s Geiger received advanced training and also spent considerable time on the development of close air-support tactics as part of the Marines developing amphibious-assault doctrine. In World War II Geiger was the commanding general of the 1st Marine Air Wing on Guadalcanal from September to November 1942. Geiger's pilots shot down 268 Japanese planes, damaged an equal number, and sank several enemy ships. Geiger then rotated back to an aviation post in Washington, D.C. before returning to the Pacific in late 1943 in command of the I Marine Amphibious Corps on Bougainville Island. Following involvement in the planning for the capture of Guam and Peleliu, Geiger's command was a part of the invasion of Okinawa in April 1945. When Lt. Gen. Simon Bolivar Buckner, Jr., was killed in June 1945, Geiger briefly held command of the Tenth Army on Okinawa. This was the first time a marine general had held a command of this size.

GROW, ROBERT W. (1895–1985). Appointed a second lieutenant in the Minnesota National Guard in 1915 while a student at the University of Minnesota, Grow graduated the next year and joined the regular army. He attended service schools in World War I and spent five months of occupation duty in Germany in 1919. More training at the Cavalry School (1923) and the Command and General Staff School (1929) followed. Grow spent time with the newly created Mechanized Force in the early 1930s and helped to develop doctrine for mechanized armor in the army. During this time Grow came to know George S. Patton, Jr. In May 1943 Grow received command of the 6th Armored Division, which the following year, as part of Patton's Third Army, broke out of the Normandy beachhead. In 1946 Grow joined the U.S. Military Mission to Iran. The Soviets under Stalin were putting pressure on Iran, Turkey, and Greece to gain access to the Persian Gulf and its oil reserves. Grow worked closely with the Iranian leadership to improve the combat readiness of the Iranian Army. In October 1948 Grow rotated back to the United States as commander at Fort Devens. Then in the summer of 1950 Grow became the army attaché in Moscow. While on a visit to Frankfurt in 1951, a communist agent photographed Grow's personal diary. The Soviets made much of the diary's contents for propaganda purposes and to embarrass Grow, a top intelligence officer. Subsequently in April 1952 the army brought charges against Grow and convened a general court martial in July. Grow was found guilty and suspended from command for six months. He retired as a major general in January 1953.

HALLAREN, MARY AGNES (1907–). Educated as a teacher, Hallaren received a commission in the Women's Army Auxiliary Corps in July 1942. A year later at the time the WAAC was redesignated the Women's Army Corps, Hallaren took command of the first battalion of WACs to go overseas. There as director of WAC personnel for the Eighth and Ninth Air Forces, Hallaren played a key role in the assignment of women in Europe. By 1945 she was director of all WAC personnel in the European theater. In May 1947 Hallaren became director of the WAC with the rank of colonel. The Women's Armed Services Integration Act of June 12, 1948 made the WAC a component of the Regular Army. Consequently Col. Hallaren became the first woman (outside of the Medical Corps) to receive a commission in the regular army. She retired from her post of director in January 1953.

HALSEY, WILLIAM FREDERICK, Jr. (1882–1959). He commanded the Third Fleet (1944–1945) at the Battle of Leyte Gulf in October 1944. James M. Merrill, *A Sailor's Admiral: A Biography of William F. Halsey* (1976).

HANCOCK, JOY BRIGHT (1898–1986). Joy Bright enlisted in the naval reserve in World War I. She continued to work for the navy as a civilian after the war's end and in 1924 married a naval aviator, Lt. Cdr. Lewis Hancock. He unfortunately died in 1925 in the crash of the airship *Shenandoah*. Despite the loss of her husband, Hancock continued her work for the navy and in 1928 earned a civil pilot's license. In July 1942 she joined the Women's Reserve of the Navy. Hancock served in the Navy throughout World War II and in July 1946 became director of the Women's Reserve with the rank of captain. She took a commission in the regular navy in 1948 and was appointed assistant chief for women in the Bureau of Personnel and continued ex officio as director of the Women's Reseve, after the organization officially passed out of existence. Hancock retired in June 1953.

HOBBY, OVETA CULP (1905–1995). Privately educated and a sometime student at Mary Hardin-Baylor College and the University of Texas Law School, Oveta Culp was appointed parliamentarian of the Texas House of Representatives in 1925. Her father, Isaac W. Culp, was a Texas legislator, and schooled his daughter in politics from the age of fourteen. Culp gave up her job of parliamentarian in 1931 when she married William Pettus Hobby, a widower and former governor of Texas, who was then the president of the *Houston Post*. Oveta Culp Hobby combined a career in journalism with a family in the 1930s and in early 1942 Gen. George C. Marshall asked her to study plans for the development of the Women's Auxiliary Army Corps (WAAC). When the WAAC became official on May 14, 1942, Hobby became the director with the relative rank of major (later colonel). The WAAC became the Women's Army Corps (WAC) on July 1, 1943. Hobby was its director throughout World War II with a peak strength of about 100,000 women. Hobby's primary concerns were the development of procedures for recruitment, training, and administering the WAC. Her high standards (for example only volunteers could join the WAC) won great respect for the WAC. After World

War II, Hobby went back to the *Houston Post* and was a successful business leader. In April 1953 she became only the second woman to serve in a presidential cabinet when President Dwight Eisenhower asked her to serve as the first secretary of Health, Education and Welfare. She resigned this post in July 1955 to return to Houston.

HORTON, MILDRED HELEN MCAFEE (1900–). A graduate of Vassar College (1920), Mildred McAfee entered teaching. She held various posts in the 1920s and 1930s and in 1936 was named president of Wellesley College. After the United States entered World War II, McAfee served on a committee that developed plans for a women's naval reserve program. The Women's Reserve of the Navy (known informally as the WAVES) came into existence on July 30, 1942 with McAfee as its director with the relative rank of lieutenant commander. Fully a part of the naval reserve from that day, the Women's Reserve numbered some 86,000 officers and enlisted by September 1945. Promoted to captain in 1943, McAfee married Captain Douglas Horton in August 1945 and resigned from her post of director in February 1946 to return to Wellesley. She stepped down from the presidency of Wellesley in 1949 and subsequently headed the National Social Welfare Assembly (1950–1958) and was a delegate to the United Nations Educational, Scientific, and Cultural Organization (1962). In 1963–1964 she served as a co-chair of the National Women's Commission on Civil Rights.

JAMES, DANIEL, Jr. (1920–1978). James learned to fly while he was a student at Tuskegee Institute from which he graduated in 1942. Appointed a cadet in the Army Air Corps in January 1943, James received a commission in July and served as an aviation instructor for the all-black 99th Pursuit Squadron for the remainder of World War II. In the Korean War James flew 101 missions as a fighter pilot and subsequently flew seventy-eight combat missions in Vietnam (1966–1967). Promoted to brigadier general in 1969, James held various posts overseas and in the United States before earning promotion to lieutenant general (1974). In September 1975 he became the first African American in U.S. military service to receive the four-star rank of general when he served as commander of the North American Air Defense Command (NORAD) from 1975–1978.

JOHNSON, CLARENCE LEONARD (1910–1990). Educated at the University of Michigan (B.A., 1932 and M.A. in aeronautical engineering, 1933), Johnson went to work for Lockheed Aircraft in California following graduation. By 1938 he had become Lockheed's chief research engineer due to his analytical abilities and the speed and insight with which he solved aviation design problems. Johnson's first complete design was the P-38 Lightning, a highly effective interceptor and fighter-bomber of World War II. In 1943 he designed the P-80 (later redesignated F-80 Shooting Star), which was the first tactical jet fighter to achieve operation status in the USAF. The F-80 saw plenty of combat in the Korean War. Johnson went on to design the C-69 Constellation (1946) and the Super Constellation (1950), both very effective commercial transports. At the height of the Cold War, Johnson's design teams turned out the F-104 Starfighter (1956), a Mach-2 fighter, and the famous U-2 high-altitude reconnaissance plane (also 1956). The A-11 (1960) and SR-71 (1964) spy planes followed. The SR-71 could fly at Mach-3 and 100,000 feet. Johnson received many honors for his genius for aeronautical design before and after his retirement in 1975.

JOHNSON, HAROLD KEITH (1912–1983). A 1933 graduate of West Point, Johnson began his army career in the infantry. In 1940 he went to the Philippines where he survived the notorious Bataan death march in the spring of 1942 and subsequent internment in Japanese prisoner-of-war camps in the Philippines, Japan, and Korea. Liberated in September 1945, Johnson received additional schooling before returning to Korea in 1950 where he saw frequent combat service. Johnson's career flourished following the Korean War with promotion to brigadier general (1956). In 1959 Johnson went to Europe as Assistant Chief of Staff, U.S. Army in Europe. Following several senior posts with NATO and in the United States, Johnson was promoted to general and appointed Chief of Staff. During his term in office (1964–1968), the Army began a build-up that rapidly increased its involvement in the Vietnam War. Gen. William C. Westmoreland succeeded Gen. Johnson as Chief of Staff when he retired in 1968.

JOY, CHARLES TURNER (1895–1956). Joy graduated from the Naval Academy in 1916. He saw service in World War I, received a master's degree in ordnance engineering from the University of Michigan in 1922, and participated in the Yangtze Patrol from 1923 to 1925. Following various tours afloat and ashore in the 1930s, Joy was promoted to captain in January 1942. He was involved in combat operations in Rabaul, New Guinea, Bougainville, the Aleutians, Solomon Islands, and the assault on Saipan (1944). Promoted to rear admiral in the spring of 1944, Joy participated in carrier operations around the Philippines, the landings at Leyte, the Iwo Jima assault (February 1945), and other actions. Following World War II, Joy was promoted to vice admiral (1949) and at the outbreak of the Korean War in June 1950 he took command of the United Nations naval forces. He had responsibility for the naval blockade of North Korea and for organizing the amphibious assault at Inchon, North Korea (September 15, 1950). From July 1951 to May 1952, Joy served as senior U.N. delegate to the Korean armistice negotiations. He retired from the Navy in 1954.

KENNEY, GEORGE CHURCHILL (1889–1977). As commanding general of the Fifth Air Force (1942–1944) he provided air support to the ground forces of Gen. Douglas MacArthur in the Southwest Pacific area. George C. Kenney, *General Kenney Reports: A Personal History of the Pacific War* (1949).

KING, ERNEST JOSEPH (1878–1956). He served as the Chief of Naval Operations during World War II, and in that capacity represented the Navy to the other service chiefs. Thomas B. Buell, *Master of Seapower: A Biography of Fleet Admiral Ernest J. King* (1980).

KINKAID, THOMAS CASSAIN (1888–1972). Kinkaid graduated from the Naval Academy in 1908. He served at sea on a variety of vessels and made advanced studies in ordnance from 1913 to 1916. He served in England in World War I before being assigned to the battleship *Arizona* (1918–1919). He graduated from the Naval War College in 1930, was a technical consultant to the Geneva Disarmament Conference in 1932, and served as a naval attaché in Rome (1938) and Belgrade (1939–1941). Following the Japanese attack on Pearl Harbor, Kinkaid commanded the carrier *Enterprise* under the overall command of Adm. William F. Halsey in the early 1942 raids on the Gilbert and Marshall Islands. He subsequently fought in the battles of the Coral Sea, Midway, and Eastern Solomons (1942). Promoted to vice admiral in June 1943, Kinkaid served as commander of the Seventh Fleet and allied naval forces in the southwest Pacific. During October 24–26, 1944 Kinkaid's naval forced protected Gen. MacArthur's ground troops at Leyte Gulf by inflicting severe losses on the Japanese naval forces. Subsequently promoted to admiral (1945), Kinkaid participated in the landings in Korea and the surrender of Seoul. He retired from naval service in 1950.

LEMAY, CURTIS EMERSON (1906–1990). Educated at Ohio State University, from which he graduated in 1932, LeMay was commissioned as a second lieutenant following completion of ROTC in 1928. He then went to aviation school where he was trained as a pursuit pilot. LeMay subsequently transferred to bombardment, where he gained a well-deserved reputation as a skilled navigator. In 1942 he trained the 305th Bombardment Group and then went with it to England, where he later commanded the 3rd Air Division in raids over Germany. Highly decorated for his combat service, LeMay found that evasive tactics during bombing runs increased the scattering of bombs and yielded no additional protection for air crews. Thus he demonstrated the value of a defensive formation in a straight-in bomb run. In 1944 LeMay became a major general with the 21st Bomber Command in Guam. LeMay, using B-29 bombers stripped of much of their defensive armament, initiated low-level night attacks on Japan with incendiary bombs to exploit the vulnerability of Japanese cities to fire. After World War II, LeMay continued to work with strategic air planning. In 1948 he directed the airlift of supplies to Berlin when it was blockaded by the Soviets. He commanded the Strategic Air Command (1948–1951) and kept it on constant alert. LeMay was chief of staff of the air force (1961–1965), and after retirement in 1965 Alabama Gov. George C. Wallace picked LeMay as his vice presidential candidate on the American Independent Party ticket in part because of LeMay's hawkish views on the Vietnam War (1968).

MCAULIFFE, ANTHONY CLEMENT (1898–1975). McAuliffe attended West Virginia University before entering the U.S. Military Academy, from which he graduated in 1918. He was commissioned in the field artillery and served at various posts in the United States and Hawaii. He graduated from the Command and General Staff School (1937) and the Army War College (1940). In August 1942 he took command of the artillery of the 101st Airborne Division. The 101st were among the first troops to parachute into France during the Normandy invasion (June 6, 1944). As deputy division commander under Gen. Maxwell D. Taylor, McAuliffe is best known for his famous reply of "Nuts!" to the surrender ultimatum of the German commander during the defense of Bastogne in December 1944. McAuliffe's troops made a resolute stand until they were relieved by elements of Gen. George S. Patton's Third Army. This helped stop the German counteroffensive known as the Battle of the Bulge. After World War II, Gen. McAuliffe went on to hold several high commands. He retired in 1956.

MACARTHUR, DOUGLAS (1880–1964). MacArthur's career was marked by brilliance and controversy throughout his service in World War I, World War II and Korea. As the commander of the American occupation forces in Japan he left an enduring legacy to a defeated foe. He guided the United Nations effort to resist the North Korean invasion of South Korea (1951) until he was relieved of his command by President Harry Truman. D. Clayton James, *The Years of Macarthur* (3 Vols, 1970–1987).

MARSHALL, GEORGE CATLETT (1880–1959). He served successively as Chief of Staff of the U.S. Army (1939–1945), Secretary of State (1947–1949) and Secretary of Defense (1950–1951). He is best remembered for his support of the European Recovery Program or Marshall Plan (1947). Forrest Pogue, *George C. Marshall* (4 Vols, 1963–1987).

MITSCHER, MARC ANDREW (1887–1947). A naval aviator, he commanded Task Force 58 (1944–1945) in the naval battles of the central Pacific, including Philippine Sea, Leyte Gulf, Iowa Jima, and Okinawa. Theodore Taylor, *The Magnificent Mitscher* (1954).

MORGAN, EDMUND MORRIS (1878–1966). Educated at Harvard University from which he received his B.A. (1902), M.A. (1903), and L.L.B. (1905), Morgan began a long career in law in private practice in Duluth, MN (1905). In 1912 he joined the law faculty at the University of Minnesota. In 1917 he left Minnesota for Yale where he taught until 1925, except for the period of World War I when he served (1917–1919) as a reserve major and lieutenant colonel in the judge advocate general's corps in Washington, D.C. under Gen. Samuel T. Ansell. In that capacity he supported Gen. Ansell in Ansell's largely unsuccessful attempt to reform the army's Articles of War during and after World War I. Morgan, who was an expert on the law of evidence, taught at Harvard (1925–1950) and Vanderbilt Universities (1950–1963) and had a distinguished career as an educator. He also chaired the war shipping panel of the War Labor Board in World War II. In 1948, Secretary of Defense James V. Forrestal appointed Morgan chair of a four-man committee that drafted legislation that subsequently became the Uniform Code of Military Justice (U.C.M.J.) for all of the armed services. The U.C.M.J. incorporated many of Gen. Ansell's earlier proposals for reform when the U.S. Congress passed it into law in 1950. Of the many changes the U.C.M.J. brought to military law, the most significant was greater protection for the rights of the accused in serious cases, especially in the establishment of the Court of Military Appeals.

MURPHY, AUDIE (1924–1971). Murphy was one of the most decorated soldiers in World War II. He enlisted in the army in June 1942 just before he turned eighteen. Murphy served in the 3rd Infantry Division as part of the Fifth Army and later the Seventh Army in Tunisia, Sicily, Italy, France, and Germany. Murphy advanced from private to lieutenant, was wounded three times, and won the Medal of Honor on January 26, 1945 when he single-handedly held off a vastly superior German force in the Colmar Pocket in eastern France. In all Murphy received 28 decorations for his wartime heroism. After the war, Murphy became an actor and businessman. One of his best films, *To Hell and Back* (1955), was based on his autobiography in which he played himself. Murphy died in a plane crash in 1971.

NIMITZ, CHESTER WILLIAM (1885–1966). As overall commander of the Pacific fleet in World War II he guided the naval war against Japan. E. B. Potter, *Nimitz* (1976).

PATTON, GEORGE SMITH (1885–1945). Although he trained as a cavalry officer, he became an exponent of armored warfare in the period just prior to World War II. While commander of the Third Army he organized a successful sweep across France into the heart of Germany (1944–1945). Martin Blumenson, *Patton: The Man Behind the Legend, 1885–1945* (1985).

POWERS, FRANCIS GARY (1929–1977). A graduate of Milligan College (1950) in Tennessee, Powers enlisted shortly thereafter in the air force. He subsequently went through flight training and earned a commission in late 1952. Powers was assigned to a jet fighter squadron, but he was not involved in the Korean War. On May 13, 1956, Powers resigned from the air force because he had been recruited by the Central Intelligence

Agency (CIA) to be a contract civilian employee at about $2,500 per month secretly piloting a high-altitude plane known as the U-2 from a base in Turkey on long-distance flights over the Soviet Union. The U-2 was designed to gather photo reconnaissance information about the Soviets' military preparedness and developing rocket program. Ostensibly used to collect weather data, the U-2 was a key U.S. intelligence tool in the Cold War at the time of the "missile gap" between the Soviet Union and the United States. Seventeen pilots, all of whom supposedly worked for the Lockheed Aircraft Corp., the developer of the U-2, made these flights between 1956 and 1960. On May 1, 1960, Powers was shot down while flying at 68,000 feet near Sverdlovsk, some 1,300 miles from the base in Pakistan that Powers had left en route to Norway. Powers, who considered himself a pilot and not a spy, survived the destruction of his U-2 and was taken prisoner. Although Powers might have committed suicide prior to his capture, the CIA had never told him he was expected to do this. Four days later Soviet Premier Nikita S. Khrushchev announced the downing of the U-2. When President Dwight D. Eisenhower explained as a "cover story" that indeed an unarmed weather plane from Turkey was missing, Khrushchev produced Powers and some of the plane's intelligence-gathering gear. Powers had confessed to the Soviets what his real mission was. Eisenhower then admitted he knew about the flights and agreed to stop them. Khrushchev retaliated by canceling a planned visit by Eisenhower to the Soviet Union and by breaking off after one day a major summit meeting in Paris (May 17). The Soviets tried Powers in August. He was found guilty of espionage and sentenced to ten years in prison, but he only served 21 months because in February 1962 the Soviets swapped Powers for Col. Rudolf I. Abel, a high-ranking Soviet spy who had been in a U.S. prison since 1957. Powers then worked briefly for the CIA, but he returned to Lockheed in late 1962 to fly the U-2 again as a test pilot. Let go by Lockheed in 1969, Powers published his version of the U-2 surveillance work in *Operation Overflight* (1970). He later flew a helicopter for a television station in Los Angeles reporting on fast-breaking stories. Powers died when his helicopter crashed on August 1, 1977.

PULLER, LEWIS BURWELL (1898–1971). Puller enlisted in the marines in August 1918 and went on to become one of the most decorated marines in history. Following service in World War I, Puller spent five years in Haiti and five years in Nicaragua where he won two Navy Crosses. Trained as an aviator as well as in infantry tactics, Puller earned the nickname "Chesty" because of his bantam rooster-like strut. He also attained a reputation as an outstanding trainer of young officers and small-unit leaders. Puller had a variety of tours of duty in the 1930s. In September 1942 Puller and the 7th Marines joined the 1st Marine Division on Guadalcanal. There Puller earned a third Navy Cross on the night of October 24–25 defending Henderson airfield. Puller later won a fourth Navy Cross during the Cape Gloucester operation on January 16, 1944. He also took part in the landings at Peleliu (September 1944). In September 1950 Puller commanded the 1st Marine Regiment in the landings at Inchon and during the fierce fighting for Seoul, South Korea. Retired as a result of physical disability in 1955, Puller held the rank of lieutenant general.

QUESADA, ELWOOD RICHARD (1904–1993). Quesada was educated at the University of Maryland and Georgetown University prior to his enlisting in the army in 1924. Assigned to the air service, Quesada went through flight training and earned a commission as a second lieutenant. Quesada had a variety of duty assignments in the 1930s including service as a technical adviser to the Argentine Air Force in 1937–1938. In July 1941 he took command of the 33rd Pursuit Group at Mitchell Field, New York. In early 1943 Quesada went to North Africa in charge of the 12th Fighter Command during the Tunisian, Sicilian, and Corsican campaigns and the invasion of Italy. In October 1943 he took command of the 9th Fighter Command in England. Quesada's planes flew cover and support missions prior to and during the D-Day invasion of France in June 1944. Quesada went to Normandy on D plus 1 to better direct tactical air operations. His planes later participated in air operations in the invasion of Germany. Following the end of the war, Quesada held several senior posts on the Air Staff and in 1947 he was promoted to lieutenant general. In 1951 he headed the Joint Task Force III that conducted the first hydrogen bomb experiments at Eniwetok Atoll in the South Pacific. Quesada retired from the Air Force in 1951 and went on to a successful career in business and public service, including two years as the first administrator of the Federal Aviation Administration (1959–1961).

RADFORD, ARTHUR WILLIAM (1896–1973). A 1916 graduate of the U.S. Naval Academy, Radford served in World War I and later completed aviation training (1920). He subsequently had various aviation assignments afloat and ashore during the 1920s and 1930s. In World War II Radford spent from late 1941 to April 1943 as director of aviation training in the Bureau of Aeronautics. Promoted to rear admiral in 1942 and ordered to sea in July 1943, he commanded the Northern Carrier Group in Adm. Raymond A. Spruance's Fifth Fleet operating in the central Pacific. Radford then rotated back to Washington in a senior aviation post. He returned to the Pacific in November 1944 in command of Carrier Division 6 in Adm. Marc A. Mitscher's Task Force 58. Radford's command participated in air operations around Iwo Jima, Okinawa, and the Japanese Home Islands. Following World War II, Radford held a series of senior posts before becoming a full admiral in command of the Pacific fleet (April 1949). A major figure in the so-called "admiral's revolt" of 1950, Radford advocated a prominent role for the navy following unification of the armed services and opposed any lessened role that favored the air force. In August 1953 Radford became chairman of the Joint Chiefs of Staff, a post he held until his retirement in August 1957.

RIDGWAY, MATTHEW BUNKER (1895–1993). As commander of the 82nd Airborne Division, he parachuted into France on June 6, 1944 (D-Day). He commanded the Eighth Army (1950–1951), and succeeded Gen. Douglas MacArthur in command of the U.N. forces in Korea (1951). Matthew B. Ridgway, *Soldier: The Memoirs of Matthew B. Ridgeway* (1956).

SHERMAN, FORREST PERCIVAL (1896–1951). Initially, Sherman attended the Massachusetts Institute of Technology before entering the U.S. Naval Academy from which he graduated in 1917. For the next two years he served in European waters in World War I. Sherman won his aviator's wings in 1922 and subsequently served ashore and afloat in various aviation posts in the 1920s and 1930s. In May 1942 he took command of the carrier *Wasp*, which was later sunk by Japanese torpedoes on September 15, during the Guadalcanal campaign. Staff aviation posts with Adm. John H. Towers and Adm. Chester W. Nimitz followed his rescue from the *Wasp*. Sherman briefly commanded Carrier Division I in late 1945 before being named deputy chief of naval operations with the rank of vice admiral. In that capacity Sherman represented the navy in the postwar negotiations involving unification of the armed services and in the establishment of the network of U.S. naval bases around the world. He and Gen. Lauris Norstad were key authors in the drafting of the National Security Act of 1947. In 1948–1949 Sherman commanded the U.S. Fifth Fleet in the Mediterranean and in November 1949 he became Chief of Naval Operations. He was very involved in European defense planning at the time of his death in 1951.

SHORT, WALTER CAMPBELL (1880–1949). Short graduated from the University of Illinois in 1901. The next year he was commissioned a second lieutenant in the infantry. He subsequently served in California, the U.S. Southwest, the Philippines, Alaska, and Oklahoma. He participated in the Punitive Expedition to Mexico (1916) and served in France with the 1st Infantry Division in World War I. In the 1920s and 1930s, Short served in a variety of posts, rising steadily from major to major general in 1940. In January 1941, Short took command of the Hawaiian Department headquartered at Pearl Harbor. He received temporary promotion to lieutenant general in February. Short held this command until December 17, 1941 when following the Japanese attack on Pearl Harbor on December 7, he, along with Adm. Husband E. Kimmel, was held responsible for the disaster. The Pearl Harbor commission headed by Supreme Court Justice Owen J. Roberts charged Short and Kimmel with errors of judgment and "dereliction of duty." Short retired in February 1942. In 1944 an army hearing on the attack at Pearl Harbor reached no conclusions about blame and a 1946 congressional investigation supported Short's interpretation of the events in which he argued that he erred in not being on the alert prior to the attack, but also that vital information had been withheld in Washington, D.C. Thus Short contended his error was one of judgment and not of dereliction. The controversy over the surprise attack was never settled.

SMITH, OLIVER PRINCE (1892–1977). Smith graduated from the University of California at Berkeley in 1916. After the U.S. entered World War I, Smith took a commission as a second lieutenant in the marines. He spent the war stationed in Guam (1917–1919). Smith then served in California, aboard the U.S.S. *Texas*, in Washington, D.C., Haiti, and Quantico, Virginia. In the early days of World War II he was stationed in Iceland. From there he went to a headquarters staff assignment. In January 1944, Smith took command of the 5th Marine Regiment and fought in several campaigns in the southwest Pacific and later as a marine deputy chief of staff of the Tenth Army in the Okinawa campaign (April–June 1945). In June 1950 Smith took command of the 1st Marine Division and went with it to Korea. The division, which constituted about half of Gen. Edward M. Almond's X Corps, participated in the amphibious assault on Inchon, the capture of Seoul, and the advance northward to the Yalu River. When a massive Chinese force attacked in November 1950, Smith's division took heavy losses, especially at the Changjin Reservoir on November 27. Smith and his marines fought a desperate thirteen-day retreat in bitter winter weather until they reached Hungnam in December. Smith retired from active service in 1955.

SPAATZ, CARL (1891–1974). He commanded the U.S. Strategic Air Force in Europe (1944) which oversaw all strategic bombing missions over Germany. He latter became the first chief of the independent air force in 1947. *Webster's American Military Biographies* (1978).

SPRAGUE, CLIFTON ALBERT FURLOW (1896–1955). A 1917 graduate of the U.S. Naval Academy, Sprague became an aviation specialist through a series of assignments in the 1920s and 1930s. On December 7, 1941 Sprague was in command of the seaplane tender *Tangier* at Pearl Harbor. His ship fired the first shots on the attacking Japanese planes. Sprague went on to command the new fast carrier *Wasp* which fought in several campaigns in the central Pacific including the first battle of the Philippine Sea in June 1944. Promoted to rear admiral in October, Sprague had command of an escort carrier group called Taffy 3 that was part of Adm. Thomas C. Kinkaid's Seventh Fleet during the action at Leyte Gulf. On October 25, 1944, Sprague's "baby flattops" suddenly confronted the previously undetected Japanese Center Force of battleships and heavy cruisers off Samar Island in the Philippines. In a remarkable display of seamanship, Sprague's outgunned ships were able to drive off the Japanese while losing two carriers, a destroyer, and a destroyer escort. The Japanese, however, lost three heavy cruisers and failed to disrupt seriously the landings at Leyte. Sprague subsequently commanded escort carrier divisions in the Iwo Jima and Okinawa campaigns. After the war (1946) he commanded the naval units at the atomic bomb tests at Bikini Atoll.

SPRUANCE, RAYMOND AMES (1886–1969). He held tactical command of the U.S. naval forces at the decisive Battle of Midway (1942). He then commanded the U.S. Fifth Fleet (1944–1945) in the drive across the central Pacific to the Japanese home islands. Thomas B. Buell, *The Quiet Warrior: A Biography of Admiral Raymond A. Spruance* (1974).

STAPP, JOHN PAUL (1910–). Stapp was born in Brazil of missionary parents. He was a graduate of Baylor University (1931) and later earned a Ph.D. in biophysics at the University of Texas (1939). Later he obtained an M.D. from the University of Minnesota (1943). Commissioned a first lieutenant in the army medical corps in October 1944, Stapp studied aviation medicine. Beginning in 1945 Stapp conducted an extensive program of research into the ability of the human body to withstand high acceleration forces. Often using himself as an experimental subject, he found the human body could endure *g* (gravity) forces nearly double the previously assumed limit. In the 1950s Stapp also experimented with the effect of high speed wind blasts, such as a pilot would experience when bailing out of a jet plane, and the responses of the human body to high altitudes. In 1960 he moved to Brooks Air Force Base in Texas to work on aerospace medical problems associated with manned space travel. From 1965 to 1967 he served at the Armed Forces Institute of Pathology in Washington, D.C. where he studied crash injuries and protection. In 1967 he furthered this work at the National Highway Safety Bureau. Stapp retired in 1970 but continued to work as a consultant for the Department of Transportation.

STILWELL, JOSEPH WARREN (1883–1946). Stilwell commanded U.S. forces in the China-Burma-Indian theater (1942–1944) and served as a military advisor to Jiang Jieshi (Chiang Kai-shek). Barbara W. Tuchman, *Stilwell and the American Experience in China, 1911–1945* (1970).

STRATTON, DOROTHY CONSTANCE (1899–). A graduate of Ottawa University (1920), the University of Chicago (M.A., 1924), and Columbia University (Ph.D., 1932), Stratton was a professor of psychology at Purdue University until she enlisted in the WAVES in 1942. Commissioned as a lieutenant, Stratton was assigned to the office of the commandant of the Coast Guard. There she developed plans for a women's reserve of the Coast Guard called SPARS from the Coast Guard motto *Semper Paratus* ["Always Ready"]. Stratton served as director of the SPARS from November 1942 to January 1946. Promoted to the rank of captain, she commanded an organization that had a peak wartime strength of over 10,000 officers and enlisted personnel. In 1946 the SPARS were completely demobilized. From 1947–1950 Stratton subsequently served as director of personnel for the International Monetary Fund and from 1950 to 1960 as national executive director of the Girl Scouts of America.

STREETER, RUTH CHENEY (1895–1990). Educated at Bryn Mawr College (1914–1916), Ruth Cheney married Thomas W. Streeter in 1917. Because her brother had been a pilot in World War I, Streeter and her mother set up the annual Cheney award for an outstanding member of the Army Air Corps. Then in 1942, Streeter earned a commercial aviation license. When a Women's Reserve of the Marine Corps was established on February 13, 1943, Ruth Cheney Streeter became its director with the rank of major. Women Marines generally served in administrative jobs and by June 1945 had a strength of over 18,000 officers and enlisted personnel. Streeter retired in December 1945, and took up an active life in civic affairs. On June 12, 1948, Congress authorized the enlistment of women in the regular Marine Corps.

SULTAN, DANIEL ISOM (1885–1947). Sultan went to the University of Mississippi from 1901–1903, but then he entered the U.S. Military Academy, graduating in 1907 and taking a commission in the engineers. For over thirty years Sultan held various engineering assignments in the United States, France during World War I, and Nicaragua. In April 1942, Sultan took command of the VIII Corps. Subsequently in January 1943 he became the deputy to Gen. Joseph W. Stilwell, then commander of the China-Burma-India theater. Sultan's task was to build the Burma Road and the Ledo Road for supplies to get through to China. When Stilwell was recalled on October 18, 1944, Sultan became commander of the India-Burma theater with Gen. Claire L. Chennault and later Gen. Albert C. Wedemeyer in command of the China theater. Sultan commanded two Chinese armies in Burma, the British 36th division, and U.S. forces as well. As a field commander Sultan not only oversaw the completion of the Ledo-Burma highway, but also directed Allied combat troops in assisting the British in the defeat of the Japanese in Burma. For his work in the Burma-India theater, he was awarded his fourth Distinguished Service Medal. He was the first army officer to receive the award four times.

TAYLOR, MAXWELL DAVENPORT (1901–1987). He commanded the 101st Airborne Division during World War II and the Eighth Army during the Korean War. He also served as Chief of Staff of the Army (1955–1959) and Ambassador to South Vietnam (1964–1965). John Taylor, *General Maxwell Taylor: The Sword and the Pen* (1989).

TWINING, NATHAN FARRAGUT (1897–1982). While in command of the Thirteenth Air Force (1943) and the Twentieth Air Force (1945), Twining supervised air operations in the southwest Pacific and later the air war against Japan. John Frisbee, *Makers of the Air Force* (1987).

VANDEGRIFT, ALEXANDER ARCHER (1887–1973). Vandegrift spent two years (1906–1908) at the University of Virginia before enlisting in the Marine Corps. He earned a commission as a second lieutenant in 1909 and then began a series of assignments that took him to Cuba, Nicaragua, the Canal Zone, Mexico, Haiti, China, and various ports in the United States. Promoted to major general in March 1942, Vandegrift took command of the 1st Marine Division. He was responsible for training the division and taking it to New Zealand to prepare to land at Guadalcanal. Vandegrift overcame many obstacles and on August 7 a beachhead was secured at Cape Esperance on Guadalcanal with the help of Adm. Richmond Kelly Turner's amphibious forces. Over the next four months the 1st Division fought a fierce jungle campaign against the Japanese forces on the island. For his efforts at Guadalcanal, Vandegrift won both the Navy Cross and the Medal of Honor. In July 1943 Vandegrift, now a lieutenant general, took charge of the I Marine Amphibious Corps for the November 1 landing on Bougainville. Vandegrift subsequently returned to Washington, D.C. and became the Commandant of the Marine Corps on January 1, 1944. On April 4, 1945, Vandegrift became the first marine officer to hold the four-star rank of general while still on active duty. He retired in March 1949.

VANDENBERG, HOYT SANFORD (1899–1954). He helped plan the tactical air support program for the invasion of Europe in 1944. He then commanded the Ninth Air Force as it provided close air support to Gen. George S. Patton's Third Army. He was Chief of Staff of the Air Force (1948–1953). Phillip S. Meilinger, *Hoyt S. Vandenberg: The Life of a General* (1989).

VAN FLEET, JAMES ALWARD (1892–1992). As commander of the 90th Division, he participated in the counter-offensive (January 1945) which ended the Battle of the Bulge. He later commanded the Eighth Army (1951–1953) during the Korean War. *Webster's American Military Biographies* (1978).

VON KARMAN, THEODOR (1881–1963). Born and educated in Budapest, von Karman took his Ph.D. at the University of Göttingen in 1908 in engineering. He then became (in 1912) the director of the Aeronautical Institute at the University of Aachen where he continued until 1930 when he came to the United States to teach at the California Institute of Technology and to serve as the director of the Guggenheim Aeronautical

Laboratory (later renamed in 1942 the Jet Propulsion Laboratory). Von Karman became a U.S. citizen in 1936. In addition to his teaching positions, he consulted for several aircraft manufacturing firms in the United States, Japan, and Europe throughout his long career. He was regarded as one of the leading aeronautical theoreticians who moved the study of aeronautics from a largely empirical enterprise to a rigorously mathematical one. Von Karman's research helped make possible the development of supersonic aircraft and guided missiles. In 1935, for example, he published his theory of air resistance to bodies moving with supersonic speed, which became known as the Karman vortex trail. In World War II he worked with the air force on the development of jet propulsion and ballistic-missile research. In 1942 he started the Aerojet Engineering Corporation to manufacture solid- and liquid-fuel rockets for use in jet-assisted take off (JATO) units, which he helped to develop.

WAESCHE, RUSSELL RANDOLPH (1886–1946). Although Waesche attended Purdue University (1903–1904), he graduated from the cadet school of the Revenue Cutter Service and was commissioned as a third lieutenant in 1906. For ten years Waesche served afloat and ashore in various posts. In 1915 Congress merged the Revenue Cutter Service with the Life Saving Service to form the U.S. Coast Guard, a part of the Department of Treasury. Waesche became head of the Division of Communications in the Coast Guard in 1916. In this job he helped develop the Guard's radio network. From that job Waesche went on to hold command of a cutter and in the 1920s command of several destroyers engaged in patrol of coastal waters against rum runners. In 1932 Waesche was named aide to the commandant of Coast Guard. Four years later he succeeded to the top post with the rank of rear admiral. He held the commandant's position until retirement in 1945. During his tenure in office, Waesche helped expand the Guard's services and from 1939 oversaw the Guard's increasing responsibility for patrol of coastal waters in antisubmarine patrol, coastal defense, port security, sabotage prevention, maintenance of communication and navigation systems (including LORAN) as well as involvement in all major amphibious operations in the Atlantic and Pacific. Waesche commanded a force that at its peak in World War II numbered over 172,000 personnel (including 10,000 SPARS) and nearly 5,000 vessels.

WALKER, WALTON HARRIS (1889–1950). Walker attended the Virginia Military Institute (1907–1908) and the U.S. Military Academy (graduated 1912). He was commissioned in the infantry and following several routine garrison assignments in the West and service in Mexico (1914), Walker went to France in 1918. He fought in the St. Mihiel and Meuse-Argonne offensives. Returning from Europe and occupation duty (1919), Walker continued his training at various army schools in the 1920s. From

1937–1940 Walker served in the War Plans Division of the General Staff. In January 1942 he took command of the 3rd Armored Division and subsequently command of the Desert Training Center on the California-Arizona border. By late 1943 Walker had command of the XX Armored Corps, which was ordered to England in early 1944. The XX Corps went to France in July 1944 as part of Gen. George C. Patton's Third Army. Walker's armored force captured Reims, then crossed the Moselle River in November, and broke the Germans' Siegfried Line in February 1945. The speed the XX Corps demonstrated earned it the nickname "Ghost Corps." Walker's troops liberated the Buchenwald concentration camp in April. Following service in Texas and Chicago (1945–1946) Walker went to Japan in command of the Eighth Army (1948). When North Korea attacked South Korea on June 25, 1950, Gen. Douglas MacArthur sent Walker and his army to South Korea, where he had command of United Nations forces. They fought a stubborn defensive withdrawal and established a 140-mile perimeter at Pusan. This gave the U.N. time to land at Inchon (September 15) and take the offensive. Unfortunately, Walker was killed in a jeep accident on December 23, 1950.

Selected Reading List

World War II

The historical study of World War II since 1945 passed through three distinct phases or generations and probably approaches a fourth. The first phase was dominated by multi-volume official histories commissioned by each of the armed services. The works were solid in research and writing style, more descriptive than analytical, and focused on the strategic, political, and institutional dimensions of the war. In short, they chronicled the war effort of American officialdom. However, having been written by eminent civilian historians who were given wide access to sources and considerable freedom of expression, these official histories were well-accepted in the profession and their view dominated the historical approach to the war for nearly twenty years.

The second phase, in the 1960s, featured battle and campaign histories written by independent scholars and popular writers. These new works differed from the official histories in that they tended to include the use of new sources, particularly German and Japanese documents and interviews and letters from soldiers. As a result, they tended to use much more vivid writing to portray military actions less as well-directed war efforts undertaken in a larger context and more as independent dramas, with distinctly human dimensions. They also tended to be more critical of American military leadership. As they appeared, the vision of the war began to fragment into a European war, with its ground, aerial, and naval dimensions, and a more complex Pacific war, fought on islands, on the seas, on the Asian continent to support China, and in the air over Japan. A final aspect of this generation of World War II historians was the revelation that the allies had cracked the German and Japanese military and diplomatic codes, which led to a flurry of books on ULTRA and MAGIC and their impact on the war.

The third phase, in the mid to late seventies, focused less on how the war was carried out than on the study of the social impact of the war on combatants, non-combatants, and society as a whole. One dimension of this has been a more critical study of American combat performance, inspired, in part, by the apparent military failure in Vietnam. These works, especially those by Weigley and Van Creveld, have been critical of American military leadership and the fighting quality of American soldiers. The dominant concern of this generation, however, is the impact of the war on society. The study of the "home front" shifted from the earlier examination of how society was mobilized to fight the war to a study of the impact of the war on society. In the 1980s, this social examination extended to the impact of the war on minority groups, especially African Americans and women. In this regard, earlier conclusions that the war acted to accelerate social changes favorable to minority groups were challenged by authors who claim that the dominant social groups controlled the war so as to minimize its social impact.

A fourth generation may be represented by authors such as Dower, Fussell, Sigal, Schaffer, and Handel, who are beginning to look at the war as an expression of political and cultural forces within society.

References, General Histories and Official Histories

Craven, Wesley F. and James L. Cate, eds. *The Army Air Forces in World War II* (Seven vols., 1948–1958). These volumes are made up of shorter histories by different authors and are largely focused on combat operations, with one volume dedicated to a study of weapons and one to non-combat activities.

Furer, Julius A. *Administration of the Navy Department in World War II* (1959). This is an in-house publication synthesizing a large number of monographs produced internally within the Navy. It covers the development of the major offices within the Navy Department, the bureaus, the fleet organization, the Marines and Coast Guard and the relations of the Navy with other agencies.

Keegan, John. *The Times Atlas of the Second World War* (1989). In this atlas, Keegan makes an effort to represent graphically the military, political, diplomatic and economic dimensions of the war with maps, charts, graphs, and multiple time lines supplemented by pictures and text.

Perret, Geoffrey. *There's a War to be Won: The United States Army in World War Two* (1991). Despite the trend toward social history, Perret's history of the army is still largely operational in its focus and emphasizes the role of leadership in developing and carrying out policies. The book is scholarly but easily accessible to a lay audience.

Morison, Samuel E. *History of U.S. Naval Operations in World War II* (Fifteen vols. 1950–1962). Morison's official history differs from that of the army in that it was largely written by one individual (with the assistance of a small staff) and focusses almost entirely on operations.

Riesenberg, Felix. *Sea War: The Story of the United States Merchant Marine in World War II* (1974). This is a popular rather than official history of the merchant marine written from an unabashedly subjective point of view. The author interlaces accounts of the operations of merchant marine in various theaters with discussions regarding its ships, structure and sailors.

Sbrega, John J. *The War Against Japan, 1941–1945: An Annotated Bibliography* (1989). This is a compilation of over 5,000 entries including books, articles, dissertations, documents, and novels topically organized and well-annotated.

Smith, Myron J., Jr. *World War II: The European and Mediterranean Theaters* (1984). Smith's compilation includes over 2,800 books, articles, dissertations, documents, and motion picture films, topically organized and cross-indexed when appropriate.

U.S. Marine Corps History and Museums Division. *History of U.S. Marine Corps Operations in World War II* (Five vols. 1958–1971). The focus of these volumes, each written by civilian and marine historians, is on operations. Overall they follow the traditional line that the war in the Pacific validated the amphibious doctrine developed earlier by the marines while stimulating major modifications including the development of assault support aviation.

U.S. Army Center for Military History. *United States Army in World War II* (80 vols. 1950–1975). The focus of this massive official history is on planning, operations, and institutional development. The entire set is broken into a number of short series, each written by a different set of authors, and each focuses on either campaigns or the role of the major operational and bureaucratic organizations in the Army.

Weinberg, Gerhard L. *A World at Arms: A Global History of World War II* (1994). This is the most recent general history of the war. As with most works of this type the focus is still primarily on military and diplomatic events, which in this case, the author attempts to discuss in a global framework.

Wheal, Elisabeth-Anne, Stephen Pope and James Taylor. *A Dictionary of the Second World War* (1990). This dictionary contains over 1,600 entries rang-

ing from a few sentences to several pages in length on military and political leaders, major events, theaters, and weapons alphabetically organized, cross-indexed, and supplemented by numerous pictures and
maps.

Willoughby, Malcolm F. *The U.S. Coast Guard in World War II* (1957).
Willoughby's book is focused almost entirely on operations, including
convoy escorts and anti-submarine duty in concert with naval operations in the Atlantic and support of landing craft operations in the Pacific.

Strategic Direction of the War

Ellis, John. *Brute Force: Allied Strategy and Tactics in the Second World War*
(1990). In a critical reevaluation of leadership in the war, Ellis argues
that the Allies relied on the relatively safe but costly strategy of using
overwhelming military and economic strength to bludgeon the enemy
to death in a war of attrition.

O'Connor, Raymond C. *Diplomacy for Victory: FDR and Unconditional Surrender* (1971). O'Connor argues that Roosevelt's call for ending the war
on the basis of "unconditional surrender" was a necessary product of
coalition warfare and domestic policy.

Steele, Richard W. *The First Offensive, 1942: Roosevelt, Marshall and the Making of American Strategy* (1973). Steele examines the process by which
political, diplomatic, and institutional pressures were integrated in the
process of making the strategic decisions that resulted in Operation
TORCH in North Africa.

Stoler, Mark A. *The Politics of the Second Front: American Military Planning
and Diplomacy in Coalition Warfare, 1941–1943* (1977). Stoler argues that
the army's efforts to establish the second front in Europe as soon as possible was based, in part, on the fear that a late start would leave Russia
in control of Europe after the war.

The War in Europe: The Air War

Crane, Conrad C. *Bombs, Cities, and Civilians: American Air Power Strategy in
World War II* (1993). In contrast with both Sherry and Schaffer, Crane
argues that the Army Air Force remained committed to a rational campaign of precision bombing of primarily industrial and military targets
all during the war.

Freeman, Roger A. *The Mighty Eighth: Units, Men, and Machines* (1970). Freeman provides a largely descriptive narrative history of the men, combat
units and planes of the Eighth Army Air Force from its origins to the
end of the War. The text is supplemented by over 400 photographs and
colored reproductions of the insignia of each of the units in the Eighth.

McFarland, Stephanie L. and Wesley P. Newton. *To Command the Sky: The Battle for Air Superiority over Germany, 1942–1944* (1991). In this study the authors argue that the Army Air Force gained the air superiority needed for the invasion of Europe in 1944 by means of a war of attrition in which bombers were used as bait to get the Luftwaffe in the air to be shot down by American fighters.

Overy, R. J. *The Air War, 1939–1945* (1980). This is a comprehensive overview of both sides of the air war in Europe. Although focused on air campaigns, it also includes the development of the air forces and doctrines involved and the impact of air operations on the conduct and outcome of the war.

Schaffer, Ronald. *Wings of Judgement: American Bombing in World War II* (1985). Following Sherry's lead (See Ch. 4), Schaffer argues that the constraints implied in the Army Air Force doctrine of precision bombing were increasingly ignored in practice so that the American bombing became indiscriminate and terroristic.

The Ground War

Allen, William L. *Anzio: Edge of Disaster* (1979). In this soldier-centered book written for a general audience, Allen argues that poor leadership allowed a planned quick strike to deteriorate into a month-long battle of attrition.

Breuer, William B. *Operation Torch: The Allied Gamble to Invade* (1986). This is a popular narrative of the planning, diplomacy and training that went into the North African landings in 1942. Breuer focuses on how unprepared the United States was to handle such an operation.

D'Este, Carlo. *Bitter Victory: The Battle for Sicily, 1943* (1988). D'Este argues, in this command-oriented study, that the Allies were able to capture the island due to superior numbers but failed to achieve their main strategic objective, the capture of the Axis defense forces.

D'Este, Carlo. *World War II in the Mediterranean, 1942–1945* (1990). D'Este provides the best introduction to the war in the Mediterranean theater. His view of the war is command-centered with its focus on strategic decisions.

Hastings, Max. *Overlord: D-Day and the Battle for Normandy* (1984). Hastings follows Van Creveld's argument that the allied soldiers were no match for the Germans in fighting skill or dedication of their German opponents and that efforts by commanders to substitute fire power for fighting power were not always successful.

Keegan, John. *Six Armies in Normandy: From D-Day to the Liberation of Paris, June 6th–August 25th, 1944* (1982). In this book, written for a general audience, Keegan looks at the conflict in Normandy from the perspective of the combatant through chapters that examine six specific units from six different nations, including an American airborne division.

MacDonald, Charles B. *The Mighty Endeavor: American Armed Forces in the European Theater in World War II* (1969). Although dated, this is still the best one-volume history of American land operations in the European war. The book is written for a general audience and tends to be more descriptive than analytic or critical.

MacDonald, Charles B. *A Time for Trumpets: The Untold Story of the Battle of the Bulge* (1985). MacDonald focuses on the American response to the German attack, arguing that Hitler's plan was foiled due to early realization by the Allied command of which strategic points needed to be held and the tenacity of allied troops in holding them.

Morris, Eric. *Salerno: A Military Fiasco* (1983). Morris sees Salerno as a fiasco because of the failure to trap Germans in southern Italy as planned and blames this on a variety of errors and miscalculations at the command level. The book is written for a general audience and views the battle from both a soldier's and command perspective.

Weigley, Russell, F. *Eisenhower's Lieutenants: The Campaign in France and Germany, 1944–1945* (1981). In this book, which is now considered by many to be the best overall study of the Allied campaign in France and Germany, Weigley is critical of American leadership for its failure to follow a single line of strategy.

Wilt, Alan F. *The French Riviera Campaign of August 1944* (1981). Wilt offers a solid, command-centered, narrative study of Operation DRAGOON from its initial planning stage to the link-up with Eisenhower's forces on the German frontier.

The Naval War

Meigs, Montgomery C. *Slide Rule and Submarine* (1991). Meigs argues that although scientists made major contributions in the anti-submarine campaigns in terms of developing new weapons and providing new ways to analyze training and operations their effectiveness was limited by conservative opposition from within the naval establishment.

Van der Vat, Dan. *The Atlantic Campaign: World War II's Great Struggle at Sea* (1988). Van der Vat presents a new synthesis of the Battle of the Atlantic that brings together the roles of systems analysis, intelligence, technological advances, and operations in a naval campaign that he feels was a rather close call for the Allies.

Y'Blood, William T. *Hunter-Killer: U.S. Escort Carriers in the Battle of the Atlantic* (1983). This is a popular study of the role of the "Jeep" carriers in the battle of the Atlantic with its focus on tactics and specific operations.

The War in the Pacific

Dower, John W. *War Without Mercy: Race and Power in the Pacific War* (1986). Dower argues that the racial stereotypes that dominated the way Americans and Japanese viewed each other influenced strategic and tactical decision-making on both sides.

Spector, Ronald H. *Eagle Against the Sun: The American War with Japan* (1985). This is now considered the best one-volume survey of the war in the Pacific available. While it is command-centered, with its principle focus on strategy and operations, attention is given to the impact of the experience of the war on various groups.

The Island War

Beck, John. *MacArthur and Wainwright: The Sacrifice of the Philippines* (1974). This is largely a documentary study of command relations between MacArthur and Washington which argues the Philippines were sacrificed due to Washington's unwillingness to risk a rescue effort.

Feifer, George. *Tennozan: The Battle of Okinawa and the Atomic Bomb* (1992). Feifer argues that the savagery of the fighting at Okinawa which inflicted nearly a quarter million casualties among troops and civilians was largely responsible for the decision to end the war by dropping the atomic bomb.

Hammel, Eric M. *Guadalcanal: Starvation Island* (1987). *Guadalcanal: The Carrier Battles: Carrier Operations in the Solomons, August–October, 1942* (1987). *Guadalcanal: Decision at Sea: The Naval Battle of Guadalcanal, November 13–15, 1942* (1988). In this trilogy, written for a general audience, Hammel examines Guadalcanal as the focal point of a giant air, land, and sea struggle that not only halted Japanese expansion to the south, but also crippled its ability to continue the naval war.

Hoyt, Edwin P. *Storm over the Gilberts: War in the Central Pacific, 1943* (1978). This is a popular account of the capture of Tarawa. Hoyt argues that the island was of negligible strategic value, but the operation gave the Navy-Marine team valuable training for later struggles.

Ross, Bill D. *Peleliu: Tragic Triumph* (1991). In this popular history, Ross argues that while the capture of Peleliu was of no strategic significance to the war, the American success in overcoming the difficulties posed by the enemy and terrain is a tribute to the fighting quality of the marines of the First Division.

Sigal, Leon V. *Fighting to a Finish: The Politics of War Termination in the United States and Japan, 1945* (1988). Sigal uses the end of the war in the Pacific as a case study about the phenomenon of war ends and sees the decision to use the bomb dictated not by needs of state to end the war but by the need of the Manhattan Project to justify costs and get funds for continued research.

Wheeler, Richard. *Iwo* (1980). In this narrative written for a popular audience, Wheeler endeavors to capture the real essence of the fighting on Iwo Jima from both a command and the soldiers' perspectives on both sides.

The Naval War

Blair, Clay, Jr. *Silent Victory: The U.S. Submarine War Against Japan* (1975). In this comprehensive account of the submarine warfare, Blair includes most major American patrols and argues that the submarines were critical in disrupting Japanese supply operations and economy.

Lindley, John M. *Carrier Victory: The Air War in the Pacific* (1978). Lindley provides a highly detailed look at how the carriers in the American, British and Japanese navies functioned in combat as well as the nature of day-to-day life on board.

Prange, Gordon W. *Miracle at Midway* (1982). Prange looks at both the command and the men in both fleets involved in this battle, arguing that the battle was also well-fought on the Japanese side so that except for American luck, the battle would have been far more even in its results.

Stewart, Adrian. *The Battle of Leyte Gulf* (1979). This is a popular narrative account of the battle at the tactical level as viewed from both the American and Japanese sides.

Willmott, H. P. *The Barrier and the Javelin: Japanese and Allied Pacific Strategies, February to June, 1942* (1983). Willmott sees the Japanese island-centered strategy in the Pacific as flawed in that it served to spread their forces, ultimately allowing the United States to concentrate its forces to stop the Japanese at the Coral Sea and then to win at Midway.

Y'Blood, William T. *Red Sun Setting: The Battle of the Philippine Sea* (1981). This popular account of the battle is largely taken from the perspective of the combatants, especially from those of the carrier pilots.

The China-Burma-India Theater

Callahan, Raymond. *Burma, 1942–1945* (1980). This is an analysis of the Allied invasion of Burma at the political and strategic level, with an emphasis on the strained nature of Anglo-American relations during the campaign.

Nalty, Bernard C. *Tigers over Asia* (1978). This is one of many books generated by Chenault and his legendary Flying Tigers in China. This book discusses both Chenault and his volunteer organization with reference to the broader strategic framework of the war in that theater.

Intelligence and Covert Operations

Drea, Edward J. *MacArthur's ULTRA: Codebreaking and the War Against Japan, 1942–1945* (1992). Drea looks at the cryptographic intelligence made available to MacArthur and his use of it. He argues that MacArthur largely used the intelligence when it fit with his own preconceptions and plans.

Calvocoressi, Peter. *Top Secret Ultra* (1980). This is considered the best of several books designed to explain ULTRA to the layman. Calvocoressi

also sets the whole question in the context of the war, arguing that UL-
TRA was helpful to the Allied side, but not alone responsible for the
victory in the war.

Handel, Michael I., et al. *Leaders and Intelligence* (1988). Eight essays examine the way leaders used military intelligence in the war, arguing that
wars of the future could be more focused on the manipulation of information rather than the deployment of men and material.

Lewin, Ronald. *The American MAGIC: Codes, Ciphers, and the Defeat of Japan*
(1982). MAGIC, the breaking of the Japanese diplomatic and military
codes, was the American counterpart to ULTRA. Lewin describes it and
claims that the obsession of the codes was of major importance in critical battles, the war on Japanese merchant marine and even the development of strategy in Europe.

Parrish, Thomas. *The ULTRA Americans: The U.S. Role in Breaking the Nazi
Codes* (1986). Parrish claims that breaking the German code was not a
one-shot affair, but that it required on-going efforts to keep up with
changes in the German code and communications practice, and that
American intelligence personnel played a significant role in these efforts.

Smith, R. Harris. *OSS: The Secret History of America's First Intelligence Agency*
(1972). In this narrative history of the cooperation of the OSS with resistance movements, Smith argues that William Donovan, in founding the
OSS, introduced the idea of combining espionage and covert activity
that still characterizes the CIA as the institutional successor to the OSS.

Winterbotham, Frederick. *The ULTRA Secret* (1974). In this book,
Winterbotham broke the story of how the British operation, codenamed
ULTRA, cracked the German military codes. This revelation promoted
a rash of literature on the subject with some American dimensions.

Social History

Bernstein, Alison R. *American Indians and World War II* (1991). Bernstein
examines Native American participation in both the civilian and military aspect of the war in the context of an extension of the "Indian New
Deal," arguing that the experience heightened the desire for Native
American self-determination.

Berube, Allan. *Coming out Under Fire: The History of Gay Men and Women in
World War Two* (1990). Estimating that close to a million homosexual
men and women entered the service in the war, Berube analyzes how
they coped with the military and how the military coped with them
arguing that the wartime experience served as a catalyst for the later
homosexual awakening as well as the development of more liberal attitudes in society towards homosexuality.

Ellis, John. *The Sharp End: The Fighting Man in World War II* (1982). Ellis offers a view of soldiers' personal experiences in the war by describing induction, training, morale, relaxation, discipline, and the combat faced by men in service.

Fussell, Paul. *Wartime: Understanding and Behavior in the Second World War* (1989). Fussell uses a study of wartime and postwar literature to get at the same issue of soldier experience as Ellis, but comes up with the far more gloomy conclusion that the soldiers saw the war as mass insanity.

Grander, Byrd H. *On Final Approach: The Women Airforce Service Pilots of W.W. II* (1991). Utilizing a "diary" format, Grander examines the organizational history, training experiences and activities of the women who flew in the service of the U.S. The work represents a compilation of material previously unavailable in a single source.

Keil, Sally. *Those Wonderful Women in Their Flying Machines: The Unknown Heroines of World War II* (1974). In this history of the Women Airforce Service Pilots (WASP), Keil argues that the women entered the force largely out of a love of flying so that the ending of the war also ended this opportunity to escape to a more exciting life. Keil also notes that, as women, the WASPs were given little credit during the war or later for their service.

Marshall, S.L.A. *Men Against Fire* (1947). This classic study of American servicemen in combat is famous for Marshall's contention that even when under fire, less that a quarter of American service men actually fired on the enemy.

Motley, Mary P., ed. *The Invisible Soldiers: The Experiences of the Black Soldier, World War II* (1975). This is a collection of edited interviews with African American military personnel regarding their experiences in the war. While African Americans found themselves confronted with discrimination, their wartime experience gave them a sense of achievement that helped inspire their later participation in the civil rights movement.

Sadler, Stanley. *Segregated Skies: All-Black Combat Squadrons of World War II* (1992). Sadler continues Jakeman's history of the Tuskeegee airmen (See Ch. 4) describing the performance of the four African American squadrons that flew in the war. Sadler claims that the combat performance of these squadrons was creditable despite their inexperience and discrimination suffered.

Soderbergh, Peter A. *Women Marines: The World War II Era* (1992). Soderbergh provides a social history of the 20,000 women who served as marines in the war, describing the varieties of their experiences. He argues that the women generally found this experience to be liberating and life-defining.

Van Creveld, Martin. *Fighting Power: German and U.S. Army Performances, 1939–1945* (1982). Using a sophisticated concept he calls "fighting power" that involves such things as the training of troops, replacement system, selection of officers and NCOs, distribution of leave and decorations, etc., Van Creveld argues that the German army was superior to the American in its "fighting power."

The Home Front in the War

Blum, John M. *V Was for Victory: Politics and American Culture During World War II* (1976). This is largely a study of social policies in America during the war which, Blum argues, established the full-employment managed economy and made Americans inward-looking, materialistic and militaristic.

Costello, John. *Virtue Under Fire: How World War II Changed our Social and Sexual Attitudes* (1985). Costello insists the uncertainty and loneliness of the war mixed with its sense of romance and exhilaration served to promote more liberal attitudes toward sex, homosexuality, and gender roles leading to the later sexual revolution of the 1960s and 1970s.

Flynn, George Q. *The Mess in Washington: Manpower Mobilization in World War II* (1979). Flynn looks at the bureaucratic efforts behind manpower mobilization to maximize production as part of the greater conflict between those who sought to conscript all resources needed for the war and those who sought to preserve the voluntarist nature of American society.

Gregory, Chester W. *Women in Defense Work in World War II: An Analysis of the Labor Problem and Women's Rights* (1974). Gregory analyzes the recruitment, training, and support provided by industries which looked to women to solve their wartime labor needs, and concludes that the war provided a liberating and permanently emancipating experience for women.

Honey, Maureen. *Creating Rosie the Riveter: Class, Gender, and Propaganda During World War II* (1984). Honey argues that the government developed separate sets of images to attract middle-class and working-class women into the war effort, but in both cases stressed that participation was to be temporary and not part of long-term social change.

Koppes, Clayton R. and Gregory D. Black. *Hollywood Goes to War: How Politics, Profits, and Propaganda Shaped World War II Movies* (1987). The authors look at the influence of the U.S. Office of Information in terms of its impact on how films portrayed allies, enemies, and problems within society.

Milkman, Ruth. *Gender at Work: The Dynamics of Job Segregation by Sex During World War II* (1987). In an analysis of the automobile and electrical manufacturing industries, Milkman sees the war having little impact on either the ideology or the practice of gender-based job discrimination.

Miller, Marc S. *The Irony of Victory: World War II and Lowell, Massachusetts* (1988). In a study focused on a single city, Miller argues that the war created greater economic dependence on war-related industries, and accelerated the development of federal intervention in the economy, erosion of local control, and increased status for traditional elites. He sees no liberation of women by the war.

Polenberg, Richard J. *War and Society: The United States, 1941–1945* (1972). Polenberg feels that the war increased the rate of change in the United States by promoting the growth of government, industrialization, urbanization, and liberalized attitudes towards race and women.

Vatter, Harold G. *The U.S. Economy in World War II* (1985). Vatter offers a comprehensive look at all aspects of the impact of the war on the American economy, arguing that the war accelerated and crystallized the establishment of a mixed economy in the United States.

Wynn, Neil. *The Afro-American and the Second World War* (1976). Wynn argues that the war produced a major upheaval in the lives of African Americans in the United States, as many moved into defense industries in northern cities, resulting in heightened political and economic expectations.

The Cold War

The four-and-one-half decade Cold War which the United States carried on with the Soviet Union continued even as hot wars were taking place in different spheres. In the United States, fears of Soviet expansion gained standing as one country after another fell into the Eastern bloc after World War II. The American response was launched with the Marshall Plan, the Truman Doctrine, the North Atlantic Treaty Organization, and the Berlin Airlift. After the Berlin Wall fell in 1990 and the Soviet Union disintegrated in 1991, even conservative American military leaders agreed the Cold War was over. But the long period of anxiety provided the U-2 incident, the Cuban missile crisis, the space race and the policies of containment, massive retaliation, and deterrence.

Nearly all writers on this period provide interpretations of how the United States gained its self-perception as the world's policeman and how that responsibility was carried out. For some, the United States had no choice but to come to the rescue of freedom-loving people everywhere; for others American motives were really self-serving and economic. All interpretations, however, stress the interrelationship of national security, military strategy, public opinion, international relations, social evolution, and diplomatic policy.

General Works

Brodie, Bernard S. *Strategy in the Missile Age* (1959). The first part of Brodie's classic treatise traces the development of certain characteristics of modern military thinking which influence national security policies in the U.S. The second part deals with new problems and approaches, discussing such topics as deterrence, limited war, and preemptive attack.

Brodie, Bernard and Fawn Brodie. *From Crossbow to H-Bomb* (1973). This is a short and generalized history of the evolution of weapons including an adequate picture of the nuclear revolution and how its science has far outpaced sentiment.

Bundy, McGeorge. *Danger and Survival* (1988). This book is about the political choices and dangers involved in the development of nuclear weapons. Bundy, a high government official from the Kennedy-Johnson administration, has evolved into a strong advocate for arms control.

Coletta, Paolo E. *The United States Navy and Defense Unification 1947–1953* (1981). Coletta records the changing character of the management authority in the Department of Defense during the Truman administration. He notes the horizontal federal structure of 1947 yielded to the vertical unitary organizational structure of 1953.

Duscha, Julius. *Arms, Money, and Politics* (1964). A searching look at the defense program and the politics involved. The economic problems of gradual disarmament are also discussed.

Endicott, John E. and Roy E. Stafford, Jr., eds. *American Defense Policy* (1965). The editors offer a framework through which to study defense policy in the United States by presenting contrasting ideas from numerous experts and decision makers as expressed in previously issued articles, speeches, and position papers.

Graebner, Norman A. *The National Security: Its Theory and Practice, 1945–1960* (1986). This volume is comprised of seven essays presented at a West Point symposium in April 1982, and focused on the efforts of Truman and Eisenhower to deal with alterations in the global balance of power.

Green, Philip. *Deadly Logic* (1966). Green discusses the theory of nuclear deterrence against the backdrop of a post-World War II world and military strategy. He notes that the principal sources of such new theory are the simulated situations of traditional "war games" and the transposition of mathematical theory of games into military-political matching of wits and threats.

Hitchcock, Walter T., ed. *The Intelligence Revolution—A Historical Perspective* (1991). These are the proceedings of the 13th Military History Symposium, held at the U.S. Air Force Academy in October 1988. Two themes run concurrently in the presentations: (1) There has been an increasing reliance on photographic, signals and electronic intelligence in the search for national security; and (2) there are inherent limitations of research into all aspects of the subject that remain sensitive today.

Kaufmann, William W., ed. *Military Policy and National Security* (1956). Kaufmann presents a series of essays which debate the military policies of the United States before the Soviet Union reached nuclear parity.

Kissinger, Henry A. *Nuclear Weapons and Foreign Policy* (1957). This early writing of Henry Kissinger gives the background for the nuclear strategy adopted by later Republican administrations. His position argues for greater communications of our intentions to the enemy to maintain the asset of deterrence.

Osgood, Robert E. *Limited War, The Challenge to American Strategy* (1957). The author deals with the question of how the United States could foster its interests (including containment) abroad without risking a nuclear war.

Rearden, Steven L. *The Formative Years, 1947–1950* (1982). This is an official history from the office of the Secretary of Defense centered on the origins and organization of the national military establishment, the progress of unification, the use of resources, and the response to the beginning of the Cold War.

Schelling, T. C. and W. H. Halperin. *Strategy and Arms Control* (1961). Schelling and Halperin develop the stability-through-deterrence thesis of which Schelling was the chief architect.

Schelling, T. C. *Strategy of Conflict* (1960). Schelling presents a series of psychological essays on games theory suggesting there is a common interest as well as conflict between adversaries in negotiations, war, and threats of war.

Steiner, Barry H. *Bernard Brodie and the Foundations of American Nuclear Strategy* (1991). This modern war study covers the career and concepts of one of the key men in the long-time debate over the stockpiling of nuclear weapons and their effectiveness as a deterrent.

Wyden, Peter. *Bay of Pigs: The Untold Story* (1979). Wyden argues that the Kennedy administration was run by enthusiastic amateurs who had no conception of the need for appropriate military command, control and communications.

Air Force

Hunter, Mel. *Strategic Air Command* (1961). This is a flattering assessment of a key element of the United States' air power and strategic thinking during the Cold War of the 1950s.

Tunner, William H. *Over the Hump* (1964 & 1985). Tunner explains in detail the principles by which he developed military air transportation and the way he applied those principles to the historic airlifts he commanded.

Vaugh, Robert V. *In the Shadow of Trinity: An American Airman in Occupied Japan* (1991). This book addresses an often overlooked facet of warrior experiences—the occupation of a defeated land during its postwar period.

Wolk, Herman S. *Planning and Organizing the Postwar Air Force 1943–1947* (1982). This excellent narrative and analysis untangles the complex history of the final year of the air force's struggle for organizational independence after its organizational structure had already been established and procedures set for the conduct of routine activity set.

Yenne, Bill. *SAC: A Primer of Modern Strategic Air Power* (1985). This is more than the assimilation of people, places, and things in the history of the Strategic Air Command. Yenne also presents "valuable perspectives on the relationship of emerging aerospace thought and technology" as they relate to world events.

Zimmerman, Carroll L. *Insider at SAC: Operations Analysis Under General Lemay* (1988). The author presents an informative narrative of the general and the people who worked with him to control strategic security and make military policy from the 1940s into the 1970s.

Navy

Armbrister, Trevor. *A Matter of Accountability* (1970). Armbrister presents a well-researched and objective account of the USS *Pueblo* affair, examining the ship's mission and the contradictions in the command structure in which it operated.

Beach, Edward L. *The United States Navy: 200 Years* (1986). A retired navy captain presents a general history of the navy. The post-World War II period is treated briefly and almost as an epilogue.

Davis, Vincent. *The Admirals' Lobby* (1967). Treating the decision makers in the navy as a political sub-culture, Davis argues that military policy emerges from the politics of the policy-making process.

Hewett, Richard G. and Francis Duncan. *Nuclear Navy, 1946–1962* (1974). This book was written at Admiral Rickover's urging to record the development of significant aspects of nuclear technology in the United States, specifically the history of the naval nuclear propulsion program.

Social/Political Issues

Scherer, Frederic M. *The Weapons Acquisition Process—Economic Incentives* (1964). Scherer focuses on the contractual and competitive incentives in the development and production of major weapon systems.

Scherer, Frederic M. and Merton J. Peck. *The Weapons Acquisition Process—An Economic Analysis* (1962). The authors focus on the non-market character of the weapons acquisition process, the structure of the defense industry and the economic criteria and relationships involved in the execution of weapons programs.

Trimble, William F. *Wings for the Navy: A History of the Naval Aircraft Factory, 1917–1956* (1990). Trimble gives an objective history of the only government-owned and operated naval aircraft production facility in the United States.

Korean War (1950–1953)

The Korean War (1950–1953) was the United States' first experience with a major "limited" conflict. It was limited not by what was technologically possible but by what seemed politically appropriate. Operating in the shadow of the atomic cloud, Truman sought to insure that the Soviet Union would find no cause to begin World War III.

Approximately 60,000 North Korean troops invaded South Korea on June 25, 1950. The United States led South Korean and United Nations' forces in a successful defense followed by an invasion of North Korea that nearly reached the Chinese border in November. Over 200,000 Chinese troops then crossed the border to drive back the United Nations' forces. A cease fire negotiated in July of 1951 placed both sides near their original positions and, after two more years of sporadic fighting, an armistice was signed on July 27, 1953.

The history of America's "Forgotten War" in Korea certainly pales in comparison to the multitude of pages written about World War II and the Vietnam conflict. However, the war and issues in it have received a fair amount of coverage. Subsequent events and the focus on the concept of "limited war" have led historians to treat the Korean War as a transitional conflict between the conventional warfare of World War II and the political warfare in Vietnam. In so doing, their own work has evolved from a limited discussion of battles and strategies to a broader concern with issues of morality, legality, and the psychological impact of the new forms of combat. One particular issue that has generated considerable discussion was the Truman-MacArthur controversy which resulted in the general's dismissal. The Army has completed three of its five planned volumes of its official history, the Air Force finished its one-volume account in 1961, and the Navy published its one-volume report in 1962.

General Works

Alexander, Bevin. *Korea, The First War We Lost* (1986). Alexander presents a comprehensive examination of the Korean War and challenges many traditional interpretations.

Condit, Doris M. *The Test of War: 1950–1953* (1988). This is volume two in a series of the history of the Office of the Secretary of Defense. It is intended to present a scholarly, objective and critical history, primarily focusing on national security policy during the period from the start of the Korean War until the end of the Truman administration.

Cumings, Bruce. *The Origins of the Korean War* (1990). Cumings argues that the origins of the war can be found more in the efforts of the U.S. and

U.S.S.R. to establish themselves on the peninsula by taking advantage of existing Korean cleavages, nourishing one against the other, and less in any conscious decisions by the Koreans to choose sides in a great struggle among super powers.

Fehrenbach, T.R. *This Kind of War* (1963). Fehrenbach views the Korean War story as a study of military unpreparedness, a test of wills, and a general lesson of caution.

Goulden, Joseph C. *Korea—The Untold Story of the War* (1982). Written by the first author to employ the Freedom of Information Act, Goulden covers military actions, political origins, peace negotiations and the war's legacy. He presents a revisionist interpretation of the war, spotlighting MacArthur's role and dismissal.

Holliday, J.K., and Bruce Cumings. *Korea: The Unknown War* (1988). This new classic on the Korean War by British authors, is the result of numerous interviews and review of official documents from all sides. The international character of the war is emphasized, as when the authors note that both the U.S. and U.S.S.R. denied the known presence of Russia in the air war for fear of a total war.

Hastings, Max. *The Korean War* (1987). Hastings suggests that Korea was a military rehearsal for the defeat in Vietnam. The United States did not learn the lessons, the Communist enemy did. The British author interviewed many participants, including members of Peking's Institute of Strategic Studies.

Higgins, Trumbull. *Korea and the Fall of MacArthur: A Précis in Limited War* (1960). Higgins discusses the overall story of the Korean Conflict with its limited effect and restrictions against attacking mainland China. He specifically addresses the power conflict between a populist politician and a self-righteous military leader—especially informative with respect to civilian control of the military.

Leckie, Robert. *Conflict: The History of the Korean War, 1950–1953* (1962). Leckie presents a generalized history of the Korean War, including both the ground and air campaigns.

Pasley, Virginia. *21 Stayed: The Story of the American GI's Who Chose Communist China: Who They Were and Why They Stayed* (1955). Pasley records a special event that few remember from the "forgotten war." She writes their stories not to condemn, but with understanding in a world of tragedy.

Poats, Rutherford M. *Decision in Korea* (1954). Poats recounts the Korean War, not as one that was lost, but the first test of the validity of the concept of collective security against centralized aggression. Uniquely, he also presents the complete text of the Korean Armistice Agreement.

Rees, David. *Korea: The Limited War* (1964). Rees views the history of the limited conflict in Korea as the first important war in American history that was not a crusade. The new purpose was an attempt to affect the opponent's will, not to crush it. Although dated, this remains one of the best studies of the conflict.

Toland, John. *In Mortal Combat: Korea, 1950–1953* (1991). Toland views the Korean War as unique in U.S. history, noting that when the armistice was finally signed, none of the issues that started the war had been settled. He asks, and attempts to answer, Who was to blame? and Was it worth it?

Vatcher, William Henry. *Panmunjom: The Story of the Korean Military Armistice Negotiations* (1958). Vatcher, a psychological warfare advisor at the negotiations, reveals the struggle and frustration that was the culmination of the Korean Conflict. The purpose of the book is to help individuals deal with the communists.

Zellers, Larry. *In Enemy Hands: A Prisoner in North Korea* (1991). This is one of the few books on prisoners during the Korean War. Zellers, a civilian missionary, describes the Death March in North Korea in 1950, the portrayal of his comrades in adversity, and the final freedom in 1953.

Army

Appleman, Roy E. *Ridgway Duels for Korea* (1990). Appleman focuses on the first six months of 1951 and describes how Ridgway took over the demoralized United Nations' command and turned it into a determined force which caused the North Koreans to seek a truce. The book contains effective maps and charts.

Appleman, Roy E. *South to the Naktong, North to the Yalu* (1961). As part of the U.S. Army five-volume series on the Korean War, Appleman's narrative portrays the grimness of a limited war and the consequences of unpreparedness. It covers U.S. Army action from the outbreak of war to the full-scale intervention of Communist China.

Appleman, Roy E. *East of Chosin: Entrapment and Breakout in Korea, 1950* (1987). This is a well written and detailed account concerning the U.S. Army's 7th Infantry Division that fought an important battle in freezing Korean weather during the early days of the conflict.

Blair, Clay. *The Forgotten War: America in Korea, 1950–1953* (1987). In one of the most extensive histories written, Blair suggests that the impact of the war on the U.S. government and society was profound and lasting. In particular, the book is about U.S. Army infantry operations in Korea. He explores the human factors of leadership, the representation of West Point graduates, and the performance of African American troops.

Gugeler, Russell A. *Combat Actions in Korea* (1954). Originally published in 1954, these accounts of small-unit actions were written primarily to acquaint American officers and soldiers who had not yet been in battle with combat realities.

Hammel, Eric. *Chosin: Heroic Ordeal of the Korean War* (1990). A total of 17 Medals of Honor were awarded to men of the U.S. Army's X Corps for their valor during the battle and retreat along the Chosin River. Hammel's detailed text puts the reader in the fox hole and the headquarters with a rapid historical narrative style.

Hermes, Walter G. *Truce Tent and Fighting Front* (1966). Part of the five-volume U.S. Army series on the Korean War, this book covers the frustrations of the truce negotiations from mid-1951 on, and the concurrent fighting.

Marshall, S.L.A. *Pork Chop Hill: The American Fighting Man in Action—Korea, Spring 1953* (1956, 1986 reprint) Marshall, who was both a general and news journalist, gives a graphic report on the actions of specific units in one season of the Korean War. His up-close and vivid detail of men and tactics gives high praise to the concept of the American soldier.

Ridgway, Matthew B. *The Korean War: How We Met the Challenge* (1967). In this review of the military history of the war, the 8th Army commander who replaced MacArthur gives most of the coverage and credit to the army while briefly commenting on air interaction. Any wider understanding of the geopolitical ramifications of the conduct of the war is spotty at best.

Air Force

Blair, Clay. *Beyond Courage* (1955). Blair tells the stories of several Air Force prisoners of war during the Korean Conflict. He suggests that the military did not prepare its personnel for the super-human trials they faced.

Futrell, Robert F. *The United States Air Force in Korea 1950–1953* (1982). Futrell documents the application of air power in the Korean conflict, stressing the accomplishments and failures which would be of interest to the military planner and student. The book contains many maps, photographs, charts and appendix items.

Navy

Cagle, Malcom W. and Frank A. Manson. *The Sea War in Korea* (1957). In this extensive survey of the naval side of the war, the authors argue that control of the sea gave the United Nations forces the advantage of mobility to defeat the initial Communist attack and limit the conflict.

Field, James A., Jr. *History of United States Naval Operations, Korea* (1962). Field has written a reliable official one-volume history of U.S. Naval activities during the conflict in Korea.

Hallion, Richard P. *The Naval Air War in Korea* (1986). Hallion discusses how carrier air power shifted to sustained operations against ground targets and reveals how much the air force had to depend on the navy for air interdiction. He also notes the impact of the technological transformation from a propeller force to jets.

Marines

Geer, Andrew. *The New Breed—The Story of the U.S. Marines in Korea* (1952). Much of what Geer presents is from both his own experiences and nearly 700 personal interviews. He believes that the real story of the Korean War is not geopolitical or even military strategy, but about those on the firing line.

Heinl, Robert D. *Victory at High Tide: The Inchon-Seoul Campaign* (1968). A retired Marine colonel sets forth the step-by-step planning and execution of the notable amphibious invasion that was inspired by the vision of MacArthur and made possible by the naval power of the United States.

Montross, Lynn, et al. *U.S. Marine Operations in Korea 1950–1953* (1954–1972). This five-volume account of Marine actions in support of the United States' limited objectives in Korea is designed to give a laudatory reflection on the Marines' efforts and accomplishments.

Montross, Lynn. *Cavalry of the Sky* (1954). Montross tells the story of the U.S. Marine Corps' helicopter operations during the Korean War, 1950–1953.

6

The Uncertain Period: 1964–1994

Two major developments made these years a time of uncertainty. The Vietnam War and its aftereffects eroded American military effectiveness and raised doubts about the nation's capacity, or willingness, to use military power to support its foreign policy. At the same time, the erosion of superpower bipolarity made it more difficult for the United States or the Soviet Union to impose their will on other nations.

The United States became directly involved in Vietnam in the mid-1950s when it replaced France as the sponsor of the South Vietnamese government. Still, despite millions of dollars of aid and extensive military advice, South Vietnam failed to stop a Communist insurgency aided and abetted by North Vietnam.

As with his predecessors, President Lyndon Johnson struggled to find a means to save South Vietnam. A brief conflict between North Vietnamese patrol boats and American naval forces in the Tonkin Gulf in August 1964 gave Johnson his opportunity. The president directed naval air attacks on North Vietnam following the incident. He also secured a resolution from Congress giving him the authority to use armed force to defend United States personnel in South Vietnam and "to prevent further aggression" there. Johnson and his successor, Richard M. Nixon, used the Tonkin Gulf Resolution as their authority to wage war in Vietnam.

Under Lyndon Johnson, the American military commitment to South Vietnam escalated rapidly. Less than 20,000 Americans served there when he assumed the presidency. They numbered 184,000 at the end of 1965, 385,000 a year later, and peaked at 543,000 early in 1969. The nation sent the best equipped and best trained force it ever fielded at the onset of a war. Yet that combined force of soldiers, marines, airmen and sailors could not eradicate the Vietnamese irregulars (Viet Cong), decisively defeat North Vietnamese regulars, or force North Vietnam to accept a cease fire.

Military historians disagree on why the American military effort failed. Some argue the armed forces unwisely fought an enemy pursuing classic counterinsurgency warfare with conventional forces too dependent on indiscriminate firepower. Others contend the United States misused its conventional power by dispersing troops in pursuit of guerilla forces who were not the real enemy. In this view, main force North Vietnamese regulars were the genuine threat and never appropriately fought. Inasmuch as the debate is unresolved, it seems appropriate to describe the conflict as a complex civil war between the Vietnamese people involving elements of revolutionary and conventional warfare.

Despite the significant increase of American personnel in Vietnam, President Johnson's concern that hostilities not precipitate a larger war with China or the Soviets led him to place constraints on the nation's military effort. As in Korea, the war would be limited in its implementation. Johnson's efforts in this regard created a strange kind of war. The White House established rules of engagement setting geographical limits where American forces could fight, and requiring them to obtain permission from South Vietnamese authorities for certain operations. Within the combat zones, however, restraints applied to the level of firepower and weaponry employed. Helicopter gunships, free fire zones, defoliants, napalm and bombing were used. This reliance on unrestrained firepower devastated large portions of the nation the United States was ostensibly trying to save. At the same time, the bombing campaign against North Vietnam was strictly regulated and modulated by the White House. President Johnson and his advisors believed a bombing campaign that punished North Vietnam in careful increments would persuade the government in Hanoi to seek peace. Unfortunately, the enemy remained intransigent, while the gradual escalation of the bombing campaign allowed the North Vietnamese to create a highly effective air defense system. Thus, an air war, prosecuted with prudence and designed to save lives, instead extracted a sanguinary sacrifice.

From 1966 onward, a minority of Americans began to protest against the war in Vietnam. Those opposed to the war took to the streets and university campuses in a sometimes calculated campaign to end American involvement in Southeast Asia. Meanwhile, an equally ardent minority stoutly defended the war effort and demanded that Johnson lift restraints on the military in order to gain victory. The inevitable public confrontations brought out the National Guard to restore order. The presence of the Guard, not only during war protests but also in urban racial disorders which racked the nation in the mid-1960s, highlighted one of the odder elements of the war. For one of the ways to avoid combat in Vietnam was to join the very reserves that ultimately patrolled the streets of American cities. Nevertheless, despite appeals from the Joint Chiefs of Staff to mobilize the reserves, Johnson refused because he feared a mobilization would intensify war protest or signal to the Soviets and the Chinese a major American escalation of the war.

The contradictions of the Vietnam War became evident in the turbulent year of 1968. Early in the year the Viet Cong and North Vietnamese launched the Tet Offensive, a major assault on urban areas in South Vietnam. Although caught by surprise, American forces smashed the offensive in six weeks of bloody fighting. The Tet Offensive nonetheless proved to be the turning point in the war. While the Communists suffered heavy losses, so too did the Americans and their South Vietnamese allies. American hopes that the new "search and destroy" approach in this war of attrition was paying off proved erroneous. Thus, when the commanders in the field sought more men, the request fell on deaf ears in Washington. In fact, Lyndon Johnson announced he did not intend to seek re-election and proposed a new peace initiative to end the war. But the level of opposition to the war increased, and the war continued to extract its bloody toll. Not surprisingly, Richard Nixon's campaign announcement that he had a secret plan to end the war contributed to his election that fall.

Nixon worked to end American participation in the war and stifle war protest by reducing American combat forces and turning the ground effort over to the South Vietnamese army (Vietnamization). In spite of this approach, American forces sustained almost as many deaths as they had up to 1969. As the American presence in Vietnam steadily declined, though, Nixon introduced a draft lottery in 1969 and ended conscription altogether in 1972. Meanwhile, the president initiated peace talks with North Vietnam. Nixon sought what he called "peace with honor," that is an American withdrawal from South Vietnam without the appearance that the United Stated had abandoned an ally. Hanoi and Washington reached a peace agreement in January 1973 following intense American bombing of the North in December. While President Nixon promised South Vietnam that the United States would continue to provide military aid and airpower, neither he nor his nation delivered on the promise. Saigon fell to North Vietnamese regulars in April 1975.

The Vietnam War affected the nation profoundly. It ruined the political careers of Lyndon Johnson and Richard Nixon, generated sharp political division in the nation, and weakened the Democratic Party. More unfortunately, the war created a gap between segments of the American people and the armed forces. The inequities of the draft and Johnson's refusal to mobilize the reserves placed too much of the burden of fighting the war on the working class and African Americans. Middle class contempt for military service generated condemnation of the armed forces generally and scorn specifically for those who served in Vietnam. Through the failures and weaknesses of some of their own, honorable professional military officers and career non-commissioned officers earned an ill-deserved stigma as warmongers which would endure for a decade.

The aftereffects of the war also left the armed forces demoralized, weakened in discipline, and ill-prepared to fight. Discipline eroded as racial tensions increased and enlisted men defied officers and non-coms. With the draft no longer in effect, the services initially found it difficult to recruit capable men and women for the new "All Volunteer Force." Military leaders faced a daunting challenge: to accept, then learn from defeat, and restore a sense of purpose and professionalism to their services. Because Lyndon Johnson refused to increase taxes to wage the war or utilize the reserves, American forces serving in NATO and composing the strategic reserve suffered a sharp decline in trained personnel and effective equipment. Nixon's decision to reduce defense spending as the war wound down prevented force modernization and the acquisition of new weapons.

The negative impact of the war fell particularly heavily on the army. In the decade following the war, the army, led by Creighton Abrams and Fred C. Weyand, rebuilt itself. Abrams, Weyand, and others restored a sense of mission to the army by emphasizing professional education, military history, and unit cohesion through intense training. General Abrams, in particular, helped develop the Total Force policy which integrated the Army National Guard and Army Reserve more closely to the active force. In consequence, no future major military effort could take place without at least a partial reserve mobilization. Army reformers developed a new military doctrine, known as AirLand Battle by the mid-1980s, which emphasized conventional warfare and was frankly shaped to fight Soviet and Warsaw Pact forces in Europe.

Ironically, while the Vietnam War occupied the nation's attention, the central feature of Cold War containment, the Soviet threat, slipped into limbo. After 1972, however, the navy and air force rediscovered the Cold War also. The navy now asserted that Soviet naval forces threatened American predominance on the high seas. Efforts to restore U.S. supremacy at sea did not take full force until Ronald Reagan's first term in the early 1980s, but as with the army, the navy defined its main mission as confronting the Soviet Union. The air force reoriented itself to Europe as well, to support AirLand Battle doctrine with interdictory attacks and to conduct strategic bombing at the theater level.

Under the Nixon Doctrine, which provided aid, but not American troops, to allies facing insurgencies policy again centered on deterrence in Europe through nuclear weapons and a strong American contingent in NATO. That emphasis continued through the presidencies of Gerald Ford, Jimmy Carter, and Ronald Reagan. In the Carter years, the fear that growing Soviet military spending would leave the United States outnumbered in conventional forces and strategic weapons as well, led to a gradual increase in military appropriations. Defense spending skyrocketed under Reagan in a drive to match the perceived Soviet threat, particularly in expanding the U.S. Navy.

Although doctrine, force structure, and military spending after 1972 focused on preparing for conventional war in Europe, overt and covert American military power was used elsewhere. Turmoil in the Middle East, for example, successively challenged Carter, Reagan, then George Bush. The triad of Arab-Israeli conflict, geographic proximity to the Soviet Union, and vast oil reserves created complex policy and strategic problems. Still, the Iran hostage situation in 1979 and the intervention in Lebanon in 1983 revealed that American power faced sharp limits in the Middle East.

Central America posed similar problems. Despite Ronald Reagan's pronouncement that with his election the nation had abandoned the sense of defeat left over from Vietnam, even this popular president could not generate sufficient congressional or public support to intervene directly in Central American insurgent struggles. Reagan fell back on thinly disguised covert support for Nicaraguan "freedom fighters" seeking to oust a Marxist government, but even that effort won only tepid public support. Reagan did rid the tiny Caribbean island of Grenada of an odd group of squabbling Marxist politicos in 1983. However, the use of aircraft carriers, fighter-bombers, Marines, and airborne troops against a motley group of locals somehow lacked the grandeur of the D-Day landing in June 1944. President George Bush sent American forces, over 22,000 strong, into Panama in December 1989 to oust and arrest Panamanian strongman General Manuel Noriega. Grandly code-named Operation Just Cause, the invasion fell short of living up to its name when it became clear that Noriega had long been in the pay of the United States. The more cynical observer might see the Panamanian operation as an overly-militarized federal posse.

From the Carter years through the end of Reagan's second term, the United States Congress appropriated nearly three trillion dollars for defense. The money not only upgraded strategic nuclear weapons but also modernized conventional forces, vastly improved the reserve components, and made the post-Vietnam All Volunteer Force the best trained, educated, and motivated volunteer military in American history. In that sense, the nation and the armed forces overcame the calamity of Vietnam. And yet in another sense the legacy of Vietnam lived on. Secretary of Defense Caspar Weinberger announced in 1984 that the Pentagon would recommend the use of combat forces only when vital American interests were clearly defined, when the Joint Chiefs of Staff could use sufficient force to complete the mission, when the political leadership was committed to winning, and when the American public clearly supported the effort. The so-called Weinberger Doctrine may explain Reagan's reluctance to push for direct intervention in Central America and the limited operations in Grenada and Panama.

President George Bush, however, found the circumstances ideal when he sent United States forces to the Persian Gulf in 1990. With the Iron Curtain crumbling and Soviet President Mikhail S. Gorbachev unopposed to American intervention, Bush organized a coalition of Western European and Middle Eastern countries eager to join the United States in facing up to Iraq's Saddam Hussein. More by accident than design, the nature of the Iraqi threat fit perfectly the emphasis on conventional, highly mobile warfare that the U.S. Army and U.S. Air Force had stressed since 1972. Moreover, Hussein unwisely gave the United States time to deploy armored and mechanized divisions from their European and United States garrisons. Mobilization of reserves, broad public support, and a congressional resolution supporting the Persian Gulf effort nearly completed the list of requirements set by Secretary Weinberger in 1984. The final ingredient, the immediate use of massive force, was added on January 17, 1991 when the American-led coalition let loose a savage air attack on Iraq which lasted five weeks. Late in February, coalition forces launched a ground attack that drove Iraqi forces out of Kuwait in less than five days and so ended Operation Desert Shield/Desert Storm.

The Gulf War stands too close in time to assess its consequences or to evaluate its impact on American military affairs. Moreover, the circumstances of the campaign are so unique that those who would draw "lessons" from this particular past must be circumspect in their analysis. Furthermore, historians in the future will need to assess how the end of the Cold War affected American military policy.

For nearly half a century the Cold War and containment, and the constant threat of nuclear warfare, governed national security thinking. With the dissolution of the Soviet Union, America has the luxury to rethink its military policy and question the national proclivity to resort to force in the protection of the nation and its interests. Indeed, the United States began to reduce its military forces even before George Bush sent troops to the Persian Gulf. Agreements with the Soviet Union to eliminate intermediate range nuclear weapons in Europe and the destruction of intercontinental ballistic missiles and their warheads marked a major turning point not only in Soviet-American relations, but American defense policy.

Furthermore, even as the Reagan defense buildup proceeded, some historians and political scientists detected an apparent decline in American power. In part this thrust represents a mode of thinking developed during the Vietnam War: that even superpowers face limits in their ability to impose their will. More importantly, the decline in power theme detects more substantive limits on the United States, especially economic. Can any one nation, it is asked, afford to maintain a global military policy over a long period of time? Some see the rapid collapse of the Soviet Union as proof that any nation which bases its approach to the world on the long-term maintenance of large military forces faces inevitable decline if not collapse.

For a considerable period, the armed forces of the United States performed a function essentially constabulary. A small army and navy sought to protect American citizens and their property on the geographic and commercial frontiers until the outbreak of the next war. At which point, the regulars mobilized, the volunteers flocked to the colors, and, after a period of confusion, stalemate, and occasionally defeat, the nation emerged victorious. In the aftermath, the military establishment was reduced, although seldom to prewar size, and those delegated to keep the peace took up their stations. The pattern was disrupted by the First World War, but consigned to the scrap heap by the second global confrontation.

Throughout the long decades of development, Americans agreed that John Adams spoke the undiluted truth when he insisted the "United States of America are a great and powerful people," and in 1945 few seriously disputed that claim. Many nations, to greater or lesser degree, offered no objection when the United States assumed a constabulary responsibility for the world. But, those who would lead the world must be aware of the ravages of time and circumstance. Just as the end of the Cold War has not inaugurated an era of universal peace, the continued position of the United States as the sole guardian of stability remains uncertain.

Chronology

1964

Jan	1	Wallace Greene (Commandant, Marine Corps)
Jan	28	Stephen Ailes (Secretary of the Army)
Jul	3	Earle Wheeler (Chairman, Joint Chiefs of Staff)
Jul	6	Harold K. Johnson (Chief of Staff, USA)
Aug	1	William Westmoreland (Military Assistance Command, Vietnam)
Aug	2	Naval action—Tonkin Gulf (USS *Maddox*)
Aug	5	Naval air action—North Vietnam
Aug	5	First pilot POW in North Vietnamese custody (Everett Alvarez, Jr., USN)
Nov	1	Viet Cong attack airbase—Bien Hoa, South Vietnam
Dec	2	President L. Johnson authorizes limited air operations against North Vietnam
Dec	24	Vietnamese irregulars (Viet Cong) bomb Brinks Hotel—Saigon, South Vietnam
Dec	24	Air/naval air action—Laos (Operation Barrel Roll)

1965

Feb	7	Naval air action—North Vietnam (Operation Flaming Dart I)
Feb	1	John McConnell (Chief of Staff, USAF)
Feb	11	Naval air action—North Vietnam (Operation Flaming Dart II)

Mar   2   Air/naval air action—North Vietnam (Operation Rolling Thunder)
Mar   8   First overt combat forces land South Vietnam (3rd Marine Regiment)
Mar 11   Naval interdiction—South Vietnam (Operation Market Time)
Mar 20   U.S. forces dispatched to Selma, AL (civil unrest)
Apr   3   Air/naval air action—Laos (Operation Steel Tiger)
Apr   3   Air action—Thanh Hoa Bridge, North Vietnam
Apr   4   First U.S. aircraft destroyed by the North Vietnam Air Force
Apr 18   First use of B-52's in South Vietnam—Binh Duong province
Apr 23   Lockheed C-141 enters operational service (first purpose designed pure-jet transport)
Apr 25   U.S. forces land Dominican Republic—ends Sep 27
May   6   Coast Guard Squadron One deployed to South Vietnam
May 20   Naval bombardment—South Vietnam (first fire support mission in connection with a land operation—USS *Hamner*)
Jun   1   First operational use of the Short Airfield for Tactical Support—Chu Lai, South Vietnam
Jun 17   First naval air victory (L. C. Page & J.E.D. Batson)
Jun 18   First tactical use of B-52s (Operation Arc Light)
Jun 30   Stanley Resor (Secretary of the Army)
Jul   1   1st Cavalry (Airmobile) activated—Ft Benning, GA
Jul   4   Battle of Ba Gia—ends Jul 7
Jul 10   First air victory (K. E. Holcombe, A. C. Clarke, T. S. Roberts & R. C. Anderson, USAF)
Jul 24   First U.S. aircraft destroyed by a North Vietnam surface-to-air missile (SA-2 Guideline)
Aug 18   Operation Starlite—ends Aug 21
Sep 11   1st Cavalry Division (Airmobile) lands South Vietnam
Sep 19   USCGC *Point Glover* & USCGC *Point Marone* initiate USCG involvement in Vietnam War (Operation Market Time)
Oct   1   Harold Brown (Secretary of the Air Force)
Nov 14   Battle of Ia Drang Valley—ends Nov 19
Dec   8   Operation Harvest Moon—ends Dec 18
Dec 25   President L. Johnson suspends the bombing of North Vietnam

1966

Jan 31   President L. Johnson resumes the bombing of North Vietnam
Feb 11   Operation Game Warden begins
Apr   1   Permanent *Route Package* system to organize the bombing of North Vietnam established
Apr 11   Air action—Mu Gia Pass (first B-52 raid against North Vietnam)
May   1   U.S. forces bombard Viet Cong positions in Cambodia

May 9   First air-cushion naval craft enters operational service (PACV)
May 30 U.S. aircraft (C-130) attempt to mine Thanh Hoa Bridge—
         North Vietnam—again May 31
Jun 8   Merle Smith (first African American graduate USCGA)
Jun 29 Air/naval air action—Hanoi & Haiphong, North Vietnam
Jun 30 Battle of Srok Dong—ends Jul 2
Jul 1   Willard Smith (Commandant, USCG)
Jul 7   Operation Hastings—ends Aug 3
Sep 14 Operation Attleboro—ends Nov 24 (first field test of the
         "search and destroy" doctrine)
Oct 25 Naval interdiction—North Vietnam (Operation Sea Dragon)

1967

Jan 2   Air action—Red River Delta (Operation Bolo)
Jan 8   Operation Cedar Falls—ends Jan 26
Feb 22 Operation Junction City—ends May 14
Mar 11 Air action—Sam Son, North Vietnam (first combat use of
         Walleye electro-optically guided bomb)
Apr 1   U.S. Coast Guard assigned to the jurisdiction of the
         Department of Transportation
Apr 5   Operation Francis Marion—ends Oct 12
Apr 24 Air/naval air action—Kep & Hoa Lac, North Vietnam
Jun 8   USS *Liberty* attacked by Israeli aircraft
Jun 22 Battle of Dak To
Jul 12 U.S. forces dispatched to Newark, NJ (racial unrest)
Jul 24 U.S. troops dispatched to Detroit, MI (racial unrest)
Jul 30 U.S. forces dispatched to Milwaukee, WI (racial unrest)
Aug 1   Thomas H. Moorer (Chief of Naval Operations)
Aug 2   Air assault—Paul Doumer Bridge—North Vietnam
Aug 31 Cobra AH-15 (first purpose designed attack helicopter enters
         operational service, USA)
Sep 1   Paul Ignatius (Secretary of the Navy)
Sep 10 Battle of Con Thien—ends Oct 4
Oct 12 Operation MacArthur—ends Jan 31, 1969
Oct 29 Battle of Loc Ninh—ends Nov 7
Nov 4   Second Battle of Dak To—ends Nov 22

1968

Jan 1   Leonard Chapman (Commandant, Marine Corps)
Jan 21 Siege of Khe Sanh—ends Apr 8
Jan 23 USS *Pueblo* seized by the forces of North Korea
Jan 25 Selected units of Air Force Reserve, Air National Guard and
         Naval Air Reserve mobilized (*Pueblo* affair)

Jan 30 Tet Offensive—ends Feb 24
Feb 27 Walter Cronkite (CBS NEWS) asserts the Vietnam War will
         "end in a stalemate"
Mar   1 Clark Clifford (Secretary of Defense)
Mar 16 My Lai massacre
Mar 31 President L. Johnson suspends the air, sea & land bombard-
         ment of North Vietnam above the 20th parallel
Apr   3 President L. Johnson suspends the air, sea & land bombard-
         ment of North Vietnam above the 19th parallel
Apr   5 U.S. troops dispatched to Baltimore, MD, Chicago, IL &
         Washington, D.C. (racial unrest)
Apr   8 Operation Toan Thang—ends May 31
Apr 11 Selected Army Reserve and National Guard units mobilized
         for service in South Vietnam
Apr 19 Operation Delaware—ends May 17
Apr 29 Battle of Dong Ha—ends May 5
May 31 20th Tactical Fighter Squadron arrives South Vietnam (first air
         guard unit so deployed)
May 12 Air Evacuation—Kham Duc
Jul   3 Creighton Abrams (Military Assistance Command, Vietnam)
Jul   3 William Westmoreland (Chief of Staff, USA)
Aug 23 U.S. troops dispatched to Chicago, IL (civil unrest)
Oct 31 President L. Johnson ends the air, sea & land bombardment of
         North Vietnam above the 19th parallel
Nov   1 Accelerated Pacification Campaign
Nov 15 Air/naval air action—Laos (Operation Commando Hunt)

1969

Jan 22 Melvin Laird (Secretary of Defense)
Jan 22 Operation Dewey Canyon—ends Mar 18
Jan 31 John Chafee (Secretary of the Navy)
Feb 15 Robert Seamans (Secretary of the Air Force)
Mar 17 Operation Atlas Wedge—ends Mar 26
Mar 18 Air action—ends May 26, 1970 (Operation Menu—Cambodia)
May 10 Battle of Hamburger Hill (Dong Ap Bia)—ends May 20
Jun   8 First combat units withdraw from South Vietnam
Jul 20 Racial unrest—Camp Lejeune, NC
Aug   1 John Ryan (Chief of Staff, USAF)
Dec 17 Lockheed C-5A (world's largest aircraft enters operational
         service, USAF)

1970

Mar 23 US troops dispatched to New York, NY (labor unrest)

May 1 Cambodian incursion—ends Jun 29 (Operation Binh Tay)
May 1 Air action—ends Aug 15, 1973 (Operation Freedom Deal-
         Cambodia)
May 4 Kent State University massacre
Jun 1 Chester Bender (Commandant, USCG)
Jun 11 First woman general (Anna Hayes)
Jul 1 Elmo Zumwalt (Chief of Naval Operations)
Jul 2 Thomas Moorer (Chairman, Joint Chiefs of Staff)
Jul 4 Racial unrest—Heidelberg, Germany
Sep 5 Operation Jefferson Glenn—ends Oct 8, 1971
Nov 21 Son Tay POW raid

1971

Jan 27 Hawker-Siddely AV-8A (first V/STOL aircraft enters opera-
          tional service, USMC)
Jan 30 Operation Dewey Canyon II—ends Feb 7
Apr 2   *The Search for Military Justice* published by the NAACP
Apr 28 First African American admiral (Samuel L. Gravely, Jr.)
May 21 Racial unrest—ends May 24—Travis AFB, CA
Jun 24 Defense Race Relations Institute, DOD (later Defense Equal
          Opportunity Management Institute) established
Jul 1   Robert Froehlke (Secretary of the Army)
Aug 17 First successful use of racism/discrimination as court-martial
          defense (*U.S. vs. Samuel Robertson*)
Sep 21 Air action—Dong Hoi (first air strike using LORAN)
Nov 12 President R. Nixon confines U.S. ground forces in South
          Vietnam to a defensive role
Nov 13 Racial unrest—Ft McClellan, AL
Nov 16 *Ad hoc* hearings on racial discrimination in the armed forces—
          ends Nov 19 (Congressional Black Caucus)

1972

Jan 1   Robert Cushman (Commandant, Marine Corps)
Mar 30 Air action—ends Sep 15 (Nguyen Hue Offensive)
Apr 25 John Warner (Secretary of the Navy)
Apr 29 First test fly-by-wire control system (USAF)
May 9   North Vietnamese harbors mined—again on May 11 (Opera-
          tion Pocket Money)
May 10 Air/naval air action—ends Oct 23 (Linebacker I)
May 10 First naval aviation ace (Randy Cunningham & William
          Driscoll)
May 13 Air assault—Thanh Hoa Bridge—North Vietnam (first combat
          use of a laser-guided bomb)

Jun   1   First woman admiral (Alene B. Duerk)
Jun   29   Frederick Weyand (Military Assistance Command, Vietnam)
Aug   5   First fully automated carrier landing (USS *Ranger*)
Aug   28   First air ace (Richard Ritchie, USAF)
Oct   12   Racial unrest—ends Oct 13 (USS *Kitty Hawk*)
Oct   12   Creighton Abrams (Chief of Staff, USA)
Nov   3   Racial unrest—ends Nov 9 (USS *Constellation*)
Nov   18   USS *Sanctuary* recommissioned (first naval vessel with a
           gender-integrated crew)
Dec   18   Air/naval air action—ends Dec 29 (Linebacker II)

1973

Jan   12   Last aerial victory North Vietnam (Walter Kovaleski & James
           Wise, USN)
Jan   23   Cease-fire agreement (U.S. & North Vietnam)
Jan   27   President R. Nixon halts all hostile acts by U.S. forces in North
           and South Vietnam
Jan   30   Elliot Richardson (Secretary of Defense)
Feb   12   POW release operation—ends Mar 29
Feb   21   Air actions Laos end—resume Feb 24–26 & Apr 16–17
Feb   27   Mine-sweep operation-North Vietnam—ends Jul 27
Mar   **   Office of Assistant Chief of Naval Personnel for Women
           abolished
Mar   29   Last organized units leave South Vietnam
May   14   Legal status of military women declared equal to that of
           military men (*Frontiero v. Richardson*)
May   15   Howard Callaway (Secretary of the Army)
May   15   John McLucas (Secretary of the Air Force)
Jul   1   Congress ends inductions under Selective Service Act
Jul   2   James Schlesinger (Secretary of Defense)
Aug   1   George Brown (Chief of Staff, USAF)
Dec   1   First Hispanic American General (Richard E. Cavazos)
Dec   3   Women authorized to serve in the Coast Guard

1974

Feb   22   First woman naval aviator (Barbara Allen)
Apr   8   William Middendorf III (Secretary of the Navy)
Apr   24   Mine-sweep operation—ends Jun 3—Suez Canal
Jun   1   Owen Siler (Commandant, USCG)
Jun   4   First woman helicopter pilot (Sally Woolfolk Murphy, USA)
Jul   1   David Jones (Chief of Staff, USAF)
Jul   1   George Brown (Chairman, Joint Chiefs of Staff)

Jul 1 James Holloway (Chief of Naval Operations)
Aug 12 Coast Guard Academy announces vacancies for women cadets
Oct 3 Frederick Weyand (Chief of Staff, USA)

1975

Jan 15 Separate promotion standard established for women (*Schlesinger v. Ballard*)
Apr 11 Phnom Penh, Cambodia evacuation (Eagle Pull)
Apr 29 Saigon, South Vietnam evacuation—ends Apr 30 (Frequent Wind)
May 14 U.S. forces land Koh Tang Island, Cambodia (*Mayaguez* incident)
May 14 Boarding party from USS *Holt* recaptures *Mayaguez*
Jun 1 Louis Wilson (Commandant, Marine Corps)
Aug 5 Martin Hoffmann (Secretary of the Army)
Oct 8 Women afforded entry to all service academies
Nov 20 Donald Rumsfeld (Secretary of Defense)

1976

Jan 2 Thomas Reed (Secretary of the Air Force)
Feb 23 Mandatory pregnancy discharge requirements eliminated all services (*Crawford v. Cushman*)
May 7 First woman AROTC cadet commissioned (Martha Hahn, South Dakota State University)
Jun ** Office of Director, Women in the Air Force abolished
Oct 1 Bernard Rogers (Chief of Staff, USA)

1977

Jan 21 Harold Brown (Secretary of Defense)
Feb 14 Clifford Alexander (Secretary of the Army)
Feb 14 W. Graham Claytor, Jr. (Secretary of the Navy)
Apr 6 John Stetson (Secretary of the Air Force)
May 1 Fairchild A-10 enters operational service (first attack aircraft since 1936)
Jun 22 First women assigned to a warship as permanent crew (Beverly Kelley & Debra Wilson, USCG)
Jun 30 Office of Director, Women Marines abolished
Sep 2 First women designated pilots, USAF
Nov 4 Women's Air Force Service Pilots accorded veteran status

1978

Feb 1 First submarine launch of a cruise missile (USS *Barb*)

Mar   7   Office, Director Women's Army Corps abolished
Mar 23   First woman to fly alert duty with the Strategic Air Command
          (Sandra M. Scott)
May 31   John Hayes (Commandant, USCG)
Jun 21   David Jones (Chairman, Joint Chiefs of Staff)
Jul   1   Lew Allen (Chief of Staff, USAF)
Jul   1   Thomas Hayward (Chief Naval Operations)
Jul 27   Non-specific restrictions prohibiting women from sea duty
          eliminated (*Owens et al. v. Brown*)
Nov   1   First woman assigned USN sea duty other than a hospital ship
          or a transport (Mary Carrol)

1979

Apr   1   First woman to command a warship (Beverly Kelly, USCG)
May 18   Hans Mark (Secretary of the Air Force)
Jun 20   First carrier-qualified woman aviator (Donna Spruill, USN)
Jun 22   Edward Meyer (Chief of Staff, USA)
Jun 28   Robert Barrow (Commandant, Marine Corps)
Oct 25   Edward Hidalgo (Secretary of the Navy)
Oct 25   First woman to command a cadet corps at a service academy
          (Linda Johansen, USCGA)

1980

Mar   1   Rapid Deployment Joint Task Force established
Apr 24   Iranian hostage rescue mission aborted (Operation Blue Light)
Dec 10   Defense Officer Personnel Management Act eliminates gender-
          based promotion lists

1981

Jan 21   Caspar Weinberger (Secretary of Defense)
Jan 29   John Marsh (Secretary of the Army)
Feb   9   Verne Orr (Secretary of the Air Force)
Feb   5   John Lehman, Jr. (Secretary of the Navy)
Aug 19   Naval air action—Gulf of Sidra

1982

May 27   James Gracey (Commandant, USCG)
Jun 18   John Vessey (Chairman, Joint Chiefs of Staff)
Jul   1   Charles Gabriel (Chief of Staff, USAF)
Jul   1   James Watkins (Chief of Naval Operations)
Aug 25   U.S. forces land Beirut, Lebanon—ends Sep 10

Sep 26   U.S. forces land Beirut, Lebanon—ends Feb 26, 1984
Dec 28   USS *New Jersey* recommissioned

1983

Jun 23   John Wickham, Jr (Chief of Staff, USA)
Jul   1   Paul Kelley (Commandant, USMC)
Oct 23   USMC Battalion Landing Team Headquarters in Beirut,
          Lebanon destroyed by a "truck bomb"
Oct 25   U.S. forces land Grenada—ends Oct 27 (Operation Urgent
          Fury)
Dec   4   Naval air action—Bekka Valley, Lebanon
Dec 18   Naval bombardment—Beirut, Lebanon

1984

Jan 15   Naval bombardment—Beirut, Lebanon
Feb   8   Naval bombardment—Beirut, Lebanon
May   2   First air-cushion landing craft (rollout)
Aug   4   Mine-sweep operation—ends Sep 18—Suez Canal/Red Sea

1985

Feb   4   Gender-specific launch crews authorized for all ICBM systems
Jul 30   First maritime prepositioning squadron operational (MPS 1)
Oct   1   William Crowe (Chairman, Joint Chiefs of Staff)
Oct 10   Naval aircraft intercept and divert an Egyptian airliner (USS
          Saratoga)
Dec   9   Russell Rourke (Secretary of the Air Force)

1986

Mar 24   Naval/naval air action—Gulf of Sidra—ends Mar 25
Apr   8   Edward Aldridge (Secetary of the Air Force)
Apr 15   Air/naval air action—Lybia (Operation El Dorado Canyon)
May 30   Paul Yost (Commandant, USCG)
Jul   1   Carlisle Trost (Chief of Naval Operations)
Jul   1   Larry Welch (Chief of Staff, USAF)
Oct   1   Congress passes Goldwater-Nichols Defense Re-Organization
          Act

1987

May   1   James Webb (Secretary of the Navy)
May 17   USS *Stark* attacked by Iraqi aircraft
Jun 23   Carl Vuono (Chief of Staff, USA)

Jul   1   Alfred Gray (Commandant, USMC)
Jul   21 Convoy escort—Persian/Arab Gulf (Operation Earnest Will)
Aug 4   Gubernatorial veto of National Guard training assignments
          disallowed (*Perpich v. U.S. Dept of Defense et al.*)
Sep 21 Army air action—Persian/Arab Gulf (*Iran Ajr*)
Oct   8   Army air action—Persian/Arab Gulf
Oct   19 Naval action—Persian/Arab Gulf
Nov 1   Naval action—Persian/Arab Gulf
Nov 23 Frank Carlucci (Secretary of Defense)

1988

Mar 31 James Ball (Secretary of the Navy)
Apr   14 USS *Samuel B. Roberts* mined—Persian/Arab Gulf
Apr   18 Naval action—Persian/Arab Gulf
Jul   3   USS *Vincennes* destroys Iranair Flight 655

1989

Jan   4   Naval air action—Gulf of Sidra
Mar 21 Richard Cheney (Secretary of Defense)
May 15 H. Lawrence Garrett III (Secretary of the Navy)
May 22 Donald Rice (Secretary of the Air Force)
Aug 14 Michael Stone (Secretary of the Army)
Oct   1   Colin Powell (Chairman, Joint Chiefs of Staff)
Dec 20 U.S. forces land Panama—ends Dec 21 (Operation Just Cause)
Dec 20 First woman to lead U.S. forces in combat (Linda Bray, USA)

1990

May 31 J. William Kime (Commandant, USCG)
Jun 29 Frank Kelso II (Chief of Naval Operations)
Jul   1   Michael Dugan (Chief of Staff, USAF)
Aug 5   Monrovia, Liberia evacuation—ends Aug 21 (Operation Sharp
          Edge)
Aug 8   U.S. aircraft land Saudi Arabia (Operation Desert Shield)
Aug 9   U.S. forces land Saudi Arabia (Operation Desert Shield)
Aug 12 USN ordered to enforce a UN-sponsored trade embargo
          against Iraq (Resolution 661)
Aug 13 First vessel Fast Sealift Squadron leaves for Saudi Arabia—
          arrives Aug 27
Aug 17 Civil Reserve Air Fleet activated (Operation Desert Shield)
Aug 22 Selected reserve units mobilized (Operation Desert Shield)
Aug 31 First Iraqi vessel (*Al Karamah*) searched (USS *Biddle*)

Sep 16 First overseas deployment of a Coast Guard Reserve unit
         (Port Security Unit, 303RD)
Sep 25 UN Security Council authorizes an air blockade of Iraq
         (Resolution 670)
Oct 30 Merrill McPeak (Chief of Staff, USAF)
Nov   5 Supreme Court orders USA to reinstate a soldier previously
         discharged for homosexuality (*Watkins v. U.S. Army*)
Nov 29 UN Security Council authorizes the use of force to compel Iraq
         to withdraw from Kuwait (Resolution 678)

1991

Jan   4 Mogadishu, Somalia evacuation—ends Jan 6 (Operation
         Eastern Exit)
Jan 16 Naval action—Persian/Arab Gulf—ends Jan 18
Jan 17 Air action—Iraq (Operation Instant Thunder)
Jan 17 First combat firing of a cruise missile from a surface vessel
         (USS *San Jacinto*)
Jan 17 First combat firing of an air-launched cruise missile
         (8th Air Force B-52Gs)
Jan 18 First combat firing of a cruise missile from a submarine
         (USS *Louisville*)
Jan 24 Naval air action—Persian/Arab Gulf
Jan 25 First Kuwaiti territory liberated (Jazirat Qurah)
Jan 29 Naval helicopter assault—Umm al Maradim (USS *Okinawa*)
Jan 29 Battle of Khafji—ends Jan 31
Jan 29 Border skirmish—ends Jan 30—Kuwait/Saudi Arabia
Jan 31 Naval air action—Persian/Arab Gulf
Feb   4 Naval bombardment—Kuwait (USS *Missouri*)
Feb   7 Naval bombardment—Kuwait (USS *Wisconsin*)
Feb 18 USS *Princeton* and *Tripoli* mined—Persian/Arab Gulf
Feb 20 Border skirmish—Kuwait/Saudi Arabia
Feb 22 U.S. forces cross Kuwait border (deception plan)
Feb 24 Operation Desert Storm—ends Feb 28
Feb 24 Iraqi anti-ship missile fired at USS *Missouri*
Feb 27 Allied forces occupy Kuwait City
Mar   2 Hammurabi Armored Division (Iraq) unsuccessfully engages
         24th Infantry Division
Mar   4 POW exchange—ends Mar 8
Apr   6 Operation Provide Comfort (Iraq)
Jun 21 Gordon Sullivan (Chief of Staff, USAF)
Jul   1 Carl Mundy (Commandant, USMC)
Sep   6 Tailhook Association episode occurs in Las Vegas, NV

Nov 22 Congress authorizes women to fly combat aircraft (USAF/ USN)

1992

May   1 U.S. forces dispatched to Los Angeles, CA—ends May 10 (civil unrest)
Jun 24 Paula Coughlin (USN) alleges sexual harassment at 1991 Tailhook Association meeting
Jul   7 Sean O'Keefe (Secretary of the Navy)
Nov 17 Congress repeals 1948 restriction against women serving on USN warships
Nov 17 Congress provides a "zone of privacy" for homosexuals serving in armed forces
Dec   9 U.S. forces land Somalia—ends Mar 25, 1994 (Operation Restore Hope)
Dec 27 Air/naval air action—Iraq

1993

Jan 13 Air/naval air action—Iraq
Jan 17 USN cruise missile attack—Iraq
Jan 17 Air action—Iraq
Jan 18 Air action—Iraq
Jan 20 Les Aspin (Secretary of Defense)
Apr 12 Air action—Bosnia (Operation Deny Flight)
Apr 28 Restrictions against women flying combat missions eliminated by Secretary of Defense
Jun 26 USN cruise missile attack—Iraq
Jul 22 John Dalton (Secretary of the Navy)
Aug   6 Sheila Widnall (Secretary of the Air Force)
Oct   1 John Shalikashvili (Chairman, Joint Chiefs of Staff)
Oct   3 Battle of Mogadishu—ends Oct 4
Oct 21 Charges against an officer facing disciplinary action in the 1991 Tailhook episode dismissed by USMC
Nov 22 Togo West (Secretary of the Army)

1994

Jan 13 Risk alone declared insufficient cause to exclude women from ground combat support roles (Secretary of Defense)
Feb   4 William Perry (Secretary of Defense)
Feb   8 Charges against officers facing disciplinary action for 1991 Tailhook episode dismissed by USN
Feb 28 Naval air action—Bosnia (Operation Deny Flight)

Apr 10   Naval air action—Bosnia (Operation Deny Flight)
Apr 11   Marine air action—Bosnia (Operation Deny Flight)
Apr 23   Jeremy Boorda (Chief of Naval Operations)
Jun   1   Robert Kramek (Commandant, USCG)
Sep 19   U.S. forces land Haiti (Operation Uphold Democracy)
Nov 21   Air action—Bosnia (Operation Deny Flight)

Military Operations

OPERATION FLAMING DART (Feb 7 and 11, 1965). In response to a Viet
Cong attack on the American airbase at Pleiku (February 7), killing eight
and wounding 109, and later Qui Nhon (February 11), killing twenty-
three, President Lyndon Johnson ordered retaliatory bombing raids
against North Vietnamese military installations north of the Demilitarized Zone (DMZ). The air attacks took place the same day as the incidents to which they responded. FLAMING DART I and II were precur-
sors to OPERATION ROLLING THUNDER.

OPERATION ROLLING THUNDER (Mar 2, 1965–Nov 1, 1968). This program of gradually escalating bombing against North Vietnam, while
supposedly retaliatory, began in an effort to stave off the collapse of
South Vietnam. Its main purpose was to convince Hanoi to halt its military activity in South Vietnam and seek a negotiated settlement. The
first attacks on March 2 hit supply and naval facilities; targets subsequently included ammunition dumps and oil supply depots, then industrial sites and power plants. Approximately 640,000 tons of bombs
were dropped, at a cost of 922 aircraft in three-and-one-half years.

SIEGE OF PLEI ME (Oct 19–26, 1965). The battle opened the campaign in
the Ia Drang valley. The North Vietnamese Army attacked an American
Special Forces camp at Plei Me on October 19, intending to destroy the
oncoming relief column. Gen. Vinh Loc of the South Vietnamese Army
(ARVN) waited for reinforcements at Pleiku before sending the column,
which was ambushed on the 23rd. The following day the American 1st
Cavalry Division, relying on helicopters for mobility, firepower, and supplies, airlifted artillery from Pleiku which freed the ARVN to break the
siege on October 26, winning "one of the war's rare decisive battles."

BATTLE OF THE IA DRANG (Nov 14–16, 1965). The first major battle between American troops and the North Vietnamese Army (NVA) occurred
here. Following the Plei Me siege (October 19–26), Gen. William
Westmoreland ordered Gen. Harry W.O. Kinnard's 1st Cavalry to comb
the Ia Drang Valley. Several small engagements ensued. On November
14, Col. Harold G. Moore's battalion encountered stiff resistance after
landing near the Chu Pong mountains. The battle continued all day; the
following day the reinforced Americans repulsed an all-out assault and

counterattacked. On the 16th, the NVA withdrew, leaving behind 600 dead and carrying off hundreds more. The Americans lost seventy-nine. The mobility of the American forces had been crucial in the battle, and North Vietnam called off plans to split the South.

OPERATION CEDAR FALLS (Jan 8–26, 1967). Gen. William Westmoreland proposed a large-unit tactical offensive against a South Vietnamese communist (Viet Cong) jungle stronghold, the "Iron Triangle," twenty miles north of Saigon. On January 8th, American infantry, airborne, and armored troops invaded. Although Viet Cong losses approximated 3,500, the enemy chose not to stand and fight. Civilian populations were relocated, vast areas of the Triangle were cleared and bases destroyed over three weeks. The operation caused North Vietnam to rethink its strategy, but enemy forces quickly returned after the Americans pulled out on the 26th.

BATTLE OF LOC NINH (Oct 29–Nov 7, 1967). The Viet Cong (VC) suffered a costly defeat in attacking Special Forces and Regional Forces camps near a large rubber plantation. On October 29, the Allies turned back repeated heavy assaults and were stoutly reinforced by helicopter the next day in time and with sufficient force to repulse more attacks on the 31st. After a day of rest, the VC, ordered to succeed at all costs, assaulted again on November 2, but to no avail. The enemy characteristically slipped away as it broke contact. Viet Cong and North Vietnamese dead numbered about 900, to eleven Americans and fifty South Vietnamese.

BATTLE OF DAK TO (Nov 1–22, 1967). North Vietnamese and Viet Cong forces attacked this American base near the borders of South Vietnam, Cambodia, and Laos, producing "one of the fiercest battles of the war." After repeated small battles, an entire division assaulted the base on the 13th. Artillery repulsed the invaders, but the attacks continued. As an American battalion then advanced on Hill 875 on the 19th, it was surrounded; a second battalion broke through the next day. Three days of bombing and napalm and an assault on the 22nd failed to dislodge the enemy, but they withdrew during the night. The Americans lost 281 and set North Vietnamese losses at 1,400.

SIEGE OF KHE SANH (Jan 21–Apr 7, 1968). The North Vietnamese Army (NVA) assaulted this isolated Marine base, located near the western edge of the DMZ, ten days prior to the Tet Offensive. President Lyndon Johnson, fearing a repeat of the French defeat at Dien Bien Phu, required that the base be held. For weeks, Col. David E. Lownd's Marines withstood mortar, rocket, and artillery fire and probes from 15–20,000 enemy troops in the area, "the heaviest bombardment endured by American forces since World War Two." Supported by heavy air strikes, the Marines held out until the NVA withdrew and Gen. John J. Tolson, III's relief column fought its way through on April 7. Marine deaths totaled 205.

TET OFFENSIVE (Jan 30, 1968). Gen. Vo Nguyen Giap's offensive assaulted every major city, town, and military base in South Vietnam beginning on January 30, the first day of celebration of Tet, the lunar New Year. The offensive achieved surprise. North Vietnamese Army troops and Viet Cong cadres carried the fight, even entering the grounds of the American embassy in Saigon. American and South Vietnamese units responded well, however, and in heavy fighting around the country beat back the attacks. Militarily, the fighting finished the Viet Cong as an effective force. But the psychological impact in America was devastating, coming on the heels of Gen. William Westmoreland's assurance that the enemy was near defeat.

BATTLE OF HUE (Jan 31–Mar 2, 1968). The Tet Offensive included a successful assault on this venerable provincial capital. Viet Cong (VC) infiltrators and two regiments of troops attacked on January 31, taking control of the inner city's walled Citadel. American and South Vietnamese troops immediately counterattacked, but the VC held the Citadel for three weeks, dispensing "revolutionary justice" to 3,000 influential citizens. Despite the city's historic importance, Allied bombing raids commenced on February 7. Under cover of a counterattack, the Viet Cong withdrew on the night of February 23/24, and the battle officially ended on March 2. Allied losses totaled 500, the Viet Cong a probable 4,000, and the city was left in ruins.

MY LAI MASSACRE (Mar 16, 1968). During the spring of 1968 Capt. Ernest Medina's C Company (11th Light Infantry Brigade, Americal Division) was operating in the Viet Cong stronghold of Quang Ngai province. On the morning of March 16, Lt. William Calley's platoon from C Company entered the hamlet of My Lai 4 to clear it of Viet Cong. Calley's troops met no armed resistance, yet he ordered his soldiers to round up and kill the inhabitants, consisting of between 100 and 500 old men, women, and children. Medina and superiors covered up the incident, but it was made public in April 1969. A subsequent army investigation and a board of inquiry resulted in 25 officers and enlisted men being charged with dereliction of duty or war crimes. Two superiors were reprimanded; only Calley was convicted of murder (on 22 or 102 counts). He was later paroled after serving about three years of his original life sentence. The massacre remains notable, one historian judges, "for sheer scale and horror" in a war punctuated by atrocities on both sides.

BATTLE OF HAMBURGER HILL (May 11–20, 1969). On May 10, an Allied force advanced into the A Shau Valley, near Laos. The following day an American unit was repulsed by enemy troops dug into Hill 937, the Ap Bia Mountain. An entire battalion attacked the hill on the 14th but was driven back, as were eight more assaults over the next five days. A four-battalion attack on the 20th succeeded, but the enemy had largely withdrawn. The "meat grinder" tactics resulted in the nickname "Hamburger Hill." Following the prescribed strategy, the mountain was abandoned soon thereafter. The seemingly senseless deaths of 241 American soldiers fueled anti-war protests in America.

CAMBODIAN INCURSION (May 1–Jun 30, 1970). Following the fall of Prince Norodom Sihanouk's government in Cambodia, Gen. Michael Davison planned a three-pronged attack under Gen. Robert Shoemaker's command against North Vietnamese sanctuaries in the "Fishhook," seeking to destroy the Viet Cong headquarters. Allied infantry, air mobile, and armored units launched into the heavy jungle on May 1, but lacked the element of surprise. The attack uncovered vast stores of supplies and disrupted North Vietnam's war plans, but the enemy's main force and COSVN had evaporated. The American force withdrew on June 30. American anti-war feeling was fueled by the apparent expansion of the war.

LINEBACKER II (Dec 18–29, 1972). President Richard M. Nixon ordered this massive air assault of Hanoi and Haiphong, known as the "Christmas bombing," to convince North Vietnam to reopen negotiations in Paris. Targets included every military installation and war-related facility in the vicinity. The Air Force and Navy flew more than 700 B-52 and 600 fighter-bomber sorties, losing twenty-six aircraft. The assault, which infuriated anti-war feeling in the United States, left "no more legitimate military targets in North Vietnam to strike." On December 26, Hanoi agreed to return to the negotiating table, but the influence of the bombing remains debatable and debated.

IRANIAN HOSTAGE RESCUE MISSION (Apr 24, 1980). Followers of Ayatollah Khomeini overran the American Embassy in Tehran on November 4, 1979, taking about 60 American hostages. In April, President Jimmy Carter ordered a military rescue mission. Col. Charles Beckwith led the assault into the desert on the 24th, where sand storms disabled two helicopters. When a third developed hydraulic problems, the mission was canceled. Another helicopter, however, crashed into a C-130 transport on the ground, resulting in eight dead and three wounded. The failed mission was a significant embarrassment to the Carter Administration.

GRENADA INVASION (Oct 25–28, 1983). President Ronald Reagan authorized Operation URGENT FURY to rescue 600 American medical students and overthrow the leftist government of Bernard Coards, who had led a coup against Maurice Bishop on October 13. About 800 armed Cubans, moreover, were constructing an air field on the island. On the 25th, the invasion began inauspiciously; Delta Force troops met stiff resistance in securing the air field. Despite inadequate intelligence and planning and several mishaps, American Marines, Rangers, and Delta Force troops secured the island by the 28th. At least eighteen Americans died and 116 were wounded.

PANAMA INVASION (Dec 20, 1989–Jan 3, 1990). The Panamanian Assembly having endorsed the rule of dictator Gen. Manuel Noriega and declared a "state of war" with the U.S., the administration of President George Bush planned an intervention (Operation JUST CAUSE). With significantly better intelligence and planning than in the Grenada episode, 11,000 American troops began to land at American bases in the Canal Zone on December 18. The attack began in the early hours of the 20th and was characterized by pockets of hard fighting and considerable civil disorder, which lasted for several days. Noriega, who sought refuge in the Vatican embassy, gave himself up on January 3. American losses totaled twenty-three dead and 323 wounded.

AIR WAR AGAINST IRAQ (Jan 17, 1991). As American and Allied troops massed against the Saudi Arabian-Kuwaiti border, Gen. H. Norman Schwartzkopf launched INSTANT THUNDER, an air and missile assault, on January 17. Gen. Charles Horner planned the operation, which continued during the following six weeks. The Allies quickly won complete air supremacy. Initially, their action focused largely on the city of Baghdad and war-related facilities in Iraq; it later emphasized the Iraqi city of Basra, near Kuwait, and the Iraqi occupying force in Kuwait. New air force and naval high-technology weaponry worked well in the battle. One commentator judged it "undoubtedly the most effective air campaign in history."

BATTLE OF KHAFJI (Jan 29–31, 1991). Iraqi troops launched a three-pronged attack across the Kuwaiti border into Saudi Arabia on the 29th. They occupied the abandoned Arabian town of Khafji and advanced along a thirty-mile front. American Marines employed aircraft and artillery to stop the advancing line and to support Saudi troops in their efforts to retake Khafji. They did so, in twelve hours of hard fighting, on the 31st. Eleven American Marines died, probably from friendly fire. The Iraqis' limited offensive crumbled, but their army demonstrated a will and capacity to fight.

OPERATION DESERT STORM (Feb 23–28, 1991). The operation comprised the American and Allied ground battle in the Persian Gulf War. Prior to opening the offensive, Gen. H. Norman Schwartzkopf arranged to move 150,000 troops to the western end of the Iraqi line along the Saudi Arabian-Kuwaiti border. Gen. William Pagonis planned the feat, which enabled Schwartzkopf to surprise his enemy. On the night of the 23rd, Allied armor and airborne forces, supported by intensive air operations, launched the attack, which by-passed the front line troops and moved toward Kuwait City and avenues of Iraqi retreat. The result was a spectacular success. Two days later, Iraqi President Saddam Hussein ordered a retreat, but his forces were subjected to constant attack until President George Bush suspended the war on February 28.

Biographical Notes

ABRAMS, CREIGHTON WILLIAMS, JR. (1914–1974). A 1936 graduate of West Point, Abrams began his army career in the cavalry. In 1940 he was assigned to the newly-created 1st Armored Division and later to the 4th Armored Division. After a series of rapid promotions, he landed in Normandy as commander of a tank battalion. Tanks under Abrams' command played a major role in the relief of Bastogne during the Battle of the Bulge. Considered one of the more aggressive and successful combat commanders of the war, Abrams was responsible for revising the postwar field manual on armored tactics. Abrams graduated from the Command and General Staff College (1949), the Army War College (1953) and held several staff positions during the Korean War. In May 1967, after holding field and staff commands in Europe, he was appointed deputy commander of the United States Military Assistance Command, Vietnam (MACV). Abrams succeeded Gen. William C. Westmoreland as Commander, MACV in 1968. In line with the decision to withdraw American troops from South Vietnam, Abrams shifted the American focus from highly visible, but sanguinary, large-unit "search and destroy" missions to small-unit operations designed to defend the village population of Vietnam. Abrams was also responsible for implementing the phased transfer of equipment (Vietnamization) to the Army of South Vietnam. Abrams became army chief of staff in 1972 at a time when budgets were shrinking and commitments remained unchanged. He mounted a successful effort to reduce costs in order to allow the U.S. Army to continue to meet its global obligations, but died (September 4, 1974) before he could fully implement his vision of the postwar army.

BROWN, GEORGE SCRATCHLEY (1918–1978). A 1941 graduate of the United States Military Academy, Brown entered flight training and later joined the initial cadre of B-24 pilots assigned to Barksdale Field, Louisiana. He was assigned to a unit of the Eighth Air Force in 1942 and participated in the attack on the oil refinery at Ploesti, Romania. He transferred to the 2nd Air Division in 1944, Air Training Command Headquarters in 1945, and Air Defense Command Headquarters in 1946. During the Korean War, Brown commanded the 62nd Troop Carrier Group, the 56th Fighter Wing and served as operations officer for the 5th Air Force. He commanded the 3525th Pilot Training Wing for three years before entering the National War College in 1956. Brown was executive officer to the Air Force chief of staff from 1957 to 1963 when he was named to command the Eastern Transport Air Force. In 1964 he helped organize a special weapons systems test unit and returned to Washington in 1966 to work for the chairman of the Joint Chiefs of Staff. In 1968, Brown assumed command of the 7th Air Force and became deputy commander for Air Operations Vietnam. In 1970, Gen. Brown became commander, Air Force Systems Command. He was appointed Air Force chief of staff in 1973 and chairman of the Joint Chiefs of Staff the following year. He retired in 1978 and died six months later.

BUCHER, LLOYD MARK (1927–). Orphaned at an early age, Bucher grew to adulthood at Father Flanagan's Boys Town in Omaha, NE. In 1945 he enlisted in the navy and returned two years later to graduate from high school at Boys Town. Enrolling at the University of Nebraska, Bucher graduated and received a commission as an ensign through the reserve officer training program (1953). He then spent most of his career aboard diesel submarines. In late 1966 Bucher received orders to take command of USS *Pueblo*, a light cargo ship, which was then being refitted and recommissioned ostensibly as an oceanographic research vessel. *Pueblo* was to be one of three ships the navy expected to deploy as Operation Clickbettle. This operation involved electronic intelligence gathering by small unarmed naval auxiliaries operating independently in international waters close to the former Soviet Union and North Korea. On January 23, 1968 armed boarders from North Korean gunboats and a submarine chaser boarded and seized *Pueblo* in international waters about 12 miles from the North Korean coast. Although one sailor out of the eighty-three officers, sailors, and civilians on *Pueblo* died during the North Koreans' attack on *Pueblo*, Bucher was not able to scuttle his ship because it lacked adequate destruct systems, especially for all the confidential documents and monitoring equipment on board. Subsequently Bucher and his crew endured great physical privation, beatings, and repeated interrogation about their "spying" from their captors. These hardships led to numerous forced "confessions" from Bucher and others. The United States meanwhile negotiated the release of the *Pueblo* crew on December 23. A court of inquiry in 1969 recommended that Bucher receive a general court martial, but the secretary of the navy, John H. Chaffee, dropped all charges against Bucher and others for signing confessions. The story of the *Pueblo* is recounted in *Bucher: My Story* (with Mark Rascovich) (1970). Bucher retired from the navy in 1973.

CADORIA, SHERIAN GRACE (1940–). Cadoria received her B.S. from Southern University in Baton Rouge, LA in 1961. She joined the Women's Army Corps (WAC) and gradually advanced in rank through the turbulent 1960s. She served in the provost marshal's office and the protocol office in Vietnam, in training assignments in the U.S., and in criminal investigation duties. Cadoria was also a student at the Command and General Staff College and the Army War College, as well as executive officer for an army unit in Europe. In 1974 Cadoria received a M.A. in social work from the University of Oklahoma. When the WAC was dissolved in 1978, Cadoria continued to receive career-enhancing assignments. In 1985 she was promoted to brigadier general—the first African

American woman in the regular army to earn the rank. From 1985 to 1987 Gen. Cadoria was director of Manpower and Personnel for the Joint Chiefs of Staff. At the time of her retirement from the army in 1990, Gen. Cadoria was the highest ranking African American woman in the U.S. armed forces.

CALLEY, WILLIAM LAWS (1944–). Calley enlisted in the army on July 26, 1966 at a time when U.S. troop strength in Vietnam was escalating. Initially trained as a clerk-typist, he was accepted for Officer Candidate School in March of 1967 after which he joined the 11th Infantry Brigade at Jungle Warfare School in Hawaii. He and the members of his company were then shipped to Quang Ngai province in South Vietnam as part of the Americal Division. Three months later, on March 16, 1968, Calley's platoon entered the village of My Lai 4 to clear it of Viet Cong. Finding only old men, women, and children, he nevertheless gave orders to kill the villagers. Between 100 and 500 people were massacred. Calley later insisted that he was simply following lawful orders from his superiors. A few men in the company however, had refused to participate in the killing. A cover-up in the army hierarchy kept the massacre hidden until April 1969 when a former member of the division brought it to public attention. An army investigation followed. On September 6, only one day before Calley was to leave the army, he was arrested and charged with the murder of 109 (later reduced to 102) Vietnamese civilians. His court martial began on November 12, 1970 and lasted seventy-seven days. On March 29, 1971 the court found him guilty of premeditated murder on twenty-two counts and sentenced him to confinement at hard labor for life. Acknowledging public sympathy for Calley, however, President Richard Nixon ordered him released under house arrest pending an appeal. Calley spent thirty-five months confined to his quarters. Meanwhile other officers and men involved in the killings were court martialed, but none was found guilty. Although his appeal was denied, Calley's sentence was reduced to twenty years, then cut in half by the Secretary of the Army. Calley entered the stockade on June 25, 1974, but received a parole after he completed one-third of his ten year sentence. Thus on November 9 he left the prison at Ft. Leavenworth a free man. During his confinement to his quarters at Ft. Benning, Calley cooperated with a journalist, John Sack, in the writing of *Body Count: Lt. Calley's Story as Told to John Sack* (1971).

COUGHLIN, PAULA (1962–). Coughlin earned a bachelor's degree at Old Dominion University and while there went through the naval reserve officers training course to gain a commission in 1984. Her father had been a naval aviator; Coughlin learned to fly helicopters in 1987. She qualified as an H-2 helicopter commander, maintenance check pilot, and instructor pilot. She made two deployments to the western Pacific while assigned to a navy oceanographic vessel in the late 1980s. In 1990 Coughlin was selected for duty as the aide to the commander of the Naval Air Test Center in Patuxent River, MD. In early September 1991, Lt. Coughlin accompanied her boss, Rear Adm. John W. Snyder, Jr. to the annual convention of the Tailhook Association, a private group of active and retired navy and marine corps aviators, at a Las Vegas hotel. While there Coughlin was one of at least twenty-six women, which included fourteen female officers, who were assaulted by other convention goers on the night of September 7. Despite Coughlin's report of her assault to Adm. Snyder shortly thereafter, the navy did little to investigate what had happened or to take disciplinary action against any men who were involved until Coughlin publicly told her side of the events in June 1992. In the aftermath of her disclosures, the secretary of the navy, Lawrence Garrett III, resigned and some 140 convention goers were implicated in the scandal, but no one was court martialed. Eighty officers, including 30 admirals, received administrative discipline and the chief of naval operations, Adm. Frank B. Kelso II, retired early. Coughlin resigned from the navy in 1994.

ELLSBERG, DANIEL (1931–). A brilliant student, Ellsberg graduated from Harvard in 1952. He won a fellowship to study advanced economics at Cambridge University and then returned to Harvard for a M.A. in economics (1953). Ellsberg then waived his student deferment and volunteered for service in the marine corps (1954–56), seeing duty in the Middle East during the Suez crisis of 1956. Returning to Harvard, Ellsberg earned a Ph.D. in economics and then joined the Rand Corporation (1959) to study game theory and risk in nuclear war. In this capacity Ellsberg was a participant in strategy sessions relating to the Cuban Missile crisis (1962), a Defense Department consultant who visited Vietnam (1961), and a rising intellectual star who joined the Defense Department in 1964 to work for Robert S. McNamara, the Secretary of Defense, on issues relating to the Vietnam War. Ellsberg went to Vietnam again in 1965 where he began to move from his previously hawkish views on the war to the position of a dove because he felt the program of pacification followed by the U.S. was not working. Between 1967 and 1969, at McNamara's request Ellsberg subsequently worked to compile a forty-seven volume classified document analyzing U.S. policy decisions on Vietnam. This material later became known as the Pentagon Papers when on June 13, 1971 the *New York Times* and other newspapers began to publish excerpts from these volumes that Ellsberg had copied and given to the newspapers. The contents of the Pentagon Papers reenforced Ellsberg's moral qualms about U.S. policy in Vietnam and documented the way successive American presidents overstepped their powers in conducting the war. The papers also revealed instances whereby the government had by-passed Congress or their advisers and misled the public about the extent of the U.S. involvement in Vietnam. Following publication of the Pentagon Papers, the government sued the *Times* and Ellsberg was charged with conspiracy against the government. The Supreme Court ruled six to three (June 30, 1971) in favor of the *Times* and Ellsberg's case was declared a mistrial (1973) when the judge learned that agents employed by the Nixon staff had illegally broken into the office of Ellsberg's psychiatrist seeking potentially damaging information on him. Ellsberg's *Papers on the War* (1972) sets out his position on the Vietnam conflict and his reasons for opposing it.

GARRETT, HENRY LAWRENCE II (1939–). Garrett earned a B.S. from the University of West Florida and then enlisted in the navy (1961). He served for three years as a machinist mate aboard submarines, including USS *Sea Poucher*, an attack sub that was deployed off the coast of Cuba during the Cuban Missile Crisis (1962). Later Garrett earned a commission as a flight officer and served in a seaplane squadron in Vietnam. In 1966 his P-5M aircraft was hit by enemy gunfire off the Cambodian coast. Garrett went to the University of San Diego Law School, graduating in 1972 and joined the navy's Judge Advocate General's Corps as an attorney. He retired from the navy in 1981 with the rank of commander and went to work for the administration of President Ronald Reagan as a lawyer, specializing in ethics. During the 1980s Garrett held various posts in government including general counsel for the department of the navy (1986–1987), undersecretary of the navy (1987–1989), and secretary of the navy (1989–1992). He was the first person in modern navy history to rise from the enlisted ranks to secretary of the service. During his tenure as secretary, Garrett dealt with reducing the size of the fleet from over 600 to about 450 vessels in the face of major budget cuts. He oversaw the probe of a deadly explosion on the battleship *Iowa* that killed 47 sailors in 1989. He also was responsible for the investigation of the Tailhook Incident that involved the sexual harassment of at least 26 women (14 of whom were female officers) at the convention of the Tailhook Association of active and retired navy and marine aviators in 1991. The problems resulting from this investigation ultimately led to his resignation in June 1992.

GOODPASTER, ANDREW JACKSON (1915–). Andrew Goodpaster's graduation second in his class at the United States Military Academy in 1939 led to a branch assignment as an engineer. He continued that association during World War II, with service in North Africa and Italy. He was reassigned to the army general staff in 1944, and his service in that capacity brought him to the attention of Gen. Dwight D. Eisenhower during the latter's term as army chief of staff. When Eisenhower assumed his duties as commander of the military wing of NATO,

Goodpaster was assigned to his staff. One of the post-World War II "army intellectuals" (he earned a Ph.D. in international relations at Princeton in 1950), Goodpaster was instrumental in the organization of the new military force and helped define the political aims of the new alliance in conjunction with W. Averell Harriman, Jean Monnet, and Edwin Plowden. In 1954, he was named presidential staff secretary and defense liaison to Dwight D. Eisenhower, and remained in that position until 1961. Goodpaster received considerable acclaim during the Eisenhower years as the consummate staff officer. He added considerable luster to that reputation during the Kennedy, Johnson, and Nixon presidencies in official and unofficial capacities. He supervised major study projects relating to the war in Southeast Asia and served as the military representative at the Paris peace talks in 1968. Although he retired in 1974, he was recalled to active duty to become superintendent of the United States Military Academy in 1977. His appointment as superintendent, which lasted until 1981, was in response to a cheating scandal which damaged the reputation of the nation's senior military academy.

GRAVELY, SAMUEL L., JR. (1922–). Educated at Virginia Union University from which he graduated in 1948, Gravely enlisted in the naval reserve in 1942. He subsequently earned a commission as an ensign at the Midshipmen School (1944), one of the first group of 12 African Americans to graduate from this program. Released from active duty in 1946, Gravely returned to active duty in 1949. During his career he had duty tours involving recruiting, communications, operations, and security. In 1962 Gravely received command of the radar picket destroyer *Falgout*. He then attended the Naval War College (1963–1964) and was the first African American line officer to be promoted to captain in the navy. In 1970 Gravely commanded the guided missile frigate USS *Jouett*. Promoted to rear admiral in 1971, Gravely commanded the Defense Communications Agency (1978–1980) and later Cruiser Destroyer Flotilla Two. He was the navy's first African American admiral. Gravely's last assignment was as commander of the navy's Third Fleet (1976 to 1980). He retired from the navy in 1980 as a vice admiral. At the time of his retirement, Gravely was the navy's highest-ranking African American.

HAIG, ALEXANDER MEIGS (1924–). Haig's extensive and frequently controversial career, began with his graduation from the United States Military Academy in 1947. He served as an aide-de-camp during the Korean conflict, and in a variety of posts during the next ten years. In 1960, he graduated from the Naval War College and the following year earned a M.A. in international relations from Georgetown University. Over the next few years he impressed his superiors in the Pentagon and the Defense Department, before accepting command of a battalion in Vietnam

(1966). Henry Kissinger, national security adviser to President Nixon, chose Haig to be his assistant in 1969, and later praised his work as "indispensable." Haig was influential in decisions regarding the war in Southeast Asia and in arranging Nixon's visit to China. Briefly returning to the Pentagon, he agreed to become Nixon's White House "chief of staff" in the midst of the Watergate turmoil (1973–1974). At the height of the crisis he reportedly functioned in place of the president and persuaded Nixon to resign (1974). Haig then became Supreme Allied Commander of NATO forces until 1981, when President Ronald Reagan selected him to be Secretary of State. His tenure was difficult. Confirmation hearings probed his involvement in decisions relating to the Vietnam war, and he made the controversial assertion that he was "in charge" at the White House after Reagan was seriously wounded in 1981. He resigned in 1982 to open a consulting firm and write his memoirs, *Caveat: Realism, Reagan, and Foreign Policy* (1984). He was an unsuccessful candidate for the Republican nomination for president in 1988.

HERSHEY, LEWIS BLAINE (1893–1977). Following education at Tri-State College (1912, 1914), Hershey entered Indiana University in 1917 to earn a Ph.D. World War I interrupted his studies and he was called up with the Indiana National Guard, which he had joined in 1911. Hershey saw brief service in France and in 1920 obtained a commission in the regular army. He then taught military science at Ohio State University (1923–1927), attended the Command and General Staff School and graduated from the Army War College (1934). From 1936 to 1940 Hershey served on the Joint Army and Navy Selective Service Committee which drew up plans for a system of national conscription. When the Selective Service System went into effect in September 1940, Hershey became its deputy director. The following July he became the director of Selective Service, a post he held until 1970. Hershey directed the operation of over 4,000 local draft boards and the registration and examination of millions of men who were eligible for service in World War II, the Korean War, and the Vietnam War. From 1970 to 1973 Hershey was a presidential adviser on the transition to an all-volunteer armed service. When Gen. Hershey retired in 1973 he was the oldest man on active status.

HOLLOWAY, JAMES LEMUEL III (1922–). The son of a distinguished naval officer, Holloway was a graduate of the wartime accelerated program at the United States Naval Academy. Although his wartime service was in destroyers, Holloway was designated a naval aviator in January 1946. After two combat tours during the Korean War, he rose through the ranks and in 1965 assumed command of the first operational nuclear-powered aircraft carrier (USS *Enterprise*). Holloway remained with *Enterprise* through two combat tours in Vietnamese waters and then returned to staff duty. As director of the strike warfare division, he was instrumental in the development of the multipurpose carrier concept. He returned to sea duty in 1970 when he took command of Carrier Division Six in the eastern Mediterranean. He succeeded Adm. Elmo R. Zumwalt as chief of naval operations in 1974 and remained in that post until his retirement in 1978. Holloway holds the distinction of commanding the first nuclear-powered naval vessel to enter combat.

HOPPER, GRACE BREWSTER MURRAY (1906–1992). A 1928 graduate of Vassar College, Grace Murray earned a M.A. (1930) and a Ph.D. (1934) from Yale in mathematics and mathematical physics. She had married Vincent F. Hopper in 1930, but they divorced in 1945. From 1931 to 1943 Grace Hopper taught mathematics at Vassar. She joined the naval reserve in 1943, got a commission in 1944, and was immediately assigned to the Bureau of Ships Computation Project at Harvard University where she worked on the Mark I computer—the first programmable digital computer made in the U.S. Following the war Hopper wanted to transfer to the regular navy, but she was turned down due to her age. Instead she remained at Harvard working on computers. She is generally credited with coining the term "bug" for an error in a program when an actual moth was found in the electrical relays of Harvard's Mark II computer. In 1949 Hopper joined the Eckert-Mauchly Corporation which then was building the Univac I electronic computer. When Remington Rand bought her employers' firm, Hopper stayed on as a mathematician and programmer. During the early 1950s she developed a new kind of program called a compiler—a software program that translated a programmer's instructions into symbolic language necessary to run the computer. In 1959 Hopper began with others to develop a programming language called COBOL (Common Business-Oriented Language), a business language for automatic digital computers. Hopper retired from the naval reserve in 1966, but the following year she was recalled to active duty to help the navy standardize its high-level programming. She retired from Sperry Corp. (the successor to Remington Rand) in 1971. By special presidential appointment, Hopper became a rear admiral in the reserve in 1983 and was the oldest navy officer on active duty when she retired again in 1986. Hopper died in 1992.

LAIRD, MELVIN ROBERT (1922–). Laird graduated from Carleton College in 1942 and joined the navy during World War II. The Wisconsin Republican then served in the state legislature before being elected to Congress in 1952, where he remained for sixteen years. He established his credentials in military affairs, enjoying a lengthy tenure on the defense subcommittee of the House Appropriations Committee. In 1969, President Richard Nixon selected Laird to be Secretary of Defense. Laird's responsibility was generally not to make policy but to explain and defend Nixon's policies to Congress, which he did quite effectively. Privately, he unsuccessfully opposed Nixon's decisions to invade Cambodia (1970) and to mine Haiphong harbor in North Vietnam (1972). He supported and encouraged, though, the Vietnamization strategy—reducing the American military presence in Vietnam by turning over greater responsibility for military operations to the army of South Vietnam. He also oversaw the replacement of the military draft with a lottery system. He resigned in 1973 but returned to counsel the embattled president on domestic affairs. When Nixon resigned in 1974, Laird left public service to become a senior advisor for *Reader's Digest.*

MCNAMARA, ROBERT STRANGE (1916–). McNamara earned a B.A. from the University of California, Berkeley (1937) and a M.B.A. from Harvard (1939). In 1940 he joined the Harvard faculty and during World War II taught special courses for army air force officers at Harvard. Then in 1943 McNamara went to England on assignment to the Eighth Air Force headquarters. There he received a commission as a captain and applied his knowledge of statistical and accounting methods to improve the B-17 bomber program. After the war (1946), the Ford Motor Company hired McNamara and eight other management experts, who came to be known as the "whiz kids," to turn around the financially troubled automaker. McNamara's advancement through Ford's management ranks was rapid due to his brilliant and innovative methods. In 1960 he became president of Ford—the first non-family member to hold that position. Shortly thereafter President-elect John F. Kennedy asked McNamara to join his cabinet as Secretary of Defense. McNamara served Kennedy and his successor, Lyndon B. Johnson, in that post until early 1968. During that time he reorganized the department, prompted cost-benefit analyses of weapons systems and procurement programs, and moved the armed services away from excessive reliance on nuclear deterrence while building more effective conventional forces. McNamara was also a principal in the build-up of U.S. troops in Vietnam from 1961 to 1967. McNamara supported the escalation of the war until late 1965 when he began to doubt the effectiveness of this policy. In 1967 he authorized a study of American involvement that came to be known as the Pentagon Papers. From 1968 to 1981 McNamara was president of the World Bank where he promoted economic growth and stability.

MOORER, THOMAS HINMAN (1912–). After graduation from the Naval Academy in 1933, Moorer served aboard the USS *Salt Lake City* and the USS *New Orleans.* In 1936, after qualifying as a naval aviator he was assigned to various aircraft carriers in the Pacific. On December 7, 1941, as a member of Patrol Squadron Twenty-two, he was one of those who sought in vain to locate the Japanese fleet after the attack on Pearl Harbor. On February 19, 1942, just north of Darwin, Australia, he evaded an attack by Japanese fighter planes and managed to land his crippled

Catalina PBY. Thus began an odyssey involving a rescue, a sinking ship, and a journey to an uninhabited island. In March 1943 Moorer was the first commander of a bombing squadron operating out of Key West. After a year in that position Moorer assumed a staff position with the Commander Air Force, Atlantic Fleet. He was later recognized for his considerable contribution to the use of aircraft in antisubmarine warfare. Moorer participated in the postwar strategic bombing survey of Japan and spent two years at a naval aviation ordnance test facility. Moorer alternated staff and sea duty and was selected for rear admiral in 1957. He advanced to the rank of vice admiral and assumed command of the Seventh Fleet in 1962, the Pacific Fleet in 1964, and the Atlantic Fleet in 1965. Adm. Moorer became the first naval officer to command both the Pacific and Atlantic fleets. He was named Chief of Naval Operations in 1967, reappointed in 1969, and named chairman of the Joint Chiefs of Staff in 1970. He retired in July 1974.

POWELL, COLIN LUTHER (1937–). The son of Jamaican immigrants, Powell entered the army in 1958 having graduated as the top cadet in ROTC at the City University of New York. Powell served two tours in Vietnam. He earned a M.A. in business administration at George Washington University in 1971, then won a coveted White House fellowship before serving as a battalion commander in Korea (1973). From that point on, Powell's career moved between military command and political appointments. He graduated from the National War College (1975), held positions with the Carter administration in the late 1970s, and returned to Washington from Fort Leavenworth in 1983 to become senior military assistant to Defense Secretary Caspar Weinberger. Involved in sensitive operations such as the sea-air raid on Libya in 1986, Powell avoided being touched by the scandal of the Reagan administration's arms sales to Iran. He briefly left Washington to command a unit in Germany, but in 1987 President Ronald Reagan appointed him deputy to the national security adviser, and then as national security adviser. In 1988, Powell once again returned to command and was promoted to general, when President George Bush named him chairman of the Joint Chiefs of Staff the following year—the first African American to hold that post. Powell proved to be a popular and telegenic chairman. During his tenure the United States conducted an operation in Panama against the regime of Manuel Noriega (1989) and engaged in Operations Desert Shield (1990–1991), to protect Saudi Arabia against Iraqi invasion, and Desert Storm (1991), the six-week war against Iraq. These operations evoked discussion at home, but the last two were especially successful and Powell was awarded a Congressional gold medal. He resigned from active duty in 1993, when his second term on the Joint Chiefs of Staff ended.

SCHLESINGER, JAMES RODNEY (1929–) A 1950 graduate of Harvard University, Schlesinger returned to the university and received a M.A.

in 1952 and a Ph.D. in 1956. As an undergraduate and graduate student Schlesinger was interested in economics and in 1955 he joined the faculty of the University of Virginia as an assistant professor. Although his first monograph, *The Political Economy of National Security* (1960), was not a success, the publication led to a position with the RAND Corporation in 1963. By 1967, Schlesinger was director of strategic studies and a consultant to the Bureau of the Budget. This latter accomplishment led President Nixon to appoint him assistant director of the Office of Management and Budget. Schlesinger was soon perceived as an abrasive individual committed to achieving an objective regardless of ideological consistency. His reputation as a problem solver led to successive appointments as Secretary of Interior (1971) and Director of the Central Intelligence Agency (1972). In 1973, Schlesinger was appointed Secretary of Defense and remained in that post until 1975. Free of the constraints imposed by the war in Vietnam, Schlesinger vigorously sought to secure the United States against the threat posed by an increasingly powerful U.S.S.R. Schlesinger's hardline approach, which involved support for limited nuclear wars, ultimately ran afoul of the desire of many within the Ford administration to reach a diplomatic accommodation with the Soviet Union and he returned to private life. In 1977, Schlesinger reemerged as Secretary of Energy in the Carter administration, but his host of enemies and the intractability of the problems he faced combined to force him from office again in 1979.

SCHWARZKOPF, H. NORMAN (1934–). Schwarzkopf, following in his father's footsteps (USMA, 1917), graduated from the United States Military Academy in 1956. He served tours in the U.S. and Germany before earning a M.A. in guided-missile engineering at the University of Southern California in 1964. That year he began a three-year teaching assignment at the Military Academy, but left in 1965 to advise a South Vietnamese airborne division, as the war in Vietnam heated up. Schwarzkopf finished his tour at the Military Academy (1966–1968), attended the Command and General Staff College, and returned to Vietnam to command a battalion. He then served in a variety of positions before being named a director in the office of the deputy chief of staff in 1982. Promoted to general the following year Schwarzkopf commanded American ground forces in the invasion of Grenada. Two years later, he was appointed deputy chief of staff for operations and then, after a year as a corps commander, deputy chief in 1987. The following year, Schwarzkopf was given command of the United States Central Command, with responsibility for drawing up plans for a possible war in the Middle East. Five days after Iraqi troops invaded Kuwait in 1990, he engineered the deployment of American forces to the region in Operation Desert Shield, to protect Saudi Arabia from invasion. When Iraq refused to leave Kuwait, the operation transformed in early 1991 into Desert Storm, an allied effort which became known as the Persian Gulf War. Following almost six weeks of devastating air and missile bombardment of Iraq, Schwarzkopf launched a 100-hour ground war which succeeded spectacularly and at minimal cost. He returned home a hero, made popular by the war's apparent success (in contrast to Vietnam) and by his televised press briefings during the engagement. Schwarzkopf subsequently retired from active duty in 1991 to write his memoirs, *It Doesn't Take a Hero* (1992).

STOCKDALE, JAMES BOND (1923–). Commissioned an ensign following graduation from the Naval Academy in 1946, Stockdale went on to flight training and earned his wings. His tours of duty included serving as a test pilot, commander of a fighter squadron, and later commander of an air wing. In 1962 he earned a M.A. from Stanford. In early August 1964, Stockdale, then a commander, flew over the Tonkin Gulf at the time that the North Vietnamese were supposed to have attacked the U.S. destroyers *Maddox* and *Turner Joy*. Stockdale later led the first U.S. bombing raid on North Vietnam. In 1965 he was shot down and spent nearly eight years as the senior navy prisoner-of-war. Much of that time he was in leg irons and solitary confinement. Following his release in 1973, Stockdale was awarded the Medal of Honor and revealed that he had observed no enemy action in the Tonkin Gulf in 1964 involving the *Maddox* and *Turner Joy*. Stockdale went on to serve as president of the Naval War College (1976–1979) and after his retirement as a vice admiral in 1979, he spent less than a year as president of The Citadel. He wrote *A Vietnam Experience* (1985) about his time in Southeast Asia. In 1992 independent presidential candidate Ross Perot selected Stockdale as his vice presidential running mate. They had known each other since the 1970s because of Perot's efforts to help POW's. As a politician, Stockdale proved to be something of a neophyte, but he held his own in the vice presidential debate on October 13 with Vice President Dan Quayle and the Democrats' Sen. Albert Gore.

WESTMORELAND, WILLIAM CHILDS (1914–). Graduating from the United States Military Academy in 1936, Westmoreland began his rapid rise as an officer in the field artillery. He served in various locations prior to World War II. In 1942 he took part in the North Africa and Sicily campaigns, then landed in France with the 9th Infantry Division in 1944. He commanded a regiment in occupied Germany and later returned to the United States for parachute training, which led to his being appointed chief of staff of the 82nd Airborne Division in 1947. After teaching at the Command and General Staff School and the Army War College, Westmoreland led a regimental combat team in Korea in 1952 and was promoted to brigadier general. Attached to the general staff for five years, he took command of an airborne division before becoming the second youngest superintendent of the United States Military Academy (1960–1963). In 1964, he was named head of the U.S. Military Assistance Command, Vietnam. Westmoreland was the tactical commander of American troops in South Vietnam and to many people in the United States he came to symbolize the American military presence in Southeast Asia. His forces took a more active role in the fighting, employing an attrition strategy labeled "search and destroy." Subsequent to the Viet Cong's Tet Offensive in early 1968, which his troops staved off but which took a heavy psychological toll back home, he was named army chief of staff. He retired from active duty four years later (1972), returned to his native South Carolina, and wrote his memoirs, *A Soldier Reports* (1976). In 1982 he charged CBS News with libel over a report he deliberately misrepresented figures on enemy troop strength during the war. The case was settled out of court in 1984.

WEYAND, FREDERICK CARLTON (1916–). After graduating from the University of California, Berkeley, in 1939, Weyand served as an intelligence officer in the Burma theater during World War II and as an infantry officer in the Korean conflict. In 1966, Major General Weyand led the 25th Infantry Division into combat in South Vietnam. The following year he took command of the corps-level II Field Force Vietnam, which played a key role in the defense of Saigon during the Tet Offensive in January 1968. After a brief assignment in the United States, Weyand was sent to Paris in 1969 to advise the American delegation negotiating an end to the war. He returned to Vietnam, however, as deputy commander of the U.S. Military Assistance Command, Vietnam (1970), and two years later was named commander. In that role, he oversaw the final withdrawal of American troops from South Vietnam in 1973. Selected as chief of staff of the army in 1974, Weyand retired from active service in 1976.

WHEELER, EARLE GILMORE (1908–1975). Wheeler graduated from the U.S. Military Academy in 1932 and served in the infantry in the U.S. and China (1937–1938). In World War II he trained troops for service in Europe and was involved in logistical operations in the European theater. Although he had no combat experience in either World War II or Korea, Wheeler became a protege of Gen. Maxwell D. Taylor. Wheeler held various administrative posts in the Pentagon and elsewhere in the 1950s. By 1959 he was the commanding general of the 2nd Armored Division. Reassigned to the Pentagon in 1960 as a staff member for the Joint Chiefs of Staff, Wheeler impressed Robert S. McNamara, the Secretary of Defense, with his nonpartisan views that stressed inter-service cooperation on policy issues. Wheeler was named army chief of staff in 1962 where he supervised a gradual modernization of army programs to achieve a balanced force capable of fighting both conventional and nuclear war. When in 1964 President Lyndon Johnson nominated Gen.

Taylor as ambassador to South Vietnam, Johnson also nominated Wheeler to succeed Taylor as the chairman of the Joint Chiefs of Staff (JCS). Wheeler served as chairman of the JCS from 1964 to 1970. There he oversaw the gradual increase of U.S. combat-forces in Vietnam from the time of the Tonkin Gulf Resolution (1964) (which Wheeler supported) to the beginning of the process of "Vietnamization" under President Richard Nixon. By 1967 Wheeler was convinced the Vietnam War had become a protracted conflict with no end in sight that required more troops and a call-up of the reserve. In consequence, Wheeler supported the 1970 bombing and invasion of Cambodia in an effort to destroy North Vietnamese sanctuaries there. Wheeler retired in 1970.

YEAGER, CHARLES ELWOOD (1923–). Shortly after he graduated from high school, Yeager enlisted in the army (1941) and after aviation training became a member of the air corps. He earned a reserve commission in 1943 and went to England as a fighter pilot. Yeager flew 64 missions in World War II, mostly in P-51 Mustangs. He shot down thirteen German planes and was once shot down himself, escaping capture with the help of the French underground. In 1947 Yeager obtained a regular commission and volunteered to test fly the then-secret experimental X-1 rocket plane built by the Bell Aircraft Co. In the X-1 Capt. Yeager was the first man to break the sound barrier (October 14, 1947) at 662 miles per hour and in the X-1A rocket plane he set a world speed record of 1,650 miles per hour (December 12, 1953). For his achievements as a test pilot, Yeager won several awards. He went on to command the Aerospace Research Pilot School (1962) and the 405th Tactical Fighter Wing (1969). Yeager subsequently retired from the air force in 1975 with the rank of brigadier general. More recently Yeager published his memoirs, *Yeager: An Autobiography* with Leo Janos (1985), and achieved celebrity status in Tom Wolfe's book *The Right Stuff* (1979), a Hollywood movie based on Wolfe's book, and TV commercials.

ZUMWALT, ELMO RUSSELL, Jr. (1920–). Zumwalt graduated from the U.S. Naval Academy in 1942 and spent most of World War II serving on destroyers in the Pacific. Following the war, he chose a naval career in part because of his concern for the threat that the Soviet Union posed for the United States. Assignments at sea and ashore such as a tour at the Naval War College (1952–1953) and two assignments (1953–1955 and 1957–1959) at the Navy Department increased his awareness of personnel issues and politics. Zumwalt commanded the guided-missile frigate USS *Dewey* (1959–1961) and subsequently worked closely with Paul Nitze, prior to and after Nitze became Secretary of the Navy in 1963. In these staff positions Zumwalt was involved in handling activities relating to NATO and the blockade of Cuba. Promoted to rear admiral in 1965, Zumwalt commanded Cruiser-Destroyer Flotilla Seven. He then served in the Pentagon where he established the navy's division of systems analysis. In September 1968 Zumwalt took command of the U.S. naval forces in Vietnam, where as a vice admiral he oversaw the "brown-water navy." He also ordered the use of the chemical defoliant Agent Orange in the Mekong Delta with the goal of driving the Viet Cong off the banks of the delta. In July 1970 Zumwalt became the youngest Chief of Naval Operations, succeeding Adm. Thomas Moorer. Zumwalt's liberalization of personnel policies helped boost recruitment and retention of personnel, but he also coped with a shrinking naval budget. His opposition to these cuts put him at odds with President Richard Nixon. Zumwalt retired in 1974 and published his memoirs, *On Watch*, in 1976.

Selected Reading List

General Works

Amme, Carl H. *NATO Strategy and Nuclear Defense* (1988). Amme looks at the strategic concepts of military confrontation and the control of nuclear weapons and makes recommendations which are often at odds with conventional wisdom.

Bertram, Christopher. *Arms Control and Military Force* (1980). These essays, published by the International Institute for Strategic Studies, provide both technical and political perspectives of the problems of arms control and the effort to reduce the risk of war.

Betts, Richard K. *Soldiers, Statesmen, and Cold War Crises* (1977). Betts analyzes the role of military advice and influence in America's Cold War decision-making process. He argues that while the military has had some influence on decision-making, this influence has been limited and often beneficial.

Blank, Stephen, Lawrence E. Grinter, Karl P. Magyar, Lewis B. Wave, and Bynum Weathers. *Low-Intensity Conflict Challenges* (1988). The authors examine the doctrines, military organizations, and strategies that Third World countries use in response to low-intensity conflicts.

Borowski, Harry R., ed. *Military Planning in the 20th Century* (1986). These are the proceedings of the 11th Military History Symposium, held at the U.S. Air Force Academy in October 1984. The papers focus on the fundamental importance of proper planning in a world of limited resources and address the problem planners often bring with them—myopic reasoning.

Brodie, Bernard. *War and Politics* (1973). This is a collection of Brodie's essays on the interaction of war and politics in the Nuclear Age. For many, Brodie was the premier strategic thinker in the United States.

Cardwell, Thomas A. *Command Structure for Theater Warfare—The Quest for Unity of Command* (1984). Cardwell discusses how the military establishments of the United States and its allies experimented with command structures in World War II, Korea and Vietnam and proposes his own views regarding appropriate command structures for future theater warfare.

Carter, Ashton B. and David N. Schwartz. *Ballistic Missile Defense* (1984). This joint study by the Massachusetts Institute of Technology and the Brookings Institute examines the controversy surrounding the Anti-Ballistic Treaty of 1972 which restricted the testing and deployment of such defenses.

Collins, John M. *American and Soviet Military Trends Since the Cuban Missile Crisis* (1978). The author examines weapon systems and types of forces employed by the two super powers since 1962. He concludes that the United States has been losing its ability to deter Soviet aggression around the world.

Gillcrist, Paul T. *Feet Wet: Reflections of a Carrier Pilot* (1990). A former navy fighter pilot provides both an historical and analytical account of the evolution of carrier aviation from the pre-World War II era to today's F-14s.

Handel, Michael J., ed. *Leaders and Intelligence* (1989). This is a collection of six essays examining the relationship between high-level leaders and their intelligence officers and the use the leaders made of the intelligence information provided.

Handel, Michael J., ed. *Intelligence and Military Operations* (1990). This is a collection of essays from U.S. Army War College conferences from 1985–1988 devoted to the study of military intelligence.

Higham, Robin. *Air Power: A Concise History* (1984). Higham surveys the rise of military air power from 1911 through the Vietnam War. This second edition adds a very short capsule of the period 1971–1983. Like his other works, this book contains Higham's own, subjective opinions as to what was important and who was great.

Hosmer, Stephen T. *Constraints on U.S. Strategy in Third World Conflicts* (1987). Hosmer writes that American military strategies in Third World conflicts and crises evolved largely from cumulative constraints so that American administrations have tended to base strategies on the politically feasible rather than optimal battlefield needs.

Kahan, Jerome. *Security in the Nuclear Age* (1975). The author clarifies the origins of the nuclear weapons problems the U.S. faced at the time of the SALT Talks by outlining the history of American policy on the subject from Eisenhower through Nixon.

Laqueur, Walter. *Guerrilla: A Historical and Critical Study* (1976). Laqueur provides what is considered by academicians as the most sophisticated treatment of guerrilla warfare.

Luttwak, Edward N. *Strategy and Politics* (1980). This collection of essays dealing with military and international affairs is a response to the pervasive pessimism and self-recrimination Luttwak found in the post-Vietnam War climate in America. Luttwak insists that America's greatest problem is a lack of confidence.

Martin, Lawrence, ed. *Strategic Thought in the Nuclear Age* (1980). Martin believes that the nuclear age caused a revolution in military affairs, public attitudes, and the study of modern strategic thought.

Morgan, Patrick M. *Deterrence* (1977). Although the book is a study for international politics, it is also important to those who analyze military strategy through political history. One chapter is devoted to crisis decision-making and the causes of war.

Rice, Edward E. *Wars of the Third Kind: Conflict in Underdeveloped Countries* (1988). Using a broad range of historical events and evidence taken from the entire twentieth century, Rice offers both insights and analyses of revolutionary warfare.

Salkeld, Robert. *War and Space: Man's Conquest of Space—Stronghold of Peace or Infinite Battlefield* (1970). Salkeld provides a broadly focused attempt to inform the American public on the history and motives of the Soviet Union's efforts to enhance its power potential by a rapid development of its military technology.

Shultz, Richard H., Jr., et al. *Guerrilla Warfare and Counterinsurgency* (1989). The authors discuss low-intensity conflicts in developing countries within the context of the Soviet-American battle for diplomatic dominance.

Shafer, D. Michael. *Deadly Paradigms: The Failure of U.S. Counterinsurgency Policy* (1988). Shafer concludes that American efforts to defeat insurgents have largely failed because American understanding of Third World societies is usually critically flawed and dangerously wrong.

Van Creveld, Martin. *Command in War* (1985). Van Creveld investigates the historical evolution of a function of war that acquired an appellation, i.e., Command, Control and Communications, in only the last two decades and now sees an increasing demand for its understanding and future employment.

Wilson, Bennie J., III, ed. *The Guard and Reserve in the Total Force: The First Decade, 1973–1983* (1985). The authors of the articles in this work provide useful introductions to the broad and complex concepts and problems associated with the military's total force policy.

Woodward, Bob. *Veil, The Secret Wars of the CIA 1981–1987* (1987). This is a rather negative history of the agency by a journalist who gathered most of his information from over 250 interviews. The story is told from the perspective of the agency director, the White House, and the Senate's Select Committee on Intelligence.

Army

Rose, John P. *The Evolution of U.S. Army Nuclear Doctrine, 1945–1980* (1980). This West Point professor argues that the U.S. military has not trained or equipped its forces for nuclear combat and has not developed a doctrinal concept for their battlefield employment.

Air Force

Armitage, M.J. and R.A. Mason. *Air Power in the Nuclear Age* (1984). The authors examine the impact of the introduction of nuclear weapons on the concepts of air operations and air power since 1945. They argue that multiple weapons, increasing defense budgets, and world wide conflicts have all been factors in the redefinition of air power.

Bright, Charles D., ed. *Historical Dictionary of the U.S. Air Force* (1992). Bright's work contains over 1,000 items, including battles, campaigns, concepts, individuals, organizations, equipment, and pertinent legislation.

Brown, Michael E. *Flying Blind—The Politics of the U.S. Strategic Bomber Program* (1992). The book is about the weapons acquisition process and examines the value of technological, economic, bureaucratic, and strategic explanations about fifteen different bomber programs. Brown believes decision makers often set performance requirements beyond the state of the art and established acquisition accidents waiting to happen.

Davis, Richard L. and Frank P. Donnini. *Professional Military Education for Air Force Officers: Comments and Criticisms* (1991). Davis and Donnini survey the efforts of the Air University to provide effective professional military training during the period 1946–1987 with a focus on the evolution of the institutions's curriculum and doctrine.

Dean, David J. *The Air Force Role in Low-Intensity Conflict* (1986). Dean examines the increasing significance of third world countries in global affairs and suggests U.S. flexibility to respond to the probability of American involvement.

Gross, Charles Joseph. *Prelude to the Total Force: The Air National Guard 1943–1969* (1984). Gross studies the origins and evolution of the Air Guard and its expanding role and close coordination with the regular force. Given a substantial peacetime mission, the Guard was able to mobilize and integrate into the previously parochial concerns of the regular air force.

Knaack, Marcelle S. *Encyclopedia of U.S. Air Force Aircraft and Missile Systems* (1978). This multi-volume work describes the development, deployment, and operational exploits of air force weapon systems.

Kreis, John F. *Air Warfare and Air Base Air Defense 1914–1973* (1988). Kreis surveys the experiences of various air forces in defending air bases

against air attack. His analysis includes command and security arrangements, positioning of defense emplacements, repair and support services, and personnel training.

Ravenstein, Charles A. *Air Force Combat Wings Lineage and Honors Histories
1947–1977* (1984). This reference provides the lineage, assignments, components, stations, commanders, aircraft, operations, service streamers,
decorations, and emblems of post-World War II combat wings of the air
force.

Ravenstein, Charles A. *The Organization and Lineage of the United States Air
Force* (1985). Ravenstein surveys the evolution of the air force field structure from earliest military aeronautical organizations to those compris-
ing the modern air force. The book also contains heraldic illustrations.

Navy

Armbrister, Trevor. *A Matter of Accountability* (1970). Armbrister presents a
well-researched and objective account of the USS *Pueblo* affair with its
emphasis on the ship's mission and the contradictions in the command
structure in which it operated.

Deacon, Richard. *The Silent War—A History of Western Naval Intelligence*
(1988). This book is the story of the development and growing sophisti-
cation of western espionage services over the last 150 years. Tracing the
unofficial activities of the intelligence network that led to the establishment of official offices, Deacon goes on to examine the technologically
advanced systems in current operation and argues the vitality of sub-
marine-based nuclear weapons.

Duncan, Francis. *Rickover and the Nuclear Navy* (1990). This is a history of
technology, not the biography of a man. It focuses on Admiral Rickover's
work: on the development of machinery, the decisions made, techniques
employed, what was built, and for what purpose.

Hooper, Edwin. *United States Naval Power in a Changing World* (1988). This
historical analysis traces the development of the U.S. Navy from its ger-
mination to the present. Its post-World War II section offers concise views
of the Cold War, Korean War, naval influence, flexible response, the shift-
ing balance of sea power and a look to the future.

Howarth, Stephen. *To Shining Sea—A History of the United States Navy, 1775–
1991* (1991). Naval strategy and its component parts (their development,
neglect, alteration, and continuity) form a recurrent theme in this history of the U.S. Navy which the author suggests is also a mirror of
America's rise from colonial to super power status.

Howe, Jonathan Trumbull. *Multicrises: Sea Power and Global Politics in the
Missile Age* (1971). Howe compares the Middle East crisis of 1967 with
the Quemoy Conflict of 1958 to determine future trends in the use of
naval power and the defense of America's interests.

Johnson, Brian. *Fly Navy—The History of Naval Aviation* (1981). Johnson attempts to record 70 years of naval aviation history by describing the significant developments and decisive battles of the men and machines. He believes the preeminence of the aircraft carrier over the battleship came without prophecy.

Ryan, Paul B. *First Line of Defense—The U.S. Navy Since 1945* (1981). The author holds that the U.S. Navy faced the complex political, diplomatic and strategic demands of the Cold War after 1945 with leaders who learned their trade during traditional warfare against Japan and Germany. As a result, mistakes were inevitable since the leaders were ignorant of alternative policies and methods, the limits of technology, and history.

Sapolsky, Harvey M. *The Polaris System Development* (1972). This is essentially a historical case study of the navy's Fleet Ballistic Missile Program, its development, procurement and deployment, which Sapolsky argued was an outstanding success.

Watson, Bruce W. *The Changing Face of the World's Navies: 1945 to the Present* (1991). Watson believes that the historical theories of sea power are still valid despite the many technological and geopolitical changes since World War II.

Marines

Fleming, Keith. *The U.S. Marine Corps in Crisis* (1990). Focussing on the Ribbon Creek incident at Parris Island as a model, Fleming discusses external pressures on the corporate body of Marine non-commissioned officers, the Corps' relationship to congress, the complex judicial system, public opinion, and the difficulty of institutional reform.

Coast Guard

Pearcy, Arthur. *A History of U.S. Coast Guard Aviation* (1989). Pearcy's book provides an abundance of photographs and extensive technical data, but little narrative.

Social/Political Issues

Art, Robert J. *The TFX Decision: McNamara and the Military* (1968). Art uses the F-111 fighter aircraft as an example of how non-technical considerations played into procurement decisions in selecting one aircraft company and plane over another.

Binkin, Martin and Mark J. Eitelberg. *Blacks and the Military* (1982). The authors trace the history of African American participation in the U.S. armed forces and describe the changes in the racial composition in the 1970s. They also discuss the burdens and benefits of military service for

African Americans and the implications of such participation for the military and society.

Bright, Charles D. *The Jet Makers: the Aerospace Industry from 1945 to 1972* (1978). Bright surveys the post-World War II history of the United States aerospace industry, giving coverage to both military and commercial aspects.

Coulam, Robert F. *Illusions of Choice: Robert McNamara, The F-111, and the Problem of Weapons Acquisition* (1977). This is the story of how General Dynamics won a multi-billion dollar aircraft contract, Pratt & Whitney captured the engines contract, and Defense Secretary Robert McNamara caused a major shift in the strategy of U.S. weapons procurement.

Fitzgerald, A. Ernest. *The Pentagonists* (1989). Fitzgerald, the patron saint of whistle blowers, presents an insider's view of the waste, mismanagement and fraud in the Department of Defense and the retribution aimed at anyone who seeks to rectify the situation.

Fox, J. Ronald. *Arming America: How the U.S. Buys Weapons* (1974). Fox, a one-time Assistant Secretary of the Army, identifies bureaucratic resistance to change as the underlying cause behind problems of cost growth, schedule slippage and technical performance shortfalls in the Department of Defense.

Gregory, William H. *The Defense Procurement Mess* (1989). Gregory's theme is that billions of dollars are lost and the military is not getting quality weapons on time due to multitudinous rules, regulations, micromanagement, bureaucratic controls, and federal legislation. Hence, the defense procurement system must be streamlined and simplified.

Goldman, Nancy Loring, ed. *Female Soldiers—Combatants or Noncombatants?* (1982). Using a comparative analysis of case studies and analysis of the historical record of women in combat, Goldman surveys and critiques the controversy surrounding this issue.

Gropman, Alan L. *The Air Force Integrates, 1945–1964* (1978). The author traces the air force's own integration struggle and its efforts for equality of treatment, from the end of World War II to the Civil Rights Act of 1964.

Kotz, Nick. *Wild Blue Yonder: Money, Politics, and the B-1 Bomber* (1988). Kotz argues that the procurement process is out of control and defense spending has become a narcotic for a country that has become economically and politically hooked on it.

MacGregor, Morris J., Jr. *Integration of the Armed Forces 1940–1965* (1981). MacGregor argues that the experiences of World War II and the postwar pressures generated by the civil rights movement compelled the services to replace their traditional attitudes toward minorities with democratic concepts of equality.

Moskos, Charles C. and Frank R. Wood, eds. *The Modern Military: More Than Just a Job?* (1988). The authors argue that the services are being transformed from institutions to occupations, a trend that could present significant dangers to our national security.

Polmar, Norman. *Strategic Weapons: An Introduction* (1975). Polmar presents a layman's discussion of the whole subject of strategic weapons, providing a non-technical outline of the history of strategic weapons development, an inventory of existing hardware, and his projection of the future.

Sammet, George, Jr., and David E. Green. *Defense Acquisition Management* (1990). The publication provides the history, structure, problems, failures and successes of defense acquisition management. The authors use their own experience in presenting an in-depth examination of both the government's and private industries' sides of the story.

Saywell, Shirley. *Women in War: First-Hand Accounts from World War II to El Salvador* (1985). This book is about equal responsibility, not equal rights. Saywell uses the experiences of twenty-two women to demonstrate that preserving the peace is no longer the patriotic duty of men only.

Useem, Michael. *Conscription, Protest, and Social Conflict—The Life and Death of a Draft Resistance Movement* (1973). Useem's book is the story of a collective movement to put a wrench in the gears of the mobilizing mechanism. It is an analysis of an American radical protest movement against participation in the Vietnam War.

Werrell, Kenneth P. *The Evolution of the Cruise Missile* (1985). Werrell looks at the historic development of the cruise missile and suggests its evolution weighs heavily on the way the military plans its deployment and employment options.

Zaroulis, Nancy L. and Gerald Sullivan. *Who Spoke Up? American Protest Against the War in Vietnam, 1963–1975* (1984). This is a sympathetic account of how individuals in a representative democracy affected public policy and "stopped the war" in Southeast Asia. It offers a counterculture view of patriotism and true Americanism.

Vietnam War

United States involvement in the on-going conflict in Southeast Asia increased after the 1964 Gulf of Tonkin Resolution and reached 543,000 troops by the spring of 1969. But the concept that a modern land force and massive air power was the key to victory failed to prove itself; and American forces were gradually withdrawn from the engagement under the cloak of the Vietnamization process.

If the Korean War was a stalemate, the Vietnam War (1965–1973) has to be construed as the United States' first military defeat, and as such it has opened a new arena for historical debate—could the United States have won, and if it could have, who was to blame for the loss? Most first-person military accounts of the war lay the blame for the loss at the feet of Lyndon

Johnson and his McNamara "Whiz Kids." However, historians with a geo-political background generally take the position that no outside power, the United States, France, or anyone else, could have intervened successfully in the war. Because the war itself was so controversial, many of the writings are aggressive attacks motivated by political opinions. While official and quasi-official studies have been numerous, there is yet to be a definitive multi-volume history written by any of the services in the style of their products on World War II. Perhaps because the media played such a key role in the conflict, more than an adequate share of the Vietnam accounts have been written by journalists. While journalists should not be automatically disqualified as authors of history, the reader must be ready to recognize overt or covert agendas in their works here just as one would in military memoirs.

General Works

Berman, Larry. *Lyndon Johnson's War: The Road to Stalemate in Vietnam* (1989). Berman provides a rather negative view of President Johnson and his policies during the Vietnam War. This work examines decision-making at the highest levels within the Johnson Administration from 1966 through early 1968.

Berman, Larry. *Planning a Tragedy: The Americanization of the War in Vietnam* (1982). Using both a political and historical survey of America's intervention in Vietnam, Berman argues that it was doomed from the beginning. This volume analyzes the increasing Americanization of the war in 1965 at the request of Lyndon Johnson.

Chandler, Robert W. *War of Ideas: The U.S. Propaganda Campaign in Vietnam* (1981). The book describes and appraises American use of propaganda in Vietnam (1965–1972) as an instrument of foreign policy in an effort to point out pitfalls to be avoided and successful techniques worthy of emulation in future psychological operations.

Fall, Bernard. *The Two Viet-Nams: A Political and Military Analysis* (1967). In this classic account, Fall surveys the political, economic, social and cultural textures of Vietnamese society as the dominant context that would shape the character of the war.

Galloway, John. *The Gulf of Tonkin Resolution* (1970). Galloway presents background history, the incident(s), the presidential response and legislative action as well as the aftermath associated with the Gulf of Tonkin Resolution, leaving open the issue as to whether it was necessary.

Hallin, Daniel C. *The "Uncensored War:" The Media and Vietnam* (1986). Hallin argues that the growing American disenchantment with the War was not merely the results of an independent media intent on demolishing the country's illusions. A powerful mythology created by the experience of previous wars played a major underlying role.

Hanna, Norman B. *The Key to Failure: Laos and the Vietnam War* (1987). Hanna argues that America's efforts to save Vietnam were doomed since the Kennedy-Johnson administrations tried to uphold the Geneva Accords of 1962, which were nullified by communist aggression.

Herring, George C. *America's Longest War: The United States and Vietnam, 1950–1975* (1986). Considered by many to be the most concise and balanced account of America's participation in the Vietnam War, Herring's book argues that the war was a logical, but flawed, continuation of Truman's policy of containment, since no president ever questioned the importance of South Vietnam to America's position in the world.

Karnow, Stanley. *Vietnam: A History* (1983). Karnow's book is a fully accurate and unusually unbiased history of America's Vietnam War. Although he attempts to bring together complex issues in the long war, the operational war story plays second fiddle to the political conditions of the day.

Maclear, Michael. *The Ten-Thousand Day War—Vietnam, 1945–1975* (1981). Maclear covers both the French and American involvement in usually unsympathetic tones.

Matsakis, Aphrodite. *Vietnam Wives* (1988). Using observations and research conducted by a Veteran's Administration therapist, Matsakis analyzes the problems faced by women and children who lived with veterans suffering post-traumatic stress disorder.

Palmer, Bruce, Jr. *The 25-Year War: America's Military Role in Vietnam* (1984). Palmer argues that while American forces were repeatedly successful in the field, the war was lost due to the strategy developed in the White House and supported by the Joint Chiefs of Staff.

Parker, Charles. *Vietnam: Strategy for a Stalemate* (1989). Accepting a global fight against Communism as the appropriate context for understanding the war, Parker argues that when the United States failed to exploit the Sino-Soviet split and abandoned military victory as its goal, the only thing left for the army in combat was to avoid defeat.

Sheehan, Neil. *A Bright Shining Lie: John Paul Vann and America in Vietnam* (1988). Sheehan presents a rather controversial portrayal of America's efforts in Vietnam by revealing the alleged arrogance, corruption, and cruelty of the United States' military-industrial complex and the South Vietnamese oligarchy.

Spector, Ronald H. *After Tet: The Bloodiest Year in Vietnam* (1993). A close examination of combat operations in 1968 and the changing nature of the war and its impact on the American forces stationed "in country" as the U.S. determined to extract itself from South Vietnam.

Stanton, Shelby L. *Vietnam Order of Battle* (1981). Stanton's book details the composition of the U.S. Army during the Vietnam conflict and is concerned primarily with ground forces and organization.

Sullivan, Michael. *The Vietnam War: A Study in the Making of American Policy* (1985). Sullivan examines the contrasting perceptions of the war held by policy makers and the public, noting how they were developed and how the two interacted.

Taylor, Maxwell D. *The Uncertain Trumpet* (1960). This was one of the military classics of the 1960s in which Taylor, a retired Army Chief of Staff, argued against the prevailing doctrine of massive retaliation and in favor of developing the capacity to offer more flexible response.

Army

Atkinson, Rick. *The Long Grey Line* (1989). Using over 200 personal interviews, Atkinson analyzes the impact of the Vietnam War on the West Point class of 1966. This work is, of necessity, somewhat uneven in coverage of individuals, but is a valuable resource for future inquiry.

Chinnery, Phillip D. *Vietnam: The Helicopter War* (1991). This is a history of the Vietnam experience as seen through the parochial eyes of helicopter crews. Chinnery includes all types of helicopters from all arms of the military service.

Clarke, Jeffery J. *Advice and Support: The Final Years, 1965–1973* (1988). This publication of the U.S. Army Center of Military History looks at the operations, efforts and aims of the United States Military Assistance Command, Vietnam (MACV) during the key years of 1965–1973. It discusses primarily the military aspects of the American intervention, but also notes some of the political questions as well.

Coleman, J.D. *Pleiku: The Dawn of Helicopter Warfare in Vietnam* (1988). Coleman, a retired U.S. Army lieutenant colonel, covers the actions of the 1st Cavalry Division (Airmobile) in the Ia Drang Campaign of 1965, the first operation in which the concept of air mobility was introduced on a large scale.

Davidson, Phillip B. *Vietnam at War: The History, 1946–1975* (1988). This retired lieutenant general in the U.S. Army and former professor at West Point provides a view of the war from its immediate post-World War II origins, focussing on military operations.

Davidson, Phillip B. *The Secrets of the Vietnam War* (1990). According to Davidson, the United States won the battles but lost the war in Vietnam because U.S. leaders at all levels, but especially Lyndon Johnson, failed to understand and adapt to Ho Chi Minh's revolutionary strategy.

Gibson, James W. *The Perfect War: Technowar in Vietnam* (1986). Gibson critically dissects the assumptions and policies behind the ground and air wars. He sees technowar (bureaucratized, technology-dependent, managed war) at the heart of the matter.

Hammel, Eric. *Khe Sanh: Siege in the Clouds—An Oral History* (1989). Using oral histories from nearly 100 Marines as well as government documents,

Hammel provides an operational narrative of the battle written for a popular audience.

Hardaway, Robert M. *Care of the Wounded in Vietnam* (1988). A doctor explains the methods and facilities used to examine, evaluate, evacuate and hospitalize Vietnam combat victims, noting that this system became the model for most trauma centers in today's civilian hospitals.

Hauser, William L. *America's Army in Crisis: A Case Study in Civil-Military Relations* (1973). Part 2 of Hauser's book is directed at the army as he looks at such issues as drugs, race, discipline, recruitment and professionalism. He believes the Army must adapt to our changing society and that society must not press too hard for immediate and radical reform.

Herbert, Paul H. *Deciding What Has to Be Done: General William E. Depuy and the 1976 Edition of FM 100-5, Operations* (1988). The creation of an operations field manual in the midst of intellectual conflict and bureaucratic politics is told with insightful quotations and illustrative incidents.

Krepinevich, Andrew F. *The Army and Vietnam* (1986). While Krepinevich believes that the war in Vietnam could have been won militarily, he agrees with many others that massive firepower is ultimately ineffective against an insurgency force. He charges General Westmoreland with the inability to shift to more flexible tactics.

Moore, Harold G. and Joseph L. Galloway. *We Were Soldiers Once...and Young* (1992). This is the story of the Ia Drang, America's first major battle in Vietnam and the deadliest one-day conflict in the entire Vietnam war. The story is told from both the American and North Vietnamese perspectives.

Sharp, U. S. Grant. *Strategy for Defeat: Vietnam in Retrospect* (1978). The former Commander-in-Chief of the Navy's Pacific Command during much of the Vietnam Conflict attributes the loss of the war to the failure of the civilian leadership in America. He believes that military autonomy would have led to victory over North Vietnam and the loss of hundreds of lives rather than thousands.

Spector, Ronald H. *Advice and Support: The Early Years, 1941–1960* (1984). This publication of the U.S. Army Center of Military History examines early American involvement—especially the operations and goals of the United States Military Assistance Advisory Group (MAAG). Spector notes the military's early reluctance to intervene in Southeast Asia.

Stanton, Shelby L. *The Rise and Fall of an American Army: U.S. Ground Forces in Vietnam, 1965–1973* (1985) This is the only strictly operational history of the ground war. The material is presented year-by-year and front-by-front.

Summers, Harry. *On Strategy: The Vietnam War in Context* (1981, rev. 1992). In one of the classic critiques of the conflict, Summers argues that the war could have been won militarily, but was lost due to a lack of appreciation for military theory and strategy which led to a faulty definition of the nature of war.

Terry, Wallace. *Bloods: An Oral History of the Vietnam War by Black Veterans* (1984). Using extensive oral history interviews with twenty African American veterans from all services, Terry concludes that the emotional suffering endured by African Americans in the war was felt more sharply than was deprivation or physical pain.

Zaffiri, Samuel. *Hamburger Hill* (1988). Zaffiri, who served in Vietnam with the 1st Infantry Division, describes this action from the point of view of both the commanders and the soldiers in the infantry.

Air Force

Bowers, Ray L. *The Air Force in Southeast Asia: Tactical Airlift* (1983). The author describes the modification necessary to combat zone airlifts in limited warfare. He focuses specifically on the involvement of C-123, C-130, and C-7 aircraft and their air crews in the Vietnam war years.

Buckingham, William A. *Ranch Hand: The United States Air Force and Herbicides in Southeast Asia, 1961–1971* (1982). Buckingham provides a critical analysis of the use of herbicides during the war, reviewing Kennedy's policy decision to allow their employment, the application of this policy and its effectiveness.

Clodfelter, Mark. *The Limits of Air Power: The American Bombing of North Vietnam* (1989). Using declassified documents and personal interviews, this air force officer argues that, despite the U.S. air doctrine and vast air power, a lasting victory could never have been won in Vietnam without linking military strategy to national policy goals.

Eastman, James N., Jr., Walter Hanak and Lawrence J. Paszek, eds. *Aces and Aerial Victories—The United States Air Force in Southeast Asia, 1965–1973* (1976). This is a collection of first-hand accounts by combat crew members who flew missions over North Vietnam.

Fox, Roger P. *Air Base Defense in the Republic of Vietnam* (1979). This official Air Force study by a military security officer who served in Vietnam looks at the concepts and efforts employed to defend ten strategic American air force installations during the Vietnam War.

Futrell, Robert F., Riley Sunderland and Martin Blumenson. *The Air Force in Southeast Asia: The Advisory Years, to 1965* (1980). This official examination of Air Force involvement in the Vietnam War is a comprehensive review of the origins of U.S. commitment and traces its evolution from Truman to Johnson.

Littauer, Raphael and Norman Uphoff, eds. *The Air War in Indochina*, revised edition (1972). This early study by the Air War Study Group (Cornell University) holds up well as an analysis of the use and impact of American air power across Southeast Asia.

Mrozek, Donald J. *Air Power and the Ground War in Vietnam* (1988). Mrozek examines expectations associated with both ground and air tactics and looks at some of their results, coming to the conclusion that battlefield strategy is often motivated by non-battlefield situations.

Nalty, Bernard C. *Air Power and the Fight for Khe Sanh* (1973). The author gives an official analysis of air operations during the important 1968 engagement in South Vietnam, describing fighters and bomber support, the use of electronic sensors, and the unified air control system.

Risner, Robinson. *The Passing of the Night: My Seven Years as a Prisoner of the North Vietnamese* (1974). General Risner recounts the horrors and humiliation of a P.O.W. during the Vietnam War. His courageous struggle is one of emotional and physical triumphs due to his strong personal foundation in love of country and belief in God.

Robbins, Christopher. *The Ravens: The Men Who Flew in America's Secret War in Laos* (1987). The Ravens' story is one of aerial conflict in Laos from at least 1964 until 1973. Engineered primarily by the CIA, these forward air controllers directed as many as 500 sorties a day despite the claim they were only conducting armed reconnaissance.

Schlight, John. *The War in South Vietnam: The Years of the Offensive, 1965–1968* (1988). Schlight looks at air force support of the ground war in Vietnam from the advisory period to the successful air campaign conducted at Khe Sanh, noting the issues that forced the air force to commit more of its resources and doctrine to the jungle war in Southeast Asia.

Tilford, Earl H., Jr. *Setup: What the Air Force Did to Vietnam and Why* (1991). This is a critical history of the air war in Vietnam from 1961 through 1973. While Tilford reports on both the successes and failures of the air war, his theme is that the air force leaders, raised on high technology and compulsive bombing, refused to adapt their strategy to the needs of limited warfare.

Tilford, E. H., Jr. *Search and Rescue Operations of the United States Air Force in Southeast Asia 1961–1975* (1980). Despite the abundance of technical information, doctrine and concepts discussion and descriptions of command and control, personnel training and aircraft capabilities, the author still presents a clear understanding of the mission of search and rescue airmen in the Vietnam War.

Navy

Hooper, Edwin B., et al. *The United States Navy and the Vietnam Conflict* (1976). Published by the Naval Institute, this work gives what could be considered an official account of naval operations in the Vietnam War from 1961 to 1975.

Hooper, Edwin B. *Mobility, Support, Endurance: A Story of Naval Operational Logistics in the Vietnam War, 1965–1968* (1972). This book was written by

Hooper to complement a planned history of U.S. naval operations in the Vietnam War and emphasize the way the navy supports its operational fleet.

Levinson, Jeffrey L. *Alpha Strike Vietnam: The Navy's Air War, 1964–1973* (1989). Rather than a comprehensive history, Levinson's book captures the contributions of naval aviation against ground targets through the stories of 22 Navy pilots.

Nichols, John B. and Barrett Tillman. *On Yankee Station: The Naval Air War in Vietnam* (1987). The authors discuss the world of carrier aviation, its doctrine of tactics, strategy, engagement and rescue, against the backdrop of personal battle stories and postwar analysis.

Schreadley, R. L. *From the Rivers to the Sea: The United States Navy in Vietnam* (1992). This Naval War College publication presents the navy's contribution to the war effort as just one part of a Greek tragedy that holds that the military ability to win was never matched by the political will.

Whlig, Frank, ed. *Vietnam: The Naval Story* (1986). In this series of essays the authors argue that while naval forces were deployed badly in Vietnam they still performed extremely well.

Wilcox, Robert K. *Scream of Eagles: The Creation of Top Gun and the U.S. Air Victory in Vietnam* (1990). Wilcox discusses the establishment and development of the navy's Fighter Weapons School. He credits the emphasis on dogfight training for increasing the enemy's aircraft loss ratio from 2 to 1 to more than 12 to 1.

Marines

Mersky, Peter B. *U.S. Marine Corps Aviation* (1983). Mersky offers one of the few books dealing with Marine aviation as he covers the history of the air arm from 1912 through the Vietnam War and after. He also offers his assessment of the post-1983 future.

Shore, Moyers S, II. *The Battle of Khe Sanh* (1969). Shore provides the Marines' point of view during the dramatic siege of 1968.

Smith, Charles R. *U.S. Marines in Vietnam: High Mobility and Standdown 1969* (1988). This book is a product of the U.S. Marine Corps History and Museums Division and addresses the Corps' operational efforts in the Vietnam War from its high water mark to the standdown in 1969.

Retrenchment and Rebuilding (1976–1994)

Although the United States was free of the military entanglement of Vietnam in the early seventies, it would take a decade-and-a-half before the mental burden would dissolve with the victories of the Cold War and the Gulf War. First the military would go through a period of downsizing and neglect until it faced the embarrassment of a bumbled rescue mission to Iran. Then a massive infusion of manpower and some minor successes against forth-rate powers renewed the nation's belief in itself. The rapid victory in the 1991 Persian Gulf War pushed the aggressor out of Kuwait and the wounds of Vietnam farther back into history.

Military history writings which report on the retrenchment and rebuilding era or the Carter-Reagan-Bush years cut across several academic disciplines and possibly more than at any other time demonstrate how modern military history involves much more than simple battle narratives. Key subjects covered include the lessons of low-intensity conflict, the Strategic Defense Initiatives, and the Gulf War. Of particular interest for the future are the divergent positions presented by Norman Friedman and Richard Hallion in the on-going struggle over the efficacy of air power and its role in future conflicts.

General Works

Atkinson, Rick. *Crusade: The Untold Story of the Persian Gulf War* (1993). Atkinson, who covered the war for the *Washington Post*, offers a personality-centered account divided between field operations and the command center which focuses on the air/land war. This work will serve as a foundation for subsequent publications.

Allen, Thomas B., F. Clifton Berry, Jr., and Norman Polmar. *CNN: War in the Gulf* (1991). The authors provide a comprehensive account of the Gulf War, not only the day-to-day events, but a historical examination of what caused the war to break out.

Bacevich, A. J., James D. Hallums, Richard H. White and Thomas F. Young. *American Military Policy in Small Wars: The Case of El Salvador* (1988). This book contains an accurate portrayal of American and Salvadoran bureaucratic problems, their military relationships, the difficulty in helping a passive ally, and the effects of high technology and advanced weaponry in low-intensity conflicts and low-budget operations.

Berman, Larry, et al. *Foreign Military Intervention: The Dynamics of Protracted Conflict* (1992). The authors look at the political, legal and military aspects of armed intervention taken by the United States in recent years.

Buckley, Kevin. *Panama: The Whole Story* (1991). Written by a journalist, this narrative of "Operation Just Cause" gives an excellent account of the military side of the intervention.

Charters, David and Maurice Tugwell, eds. *Armies In Low-Intensity Conflict* (1988). An anthology of case studies of U.S. and allied countries as they face the difficult transition between conventional warfare and low-intensity conflicts. Each case study explores a different aspect of the expectation that armies can respond to non-conventional and conventional requirements.

Guerrier, Steven W. and Wayne C. Thompson. *Perspectives on Strategic Defense* (1987). This book provides an introduction to the many complex issues involved in the Strategic Defense Initiative and explores such topics as its technical feasibility, its impact on U.S.-U.S.S.R. relations and its impact on our NATO allies and on arms control in general.

Hall, David Locke. *The Reagan Wars: A Constitutional Perspective on War Powers and the Presidency* (1991). Hall's book is essentially one for political scientists who study American institutions. However, it gives a narrative account of four significant acts of military force that Reagan employed in Lebanon, Grenada, Libya, and the Persian Gulf.

Halperin, Martin. *Defense Strategies for the Seventies* (1971). Halperin examines the policy objectives of the super powers and argues the results of limited wars are difficult to determine. He also analyzes the reasons for the importance of limited wars in the contemporary world and the attitude of the United States toward such conflicts.

Hartmann, Frederick H. and Robert L. Wendzel. *Defending America's Security* (1988). This is a useful introduction to American security concerns in the international environment. Hartmann describes the policy process in the security organization and addresses threats, responses, and issues.

Holm, Jeanne. *Women in the Military, An Unfinished Revolution* (1992). General Holm gives her views and analysis of the evolving role of American military women in post-Vietnam operations. Originally published in 1982, the work was revised to include Grenada, Panama and Desert Shield/Storm.

Luttwak, Edward N. *The Pentagon and the Art of War* (1985). Luttwak states that U.S. armed forces have failed the country, supporting his argument by citing the specific examples of Vietnam, the *Mayaguez* affair, the aborted Iran rescue and others, while repeating frequently heard claims regarding fraud, waste and mismanagement in the government.

Martin, David C. and John Walcott. *Best Laid Plans: The Inside Story of America's War Against Terrorism* (1988). This is a series of narratives about anti-terrorist operations such as the 1980 Iranian hostage rescue mission, encounters with Gadhafi, the Dozier kidnapping, the Lebanon debacle, the TWA hijacking, the *Achille Lauro*, the Beirut hostages and the Iran-Contra episode.

Payne, Keith B. *Strategic Defense: Star Wars in Perspective* (1986). In an effort to help sell SDI, Payne provides layman's explanations of technologies such as lasers and particle beam weapons, and, using illustrations, describes how the layered defense system would work.

Sloan, Stanley R., ed. *NATO and the 1990s* (1989). Sloan offers a series of essays which suggest that NATO would be just as relevant in the 1990s as it was in the 1950s.

Smith, Perry. *How CNN Fought the War* (1991). General Smith looks at how television broadcasting of military events in the 1991 Gulf War influenced public opinion, the U.S. decision makers, and the enemy.

Air Force

Bergquist, Ronald E. *The Role of Airpower in the Iran-Iraq War* (1988). Bergquist demonstrates how the values and needs of Iranian and Iraqi leaders caused them to use air power in contrast to the expectations of western thought.

Coyne, James P. *Airpower in the Gulf* (1992). This is a well-written and positive in-house account of the successful build-up to the Gulf War and the airmen who fought in it.

Hallion, Richard P. *Storm over Iraq: Air Power and the Gulf War* (1992). This is a detailed survey of lessons learned in Operation Desert Storm by the Chief of the U. S. Air History Program. The author argues that the battle, fought with high technology, radicalized campaign strategy and marks the ascendancy of air power as supreme in warfare.

Navy

Ennes, James M., Jr. *Assault on the Liberty* (1979). Ennes presents the story of the Israeli attack on an American intelligence ship in June of 1967 and argues that both governments participated in a cover-up. He reveals the human faces that participated and the disturbing story of navy bungling.

Friedman, Norman. *Desert Victory: The War for Kuwait* (1991). This first examination by a specialist leans heavily on the joint operations element and the technological aspect of the war. Friedman does not accept the USAF contention that the ground and sea forces played only a minor role in the coalition victory.

Hartmann, Frederick H. *Naval Renaissance—The U.S. Navy in the 1980s* (1990). This is a presentation of the navy's overall program from 1980 to 1987, especially the "payoff" years of 1982 to 1986. Initially, the analysis discusses serious problems in leadership, management, and morale. Ultimately, it focuses on what those in-house called the successes of a Naval renaissance.

Lehman, John F., Jr. *Command of the Seas: Building the 600 Ship Navy* (1989). The Secretary of the Navy during most of the Reagan years gives his perspective and defense for the greatest naval buildup since World War II. He discusses eight principles of naval strategy as well as the petty fights within the bureaucratic maze which were a feature of the buildup.

Rowan, Roy. *The Four Days of the Mayaguez* (1975). Rowan tells the story of the seizure of the *Mayaguez* by Cambodian forces in May of 1975 and the response directed by President Ford.

Marines

Hammel, Eric. *The Root: The Marines in Beirut* (1985). Hammel describes the U.S. Marines in Beirut during turbulence in August of 1982–February of 1984 largely from the point of view of the marines themselves.

Moore, Molly. *A Woman at War* (1993). A highly personal account by the *Washington Post*'s Pentagon correspondent. The author viewed the war from a vantage point of her access to the headquarters of the lst Marine Expeditionary Force and its commander Gen. Walter Boomer.

7

The Asymmetric Period: 1995–2004

For several decades during the Cold War, the American military prepared to fight either a large-scale conventional war or a nuclear war against the Soviet Union and its allies. The Cold War ended without a cataclysmic conflict between the United States and the Soviet Union. By 1991 communism's containment ceased to be a strategic priority.

The First Gulf War in early 1991 represented the type of large-scale operation that the American military expected to fight, a "Second Generation" conflict in which massive forces would face off against each other on a conventional battlefield. After a thorough air attack beginning in January 1991, multinational ground forces under American leadership launched a mechanized ground attack from Saudi Arabia into southern Iraq in February 1991. Operation Desert Storm achieved its objectives sooner than expected. American troops and their allies liberated Kuwait and pushed the reeling Iraqi forces far back into Iraq by March 1991. On an operational level, this represented a decisive victory. Victory was also achieved on a political level. President George H. W. Bush decided to allow Saddam Hussein to remain in power, albeit in a much weaker position. This would maintain a balance of power in the Middle East.

With victory in the First Gulf War, the United States stood as the sole superpower with military forces to match this title. Indeed, some Americans believed that the globe was poised to enter an era of Pax Americana. This conflict, however, did not end violence in the Middle East. Nor was it the only time when Americans would take up arms against Iraq. Global peace did not develop in the 1990s.

Multipolarity emerged in the new international arena. Although the United States remained dominant in nuclear and conventional warfare capabilities, other powerful actors emerged in the form of nation-states or nonstate actors. Regional conflicts became the most pressing threats to American security: in the Middle East, with Iraq remaining a threat and with the Israeli-Palestinian conflict no closer to resolution; in Asia, with tensions remaining high between North and South Korea and between India and Pakistan; in Europe, with ethnic and religious conflict arising in the Balkans; in Latin America, with efforts to interdict the narcotics trade while maintaining the region's political stability; and in Africa, with ongoing turmoil among political, economic and ethnic groups. Beyond these dangers, nonstate actors such as the terrorist group al-Qaeda loomed as threats to Americans and global stability. Effective symmetric responses to terrorism could not be found in America's contingency plans.

Historical analogues offered no clear-cut lessons about how the United States should reposition itself in this new environment. Americans wrestled with how to meet the dual challenges of protecting interests and projecting force around the globe. The Department of Defense's *Quadrennial Defense Reviews* (1997 and 2001) represented halting attempts by the American military to develop new strategic contingencies and address new operational realities. These reports outlined a new military posture that stressed speed, versatility and cooperation.

Aside from transformations of its mission, size and structure, the U.S. military also experienced social changes. Minorities in uniform achieved greater levels of promotion and acceptance, though this has not occurred without tensions, nor have minorities yet realized complete equality. The American military thus reflected increasing racial, gender and sexual equity in the nation as a whole.

Despite international tensions, President William J. Clinton continued his predecessor's reduction of American military forces from their strength levels during the Cold War and the First Gulf War. Both the Bush and Clinton administrations deemed it unnecessary to maintain a large active-duty military force designed to fight another superpower in a conventional or nuclear conflict. As the regular military forces shrank, the Reserves and the National Guard assumed many logistical responsibilities and combat components from the regular services. When necessary, the Reserves and the Guard received calls to active duty and federal service to augment the regular services.

Force structures in the army, air force, navy and marine corps slowly evolved toward employing smaller, more integrated, more flexible units. For example, in the late 1990s U.S. Army Chief of Staff Eric Shinseki and U.S. Marine Corps Commandant Charles Krulak called for "joint operations" capabilities which combine land, sea and air units from different services into a single fighting force. New technologies such as global positioning systems and laser-guided aerial munitions added to the possible effectiveness of joint operations. Yet, the branches of armed services only reluctantly abandoned some of their weapons systems, despite the fact that these time-honored symbols of the services might not be relevant to asymmetric warfare. In other cases, the military services refused to upgrade or replace some aging equipment.

Military forces were designed to destroy enemy forces in service of political goals. In the post–Cold War era, these goals became confusing and complex. The American military seldom exercised its overwhelming force; on the contrary, it engaged in dozens of humanitarian, peacekeeping, peacemaking and special operations. The American military acted both inside and outside the United States, either unilaterally or under the auspices of the United Nations, the North Atlantic Treaty Organization (NATO) or some other alliance. These actions took the form of relief activities in the wake of natural disasters as well as preemptive strikes against terrorists or supporters of terrorists. Such asymmetric activities, especially those combating terrorism, entailed pitting military might against an enemy without national allegiances or moral inhibitions.

Examples of activities other than making war are the American operations in Bosnia and Kosovo from 1995 through 2000. American-led NATO forces entered the region to protect the ethnic and religious minorities, all of whom fought each other in bloody civil wars once the Cold War's end unleashed old hatreds. Between 20,000 and 30,000 American troops deployed to Bosnia and Kosovo during the late 1990s. Their mission required not only peacekeeping but also peacemaking. In Bosnia, they attempted to prevent the resumption of the civil war, protect refugees from further persecution and establish a freely elected government. American troops spent much of their time manning checkpoints and conducting heavily armed patrols. By 1999 most American troops had withdrawn from the still-tense region.

In nearby Kosovo, more force was required to stop Serbian president Slobodan Milosevic from undertaking genocide and terrorism against Albanian and Muslim minorities living in Kosovo. NATO forces under the command of General Wesley K. Clark initiated massive attacks against Serbian forces with aircraft and cruise missiles in early 1999. These attacks gradually crippled Milosevic's capability to make war and brought him to the peace table in summer 1999, where he agreed to withdraw his troops from Kosovo. More peacekeeping troops entered Kosovo, this time under the auspices of the United Nations. Complete success in the Balkans, however, was not achieved because the ethnic and religious tensions remained entrenched among the factions.

President George W. Bush assumed the presidency in 2001. Solutions to problems around the globe were not apparent to the new administration. President Bush staffed his administration with several experienced individuals such as Vice President Dick Cheney, Secretary of State Colin Powell, Secretary of Defense Donald Rumsfeld and National Security Advisor Condoleezza Rice. A scandalous election and a moribund economy marred the new president's first months in office. Indeed, little about the new American leader looked extraordinary.

The lackluster atmosphere changed on September 11, 2001. In midmorning, 19 radical Muslims from Osama bin Laden's terrorist group al-Qaeda hijacked four American civilian airliners. Using these aircraft as aerial bombs, the terrorists flew two of them into the World Trade Center towers in New York City and one into the Pentagon in Washington DC. More than 3,500 American civilians and military personnel were killed in the worst terrorist attack in American history. Exposing the nation's vulnerability to unconventional attacks by nonstate actors, this dramatic event posed unheralded challenges to the American military.

The American president reacted by establishing what would become the "Bush Doctrine" for national security—a doctrine which allowed preemptive strikes against possible threats to American security. Bush also strengthened the defense of the United States with the establishment of the Department of Homeland Security and passage of the so-called Patriot Act. Bush received consent from Congress to use military force against terrorists as nonstate actors or against nation-states supporting their activities. The United States then embarked on what was euphemistically called the "war on terror." Finding and fighting the terrorists represented a new type of warfare, termed "Fourth Generation" warfare by civilian and military observers alike.

The American military of 2001 was not designed to fight an asymmetrical conflict against opponents with neither sovereign nor legal status. Organizations like al-Qaeda function in decentralized cells of terrorists capable of acting independently or in concert with others. They cross national borders with ease, attack military or civilian targets at will and possess little or no infrastructure for a retaliatory strike. This made fighting a war against terrorists problematic at best. To meet such an enemy, some civilian and military leaders in the Department of Defense moved still further toward restructuring American forces. The army, for example, laid plans to replace its ten large divisions with 50 brigade-sized combat teams. These smaller units, it was hoped, would possess greater mobility and more special operations capabilities on battlefields.

Two examples illustrate President Bush's attempts to combat terrorism. Weeks after the September 11 attack, the United States launched Operation Enduring Freedom against the Taliban, the oppressive government in Afghanistan that harbored al-Qaeda's leadership and supported its terrorist activities. Utilizing sea, air, ground and special operations units, the American military quickly liberated Afghanistan and slowly started to eliminate terrorist forces there. The latter activity represented a tougher task than the former. Although the new American-supported government of Afghanistan ruled the populated areas of that nation, the countryside proved more difficult to control because of rugged, mountainous terrain. American troops found themselves conducting special operations beyond the usual scope of military activities: rebuilding political infrastructure, establishing as free a society as possible and searching for surviving terrorists or Taliban supporters.

A second example of combating terror came in March 2003, when the United States and several allied nations attacked Iraq in the Second Gulf War. President Bush ostensibly launched a preemptive strike to eliminate weapons of mass destruction (WMD) that the American intelligence community had assured him were in Iraq. At the same time, this attack would remove brutal dictator Saddam Hussein from power and it would also give the United States more control over Iraqi oil.

In Operation Iraqi Freedom, American and allied forces moved quickly into action. The fast-moving units included coordinated air, sea, land and special operations forces working jointly in a single, unified command structure. They easily neutralized Iraqi forces by destroying them where they stood or cutting off their lines of retreat. Once Saddam Hussein was ousted and major combat operations were stopped in early May 2003, American troops turned to rebuilding Iraq, laying foundations for a freer society and mopping up pockets of armed resistance.

Operation Iraqi Freedom was a costly undertaking. At the end of 2004, 1,500 American military men and women had lost their lives, with billions of dollars expended. Unlike the First Gulf War, this one did not end quickly, and international support waned. Moreover, the troops in the field could not find the WMD the experts in Washington DC were so sure existed. Such developments called into question the decisions, efforts, and motivations of President Bush and his key advisors. As each day passed, more people wondered if the United States could sustain its will around the world and whether terrorism could be defeated by establishing democracy in a new Iraq.

In Bosnia, Kosovo, Afghanistan and Iraq, the American military gradually adapted to new requirements of warfare such as joint operations and mobile expeditionary force structures. However, even as the transformation progressed, questions remained about the correctness of such operational adaptations. The small, brigade-size units offered increased mobility in battle but lacked the war-fighting power to destroy a large or concentrated enemy force.

Clearly, the American military leadership continued to grapple with how to win the asymmetric, or Fourth Generation, warfare of the 21st century. The new environment necessitated not only winning the war but also winning the peace. The concepts of success and failure were not as apparent as in past conflicts. Indeed, some scholars and soldiers believed that a decisive, long-term political victory against terrorist groups might never be achieved. Whereas the American military may have proven adaptable at the operational level, its civilian decision makers seemed less apt at responding to the ever-changing forces of geopolitics. As a result, members of the military continued to ponder both their strategic and political missions.

Some commentators suggested that many within the Bush administration possessed an anachronistic view of the world, that they cut their teeth during the Cold War when containment of the Soviet Union and communism stood as the ultimate goal of American foreign policy. In consequence, the administration, it was charged, was wont to view the current war on terrorism in the same manner as the Cold War, viz., a zero-sum game. Meantime, others, both within and without the U.S. government, insisted the post–Cold War world was more complex and confusing, especially with asymmetric warfare. If these concepts of absolute victory and complete defeat hold sway, subsequent administrations could be constrained from selecting a wider range of viable military options or achieving a wider range of successful political outcomes.

Chronology

1995

Jan   3   Operation United Shield—ends Mar 25, 1995 (Somalia)

Feb   3   First woman to pilot a space shuttle (Eileen Collins, USAF)

Feb   28   U.S. forces land in Mogadishu, Somalia (Operation United Shield)

Mar   10   Operation Safe Border—ends Jun 30, 1995 (Peru-Ecuador)

Mar   31   Operation Restore Democracy ends (Haiti)

Apr   19   Humanitarian Service Operation—ends May 3, 1995 (Oklahoma City, OK)

Apr   21   First woman pilot, U.S. Marines (Sarah Deal, USMC)

May   30   Humanitarian Service Operation—ends Sep 30, 1995 (Eritrea & Ethiopia)

Jun   2   U.S. aircraft shot down in Bosnia-Herzegovina—pilot retrieved Jun 8, 1995 (Scott O'Grady)

Jun   3   First woman graduate top of class, USMA (Rebecca Marier, USA)

Jun   13   Humanitarian Service Operation—ends Oct 17, 1995 (Vladivostok, Russia)

Jun   20   Dennis J. Reimer (Chief of Staff, USA)

Jul   1   Iraq admits existence of offensive biological weapons program but denies weaponization

Jul   1   Charles C. Krulak (Commandant, USMC)
Jul   12   Humanitarian Service Operation—ends Aug 10, 1995 (Wake
            Island)
Aug   4   Homosexuality no longer grounds for denial of security
            clearance (Executive Order)
Aug   29   Operation Deliberate Force—ends Sep 20, 2004 (Bosnia-
            Herzegovina)
Aug   30   First combat use of Low Altitude Navigation and Targeting for
            Night system (Operation Deliberate Force)
Sep   9   Tomahawk fire mission (Operation Deliberate Force)
Sep   16   Humanitarian Service Operation—ends Oct 31, 1995 (Virgin
            Islands & Puerto Rico)
Oct   1   Humanitarian Service Operation—ends Sep 30, 1996 (Laos)
Oct   4   Humanitarian Service Operation—ends Oct 13, 1995 (Alabama
            & Florida)
Oct   21   U.S. Supreme Court refuses appeal of previous ruling
            Thomasson v. Perry (Don't Ask, Don't Tell)
Dec   1   Operation Zorro II—ends May 2, 1996. Interdiction effort
            (Mexico)
Dec   14   Operation Joint Endeavor—ends Dec 20, 1996 (Bosnia-
            Herzegovina)
Dec   30   First U.S. casualty in Bosnia-Herzegovina (Martin J. Begosh)

1996

Mar   22   First woman guard, Tomb of the Unknowns at Arlington
            National Cemetery (Heather L. Johnson, USA)
Apr   8   Humanitarian Service Operation—ends Aug 12, 1996 (Liberia)
Jun   25   Khobar Towers complex is target of truck bomb (Saudi Arabia)
Jun   26   Virginia Military Institute becomes coeducational (*U.S. v.
            Virginia et al.*)
Aug   2   Jay L. Johnson (Chief of Naval Operations)
Aug   12   Humanitarian Service Operation—ends Sep 11, 1996 (California
            & Oregon)
Aug   24   The Citadel (Charleston, SC) becomes a coeducational
            institution
Sep   3   Operation Desert Strike—ends Sep 4, 2004 (Iraq)
Sep   5   Humanitarian Service Operation—ends Sep 13, 1996 (North
            Carolina)
Sep   15   Humanitarian Service Operation—ends Apr 30, 1997 (Guam)
Sep   16   Humanitarian Service Operation—ends Dec 15, 1996 (Iraq)
Sep   29   Humanitarian Service Operation—ends Apr 7, 1997 (Republics
            of Korea and Palau)

Oct   1   Humanitarian Service Operation—ends Sep 30, 1999 (Laos)
Oct   1   Humanitarian Service Operation—ends Sep 30, 2001
          (Cambodia)
Oct   10 Humanitarian Service Operation—ends Nov 21, 1996 (Wake
          Island)
Nov   7   USA establishes sexual harassment hotline—ends Jun 13, 1997
Nov   15 Operation Guardian Assistance—ends Dec 27, 1996 (Uganda)
Nov   15 Operation Phoenix Tusk—ends Dec 27, 1996 (Zaire)
Nov   22 USA Senior Review Panel on Sexual Harassment established—
          report released Sep 11, 1997
Dec   19 First USN warship transits Taiwan Straits since 1979 (USS
          Nimitz)
Dec   20 Operation Joint Guard—ends Jun 10, 1998 (Bosnia-
          Herzegovina)
Dec   31 Operation Provide Comfort ends (Iraq)

1997

Jan   1   Operation Northern Watch—ends May 1, 2003 (Iraq)
Jan   4   Humanitarian Service Operation—ends Feb 24, 1997
          (California)
Jan   4   Humanitarian Service Operation—ends Feb 6, 1997 (Nevada)
Jan   4   Humanitarian Service Operation—ends Feb 20, 1997 (Idaho)
Jan   10 Humanitarian Service Operation—ends Feb 7, 1997 (South
          Dakota)
Jan   12 Humanitarian Service Operation—ends Feb 7, 1997 (North
          Dakota)
Jan   27 William S. Cohen (Secretary of Defense)
Feb   18 Operation Assured Lift—ends Mar 7, 1997 (Liberia)
Mar   1   First woman State Adjutant General (Martha T. Rainville,
          Vermont National Guard)
Mar   14 Operation Silver Wake—ends Mar 26, 1997 (Albania)
Mar   17 Operation Guardian Retrieval—ends Jun 5, 1997 (Congo)
Apr   7   Humanitarian Service Operation—ends Jun 3, 1997 (North
          Dakota)
Apr   7   Humanitarian Service Operation—ends May 6, 1997 (South
          Dakota)
Apr   9   Humanitarian Service Operation—ends Apr 29, 1997
          (Minnesota)
May   29 Operation Noble Obelisk—ends Jun 5, 1997 (Sierra Leone)
Aug   13 Anthony C. Zinni (Commander in Chief, U.S. Central
          Command)
Sep   3   Air action—Iraq (Operation Northern Watch)

Dec 16 Kassebaum-Baker Committee recommends gender segregation for training purposes (Secretary of Defense rejects Mar 16, 1998)

Dec 17 Humanitarian Service Operation—ends Jan 24, 1998 (Guam)

1998

Jan 10 Humanitarian Service Operation—ends Jan 19, 1998 (New York)

Jan 13 Humanitarian Service Operation—ends Jan 21, 1998 (Maine)

Jan 21 Humanitarian Service Operation—ends Mar 25, 1998 (Kenya)

Mar 7 Hugh Thompson, Lawrence Colburn and Glenn Andreotta receive Soldier's Medal for actions at My Lai, Republic of Vietnam (Mar 16, 1968)

Mar 19 Humanitarian Service Operation—ends Jun 20, 1998 (Portuguese Azores)

Apr 22 U.S. Supreme Court affirms that courts may treat fathers and mothers differently in deciding U.S. citizenship of children born out of wedlock and outside the United States (*Miller v. Albright*)

May 9 Humanitarian Service Operation—ends May 24, 1998 (Ecuador)

May 25 Humanitarian Service Operation—ends Jun 6, 1998. (Sierra Leone)

May 30 James M. Loy (Commandant, USCG)

Jun 10 Operation Shepherd Venture—ends Jun 17, 1998 (Guinea-Bissau)

Jun 10 Operation Joint Forge begins (Bosnia-Herzegovina)

Aug 7 Humanitarian Service Operation—ends Aug 31, 1999 (Kenya & Tanzania)

Aug 8 Humanitarian Service Operation—ends Aug 17, 1998 (Republic of Congo)

Aug 20 Air operation—Afghanistan and Sudan (Operation Infinite Reach)

Sep 9 Humanitarian Service Operation—ends Sep 23, 1998 (Bangladesh)

Sep 20 Humanitarian Service Operation—ends Oct 10, 1998 (Liberia)

Sep 23 *Able v. United States* (2nd Circuit Court of Appeals upholds constitutionality of Don't Ask, Don't Tell. End of multiple challenges until *Cook v. Rumsfeld*, Dec 6, 2004)

Sep 25 Humanitarian Service Operation—ends Nov 1, 1998 (Puerto Rico, Dominican Republic & Haiti)

Oct 28 Humanitarian Service Operation—ends Feb 20, 1999 (Central America)

Nov 11 Operation Desert Thunder II—ends Dec 16, 1998 (Kuwait)

Nov 22   Operation Strong Support—ends Feb 10, 1999 (Central
          America)
Dec 16   Operation Desert Fox—ends Dec 19, 1998 (Iraq)
Dec 16   First woman to fly B-52 combat air mission (Cheryl Lamoureux,
          USAF)
Dec 16   First woman to fly combat naval air mission (Kendra Williams,
          USN)
Dec 17   First combat deployment USAF B-1 (Operation Desert Fox)
Dec 18   First woman to command USN warship (Kathleen McGrath,
          USN)
Dec 30   Air action—Iraq (Operation Northern Watch)

1999

Jan   1   Humanitarian Service Operation—ends Sep 30, 2001 (Thailand)
Jan 17   Humanitarian Service Operation—ends Jan 26, 1999
          (Clarksville, TN)
Feb 24   Humanitarian Service Operation—ends Feb 28, 1999 (Austria)
Feb 28   Significant air action—Iraq (Operation Northern Watch)
Mar   1   Significant air action—Iraq (Operation Northern Watch)
Mar 16   First general officer subject to court-martial since 1952 (David
          Hale, USA)
Mar 24   Operation Noble Anvil—ends Jun 20, 1999 (Serbia)
Mar 24   First air victory, Operation Noble Anvil (Cesar Rodriquez &
          Michael Showers)
Mar 24   First combat use, Joint Direct Attack Munition (Operation
          Noble Anvil)
Mar 24   First combat deployment, USAF B-2 (Operation Noble Anvil)
Mar 27   USAF F-117 destroyed (Serbia)
Apr   3   Humanitarian Service Operation—ends Jun 5, 1999 (Albania)
Apr 17   Significant air action—Iraq (Operation Northern Watch)
Apr 29   Significant air action—Iraq (Operation Northern Watch)
Apr 30   Significant air action—Iraq (Operation Northern Watch)
May   1   Humanitarian Service Operation—ends Jul 31, 1999 (Fort Dix,
          NJ)
May   1   USAF F-16 destroyed (Serbia)
May   4   Humanitarian Service Operation—ends Aug 20, 1999
          (Oklahoma)
May   8   First woman graduate, The Citadel (Nancy Mace)
Jul   1   James L. Jones (Commandant, USMC)
Jul 23   First woman to command U.S. space flight (Eileen Collins,
          USAF)

Jul	28	Humanitarian Service Operation—ends Aug 16, 1999 (West Point, NY)
Aug	3	F. Whitten Peters (Secretary of the Air Force)
Aug	17	Humanitarian Service Operation—ends Sep 11, 1999 (Southern Europe)
Sep	13	Humanitarian Service Operation—ends Dec 14, 1999 (Kingdom of Jordan)
Sep	15	Humanitarian Service Operation—ends Nov 9, 1999 (North Carolina)
Sep	16	Humanitarian Service Operation—ends Sep 23, 2000 (East Timor)
Dec	17	Humanitarian Service Operation—ends Mar 7, 2000 (Venezuela)

2000

Feb	24	Humanitarian Service Operation—ends Apr 11, 2000 (Mozambique & South Africa)
Mar	1	Humanitarian Service Operation—ends May 11, 2001 (Djibouti)
Mar	1	Humanitarian Service Operation—ends May 10, 2001 (Oman)
Jul	21	Vern Clark (Chief of Naval Operations)
Oct	1	Humanitarian Service Operation—ends Oct 8, 2000 (Belize)
Oct	12	USS *Cole* attacked (Yemen)

2001

Jan	14	Humanitarian Service Operation—ends Feb 28, 2001 (El Salvador)
Jan	20	James G. Roche (Secretary of the Air Force)
Jan	20	Donald H. Rumsfeld (Secretary of Defense)
Jan	26	Humanitarian Service Operation—ends Feb 19, 2001 (India)
Feb	21	First successful launch of missile from unmanned aerial vehicle
Mar	1	Humanitarian Service Operation—ends Dec 31, 2002 (East Timor)
Apr	1	USN aircraft collides with People's Republic of China aircraft. (U.S. aircraft lands successfully, Chinese aircraft does not)
Apr	5	First woman Chief of Chaplains (Lorraine K. Potter, USAF)
May	8	Operation Focus Relief—ends Aug 3, 2001 (Ghana & Senegal)
May	19	First women complete four-year program (Virginia Military Institute)
May	24	Gordon R. England (Secretary of the Navy)
May	31	Thomas H. White (Secretary of the Army)
Jun	2	Humanitarian Service Operation—ends Aug 9, 2001 (Egypt)

Sep   6   John P. Jumper (Chief of Staff, USAF)
Sep 11   Terrorist attack (World Trade Center, New York; United Airlines
          Flight 93, Somerset County, PA; Pentagon, Washington DC)
Oct   1   Richard B. Myers (Chairman, Joint Chiefs of Staff)
Oct   1   Naval Special Clearance Team One operational (maritime
          mines)
Oct   7   Operation Enduring Freedom—ends May 1, 2003 (Afghanistan)
Oct 11   U.S. forces deployed Pakistan (Operation Enduring Freedom)
Nov   3   Battle of Bai Beche, Afghanistan—ends Nov 5, 2001
Nov 14   Siege of Konduz, Afghanistan—ends Nov 26, 2001
Nov 18   Battle at Tarin Kowt, Afghanistan
Nov 28   First American combat death in Afghanistan (Johnny Michael
          Spann)
Nov 30   Battle of Kandahar, Afghanistan—ends Dec 7, 2001
Nov 30   Battle of Tora Bora, Afghanistan—ends Dec 17, 2001

2002

Jan   9   First woman marine killed in hostile fire zone (Jeannette L.
          Williams)
Jan   9   Office of Legal Counsel (Department of Justice) avers that
          captured members of al-Qaeda and the Taliban are unprotected
          by Geneva POW Convention
Jan 15   Operation Balikatan—ends Jul 31, 2002 (Republic of the
          Philippines)
Jan 19   Secretary of Defense directs Chairman, Joint Chiefs of Staff, to
          inform field commanders that al-Qaeda and Taliban not
          entitled to POW status (Yoo-Delahunty memorandum).
          President G. Bush validates order on Feb 7, 2002
Feb   7   First use of unmanned aerial vehicle in offensive combat role
          (Yemen)
Feb 19   Humanitarian Service Operation—ends Apr 15, 2002 (Nigeria)
Mar   2   Operation Anaconda—ends Mar 17, 2002 (Afghanistan)
Apr 17   Charter of Defense Department Advisory Committee on
          Women in the Service significantly revised (DACOWITS)
Apr 19   USS *Cole* rejoins U.S. Atlantic Fleet
May 30   Thomas H. Collins (Commandant, USCG)
Jun   1   Doctrine of preemptive action announced (President G. Bush)
Jun 24   U.S. Congress enjoins Department of Defense from requiring
          servicewomen to wear specific clothing while off duty (Saudi
          Arabia)
Aug 19   Operation Mountain Sweep—ends Aug 26, 2002 (Afghanistan)

Sep   4   David D. McKiernan (Coalition Forces Land Component Commander, Iraq)
Sep   7   Operation Champion Strike—ends Sep 10, 2002 (Afghanistan)
Sep 17   National Security Strategy of the United States (Bush Doctrine)
Sep 22   Humanitarian Service Operation—ends Oct 4, 2002 (Ghana & Ivory Coast)
Sep 29   Operation Alamo Sweep (Afghanistan)
Oct 29   Humanitarian Service Operation—ends Nov 3, 2002 (Central African Republic)
Dec   8   Humanitarian Service Operation—ends Dec 31, 2002 (Guam)
Dec 12   Combined Joint Task Force–Horn of Africa established (Djibouti)
Dec 21   Deployment of U.S. forces to Persian Gulf region authorized (President G. Bush)

2003

Jan 13   Michael Hagee (Commandant, USMC)
Jan 27   Operation Mongoose (Afghanistan)
Feb 10   Operation Eagle Fury (Afghanistan)
Feb 25   U.S. Coast Guard moves from Department of Transportation to Department of Homeland Security
Feb 29   Humanitarian Service Operation—ends Jun 1, 2004 (Haiti)
Mar 18   Significant air action—Iraq (Southern Watch)
Mar 20   Operation Iraqi Freedom—ends May 1, 2003
Mar 20   First combat use XM898 SADARM artillery submunition (Tallil, Iraq)
Mar 20   Operation Valiant Strike—ends Mar 28, 2003 (Afghanistan)
Mar 22   First missile strike using Predator UVA platform (Al Amarah, Iraq)
Mar 23   Battle of An Nasiriyah, Iraq—ends Mar 24, 2003
Mar 23   First Native American woman to die in combat (Lori Piestewa, USA)
Mar 23   First African American woman taken prisoner of war (Shoshana Johnson, USA)
Mar 23   First operational use unmanned underwater vehicle (REMUS) maritime mine clearance—ends Mar 26, 2003 (Umm Qasr, Iraq)
Mar 24   Shamal (sandstorm) affects combat operations in Iraq—ends Mar 27, 2003
Mar 26   First operational airdrop by USAF C-17 (Bushur, Iraq)
Mar 27   Operation Viking Hammer—ends Mar 28, 2003 (Afghanistan)
Mar 30   Battle of An Najaf, Iraq—ends Apr 1, 2003
Mar 30   Siege of Basra, Iraq—ends Apr 7, 2003

Apr   1   First B-2 combat mission by woman (Jennifer Wilson, USAF)
Apr   1   Battle of Karbala Gap, Iraq—ends Apr 2, 2003
Apr   1   Jessica Lynch (USA) removed from Iraqi custody
Apr   2   Battle of Al Hillah, Iraq—ends Apr 10, 2003
Apr   2   First combat use Wind-Corrected Munitions Dispenser with
          Sensor Fuzed Weapon (Al Hillah, Iraqi)
Apr   3   Battle of Baghdad International Airport—ends Apr 4, 2003
Apr   3   Battle of Al Aziziyah, Iraq
Apr   5   Siege of Baghdad, Iraq—ends Apr 9, 2003
Apr   7   Battle of Strongpoints Larry, Curly and Moe—ends Apr 8, 2003
          (Baghdad, Iraq)
Apr 13   Additional U.S. forces removed from Iraqi custody
May   1   U.S. declares end of major combat operations in Iraq (Attacks
          on U.S. forces continue)
May 15   Operation Planet X (Iraq)
Jun   3   Humanitarian Service Operation—ends Jun 20, 2003 (Liberia)
Jun   9   Operation Peninsula Strike—ends Jun 12, 2003 (Iraq)
Jun 14   Ricardo S. Sanchez (Commander, Combined Joint Task Force 7)
Jun 15   Operation Desert Scorpion—ends Jun 28, 2003 (Iraq)
Jun 15   Operation Spartan Scorpion—ends Jun 16, 2003 (Iraq)
Jun 29   Operation Sidewinder—ends Jul 7, 2003 (Iraq)
Jul   2   Operation Haven Denial—ends Jul 6, 2003 (Afghanistan)
Jul   7   John Abizaid (Commander, U.S. Central Command)
Jul 12   Operation Soda Mountain—ends Jul 17, 2003 (Iraq)
Jul 14   Operation Ivy Serpent—ends Jul 17, 2003 (Iraq)
Jul 16   First public acknowledgment of fighting in Iraq as guerrilla
          war (John Abizaid, USA)
Jul 20   Operation Warrior Sweep—ends Sep 13, 2003 (Afghanistan)
Jul 22   Uday and Qusay Hussein die in firefight (Mosul, Iraq)
Jul 25   Humanitarian Service Operation—ends Oct 15, 2003 (Liberia)
Aug   1   Peter J. Schoomaker (Chief of Staff, USA)
Aug 26   U.S. court restricts global deployment of high-intensity sonar
          system (USN accepts limits peacetime use, Oct 14, 2003)
Aug 26   Operation Ivy Needle—ends Sep 9, 2003 (Iraq)
Oct 15   Operation Chamberlain begins (Iraq)
Oct 15   Operation Sweeney begins (Iraq)
Nov   7   Operation Ivy Cyclone (Tikrit, Iraq)
Nov 12   Operation Iron Hammer (Baghdad, Iraq)
Nov 17   Operation Ivy Cyclone II (Ba'quba, Kirkuk & Balad, Iraq)
Dec   4   Operation Bulldog Mammoth (Abu Ghurayb, Iraq)
Dec 13   Saddam Hussein captured by U.S. forces (Operation Red
          Dawn)
Dec 18   Operation Iron Justice begins (Iraq)

Dec 21 Operation Rifles Fury (Rawah, Iraq)
Dec 24 Operation Iron Grip (Baghdad, Iraq)

2004

Jan 12 Operation Mountain Blizzard—ends Mar 12, 2004 (Afghanistan)
Jan 13 Operation Market Sweep (Fallujah, Iraq)
Feb 28 U.S. pledges to abandon use of persistent land mines after 2010
Mar 7 Operation Mountain Storm—ends Jul 28, 2004 (Afghanistan)
Mar 31 Four American civilian contract workers killed under extreme circumstances (Fallujah, Iraq)
Apr 4 Operation Vigilant Resolve—cease-fire Apr 9, 2004 (Fallujah, Iraq)
Apr 4 Coordinated attacks on Iraqi opposition forces (Kufa, Karbala, Najaf, Al Kut & Sadr City, Iraq)
Apr 11 Operation Danger Fortitude—ends Apr 17, 2004 (Najaf, Iraq)
Apr 23 Operation Yellow Stone (Al-Rashida, Iraq)
Apr 30 Photographic evidence of abuse of persons detained in Iraqi prison released to U.S. media (Abu Ghurayb)
May 4 Operation Iron Saber—ends Jun 24, 2004 (Najaf, Diwaniyah, Al Kut & Karbala, Iraq)
May 4 Operation Wolfpack Crunch—ends May 5, 2004 (Diwaniyah, Iraq)
May 19 Operation Disarm (Baghdad, Iraq)
May 27 Truce arranged U.S. forces and Iraqi opposition elements
May 27 First National Guard division scheduled for deployment to combat zone since Korean War mobilized (42nd Division, New York National Guard)
Jun 1 Operation Slim Shady (Kirkuk, Iraq)
Jun 17 Operation Striker Tornado (Baghdad & Karbala, Iraq)
Jun 24 Operation Gimlet Crusader (Kirkuk, Iraq)
Jul 1 Multinational Force–Iraq (George W. Casey, Jr.)
Jul 19 First woman fighter squadron commander (Martha McSally, USAF)
Aug 2 Truce between U.S. forces and Iraqi opposition elements ends (Najaf, Iraq)
Aug 4 Operation Phantom Linebacker (Iraqi-Syrian border)
Aug 5 Operation Cajun Mousetrap III—ends Aug 15, 2004 (Samarra, Iraq)
Aug 12 U.S. and Iraqi forces launch combined offensive against Iraqi opposition elements (Najaf, Iraq)
Aug 23 Operation Clean Sweep—ends Aug 24, 2004 (Fallujah, Iraq)

Sep   9   Operation Black Typhoon—ends Sep 14, 2004 (Tal Afar, Iraq)
Sep   30   USN closes ELF (extremely low frequency) communications
            sites (Republic, MI & Clam Lake, WI)
Oct   1   Operation Baton Rouge (Samarra, Iraq)
Oct   14   Siege of Fallujah, Iraq, begins—ends Dec 19, 2004 (Operation
            Phantom Fury)
Oct   23   First submarine designed for post–Cold War service
            commissioned (USS *Virginia*)
Nov   3   Combined operation—Afghan, Pakistan and U.S. forces (Shkin,
            Afghanistan)
Nov   23   Operation Plymouth Rock—ends Dec 1, 2004 (Babil Province,
            Iraq)
Dec   6   *Cook v. Rumsfeld* (Lawsuit challenging constitutionality of Don't
            Ask, Don't Tell)
Dec   31   Department of Justice disavows many of the assertions made
            in the Yoo-Delahunty memorandum of Jan 9, 2002

Military Operations

OPERATION RESTORE DEMOCRACY (Sep 19, 1994–Mar 31, 1995). More
    than 20,000 U.S. military personnel were involved in the U.S.-led multi-
    national force acting on behalf of the United Nations to restore elected
    president Jean Bertrand Aristide to power in Haiti. Diplomatic efforts by
    former president Jimmy Carter averted violence, as the troops entered
    the country peacefully on September 19. By mid-December the U.S.
    presence was drawn down to 6,000 and the mission was transferred to
    the United Nations on March 31, 1995. Some U.S. troops remained until
    February 29 of the next year. Total U.S. casualties at that point numbered
    two dead and three wounded.

OPERATION JOINT ENDEAVOR (Dec 14, 1995–Dec 20, 1996). After four
    years of destruction in Bosnia-Herzegovina, the United Nations inter-
    vened on December 14, ordering the 1st Armored Division to deploy
    troops as part of a multinational effort. A powerful task force—Eagle—
    was formed and reached its area of operation by December 20. More
    than 20,000 strong, it successfully enforced the U.N.-mandated cease-
    fire. On November 10, 1996, members of the 1st Infantry Division re-
    placed Task Force Eagle and, when the U.N. Implementation Force dis-
    banded on December 20, the 1st Infantry Division remained as part of
    the Stabilization Force. American military forces continue to participate
    in the Stabilization Force, successively labeled Operation Joint Guard
    and Operation Joint Forge.

OPERATION INFINITE REACH (Aug 20, 1998). Retaliating for the August 7 bombings of U.S. embassies in Nairobi and Dar es Salaam, President Clinton authorized a military assault on training camps and facilities associated with Osama bin Laden, whose radical Islamic organization al-Qaeda carried out the attacks. Under the command of Gen. Anthony Zinni, U.S. warplanes and cruise missiles targeted several al-Qaeda camps in Afghanistan's rugged countryside and a pharmaceutical factory in the Sudan, destroying the targets and killing at least 20 people, but failing in their primary objective to eliminate bin Laden and his advisers. The Sudanese later asserted that the plant had no connection to bin Laden, making quality of intelligence a sensitive issue for future operations.

OPERATION DESERT FOX (Dec 16–19, 1998). After repeatedly warning Iraq to give U.N. Special Commission inspectors unfettered access to search thoroughly for weapons of mass destruction, and after Iraqi air defense systems fired on allied aircraft, President Clinton ordered cruise missile attacks against military targets across Iraq beginning on December 16. About 29,000 U.S. forces were involved, joined by 1,500 from Britain. American and British warplanes, including the first combat role for the B-1B Lancer, attacked 97 military targets during a 70-hour period. The effort to degrade Iraq's ability to produce and deliver WMD successfully damaged Iraqi command and control operations and units of the elite Republican Guard force, among other targets.

OPERATION NOBLE ANVIL (Mar 24–Jun 20, 1999). When diplomacy failed to end a crisis in the Serbian province of Kosovo in the former Yugoslavia, NATO undertook Operation Allied Force, commanded by Gen. Wesley Clark, to stabilize the region. Calling the American joint force component "Operation Noble Anvil," the Clinton administration supported NATO's intervention to protect Kosovo's ethnic Albanian majority from the depredations of Serbian troops controlled by President Slobodan Milosevic. American air and sea units cooperated with British forces to target Yugoslav military capabilities within Kosovo and around Belgrade in Serbia, beginning on March 24. The campaign involved more than 31,000 U.S. military personnel and saw the combat debut of the B-2 Stealth bomber. After Serbian forces withdrew from Kosovo, the air campaign was suspended on June 10 and formally ended ten days later.

OPERATION ENDURING FREEDOM (Oct 7, 2001–May 1, 2003). In the wake of the devastating September 11 terrorist attacks on the World Trade Center and the Pentagon orchestrated by Osama bin Laden's al-Qaeda organization, U.S. planners commanded by Gen. Tommy R. Franks designed a campaign to eliminate al-Qaeda training camps in Afghanistan and the Taliban government that harbored them. On October 7 a U.S.-led coalition (Britain was the major partner, although 21 nations eventually contributed 8,000 troops) relied on U.S. and British aircraft and cruise missiles to open this war, achieving air supremacy by October 20. Precision-guided weapons accounted for more than half of the 18,000 munitions dropped over the next five months, and unmanned surveillance aircraft contributed significantly. The ground war largely employed Special Forces and Special Operations Forces which cooperated with armed local anti-Taliban groups formed into the Northern Alliance. Battlefields ranged from the mountainous countryside to major population centers such as Kandahar, Kabul and Jalalabad. Simultaneously, the United States supplied humanitarian aid and helped establish an interim government, inaugurated on December 22. Al-Qaeda's camps were crushed by March 2002, although most leaders (including bin Laden) escaped. President Bush declared an end to major combat operations on May 1, 2003, but sporadic fighting continued while U.S. forces engaged in nation building.

ASSAULT AT BAI BECHE (Nov 3–5, 2001). Working with Afghani Northern Alliance cavalry led by Rashid Dostum, teams of U.S. Special Forces (part of Task Force Dagger commanded by Col. John Mulholland) ran up against well-trained, determined al-Qaeda fighters who made a stand at Bai Beche, on the road to Mazar-e-Sharif. The Special Forces teams were led by Capt. Mark Nutsch and Lt. Col. Max Bowers. Two days of air strikes failed to break the opposition, and a ground assault followed on November 5. After al-Qaeda repulsed one cavalry charge, Dostum's forces fortuitously launched a second just as U.S. air strikes hit the enemy lines, allowing the cavalry to charge through the resulting gap. Fearing encirclement, the al-Qaeda fighters fled, opening the way to Mazar-e-Sharif, a crucial strong point in the north that the allied force occupied on November 9.

BATTLE AT TARIN KOWT (Nov 18, 2001). Afghanistan's Taliban forces sent a convoy of 1,000 troops from Kandahar to this small town in south-central Afghanistan, whose inhabitants had overthrown their Taliban governors and which was being occupied by a team of U.S. Special Forces commanded by Capt. Jason Amerine and a few dozen anti-Taliban militia loyal to local leader Hamid Karzai (later elected president of the transitional post-Taliban state). The Special Forces team directed air support using lasers to identify targets for the precision-guided weapons, which devastated the approaching convoy in about four hours. The remnants of the Taliban force retreated to Kandahar, and the Taliban never mounted another assault in the south again.

SEIGE OF KONDUZ (Nov 14–26, 2001). Northern Alliance troops finally occupied this last northern stronghold of the Taliban on November 26 after a two-week bombardment by U.S. warplanes. Capt. Patrick

O'Hara commanded a Special Forces team that served as combat advisers for the forces of anti-Taliban insurgent Gen. Mohammad Daoud and spotted for the close air support that decimated the Taliban and al-Qaeda enemy around Konduz. Encircling the city by November 23, General Daoud engaged in negotiations for the surrender of more than 5,000 troops in the city. Most of the Taliban and al-Qaeda forces capitulated, but Daoud's troops had to subdue some diehard resisters in order to occupy the city completely. Much later, allegations arose that Northern Alliance troops had massacred many prisoners, but U.S. personnel denied knowledge of the incident.

ASSAULT ON KANDAHAR (Nov 30–Dec 7, 2001). Under the command of Lt. Col. Dave Fox, U.S. Special Forces working with two groups of anti-Taliban forces, led by Hamid Karzai and Gul Agha Sharzai, began to move on the city of Kandahar from the north and south, respectively, while bombing attacks weakened the enemy. The northern force began its advance on November 30, meeting light resistance except for firefights at Sayed Alam-a-Kalay (Dec 3) and Shalawi Kowt (Dec 5), when a friendly fire incident at the latter site killed three Americans and 23 or more of Karzai's irregulars. The advance, however, continued. Meanwhile, Sharzai's force captured the airfield and cut a main road from south of the city. Negotiations for a surrender ensued, but the Taliban forces fled their last remaining stronghold in the country and Kandahar was occupied on December 7.

ASSAULT ON TORA BORA (Nov 30–Dec 17, 2001). About 40 U.S. Special Forces troops from Task Force Dagger directed the efforts of three separate tribes of indigenous anti-Taliban militia against this complex of caves and trenches at an al-Qaeda training base in the rugged Tora Bora mountains, south of Jalalabad. British Special Air Service commandos also participated. Following an aerial bombardment starting on November 30, ground forces began their assault on December 5, meeting determined opposition. Repeated air strikes (including use of the 7.5-ton "daisy cutter" bomb) and ground skirmishes resulted in an estimated 300 enemy dead and between 60 or more (some estimated 150) captured. Yet, because the encirclement was incomplete on the porous Pakistani border and Afghan forces proved hesitant in battle, at least 1,000 al-Qaeda fighters slipped away, likely including their leader Osama bin Laden, a key target for the Americans. Afghan guerrilla leaders declared victory on December 17. Disappointed U.S. strategists, however, altered their methods, choosing to rely more heavily on American troops and less on indigenous forces as they continued to search the caves during the next few months.

OPERATION ANACONDA (Mar 2–17, 2002). The purpose of this operation was to root out bands of Taliban and al-Qaeda fighters over 60 to

70 square miles in the Shah-i-Kot Valley and its rugged, snowy mountains (8,000–12,000 ft.) in eastern Afghanistan near Gardez. Under the command of Gen. Franklin L. Hagenbeck, about 900 troops from the 10th Mountain Division, the 101st Airborne and Special Forces teams joined with 200 soldiers from six Coalition partners and eventually 2,000 Afghan troops. They also utilized close air support. Designed quickly to encircle and squeeze the enemy, the operation instead ran into heavy resistance in close fighting in cave complexes on March 2, and fierce fighting at the Takur Ghar ridge on March 4 cost the lives of seven U.S. Rangers. Heavy combat continued to March 12, and the operation ended on March 17. Coalition casualties totaled 11 dead—eight of them American. U.S. command estimated over 500 enemy dead, but few bodies were found; hundreds of enemy likely escaped. Although Gen. Tommy R. Franks, the operational commander, declared it "an unqualified and complete success," the operation provoked controversy as several reports presented grimmer assessments.

OPERATION IRAQI FREEDOM (Mar 20–May 1, 2003). After President Saddam Hussein refused to comply with U.N. inspections for weapons of mass destruction (WMD), President George W. Bush authorized military action, asserting that Iraq maintained ties to terrorist networks and did indeed possess WMD. The operation opened with a predawn aerial bombardment on March 20 designed to "shock and awe" the enemy and "decapitate" its leadership. The leaders survived, but Coalition air forces (American, British and Australian) controlled the skies throughout the campaign. Coalition ground troops, meanwhile, invaded rapidly from Kuwait on March 20, the British assaulting the Al Faw Peninsula while American troops proceeded north along three routes converging on Baghdad. Special operations in northern Iraq added another dimension. Gen. Tommy R. Franks had overall command, assisted by Gen. David McKiernan and Gen. T. Michael Moseley. Their strategy relied on the use of task forces and on speed. U.S. troops, numbering 242,000, were augmented by 45,000 British and 14,000 Australians. After 43 days, President Bush announced the end of major combat operations. To that point, U.S. casualty figures listed 138 dead. However, a surprisingly strong insurgency continued well into the following year. By June 28, 2004, when an interim Iraqi government took control, the U.S. death toll had reached 855, with more than 5,000 wounded. In the months that followed, new casualties were reported frequently, reaching almost 1,500 killed by January 2005. Securing the peace presented the Coalition with some of its sternest challenges in this effort.

BATTLE FOR AN NASIRIYAH (Mar 23–24, 2003). Gen. Rick Natonski's Task Force Tarawa, comprised of 5,000 marines, sought to capture two bridges across the Euphrates River and the Saddam Canal in Iraq's An

Nasiriyah, allowing elements of Gen. James Mattis's 1st Marine Division to advance toward Al Kut as the eastern prong of Operation Iraqi Freedom. On March 23, the Task Force engaged in intense urban warfare with Iraqi regulars and "fedayeen," determined volunteers often from outside Iraq, resulting in 28 U.S. deaths. Unexpectedly strong resistance and U.S. battlefield errors that day and the next led to the war's sharpest fighting to that point, but the marines eventually captured the bridges. On March 25 Mattis's troops and supplies traversed the not fully pacified "Ambush Alley" to and through An Nasiriyah and across the bridges. Task Force Tarawa, meanwhile, continued to combat insurgents in the town and finally secured it in early April.

OPERATION VIKING HAMMER (Mar 27–28, 2003). Col. Charlie Cleveland, assisted by air force Col. O. G. Mannion, commanded Task Force Viking, comprised mainly of the U.S. 10th Special Forces Group and British special operations troops. Tasked with opening a second front in northern Iraq, some of its 15,000 soldiers had infiltrated the country before Operation Iraqi Freedom began in order to ally with 65,000 Kurdish militia. Subsequently, Cleveland ordered Lt. Col. Ken Tovo to lead a joint assault, code named Operation Viking Hammer, to eliminate camps of the Islamic terrorist organization Ansar al-Islam that were spread over 300 square kilometers. Tovo's six groups of Kurdish peshmerga fighters and "A team" special operations soldiers attacked from six different prongs early on March 27, met intense resistance and used limited close air support with tremendous success. By the following afternoon, the raid had weakened Ansar al-Islam's 1,000 fighters, freeing Task Force Viking to move against Iraqi forces to its south.

BATTLE FOR AN NAJAF (Mar 30–Apr 1, 2003). Elite Iraqi Republican Guard troops and fedayeen irregulars slowed the advance of the U.S. Army's 3rd Infantry Division toward Karbala and Baghdad on the western flank of Operation Iraqi Freedom. Attacking from An Najaf, a Muslim holy city of 500,000, the Iraqis threatened the 3rd Division's narrow supply lines. Changing strategy, Gen. Buford Blount ordered his troops to isolate the city, which they did in very heavy fighting (Mar 24–25). V Corps' commander, Gen. William Scott Wallace, then ordered an assault by 8,000 troops from the 101st Airborne, commanded by Gen. David Petraeus, to eradicate opposition within An Najaf. Landing at several points on the city's periphery on March 30, combined infantry and helicopter units fought the paramilitaries, in particular, often in fierce block-by-block conflict. Two days later the 101st had achieved control of the city.

BATTLE FOR THE KARBALA GAP (Apr 1–2, 2003). The 3rd Infantry Division's advance on Baghdad from the southwest depended on its control of the Karbala Gap, a strip of land 25 miles wide with bridges over the

Euphrates River. Following a series of air attacks on the Iraqi Republican Guard units defending the area, the 1st and 2nd Brigade Combat Teams launched an offensive on April 1, meeting stiff resistance. Rangers captured the important Hadithah Dam, the destruction of which would have flooded the invasion route, and defended the dam while enduring heavy fighting for two weeks. Late in the afternoon of April 2, a platoon managed to cross a bridge that the Iraqis then tried to blow up. When the bridge failed to collapse, U.S. engineers secured it and built a second crossing. The path to Baghdad was open.

ASSAULT ON AL HILLAH (Apr 2–10, 2003). 101st Airborne commander Gen. David Petraeus was ordered to attack Iraqi forces in Al Hillah, pinning them down so that coalition forces could approach Baghdad from the southwest after having secured the Karbala Gap. His 2nd Brigade Combat Team was opposed by irregular forces—fedayeen—but also by soldiers from the elite Republican Guard's Hammurabi Division, resulting in one of the few instances of a determined defense by Iraq's regular army. The battle began on April 2 and consumed an enormous amount of ordnance as helicopters, fighter-bombers and artillery supported a ground assault on the stronghold. As the fighting intensified, Petraeus committed his 3rd Brigade Combat Team to clear the city, which was accomplished by April 10 in heavy urban fighting.

BATTLE NEAR BAGHDAD INTERNATIONAL AIRPORT (Apr 3–4, 2003). Commanding the 3rd Infantry Division, Gen. Buford Blount ordered a company-sized unit of cavalry from A Troop to advance to a key intersection on the western periphery of the airport. The company, including 20 fighting vehicles, met strong but suicidal resistance from fedayeen and armored units. Accompanied by close air support, the troopers eventually killed an estimated 500 fedayeen militia and destroyed 34 T-72 tanks arrayed against them in close combat.

BATTLE OF BAGHDAD (Apr 5–9, 2003). While the 1st Marine Division approached Baghdad from the south and east, the 3rd Army Infantry Division was poised west of the city. On April 5 Col. Dave Perkins's 2nd Brigade Combat Team (BCT) made the initial ground assault on Baghdad, executing a rapid "thunder run" by Task Force 1–64 Armor into and out of the city center. After the 3rd BCT blocked the city's northern exit on April 6, Perkins conducted a second run on April 7 and into the morning of April 8, the troops and armored vehicles remaining in the heart of the city despite determined and skilled opposition from fedayeen fighters. Marine infantry, meanwhile, entered the city from the south and east at four separate points, having fought their way across a makeshift bridge spanning the Diyalah River while the U.S. Naval Construction Force (Seabees) constructed another in 20 hours. The allied military fully occupied the city on April 9.

OPERATION WARRIOR SWEEP (Jul 20, 2003–Sep 13, 2003). U.S. troops, including Special Forces and members of the 82nd Airborne, formed a joint force with about 1,000 troops in the Afghan National Army (ANA) as well as Italian soldiers in this search for regrouped units of Taliban and al-Qaeda fighters in mountainous eastern Afghanistan. It was the first operation for the ANA, created after the overthrow of the Taliban in Operation Enduring Freedom. Large caches of arms were uncovered, at one point more than 75,000 pounds of ordnance were destroyed, and with the help of air support, a reported 35 enemy combatants were killed before the operation ended in mid-September.

ASSAULT ON FALLUJAH (Nov 8–13, 2004). Following the official end of Operation Iraqi Freedom on May 1, Fallujah, a city of 300,000 inhabitants west of Baghdad, remained a stronghold for insurgent groups, mainly Sunni Muslims. After months of unrest in the city, the U.S. leadership assembled a force of approximately 10,000 soldiers and marines, joined by a few thousand British forces and Iraqi national guardsmen. Code named "Operation Phantom Fury," the plan was to weaken the insurgents through several weeks of aerial attacks and then use overwhelming force in a classic "hammer and anvil" maneuver. With a blocking force established south of the city, and after a small U.S. force captured two key bridges on November 7, ground troops began their push from the north on November 8 following an aerial bombardment unmatched since the start of the war. Initial opposition was relatively light, as many insurgents, most prominently the leadership, evacuated the city prior to the barrage along with about two-thirds of the civilian population. The fighting intensified, however, as the troops pushed the insurgents farther into the city. Fighter planes, helicopter gunships and armored vehicles devastated much of Fallujah as the ground force engaged in intense urban combat. The heavy fighting ended by November 13, but skirmishing continued for several more days. Of the 3,000 insurgents remaining, an estimated 1,200 were killed at a cost of 71 U.S. dead and 450 wounded. U.S. leaders immediately promised millions of dollars in aid to help rebuild the city.

Biographical Notes

ABIZAID, JOHN P. (1951–). A 1973 graduate of West Point, Abizaid began his army career in the infantry, first serving as rifle and scout platoon leader in the 504th Parachute Infantry Regiment. He subsequently commanded the 2nd and 1st Ranger Battalions, which included combat operations in Grenada (1983). Abizaid went on to command the 325th Airborne Battalion Combat Team during the First Gulf War (1991) and saw service in Kurdistan in northern Iraq. He then commanded the 504th Parachute Infantry Regiment of the 82nd Airborne Division, served a tour as assistant division commander of the 1st Armored Division in Bosnia-Herzegovina (mid-1990s) and was commandant at West Point (1997–1999). From 1999 to 2000 Abizaid commanded the 1st Infantry Division in Germany, served as the director of strategic plans and policy on the Joint Chiefs of Staff in Washington DC (2000–2001) and served as deputy commander (forward) of the Combined Forces Command, U.S. Central Command (2001–2003), during Operation Iraqi Freedom. Promoted to the rank of general, he took command of the U.S. Central Command in July 2003.

BIN LADEN, OSAMA (1957–). Born in Saudi Arabia to a wealthy Yemeni family, Osama bin Laden left his homeland in 1979 to fight the Soviet military forces following their invasion of Afghanistan. Both the United States and Saudi Arabia supplied money and training to anti-Soviet fighters in Afghanistan. While he was in Afghanistan, bin Laden founded the Maktab al-Khidimat (MAK), which recruited fighters, especially Muslims, from other nations to fight the Soviets using equipment supplied mainly from the United States. Following the Soviets' withdrawal from Afghanistan, these "Arab Afghans," as the MAK fighters were called, shifted their opposition to the United States and its supporters in the Middle East, and bin Laden returned to Saudi Arabia to work in the family construction business. The Saudi government expelled bin Laden in 1991 for antigovernment activities, so he moved to Sudan, where he continued his opposition to the United States. The presence of U.S. troops in Saudi Arabia during and after the First Gulf War (1991) further radicalized bin Laden, who was considered by many at the time to be primarily a financier of terrorists. In 1994 the Saudi authorities stripped bin Laden of his citizenship. In 1996, under pressure from the United States, the Sudanese government expelled bin Laden, who then returned to Afghanistan, where he allied with the fundamentalist Taliban government and has continued his efforts to liberate Islam's three holiest places—Mecca, Medina and Jerusalem. In time, he surfaced as the leader of an international terrorist organization known as al-Qaeda. Bin Laden became the object of an international manhunt in connection with the 1993 bombing of the New York World Trade Center, the 1996 killing of 19 U.S. soldiers in Saudi Arabia, the 1998 bombings of the U.S. embassies in Tanzania and Kenya, and the 2001 destruction of the World Trade Center and attack on the Pentagon in Washington. The Federal Bureau of Investigation considered bin Laden as one of its ten most wanted fugitives and offered a reward of $25 million for information leading to his arrest or conviction.

CASEY, GEORGE W., JR. (1948–). Graduating from Georgetown University in 1970, Casey received a commission as an infantry second lieutenant in the army. His initial service was as a mortar platoon leader in Germany. He then had subsequent assignments in which he commanded a battalion in the 10th Infantry Regiment (1982–1984) and the 3rd Brigade in the 1st Cavalry Division (1993–1995), served as assistant division commander for the 1st Armored Division in Bosnia and Germany (1996–1997) and then commanded the 1st Armored Division (1999–2001). Promoted to brigadier general in 1996, Casey served on the Joint Staff in Washington (2001–2003). In October 2003 Casey was named the army's vice chief of staff, a position that he held until mid-2004 when he was promoted to general and named to the newly created post of commander of the Multinational Force–Iraq. General Casey replaced Gen. Ricardo S. Sanchez and became the highest-ranking U.S. officer in Iraq with responsibility for overseeing the U.S.-led operations in that country and for working with the new Iraqi government. Little of Casey's career was spent in the Middle East, and he had not commanded soldiers in combat. In the new job, Casey focused on reconstruction issues

CLARK, WESLEY K. (1944–). Born in Little Rock, Arkansas, Wesley Clark graduated first in his class from the U.S. Military Academy in 1966. He then studied as a Rhodes scholar at Oxford University, where he received a master's degree in philosophy, politics and economics. Clark subsequently went through armor, Ranger and Airborne training. In 1975–1976 he was a White House fellow and served as a special assistant to the director of the Office of Management and Budget. He also served on the faculty at West Point. Clark then commanded an armor brigade in the 4th Infantry Division (1986–1988) and the 1st Cavalry Division (1992–1994). As the director of strategic plans and policy of the Joint Staff in Washington (1994–1996), Clark participated in the negotiations for the Bosnian Peace Accords at Dayton, OH, which established the political divisions of Bosnia and Herzegovina out of the former Yugoslavia. Clark went on to serve as commander-in-chief, U.S. Southern Command, Panama (1996–1997), and as NATO's supreme allied commander and commander-in-chief, U.S. European Command (1997–2000). Thus, Clark directed NATO's first major combat action (1999), protecting millions of Albanians in Kosovo from ethnic cleansing attacks by neighboring Serbians. He retired from the army in 2003. Clark is the author of a memoir, *Waging Modern War* (2001), and in 2004 campaigned for the Democratic presidential nomination.

FALLOWS, JAMES M. (1949). Fallows, who was born in Philadelphia, PA, and grew up in Redlands, CA, graduated from Harvard College, where he was the editor of the school's daily newspaper, the *Harvard Crimson*. He then spent two years (1970–1972) studying economics at

Oxford University as a Rhodes scholar before entering the field of journalism as a magazine editor and writer. During the 1970s he also served for a time as one of "Nader's Raiders" for Ralph Nader's nonprofit organization, Public Citizen, and as chief speechwriter for President Jimmy Carter. From 1979 to 1996 Fallows was the Washington editor for the *Atlantic Monthly*. During that time he spent four years traveling in Asia and wrote numerous articles dealing with U.S. domestic and defense issues. In 1981 he published a book that analyzed U.S. defense spending (*National Defense*) and in 1994 he published an insightful book on East Asian economic and political systems. Between 1996 and 1998 Fallows was the editor of *U.S. News & World Report*. Then, in 1998, he became chairman of the New America Foundation, a nonprofit, nonpartisan think tank located in Washington DC. In addition to his writings, Fallows offered journalistic commentary on military and public policy questions through National Public Radio and the Public Broadcasting System.

FRANKS, TOMMY RAY (1945–). As commander-in-chief of the U.S. Central Command from 2000 until his retirement in 2003, General Franks oversaw the initial campaign in Afghanistan against al-Qaeda and the Taliban following the attack on the World Trade Center and the Pentagon in 2001. He also had oversight of the subsequent invasion of Iraq in 2003 that overthrew Saddam Hussein. Born in Oklahoma, Franks received his early education in Texas and in 1967 earned a commission as a second lieutenant in the artillery. He first saw combat in South Vietnam, where he served as a forward observer in the 4th Field Artillery. Returning to Texas, Franks graduated (1971) from the University of Texas, Arlington, with a degree in business administration. He subsequently served in Germany, graduated from the Armed Forces Staff College and served in the Office of the Chief of Staff, Army, in Washington. In the decades that followed, Franks moved steadily through the ranks. Promoted to general in 2000, Franks succeeded Gen. Anthony Zinni in command of the U.S. Central Command. General Franks retired from the army in 2003. He published his autobiography, *American Soldier*, in 2004.

HUSSEIN AL-TIKRITI, SADDAM (1937–). Born in the small northern Iraqi village of al-Auja, near the town of Tikrit, Hussein joined the revolutionary Iraqi Baathist party and was involved in a failed coup against Iraq's president (1959). Hussein escaped to Egypt, where he fell under the influence of Egyptian nationalist Gamal Abdel-Nasser (1918–1970). After a 1963 Baathist-Nasserist coup succeeded, Hussein returned to Iraq. In 1969 Hussein became Iraq's vice president. In the 1970s with the help of the Soviet Union, Hussein nationalized the oil industry in Iraq, gained control over the country's oil revenues, and through an alliance with the local Communists was able to suppress Kurdish opposition in the country. In 1979 he took full control of Iraq and consolidated his power by executing a number of potential rivals. Israel's 1981 covert attack on Iraq's nuclear plant near Baghdad fueled Hussein's intense hatred for Israel. In 1980 Hussein, a Sunni Muslim, attacked neighboring Iran, home to many Shiite Muslims. The war turned into a stalemate that lasted eight years, in part due to arms that the United States and the Soviet Union supplied to Iraq. Hussein also used this conflict to further the cult of his personality. In August 1990 he invaded neighboring Kuwait, which led to the formation of a coalition of U.N. forces, including the United States. Coalition ground forces invaded Kuwait, drove Iraq's military back toward Baghdad in February 1991 and forced Hussein to agree to a cease-fire after five days of combat. Iraq then suffered under U.N.-imposed sanctions and no-fly zones, but Hussein continued in power despite several failed assassination attempts. Beginning in March 2003 with Operation Iraqi Freedom, the United States began combat operations against Hussein and his army. On May 1 the United States declared the end of major combat in Iraq and that Hussein and the Baathists had been overthrown, but the former president was still at large. On December 13, 2003, U.S. forces captured Hussein and turned him over to the new interim Iraqi government for trial.

JENKINS, CHARLES ROBERT (1940–). The U.S. Army alleged that Sergeant Jenkins deserted to North Korea in 1965 while on patrol along the Demilitarized Zone that separates North and South Korea. Jenkins, who had received only a seventh-grade education in his native North Carolina, enlisted in the National Guard in 1955. Three years later he enlisted in the regular army. In 1960 he was sent to South Korea, where he was promoted to sergeant. In September 1964 Jenkins returned to Korea for a second tour of duty. He disappeared on January 5, 1965. The army charged he had deserted to North Korea and had letters that Jenkins had written to his family prior to his disappearance that supported its claim. Jenkins's family denied the charges; they claimed the North Koreans had captured him. Independent of the disappearance of Jenkins, North Korean spies kidnapped at least 13 Japanese nationals from their homeland in the 1970s and '80s for the purpose of teaching Japanese to North Korean agents. One of those kidnapped was Hitomi Soga, who was abducted in 1978. In 1980 Soga married Jenkins and they had two daughters. When in 2002 the Japanese prime minister went to North Korea and negotiated the return of the five surviving abductees, Soga returned to her native land, but Jenkins refused to leave, saying that he feared he would be court-martialed upon reaching Japan. In 2004 the Japanese prime minister went to North Korea a second time and was able to convince the North Koreans to allow the former American soldier and his daughters to travel to Indonesia, which has no extradition treaty with the United States. Once Jenkins and his daughters reached Indonesia, they proceeded to Japan, where in November 2004 Jenkins was court-martialed and found guilty of desertion and aiding the enemy. The court demoted Jenkins to private, stripped him of all back pay and allowances, gave him a dishonorable discharge and ordered him imprisoned for 30 days.

JOHNSON, SHOSHANA (1973–). Born in the Republic of Panama, Johnson participated in Junior ROTC at Andress High School in El Paso, Texas. Her father, an army retiree, fought in the First Gulf War. In 1998 Johnson joined the army and was assigned to the 507th Ordnance Maintenance Company, which was headquartered in El Paso. Johnson trained as a cook for her unit. When the 507th deployed to Iraq in 2003, Specialist Johnson was caught in an ambush on March 23 on the road to An Nasiriyah. She received a bullet wound in one ankle and injuries to both legs. Along with Private Jessica Lynch and five other Americans, Johnson was taken prisoner by her Iraqi attackers. Thus, Johnson became the first female African American POW in U.S. military history. Shortly thereafter, a videotape surfaced showing Johnson and the other American POWs undergoing interrogation by their captors. The Iraqis held these Americans for 22 days before they were unexpectedly released unharmed on April 13 to a marine unit near Tikrit (Lynch had been rescued earlier on April 1). Johnson subsequently recovered from her wounds and received the Bronze Star, Purple Heart, and Prisoner of War Medal in recognition of what she had endured. She received an honorable medical discharge from the army in December 2003.

KARPINSKI, JANIS L. (c. 1953–). The 2004 allegations of detainee abuse in Iraqi prisons, particularly at Abu Ghurayb, following the U.S. defeat of the military forces of former President Saddam Hussein have given prominence to Brig. Gen. Janis L. Karpinski. In 2003 General Karpinski took command of 15 detention facilities in central and southern Iraq, including three large prisons that were run by troops from the United States or Great Britain. Karpinski had begun her military career in the regular army, but in 1987 she moved to the Army Reserves, while handling intelligence and military police duties in the Middle East and United States. In 1991 Karpinski served in the First Gulf War in Saudi Arabia. Although General Karpinski had no prior experience operating prison or detention facilities, in June 2003 she took charge of the 800th Military Police Brigade, the organization nominally responsible for operating prisons such as Abu Ghurayb. She also had command of the National Guard and Reserve units in the city of Mosul. By October 2003 allegations of prisoner abuse at Abu Ghurayb, a notorious prison under the Hussein regime, began to surface. In January 2004 Lt. Gen.

Ricardo Sanchez, the senior army commander in Iraq, replaced General Karpinski with Maj. Gen. Geoffrey Miller, who had previously been in charge of the detention facility at Guantanamo Bay, Cuba. An army investigation followed, Karpinski was subsequently suspended from her brigade command and she returned to the United States. President Bush approved her demotion to colonel on May 5, 2005.

LYNCH, JESSICA (1983–). When Jessica Lynch's 507th Ordnance Maintenance Company deployed to Iraq in 2003, she was a 19-year-old private first class performing the duties of a supply clerk. Born in Palestine, WV, Lynch came to public attention when, on March 23, 2003, she was traveling in a convoy toward An Nasiriyah, Iraq, and her vehicle, along with others, took a wrong turn and was ambushed by enemy fighters. The Humvee in which Lynch was riding was hit by a rocket-propelled grenade and crashed into another vehicle in the convoy. Although 11 Americans, including Lynch's best friend in her unit, Private First Class Lori Ann Piestewa, died in that ambush, Lynch and six other Americans were captured. The Iraqi troops who initiated the attack subsequently took Lynch to a local hospital because she was injured. Eight days later a force of Army Rangers, Marine commandos and Navy SEALs located Lynch and removed her without opposition from the hospital. Accounts of exactly what happened while Lynch was in the Iraqi hospital and during this action are in dispute. Lynch herself said afterward that she did not fire her weapon during the ambush because her gun jammed, she did not resist capture, and she has no memory of mistreatment during her time in the hospital. Physicians who treated Lynch in a hospital in Germany indicated she suffered injuries to her head, spine, and fractures of her right arm, both legs, and right foot and ankle. On July 22, 2003, Lynch was released from the hospital in Germany. She was awarded the Purple Heart and Bronze Star and given an honorable medical discharge. Lynch subsequently wrote an autobiography (with Rick Bragg) titled *I Am a Soldier, Too: The Jessica Lynch Story* (2003).

MCSALLY, MARTHA (1966–). In 1984 McSally, who grew up in Rhode Island, enrolled at the U.S. Air Force Academy with the goal of becoming a fighter pilot. At the time, military regulations barred women from flying combat missions. Following her graduation in 1988, McSally earned a master's degree from the School of Public Policy at Harvard. After the Department of Defense eliminated its restrictions on women flying combat missions (1993), McSally was one of the first seven women in the air force selected for assignment to operational units flying combat jets. She is credited with being the first woman in the air force to fly a combat aircraft into enemy territory (Iraq). In 1995 and 1996, while serving in Kuwait, McSally, who had been promoted to lieutenant colonel in 1993, accumulated 100 hours flying missions over the southern no-fly zone in Iraq. Subsequently McSally was assigned as the director of the Joint Search and Rescue Center at a base near Riyadh, Saudi Arabia. In December 2001 this assignment brought McSally, who was then the highest-ranking female fighter pilot in the air force, into conflict with her superiors. She objected to the mandatory requirement established years before by American commanders in Saudi Arabia that female military personnel wear an abaya, a black, shapeless robe that extends from head to toe, when they were off the base. McSally argued that this requirement was offensive to her as a Christian. Consequently, she sued the secretary of defense in 2001 to have this regulation changed so that she and other women in the service who were stationed in Saudi Arabia could wear appropriate American clothing off base, as their male counterparts are permitted to do. When the dress requirements were modified in 2002, McSally dropped her lawsuit. In July 2004 Lieutenant Colonel McSally became the first female commander of an air combat unit at an air force base in Arizona.

MILOSEVIC, SLOBODAN (1941–). Milosevic is the former president of Serbia and of the Federal Republic of Yugoslavia. Born in Poarevac, Serbia, Milosevic earned a law degree from Belgrade University (1964) but worked as a banker. He came to prominence in Serbian politics in the 1980s. In 1988 he deposed the head of the Belgrade Committee of the Communist Party. The following year the Serbian National Assembly elected him president. Milosevic led a nationalist campaign to exert hegemony over Kosovo, an area of the Yugoslav republic where ancient hatreds between Serbs, who were predominantly Orthodox Christians, and Albanians, who were mostly Muslims, flared out of control after communism collapsed in the early 1990s. Milosevic took advantage of this nationalism to embrace the cause of the Kosovo Serbs and their resentment of Kosovar Albanian autonomy, which also encouraged Slovene, Croat and Bosnian nationalist movements. Milosevic ceded independence to Slovenia (1991), but he supported indigenous Serb communities with his Yugoslav army and paramilitary forces in fighting bloody wars in Croatia (1991) and Bosnia (1992–1995) that included ethnic cleansing of non-Serbs in those countries. In 1994 NATO, with strong U.S. support, intervened militarily by bombing Serbian forces in Bosnia. A compromise settlement that ended the fighting was reached in 1995 at Dayton, OH. Then, in 1998, fighting again broke out in Kosovo, but more NATO air strikes (1999) forced the Serbs to withdraw. The United Nations had indicted Milosevic for war crimes and crimes against humanity in the fighting in Kosovo. Arrested by the Serbian government (2001) and turned over to the U.N. International Criminal Tribunal for the Former Yugoslavia, Milosevic was tried at The Hague on 66 counts of genocide and other crimes.

MYERS, RICHARD B. (1942–). Born in Kansas City, MO, and educated at Kansas State University (BSME, 1965) and Auburn University (MBA, 1977), Myers is the 15th chairman of the Joint Chiefs of Staff. He received his commission as a second lieutenant in the air force (1965) through the ROTC program at Kansas State. Following his pilot training, Myers held a succession of air force operational and staff assignments during which he accumulated more than 4,100 flying hours in a variety of aircraft, including 600 combat hours. Myers holds the command pilot rating. Myers served in Germany in the late 1960s and in various assignments in Thailand, Japan and the United States in the 1970s. His duties in the 1980s included staff assignments, tactical fighter jobs, training positions and attendance at the Army War College. Promoted to brigadier general in 1990, Myers was subsequently commander of U.S. Forces Japan and 5th Air Force (1993–1996), assistant to the chairman of the Joint Chiefs of Staff (1996–1997), Commander, Pacific Air Forces (1997–1998), Commander-in-Chief of the North American Aerospace Defense Command (1998–2000) and vice chairman of the Joint Chiefs (2000–2001). He was promoted to general in 1997 and became chairman of the Joint Chiefs on October 1, 2001.

PETERS, RALPH (1952–). Born in Pottsville, PA, Peters enlisted in the U.S. Army in 1976 and earned a commission in 1980. He served in a variety of jobs, including as intelligence analyst for the 1st Armored Division, during an army career that took him to Bolivia, Peru, Colombia, Venezuela and Panama. When in the service, Peters learned Russian and German and earned a master's degree in international relations from St. Mary's University (1988). He retired from the army in 1999 as a lieutenant colonel so that he could focus on his work as a military strategist, news correspondent and novelist. Although Peters has published a number of Civil War novels under the pen name Owen Parry, his writing on U.S. military and defense policy reflects not only his wide experience as a soldier, but also considerable reading and reflection on a wide range of classic and contemporary writing on combat and strategic issues. As a military theorist, Peters's most influential books are *Fighting for the Future: Will America Triumph?* (1999), *Beyond Terror: Strategy in a Changing World* (2002) and *Beyond Baghdad: Postmodern War and Peace* (2003).

PETRAEUS, DAVID HOWELL (c. 1953–). A native of Cornwall, NY, Petraeus graduated from West Point in 1974 with a commission as a second lieutenant and then went through training at the army's Ranger School. During his army career, Petraeus has held a variety of command and staff jobs, including serving as an aide to three different generals. In 1985 he earned a master's of public affairs and in 1987 a PhD from the Woodrow Wilson School of Public and International Affairs at Princeton

University. During the First Gulf War, Petraeus served as aide to the army chief of staff. In 1991 he took command of a battalion in the 101st Airborne Division. Petraeus subsequently served as assistant chief of staff for operations of the NATO force in Bosnia and as deputy commander of the U.S. Joint Interagency Counter-Terrorism Task Force in Bosnia. In July 2002 he took command of the 101st Airborne Division at Fort Campbell, KY. In 2003 Petraeus's division deployed to Iraq where it participated in combat operations in March and April and was subsequently responsible for peacekeeping operations in the northern Iraqi city of Mosul. In early 2004 Petraeus returned with his division to duty in the United States. He was promoted to lieutenant general and assigned as chief of the Office of Security Transition–Iraq. Returning to Iraq, Petraeus took charge of training and equipping all of Iraq's security forces.

PIESTEWA, LORI ANN (1980–2003). A member of the Hopi tribe, Piestewa was the first Native American woman killed in combat. Piestewa was born and raised in Tuba City, AZ, where she participated in the Junior ROTC program in high school and graduated in 1997. Both her father and grandfather served in the army, so she joined the army in 2001, in part to support herself and her two children. Following basic and advanced training, Piestewa was assigned to the 507th Ordnance Maintenance Company at Fort Bliss, TX. While she was at Fort Bliss, Piestewa met Private Jessica Lynch and the two became close friends. In early 2003 the 507th deployed to Kuwait as part of Operation Iraqi Freedom. On March 23, 2003, Private First Class Piestewa, whose job was to keep track of the supplies used by her unit, was driving a Humvee in a convoy toward An Nasiriyah, Iraq, when her vehicle, along with others, took a wrong turn and was ambushed by enemy fighters. In the shooting that followed, a rocket-propelled grenade hit Piestewa's Humvee, causing it to crash into a stationary tractor-trailer rig that was part of the convoy. Piestewa survived the crash but was seriously injured and died later in Iraqi custody. Ten other American troopers died in the firefight, and Jessica Lynch and five other soldiers were captured. On April 4 Piestewa's body, along with the bodies of the other dead Americans, was found in a shallow grave near the hospital where the injured Lynch had been taken. Piestewa was posthumously promoted and awarded the Purple Heart.

QADDAFI, MUAMMAR (1941–). Born in Surt, Libya, Qaddafi received a mosque-based education. In 1961 he entered Benghazi Military Academy, where he was greatly influenced by the Arab nationalist ideas of Egyptian leader Gamal Abdel-Nasser (1918–1970). Following graduation (1966), Qaddafi went on to receive advanced training at the Royal Signal Corps School in Great Britain. From the early 1960s Qaddafi was involved with a politically active group known as the Free Officers Movement. In 1969 the group staged a successful coup against the existing Libyan monarchy. Within a year, Colonel Qaddafi became head of state in Libya, a position in which he advocated a mix of arab nationalism, revolutionary socialism and Islamic orthodoxy, which is sometimes identified as "Islamic socialism." Stridently anti-Western, Qaddafi nationalized Libya's oil industry (1973) and used oil revenues to support international terrorism. In the 1980s Qaddafi strengthened his country's ties to the Soviet Union and bought Soviet weaponry. Qaddafi's support for Palestinian independence, his backing of revolutionary Iran in that country's war with Iraq (1980–1988) and his support for other liberation activities in the developing world led to a U.S. ban (1982) on Libyan oil imports and other economic sanctions. U.S. accusations of Libyan involvement in terrorist activities led to U.S. bombing attacks on several Libyan sites (1986). Following the 1988 destruction of Pan American Flight 103 over Lockerbie, Scotland, Qaddafi refused to allow extradition of two Libyan suspects for trial. More economic sanctions and greater diplomatic isolation followed throughout the 1990s. Then, in 1999, Libya turned over the two suspects for trial and in 2002 Qaddafi apologized for the Pan Am bombing and agreed to pay compensation to the victims' families. Qaddafi later allowed U.N. inspectors to dismantle his nuclear weapons program with the goal of opening Libya to Western investment. The United States and the United Nations, in turn, have lifted most of their sanctions on Libya.

RUMSFELD, DONALD H. (1932–). Born in Chicago, IL, Rumsfeld graduated from Princeton University in 1954. Before embarking on a long career in both the public and private sectors, Rumsfeld served as a naval aviator (1954–1957). In the late 1950s Rumsfeld was an administrative assistant in the U.S. House of Representatives, then worked as an investment banker before being elected to the House in 1962. He served four terms and then was a member of President Richard Nixon's cabinet (1969–1973). Rumsfeld served as the U.S. ambassador to NATO (1973–1974), chief of staff for President Gerald Ford (1974–1975) and then secretary of defense (1975–1977). He was the youngest person to hold the position to date. From 1977 to 1985 he was president and chief executive officer and later chairman of G. D. Searle, a Fortune 500 pharmaceutical company. Returning to public service in 1983, Rumsfeld was President Ronald Reagan's special envoy to the Middle East, during which time he met with Saddam Hussein, whom the United States was supporting in Iraq's war with neighboring Iran. In 1985 he returned to the private sector, serving as an executive for several companies between 1985 and 2001. President George W. Bush appointed Rumsfeld secretary of defense in 2001. As a key Bush cabinet member, Rumsfeld oversaw a major reorganization of the military's command structure, adopted a new defense strategy for post–Cold War conflicts, and after September 11, 2001, aggressively promoted the use of force against the Taliban in Afghanistan and the invasion of Iraq in 2003.

SANCHEZ, RICARDO S. (1953–). Born and raised in Rio Grande City, TX, Sanchez participated in Junior ROTC in high school, spent one year at the University of Texas and then transferred to Texas A&I University (now Texas A&M University–Kingsville), where he majored in math and history. Graduating in 1973, Sanchez was commissioned a second lieutenant and was initially assigned to the 82nd Airborne Division, where he served in a variety of positions in the 1970s as he advanced in rank. He served in Korea, Panama and Germany and earned a master's degree in operations research and systems analysis. In addition, he attended the Command and General Staff College and the Army War College. In 1991 Sanchez was a battalion commander in the First Gulf War. Promoted to brigadier general in 1991, he commanded the 2nd Brigade of the 1st Infantry Division at Fort Riley, KS, and then served as deputy chief of staff and later as director of operations for the U.S. Southern Command. On July 1, 2001, Sanchez took command of the 1st Armored Division, which was part of the U.S. Army's V Corps. On June 14, 2003, Lieutenant General Sanchez became commander of Combined Joint Task Force 7 in Iraq. As such, he was responsible for all offensive operations in Iraq and for support of Iraq's provisional government. In 2004 Sanchez was the highest-ranking Hispanic in the U.S. Army. When in May 2004 Combined Joint Task Force 7 was replaced by the Multinational Corps–Iraq and the Multinational Force–Iraq, Sanchez headed the Multinational Force–Iraq where he focused on strategic issues until he was replaced on July 1 by Gen. George W. Casey, Jr. From Iraq, General Sanchez went to Heidelberg, Germany, where he took command of the V Corps.

SHALIKASHVILI, JOHN MALCHASE DAVID (1936–). General Shalikashvili served as chairman of the U.S. Joint Chiefs of Staff from 1993 to 1997. Born in Warsaw, Poland, Shalikashvili's father fought with the Nazis in World War II and was captured in Normandy in 1944. When the Soviet army approached Warsaw in 1943, Shalikashvili, his mother and his two siblings fled to Germany, where they were reunited with Shalikashvili's father. In 1952 the Shalikashvili family immigrated to Peoria, IL, where a distant relative sponsored the family and helped them adjust to the United States. Shalikashvili subsequently learned to speak English by watching movies. After graduating from high school, Shalikashvili earned a bachelor's degree in mechanical engineering in 1958 from Bradley University. That same year Shalikashvili and his family became American citizens. Drafted into the army as a private in

1958, Shalikashvili subsequently earned a commission in 1959 as a second lieutenant by completing training at the army's Officer Candidate School. From 1959 to 1979 he served in various troop and staff posts. In 1979 he took command of division artillery for the 1st Armored Division in Germany. His later assignments included command of the 9th Infantry Division (1987–1989), Supreme Allied Commander Europe, Commander-in-Chief U.S. Forces Europe (1992–1993) and chairman of the Joint Chiefs of Staff (1993–1997). In those last two positions, General Shalikashvili participated in all the operational planning that dealt with U.S. military operations in Bosnia and Kosovo.

SPANN, JOHNNY MICHAEL ("MIKE") (1969–2001). Spann hailed from Winfield, AL. He graduated from high school in 1987 and from Auburn University in 1992 with a degree in criminal justice and law enforcement. Spann then entered the marine corps through its officer-training program. Before leaving the marines to join the Central Intelligence Agency in 1999, Spann spent part of his service in Okinawa (1994–1995). In the CIA, Spann was assigned to the Directorate of Operations, which typically arms and trains local forces and conducts covert assaults. In the fall of 2001 Spann went to Afghanistan to work with indigenous opponents of the Taliban. He was killed in a Taliban prison uprising at Mazar-e-Sharif fortress on November 25, 2001, while questioning prisoners. Spann is believed to be the first American to die in combat in Afghanistan and the first CIA officer killed in a military operation since the Vietnam War. Although Spann did not initially qualify for burial at Arlington National Cemetery due to the strict regulations regarding eligibility, the regulations were waived and Spann was buried there with full military honors.

TILLMAN, PATRICK DANIEL (1976–2004). Pat Tillman was born in San Jose, CA, graduated from high school and entered Arizona State University on a football scholarship. Although he was small for the position of linebacker, Tillman earned conference defensive player of the year honors in 1997 and graduated from the university in three-and-one-half years with a degree in marketing. The Arizona Cardinals professional football team in the National Football League drafted Tillman in 1998. Tillman played well as a professional athlete, but following the attacks of September 11, 2001, he and his brother enlisted in the army in May 2002. In making this choice, Tillman passed up a three-year, $3.6 million contract with the Cardinals. Both brothers successfully completed training as Army Rangers, an elite unit. Assigned to the 75th Ranger Battalion, Tillman went to Iraq in March 2003 as part of Operation Iraqi Freedom. He then returned to the battalion's base at Fort Lewis, WA, before deploying to Afghanistan in early 2004. On April 22, 2004, Tillman's unit was on patrol against Taliban and al-Qaeda fighters as part of

Operation Mountain Storm when they were ambushed near the village of Sperah, along the border with Pakistan. During the ensuing firefight, Tillman was killed, probably by friendly fire from his own unit, and two other soldiers were injured. The army posthumously awarded Tillman the Silver Star and Purple Heart and promoted him from specialist to corporal.

WALLACE, WILLIAM SCOTT (c. 1948–). A 1969 graduate of the U.S. Military Academy, Wallace was commissioned a second lieutenant and subsequently became a platoon leader in the 6th Armored Cavalry Regiment. He then served (1971–1972) as a district advisor on the staff of the Military Assistance Command, Vietnam, and as company commander in the 82nd Airborne Division (1973–1974). Various operational and staff assignments in the United States and Germany followed. During the middle years of his career, Wallace earned a master's degree and attended the Army Command and General Staff College and the Naval War College. Promoted to brigadier general in 1995, Wallace commanded the National Training Center in California (1995–1997), the 4th Infantry Division at Fort Hood, TX (1997–1999) and the army's V Corps. As V Corps commander, General Wallace led all U.S. ground forces in the invasion of Iraq in March 2003. In July 2003 he became the commanding general at the army's Combined Arms Center and Fort Leavenworth in Kansas.

WOLFOWITZ, PAUL DUNDES (1943–). Born into a New York City Jewish family, Wolfowitz's career included academic and public service at the highest levels of government. Wolfowitz earned an undergraduate degree in mathematics and chemistry from Cornell University (1965) and a master's degree (1967) and PhD in political science (1972) from the University of Chicago. He taught at Yale University (1970–1973) and Johns Hopkins University (1980–1981) and served in the U.S. Arms and Disarmament Agency (1973–1977), which represented the United States in the Strategic Arms Limitation Talks (SALT) that dealt with nuclear nonproliferation issues. During the administration of President Ronald Reagan, Wolfowitz was the director of policy planning for the State Department (1981–1982) and assistant secretary of state for East Asian and Pacific affairs (1982–1986). He then served as U.S. ambassador to Indonesia from 1986 to 1989. When George H. W. Bush became president, Wolfowitz served as undersecretary of defense for policy (1989–1993). At the time, Richard B. Cheney was the secretary of defense. From 1994 to 2001 Wolfowitz was the dean of the Paul H. Nitze School of Advanced International Studies at Johns Hopkins. President George W. Bush subsequently appointed Wolfowitz deputy secretary of defense in early 2001. Considered by many observers to support the use of power to create more power, Wolfowitz tended toward a "hawkish" stance on the use of military force against potential aggressor states and, after September 11, 2001, advocated the use of preemptive force against Saddam Hussein.

ZARQAWI, ABU MUSAB AL- (1966?–). Little is accurately known about Zarqawi. He is thought to have had the birth name of Ahmed Fadell al-Khalayeh and to have grown up in the Jordanian city of Zarqa, located north of Amman, from which he fashioned the name of Zarqawi. He is believed to have dropped out of school at age 17, to have been jailed for criminal activities in the 1980s and in 1989 to have gone to Afghanistan to fight a holy war against the Soviets. In 1992 Zarqawi, who is a Sunni Muslim, returned to Jordan, where he is said to have joined a militant Islamic group whose antigovernment activities led the Jordanian authorities to arrest him in 1993. Five years later Zarqawi was released from prison under an amnesty for political prisoners. He subsequently went to Pakistan and then returned to Afghanistan in 2000, where he is thought to have established a chemical weapons camp near Herat and may have met with al-Qaeda leaders such as Osama bin Laden. In 2002 Zarqawi is believed to have illegally reentered Jordan, established a militant group he called Tawid and Jihad Movement, and played a key role in the slaying of Laurence Foley, a senior American diplomat, in Amman. The Jordanian authorities sentenced Zarqawi to death in absentia. Zarqawi probably then moved to northeastern Iraq, where he is thought to have established ties with Ansar al-Islam, another militant Islamic group. Since then his whereabouts have been uncertain, although some reports claimed that in 2002 Zarqawi had set up a camp in Khurmal in an isolated part of the mountains of northeastern Iraq where he trained recruits and worked on making chemical weapons. Zarqawi was linked to numerous bombings and attacks in various places in Iraq, including the May 2004 beheading of American hostage Nicholas Berg. As with bin Laden, the United States offered a reward of $25 million for his capture. At one point Zarqawi appeared to rename his group the Al-Qaeda Organization for Holy War in Iraq, indicating his alliance with al-Qaeda.

ZINNI, ANTHONY C. (1947–). Born and raised in Philadelphia, PA, Anthony Zinni graduated from Villanova University in 1965 with a bachelor's degree in economics and was commissioned a second lieutenant in the marine corps. Zinni had his initial training and then in 1967 went to Vietnam as an infantry advisor to the South Vietnamese marines. While he was in Vietnam, Zinni studied the local culture and learned the Vietnamese language. In 1970 Zinni returned to Vietnam, where he was wounded in action. While serving as regimental commander of the 9th Marines and commanding officer of the 31st Marine Expeditionary Unit on Okinawa (1987–1989), Zinni twice oversaw the deployment of the 31st Marine Expeditionary Unit to the Philippines to carry out emergency security operations and disaster relief. Promoted to brigadier general, Zinni then served as deputy director of operations at the U.S. European Command. After the First Gulf War (1991), Zinni led U.S. relief operations in Turkey and northern Iraq. He then was in charge of relief efforts following an earthquake in the former Soviet Union and subsequently was the director for operations for relief efforts in Somalia (1992). From 1994 to 1996 General Zinni was commanding general, 1st Marine Expeditionary Force. As part of his duties, he supervised the 1995 operation during which the United Nations withdrew its forces from Somalia. In 1997 Zinni became commander in chief of the U.S. Central Command, which, because of its involvement in the security of the Middle East, led him to study Arabic. General Zinni retired in 2000. In 2001 President George W. Bush appointed him U.S. Peace Envoy to the Middle East. While in this position, Zinni attempted to negotiate a peace settlement between Israel and the Palestinian Authority (2002).

Selected Reading List

In the decade and a half after the end of the Cold War, some commentators on military affairs asserted the period was marked by two major developments. The first was an increasing focus by American forces on wars of intervention, or policing actions, designed to promote American and allied security and to further humanitarian concerns. Although this form of warfare began with Vietnam, it took on its current character after the end of the Cold War. The second major development was what some interpreted as a kind of military revolution that was transforming the way armed forces fight, the way they are organized, and the military cultures that give them cohesion and identity. This revolution is not only a product of the special character of the wars of intervention that characterize this period, but was also the result of the advent of information-age technology and major social changes.

The writing of military history for this period, therefore, tends to be of two types. First, traditional military history made up of narratives and analyses of operations continued to flourish, although participants or journalist observers rather than historians initially wrote much of it. The second type involved analyses of the nature of wars of intervention or of the nature of the forces causing a military transformation. Here, too, observers, social scientists and other nonhistorians did much of the writing. In these works, history was often used to provide case studies from which models, policy recommendations or lessons are to be drawn. The selected reading list below follows this division, with books related to the military transformation appearing first.

Military Transformation in the Post–Cold War World

General

Boot, Max. *The Savage Wars of Peace: Small Wars and the Rise of American Power* (2002). Thought-provoking and controversial, Boot believes the United States has good reasons for a 200-year history of involving itself in the internal affairs of other countries.

Cimbala, Stephen J. *Coercive Military Strategy* (1998). Cimbala analyzes Vietnam and Desert Storm as case studies of what he calls "coercive military strategies" and argues that such conflicts will become an even more important part of overall American security strategy in the future.

Downie, Richard D. *Learning from Conflict: The U.S. Military in Vietnam, El Salvador, and the Drug War* (1998). Using the conflicts noted in the title, Downie argues that the U.S. military has failed to create a "learning cycle" sufficiently flexible to allow itself to create an adequate and dynamic counterinsurgency doctrine.

Fleitz, Frederick H., Jr. *Peacekeeping Fiascos of the 1990s: Causes, Solutions and U.S. Interests* (2002). Fleitz argues that the United States' expanded peacekeeping operations failed because military reality could not match political considerations. The use of military force for nation building requires a completely new set of skills and training that leads to stabilization in different cultures. High tech has little to do with sustained peacekeeping.

Gaddis, John L. *We Now Know: Rethinking Cold War History* (1997). This diplomatic historian believes that the fall of the Soviet Union was inevitable since it was coercive in nature as opposed to democratic and capitalistic. The book enhances the traditional view of Western thought with recently released documentation from behind the former Iron Curtain. Gaddis offers a balance to the self-flagellation of many current revisionist historians.

Halberstam, David. *War in a Time of Peace: Bush, Clinton and the Generals* (2002). Halberstam analyzes the domestic and international political and cultural contests in which the United States fought its police-action wars in the 1990s.

von Hippel, Karin. *U.S. Military Intervention in the Post–Cold War World* (2000). As a political scientist, von Hippel examines four interventions—Panama, Somalia, Haiti and Bosnia—undertaken by the United States to rescue people from barbarous rulers and to extend democracy, and draws conclusions regarding policies that should be followed in such efforts.

Huchthausen, Peter. *America's Splendid Little Wars: A Short History of U.S. Military Engagements, 1975–2000* (2003). The author, a retired American naval officer, reviews the operational aspects of American wars of intervention with an emphasis on determining the factors that led to both successes and failures.

Kaplan, Robert D. *The Coming Anarchy: Shattering the Dreams of the Post–Cold War* (2000). This collection of essays on the strategic environment covers a myriad of subjects that include pushing democracy on nonprepared people, tribal brutality, an application of Gibbons's theory from his *Rise and Fall of the Roman Empire,* and the pitfalls of peace.

Kaplan, Robert D. *Warrior Politics: Why Leadership Requires a Pagan Ethos* (2003). Kaplan believes that the new world conflict requires a ruthless strategy that justifies nearly any means to win.

Keegan, John, ed. *The Book of War: 25 Centuries of Great War Writing* (1999). Keegan has collected 82 edited works that he believes capture the widest range of experience and historiography.

Moskos, Charles C., John Allen Williams and David R. Segal, eds. *The Postmodern Military: Armed Forces after the Cold War* (2000). This is a series of essays in which the authors analyze developments in the armed forces of Atlantic-community nations seeking to define a theoretical model for analyzing the changing nature of armed forces in a postmodern world. They note in particular the continued blurring of distinctions between civilian and military.

Priest, Dana. *The Mission: Waging War and Keeping Peace with the American Military* (2003). Priest, a military affairs correspondent, argues that since the end of the Cold War the United States has increasingly turned to the military to deal with a variety of international problems, including drug traffic, terrorism and even nation building.

Social Issues

Brodie, Laura F. *Breaking Out: VMI and the Coming of Women* (2000). In this book, Brodie, a part-time member of the VMI faculty, reviews positively the efforts made by VMI to comply with court-imposed coeducation without destroying what the school considered its essential culture.

Gulman, Stephanie. *The Kinder, Gentler Military: Can America's Gender-Neutral Fighting Forces Still Win Wars?* (2000). In analyzing the efforts by American armed forces to conform to a social agenda given to them in the 1990s, Gulman argues that gender integration has weakened American fighting ability.

Katzenstein, Mary F. and Judith Reppy, eds. *Beyond Zero Tolerance: Discrimination in Military Culture* (1999). This collection of essays notes efforts made in the American armed forces to contain harassment and discrimination but argues that the institutional and social culture continues to condone and even encourage such practices.

Snyder, R. Claire. *Citizen-Soldiers and Manly Warriors: Military Service and*

Gender in the Civic Republican Tradition (1999). Snyder argues that the bonding rituals used in citizen-soldier armies produce a highly masculinized military organization and culture, but that such practices could be retooled in a way that celebrates gender and creates transgendered bonding in new armies.

Technological Change

Gongora, Thierry and Harald von Riekoff. *Toward a Revolution in Military Affairs?: Defense and Security at the Dawn of the Twenty-First Century* (2000). The authors discuss what they see as a "revolution in military affairs" created by the integration of information technologies into weapon systems, military units and operations since the Gulf War in 1991 and analyze its impact on American security strategies.

Owens, Bill. *Lifting the Fog of War* (2000). Owens surveys the many ways in which computers, electronic surveillance and satellites have helped illuminate the battlefield.

Price, Alfred. *War in the Fourth Dimension: U.S. Electronic Warfare from Vietnam to the Present* (2001). Writing for a popular rather than technical audience, Price reviews the history of electronic warfare in the United States, focusing on the development of equipment and theories rather than on policies.

Richelson, Jeffrey T. *America's Space Sentinels: DSP Satellites and National Security* (1999). Richelson provides a history of the Defense Satellite Program (DSP) devised to create a network of satellites to warn against Soviet missile attacks but which, since the end of the Cold War, has been used to monitor missile activity in the Gulf region.

Impact on the Services

ARMY

Ambrose, Stephen E. *Duty, Honor, Country: A History of West Point* (1999). Ambrose traces the evolution of West Point from its inception to the end of the 20th century. He looks at the extent to which the education of its graduates was affected by the military academy's tradition and culture.

Bolger, Daniel P. *Death Ground: Today's American Infantry in Battle* (2003). Bolger, a serving army officer, surveys what he sees as the transformation of American infantry over the past 60 years, moving from a mass force of citizen soldiers to a small group of highly trained and specialized professional soldiers.

Currie, James T. and Richard B. Crosland. *Twice the Citizen: A History of the United States Army Reserve, 1908–1995* (1997). This revised and updated edition records the evolution of the organization from its genesis as the

Medical Reserve Corps to being part of the total force concept employed in the First Gulf War.

English, John A. and Bruce I. Gudmundsson. *On Infantry* (2000). The authors present the development of warfare in the last century by spotlighting small unit training and tactics.

Hogan, David W., Jr. *Centuries of Service: The U.S. Army, 1775–2004* (2004). This official U.S. Army publication shows that the nature of the army's mission has reached far beyond simply fighting a war to being engaged in engineering support for national infrastructure, providing disaster relief, quieting civil disturbances and supporting diplomatic goals.

Romjue, John L. *American Army Doctrine for the Post–Cold War* (1996). The book presents background on the process used to change the Air Land Battle Doctrine to a post–Cold War one. The most necessary addition was of "operations other than war."

NAVY

Gray, Colin S. *The Navy in the Post–Cold War World: The Uses and Value of Strategic Sea Power* (1994). Basing his argument on historic analogies related to the experience of the Royal Navy, Gray claims that sea power will remain relevant as a strategic option for the United States well into the 21st century.

AIR FORCE

Boyne, Walter J. *Beyond the Wild Blue: A History of the United States Air Force, 1947–1997* (1997). This veteran air historian captures the 50-year history of the newest service better than anyone. He covers the key events and prime players in a concise and insightful way. The appendix is especially helpful, with a list of leaders, commands and important dates.

Cameron, Rebecca H. and Barbara Wittig. *Golden Legacy, Boundless Future: Essays on the United States Air Force and the Rise of Aerospace Power* (2000). These essays come from a golden anniversary symposium and cover the air service from its early days to modern times. Topics include personalities, doctrine, bureaucracy, operations, logistics, airlift, reconnaissance, space and technology.

Gross, Charles J. *The Air National Guard and the American Military Tradition* (1995). Gross traces the Guard's growth from colonial times through its participation in the First Gulf War. He discusses key events, people and political factors that gave impetus to its development.

Lambeth, Benjamin, ed. *The Transformation of American Air Power* (2000). The author contends that the United States' air power has been transformed over the past two decades to where it has finally become truly strategic in its potential effects.

Nalty, Bernard C., ed. *Winged Shield, Winged Sword: A History of the United States Air Force, 1907–1997* (1997). This is the official, two-volume history from the Air Force History and Museums Program.

Military Operations: 1990–2004

First Gulf War

GENERAL

Gordon, Michael R. and Bernard E. Trainor. *The Generals' War* (1995). This book has been labeled a critical analysis, sweeping account and warts-and-all history of the First Gulf War. It focuses on the military leaders who planned and executed the war and lays blame on specific individuals. It clearly dispels the common belief that the war's success was a model for joint operations.

Mandeles, Mark D., Thomas C. Hone and Sanford S. Terry. *Managing "Command and Control" in the Persian Gulf War* (1996). The authors argue that existing command and control systems in the First Gulf War were not adequate to meet the demands of a fast-paced air campaign and had to be overridden by ad-hoc systems.

Newell, Clayton R. *Historical Dictionary of the Persian Gulf War, 1990–1991* (1998). This is a reference work that contains short articles on key persons, events and other items associated with the First Gulf War along with a useful chronology and narrative history of the conflict.

ARMY

Houlahan, Thomas. *Gulf War: The Complete History* (1999). With a focus on the ground campaign, Houlahan's main point is that despite overwhelming air superiority, the lack of lethality of air-to-ground weapon systems proved the necessity of ground forces to force the enemy to surrender.

Kitfield, James. *Prodigal Soldiers* (1995). This book attempts to explain how the loss of the Vietnam conflict led to the victory in the First Gulf War. Specific credit goes to increased funding and the influence of commanders in the theater.

Scales, Robert H., Jr. *Certain Victory: The U.S. Army in the Gulf War* (1993). This official history gives a detailed survey of the conflict from the army's perspective. Both tactical and operational aspects are presented.

Swain, Richard M. *"Lucky War": Third Army in Desert Storm* (1994). Swain gives an honest appraisal of the war and the problems overcome. Interestingly, the author cautions against any overconfidence in future military actions.

AIR FORCE

Hallion, Richard P. *Storm over Iraq: Air Power and the Gulf War* (1992). This prominent Air Force historian presents a picture of the lessons learned from the standpoint of an insider. His access to key players and official documentation allows him to write current history with a unique understanding. He argues that aerospace technology enabled air power to win a war in a manner supporters had claimed was possible since air doctrine was born.

NAVY

Maralda, Edward J. and Robert J. Schneller, Jr. *Shield and Sword: The United States Navy and the Persian Gulf War* (2001). Written by two senior historians at the Naval Historical Center, this is an official history of U.S. naval operations in the First Gulf War. The focus of the book is on command and control, interservice relations and weapons effectiveness.

MARINES

Michaels, G. J. *Tip of the Spear: U.S. Marine Light Armor in the Gulf War* (1998). Michaels was a company commander during the First Gulf War, and his book provides a firsthand account of a Light Armor Vehicle (LAV) company in the race to liberate Kuwait City during the war as well as some observations on the use of LAV units in such operations.

BOSNIA-HERZEGOVINA AND KOSOVO

Bacevich, Andrew J. and Eliot A. Cohen, eds. *War over Kosovo: Politics and Strategy in a Global Age* (2001). The editors use "this strange little war" as a stage to support their contention that a new way of war has emerged in the world. It consists of an allied effort fought in a failed nation, for limited objectives with the fewest casualties possible. Thus, an aerial bombardment strategy is the cleanest and quickest.

Burg, Steven L. and Paul S. Shoup. *The War in Bosnia-Herzegovina: Ethnic Conflict and International Intervention* (1995). This survey of the background, operations and conclusion of the war in Bosnia-Herzegovina is focused on the complex nature of the conflict, which made the creation of a peaceful settlement so difficult.

Clark, Gen. Wesley K. *Waging Modern War: Bosnia, Kosovo, and the Future of Combat* (2001). This is Clark's own account of the war he waged with an emphasis on the erosion of his position as commander due to political divisions within the Clinton administration.

Cordesman, Anthony H. *The Lessons and Non-Lessons of the Air and Missile Campaign in Kosovo* (2001). Cordesman provides a detailed and technical analysis on air operations in Kosovo and argues that the experience revealed deep flaws in the way the United States wages war.

AFGHANISTAN

Cordesman, Anthony H. *The Lessons of Afghanistan: War Fighting, Intelligence, and Force Transformation* (2002). Cordesman analyzes the conflict in Afghanistan in the context of issues of force transformation. He sees the war as asymmetric, with each side using different means to secure different goals in a struggle highly interconnected with the larger global conflict related to terrorism.

Smucker, Philip. *Al Qaeda's Great Escape: The Military and the Media on Terror's Trail* (2004). Smucker, a war reporter, argues that American military forces in Afghanistan were under pressure to focus on the Taliban and produce a quick victory, and in doing so allowed Osama bin Laden and much of the al-Qaeda leadership to escape.

Second Gulf War

GENERAL

Cordesman, Anthony H. *The Iraq War: Strategy, Tactics, and Military Lessons* (2003). This is a highly analytical review of the Second Gulf War by a leading military analyst. The focus is on operations and interaction between the services.

Murray, Williamson and Robert H. Scales, Jr. *The Iraq War: A Military History* (2003). The authors not only present an overview of the American military campaign but also address debates within the State Department about global strategy and military power.

Ryan, Mike. *Baghdad or Bust: The Inside Story of Gulf War* (2003). This is a good and concise guide to the campaign to overthrow the regime of Saddam Hussein. Described are the political and logistical successes and their accompanying problems. Juxtaposed are such topics as precision bombing and collateral damage along with heroic actions and accidental deaths.

ARMY

Zucchino, David. *Thunder Run: The Armored Strike to Capture Baghdad* (2004). Written by an embedded reporter, the book is a well-written account of the good, the bad, and the ugly situation faced by those fighting the tank battles churning to the capital city. The death and destruction wrought by both sides are described in careful detail.

AIR FORCE

Boyne, Walter J. *Operation Iraqi Freedom: What Went Right, What Went Wrong, and Why* (2003). Boyne offers an early assessment of the war with emphasis on the positive role and effectiveness of air power and high-tech weapons.

MARINES

West, Bing and Robert H. Scales, Jr. *The March Up: Taking Baghdad with the 1st Marine Division* (2003). Two military veterans present a behind-the-scenes account of the famed 1st Division as it raced to the finish line in Baghdad. This work presents the war as seen through the eyes of the strategists, commanders and corporals. The book presents the true nature of ground combat in a new century of warfare.

TERRORISM

Benjamin, Daniel and Steven Simon. *The Age of Terror: Radical Islam's War Against America* (2002). The authors present a history of radical Islam and recent terrorist activities and review how national security concepts changed under the last three administrations. They propose that the spread of democracy is the only way to negate such radicalism.

Burke, Jason. *Al-Qaeda: Casting a Shadow of Terror* (2003). Burke's firsthand investigation of Islamic extremist groups in Afghanistan leads him to conclude that the U.S. focus is unfounded and unfruitful. He reasons that Islamic hatred of the West is so deep and pervasive that the defeat of al-Qaeda and Osama bin Laden would have little impact.

Juergensmeyer, Mark. *Terror in the Mind of God: The Global Rise of Religious Violence* (2000). The book addresses a blind spot in America's understanding of world terrorism in that secular societies fail to grasp the intensity of true believers' hatred of their enemies. The author identifies common elements of the conflicts.

Ullman, Harlan. *Unfinished Business: Afghanistan, the Middle East and Beyond: Defusing the Dangers that Threaten America's Security* (2002). A national security expert reviews history, policy, doctrine and strategy to find recommendations for the United States in the world after September 11, 2001.

OTHER

Haulman, Daniel L. *The United States Air Force and Humanitarian Airlift Operations, 1947–1994* (1998). This seven-chapter reference book describes humanitarian airlifts by specific regions. Each mission is described by name, location, date, cause of emergency, units involved, type of cargo, aircraft used and a brief narrative.

Glossary

AAA: Antiaircraft artillery.

ABATIS: Felled trees, usually with branches facing the direction of the enemy, used to obstruct an attack.

ABSENT WITHOUT LEAVE: An unauthorized absence from official duties, usually considered a court martial offense (AWOL).

ACE: Those who destroy five enemy aircraft (normally in the air).

ACTIVE DUTY: Full-time military service.

ADMINISTRATIVE LOADING: A process that emphasizes speed and convenience of loading ships in those situations where combat is considered unlikely.

ADMIRAL: The highest ranking commissioned naval officer.

ADVANCE GUARD: That element which precedes the main body of a unit for the purpose of discovering unwelcome surprises.

AEROSTAT: An aircraft that derives its buoyancy from lighter-than-air gas contained within a compartment.

AFTER ACTION REPORT: Written commentary of an operation from an individual perspective—usually the commanding officer of a unit.

AID MAN: Individual attached to a unit to provide emergency medical care.

AIR ASSAULT: Deployment of troops by helicopter.

AIRBORNE WARNING AND CONTROL SYSTEM: A radar system aboard an aircraft designed to identify an enemy and place friendly aircraft in a position to destroy same (AWACS).

AIREDALE: Naval aviator (slang).

AIRHEAD: The area surrounding a landing zone which must be controlled to ensure safe air landing operations.

AIRLAND BATTLE: Current U.S. doctrine for conducting military activity at the operational level.

AIRMOBILE: A unit or equipment capable of transport by aircraft.

AIRSHIP: An aerostat with a propelling system and directional control.

ALL VOLUNTEER FORCE: An attempt, begun in 1973, to create a military establishment that does not rely on conscription to fill the ranks.

AMPHIBIOUS OPERATION: A surface attack launched from naval craft against a hostile shore.

AMPHIBIOUS VEHICLE: A motorized conveyance capable of carrying troops and material through shallow water. Such units may also provide fire support for an amphibious operation.

ANTI-BALLISTIC MISSILE SYSTEM: A defensive system designed to destroy ballistic missiles while airborne.

ARMED RECONNAISSANCE: Locating and attacking targets of opportunity.

ARMORED PERSONNEL CARRIER: Lightly armored, tracked vehicle for troop transport; see also infantry fighting vehicle.

ARTICLES OF WAR: Those regulations that governed the activities of soldiers until the creation of the Uniform Code of Military Justice in 1951.

ASHCAN: A depth charge (slang).

ASW: Antisubmarine warfare.

ATTACHE: An individual assigned to assist diplomats regarding military matters and occasionally to gather information.

ATTACK CARRIER: A vessel whose primary tactical role is offensive air operations against an enemy, afloat or ashore (CVA).

BAILOUT: An emergency departure from a damaged aircraft or a vehicle, particularly of the armored variety.

BALLISTIC MISSILE: A self-powered projectile without aerodynamic lifting surfaces that assumes a ballistic trajectory when power is lost.

BATTALION: A unit of organization below a brigade and above a company/battery.

BATTERY: An artillery unit below a battalion and above a platoon.

BATTLEFIELD AIR INTERDICTION: A tactical air mission (BAI).

BATTLESHIP: The largest vessel in the line of battle, replaces ship of the line (BB).

BEACHHEAD: The designated area on a hostile shore the possession of which ensures the continuous landing of troops and material.

BOARD: To set foot on a ship for an authorized purpose of duty, to capture a ship with an armed party, or a group of officers convened for a specific purpose such as a court-martial or promotion.

BOUNTY MONEY: A monetary award to officers and crew for the destruction of an enemy warship.

BRACKETING: Adjust artillery fire by firing to either side of a target and halving the distance until the target is hit.

BREACH: To create a passage through a fortification or obstacle.

BREACHBLOCK: Steel block that closes the rear of a cannon.

BREASTWORK: Defensive earthwork built above-ground that provides cover for a standing soldier.

BREVET RANK: An honorary title, awarded for meritorious action in time of war, which does not normally confer authority or pay.

BRIG: Sailing vessel with two square-rigged masts or a naval penal facility.

BRIGADE: A unit of organization below a division and above a battalion.

BROADSIDE: The simultaneous discharge of the main armament of a ship, all the guns on one side of a warship, or the side of a ship above the water line.

BULK-BREAK: Cargo ships which require cargo to be disassembled for loading.

CAISSON: A two-wheeled vehicle for carrying ammunition attached to a limber.

CANISTER: A short-range anti-personnel projectile from artillery or small arms.

CAPITAL SHIP: A warship of the largest size and heaviest armament, e.g., a battleship.

CARRIER: A naval vessel which allows aircraft to take-off and land (CV).

CARRONADE: Naval cannon throwing ball of at least 32 pounds over a short distance.

CHAIN OF COMMAND: Organizational structure through which authority is exercised.

CINC: Commander-in-Chief.

CIRCULAR ERROR PROBABLE: As a method to determine the accuracy of ballistic missiles, the radius of a circle within which half the missiles land (CEP).

CLASS: Any group of ships built to a common plan, or a group of supplies with numerical designations.

CLOSE AIR SUPPORT: Aircraft employed in direct support of ground operations.

COLONEL: A commissioned officer in the air force, army or marines above major but below general.

COMBAT ARMS: Those branches of the army directly involved in combat.

COMBAT LOADING: A process for loading ships that emphasizes rapid retrieval of items needed for immediate combat.

COMBAT AIR PATROL: A force assigned to protect a specific area or target, e.g., aircraft launched to intercept aircraft approaching a carrier (CAP).

COMBINED CHIEFS OF STAFF: A combination of American service chiefs and representatives of British service chiefs developed to control allied operations during World War II (CCS).

COMMANDER: A commissioned naval officer above a lieutenant commander, but below a captain.

COMMISSION: To declare a ship ready for service or designate an individual an officer.

COMMODORE: A commissioned naval officer above captain, below admiral, normally bestowed only in wartime. It was the highest rank in the United States Navy until 1866.

COMPANY: A unit of organization below a battalion and above a platoon.

CONVENTIONAL WEAPONS: Weapons that are not nuclear, biological or chemical.

CORPS: A unit of organization larger than a division and smaller than an army.

COUNTER-VALUE STRATEGY: Targeting population centers vs. military forces.

COUNTER-FORCE STRATEGY: Targeting military forces vs. population centers.

COURT-MARTIAL: A tribunal authorized to judge infractions of a military code of justice.

CROSSING THE T: Naval maneuver whereby the intended track of one force is at a right angle to an opponent's projected course, thereby allowing the discharge of an unhindered raking broadside.

CRUISE MISSILE: A self-powered guided projectile with aerodynamic lifting surfaces programmed to follow a specific route.

CRUISER: A warship which sacrifices armor and firepower to achieve extensive cruising radius. These vessels were intended to accompany convoys and conduct reconnaissance operations for battleships (CA).

CSA: Confederate States Army.

C.S.A.: Confederate States of America.

CSN: Confederate States Navy.

CSS: Confederate States Ship.

D-DAY: The date on which an operation is to begin, e.g., June 6, 1944.

DEFENSE READINESS CONDITION: A numerical designation that identifies the degree to which the outbreak of war is considered likely (DEFCON).

DEFILADE: Protection from enemy fire by use of a natural or artificial obstacle.

DEMILITARIZED ZONE: An area, usually between two countries, within which fortifications and troops movements are presumably banned (DMZ).

DEPTH CHARGE: An explosive device used against underwater targets—especially submarines.

DESTROYER: A short-range, fast vessel with torpedoes as its main armament. These vessels were called torpedo-boat destroyers for that was their task. World War II saw an alteration in their mission to one of anti-submarine warfare with corresponding changes in armament (DD).

DIVISION: The basic personnel working unit of the navy, or an army unit of organization below a corps and above a brigade; a number of naval vessels of the same type grouped for operational control and more than two aviation wings.

DOGFACE: Infantry personnel or ordinary solider (WW II slang).

DOUGHBOY: Infantry personnel (WW I slang).

ELECTRONIC COUNTERMEASURES: Actions taken to degrade an enemy's ability to use the electromagnetic spectrum (ECM).

ENFILADE: To rake with gunfire a column, troops or a fortification in a lengthwise direction.

ENLISTED: An individual whose term of service is governed by a contract.

ENSIGN: The lowest ranking commissioned naval officer, or the national flag when flown from a warship.

ENVELOPMENT: An attack directed toward an enemy flank(s) or rear.

ESCORT CARRIER: Although created for convoy defense, the escort carrier undertook a variety of missions during WW II (CVE).

EXTERIOR LINES: A situation in which a previously dispersed unit is unable to concentrate faster than an opponent can mount a counter-attack.

FIELD TRAIN: Logistics units which do not directly support combat operations.

FIRE-SHIP: A ship filled with combustibles deliberately set afire and steered toward an anchored enemy.

FIXED WING: Non-helicopter aircraft.

FLAG OFFICERS: Those officers allowed their own starred flag, usually generals or admirals.

FLANK: The side of an element or formation.

FORAGE: The collection of food for troops and animals by the acquisition of such items from the civil population. This process is frequently marred by an unwillingness on the part of the civil population to participate.

FORWARD AIR CONTROLLER: An individual directing attacks by aircraft away from friendly troops, or alternatively against enemy targets (FAC).

FORWARD EDGE OF BATTLE AREA: The area in which two opposing forces interact (FEBA).

FORWARD OBSERVER: A person in a position to visually direct artillery fire.

FORWARD SLOPE: Terrain in full view of the enemy.

FRIENDLY FIRE: The misguided attempt, all too often successful, to destroy personnel, vehicles, vessels or aircraft of one's own country.

FRIGATE: Sailing ship with a single enclosed gundeck carrying from 24 to 44 guns. Also an escort ship in size between destroyer and cruiser.

FRONT: The line of lateral contact at which two opposing forces come together.

GENERAL: The highest ranking commissioned officer in the air force, army or marines.

GOB: An enlisted sailor (slang).

GROUP: Several aircraft assigned to a specific purpose; a flexible administrative/tactical unit; or a unit of variable size normally involving two or more battalions.

GRUNT: Infantry personnel (slang).

GYRENE: Marine (slang).

HAND: A member of a ship's crew.

HIGH EXPLOSIVE ANTI-TANK: An artillery shell designed to penetrate armor with an explosive charge (HEAT).

HIGH-SUBSONIC, OPTICALLY-GUIDED, TUBE-LAUNCHED: An anti-vehicle wire-guided missile (HOT).

IN THE AIR: A flank unsecured by a geographic obstacle and thus vulnerable (19th century).

IN THE CLEAR: The transmission of an uncoded message.

INFANTRY FIGHTING VEHICLE: An armored troop transport capable of supporting an infantry assault with light artillery or missile fire.

INTERCONTINENTAL BALLISTIC MISSILE: A missile with a range between 3,000 to 8,000 miles (ICBM).

INTERIOR LINES: A situation in which a previously dispersed unit is able to concentrate faster than an opponent can mount a counter-attack.

INTERMEDIATE RANGE BALLISTIC MISSILE: A missile with a range between 1,500 to 3,000 miles (IRBM).

INTERROGATION FRIEND OR FOE: An electronic transponder device which responds to a radar signal in an attempt to preclude a friendly fire episode (IFF).

ISLAND: The structure above the flight deck of an aircraft carrier.

JAM: To render a firearm inoperative or to make enemy radar/radio transmissions unintelligible.

JOINT CHIEFS OF STAFF: General officers who individually head the Air Force, Army, Marine Corps and Navy (JCS).

KIA: Killed in action.

LANDING SHIP TANK: A ship designed to transport large vehicles and land them directly on a beach (LST).

LANDING ZONE: The area selected for the delivery of cargo by transport helicopters (LZ).

LAWS OF WAR: International traditions that delimitate the conduct of combat.

LEATHERNECK: Marine (slang).

LIBERTY: Authorized absence from assigned duty for naval and marine personnel.

LIEUTENANT: The lowest ranking commissioned officer in the air force, army or marines.

LIMBER: The detachable front of a caisson to which horses are attached.

LINE ASTERN: Aircraft in a column.

LINE OF COMMUNICATION: The connection between commanders and those they command (LOC).

LINE AHEAD: Naval vessels in a column formation.

LINE OF SUPPLY: The connection between consumers and producers (LOS).

LINEAR TACTICS: The use of successive lines of infantry who fire and reload in sequence.

LOGISTICS: The science of moving and maintaining troops and supplies.

LONG-RANGE ELECTRONIC NAVIGATION: A navigation position fixing system using transmissions of two or more fixed radio transmitters (LORAN).

MACH NUMBER: The ratio of the speed of an aircraft to the speed of sound. Mach 2 is twice the speed of sound.

MAGNETIC ANOMALY DETECTOR: A device to locate submerged submarines (MAD).

MAJOR: A commissioned officer in the air force, army or marines above captain but below colonel.

MARITIME PREPOSITIONING SQUADRON: Pre-positioned material placed aboard a cargo ships designed to provide a unit, normally a Marine Amphibious Brigade, with the necessities of combat for several weeks.

MAYDAY: International voice distress call probably derived from the French phrase m'aider (help me).

MEDIC: See aid man.

MEDIUM RANGE BALLISTIC MISSILE: A missile with a range between 600 to 1,500 miles (MRBM).

MEETING ENGAGEMENT: Combat when a maneuvering force unexpectedly contacts the enemy.

MIA: Missing in action.

MULTIPLE INDEPENDENTLY TARGETABLE RE-ENTRY VEHICLES: Warheads discharged from a single missile to strike several targets (MIRV).

NAPALM: An incendiary used as filler for bombs or as fuel for flamethrowers (naphthenic acid and palmetate).

NORTH ATLANTIC TREATY ORGANIZATION: A mutual defense pact organized in 1949 to coordinate the defense of the signatory nations (NATO). The Warsaw Pact was viewed as the organization's chief opponent.

OPEN SIGHTS: To fire an artillery piece at minimum range.

OPERATION: Organized military activity cared out within a single theater.

PASS: An attack with an aircraft against aerial or ground targets, or a written leave of absence from duty for a soldier.

PENTAGON: Office building containing the principle executive offices of the Department of Defense, the Air Force, Army, Marines and Navy.

PLATOON: The subdivision of a company, battery or troop.

POL: Petroleum, oil and lubricants.

POMCUS: Pre-positioned material located outside the United States designed to provide a unit, normally an army division, with the necessities of combat for several weeks.

POW.: Prisoner of War.

PRIVATEER: An armed private ship authorized to attack enemy vessels. Their use was generally abolished by the Declaration of Paris (1856).

PRIZE: A merchant ship captured during wartime.

PRIZE MONEY: A monetary award to officers and crew for the sale of a captured ship and any cargo.

QUARTERMASTER CORPS: The branch and the people responsible for delivering supplies.

REDLEG: Artillery personnel (slang).

REGIMENT: A unit of organization below a division and above a battalion.

REGISTER: To adjust artillery fire on a particular location so as to furnish a point of reference for later targets.

REGULAR: The permanent component of the military establishment; also those who volunteer for service in contrast to individuals either conscripted or a part of the militia/reserve system.

RESERVE OFFICERS' TRAINING CORPS: An organization within an educational system to train prospective commissioned officers (ROTC).

REVERSE SLOPE: That terrain which is not in view of the enemy.

ROLL ON-ROLL OFF: Ships that allow self-assisted loading for motorized vehicles.

SAC: Strategic Air Command, USAF.

SAM: Surface-to-Air Missile.

SCRAMBLE: The movement of an aircraft from ground to air in the shortest possible time, or altering electronic communications to make them unintelligible to unauthorized listeners.

SHIP OF THE LINE: A sailing ship with two or more enclosed gundecks and at least 64 guns.

SHORT-TAKE-OFF AND LANDING: Aircraft which do not require lengthy runways (STOL).

SLOOP: A ship-rigged vessel carrying more than 18 but less than 22 guns on a gundeck.

SORTIE: The dispatch of an aircraft or ship to accomplish a specific task and an attack by from a place surrounded or blockaded by an enemy.

SORTIE RATE: The number of sorties mounted in a specified amount of time.

SPARS: Women's component of the USCG.

SQUAD: The final subdivision of a platoon—the army's smallest tactical unit.

SQUADRON: A cavalry unit above a troop and below a division; two or more divisions of naval vessels; and the basic administrative designation for aviation units.

SS: Submarine or merchant steamship, the addition of letter N indicates nuclear power.

SSB: Fleet ballistic missile submarine, the addition of letter N indicates nuclear power.

STAND DOWN: To relax an alert status or withdraw a unit from action entirely.

STOCKADE: Wooden fortification or army penal facility.

STRAIGHT LEG: Non-airborne personnel (slang).

STRATEGIC ARMS LIMITATION TALKS: Negotiations between the U.S. and U.S.S.R. designed to limit offensive ballistic missile deployment (SALT).

STRATEGIC ARMS REDUCTION TALKS: Negotiations between the U.S. and U.S.S.R. designed to limit offensive ballistic missile deployment (START).

STRATEGIC DEFENSE INITIATIVE: Research program to develop an effective antiballistic missile defense system (SDI).

STRATEGY: The art of developing and using resources to achieve objectives defined by an executive authority.

SUBMARINE LAUNCHED BALLISTIC MISSILE: A ballistic missile launched from a submarine (SLBM).

TACTICS: The art of using armed forces in battle.

TEETH-TO-TAIL RATIO: The relationship between combat forces and support forces.

TIME ON TARGET: The time of arrival at an objective of personnel or explosive ordnance.

TINCAN: Destroyer (slang).

TOW: Tube-Launched, Optically Tracked, Wire Command-Link Guided anti-vehicle missile.

TROOP: A cavalry unit below a squadron.

TURNING MOVEMENT: An envelopment that avoids an enemy main body to threaten a vital point to the rear, thereby forcing them to withdraw.

TURRET: An armored, usually rotating, structure atop the hull of a tank or ship.

UNIFORM CODE OF MILITARY JUSTICE: Those regulations that govern the activities of the entire military establishment since 1951 (UCMJ).

USA: United States Army.

U.S.A.: United States of America.

USAAC: United States Army Air Corps.

USAAF: United States Army Air Forces.

USAF: United States Air Force.

USAFA: United States Air Force Academy.

USCG: United States Coast Guard.

USCGA: United States Coast Guard Academy.

USMA: United States Military Academy.

USMC: United States Marine Corps.

USN: United States Navy.

USNA: United States Naval Academy.

USRC: United States Revenue Cutter.

USRCS: United States Revenue Cutter Service.

USS: United States Ship.

VERTICAL AND/OR SHORT TAKEOFF AND LANDING: Aircraft able to use limited runways or dispense with same altogether. (V/STOL).

VERTICAL TAKEOFF AND LANDING: Aircraft able to dispense with runways (VTOL).

WAAC: Women's Army Auxiliary Corps.

WAC: Women's Army Corps.

WAFS: Women's Auxiliary Ferrying Squadron.

WARSAW PACT: A mutual defense pact organized in 1955 to coordinate the defense of the signatory nations. NATO was viewed as the organization's chief opponent.

WASP: Women's Airforce Service Pilots.

WAVES: Women Accepted for Voluntary Emergency Service (informal designation for Women's Reserve of the Navy).

WIA: Wounded in action.

WING: The basic operational unit of air and naval air forces.

YELLOWLEG: Cavalry personnel (slang).

ZULU: Greenwich Mean Time.

Contributors

Kevin B. Byrne is Professor of History at Gustavus Adolphus College.

Jerry M. Cooper, now retired, was Professor of History at the University of Missouri–St. Louis.

James L. Crowder is Chief of the Office of History for the Oklahoma City Air Logistics Center, Tinker Air Force Base.

John M. Lindley is an independent scholar and editor.

Jerry K. Sweeney, now retired, was Professor of History at South Dakota State University.

David J. Ulbrich is Instructor of History at Ball State University.

William J. Woolley, now retired, was Helen Swift Nielson Professor of Cultural Studies at Ripon College.

Index